DISCOVERING

CHRISTIAN HOLINESS

THE HEART OF
WESLEYAN-HOLINESS THEOLOGY

DISCOVERING

CHRISTIAN HOLINESS

THE HEART OF
WESLEYAN-HOLINESS THEOLOGY

DIANE LECLERC

BEACON HILL PRESS
OF KANSAS CITY

ISBN 978-0-8341-2469-1

Printed in the
United States of America

Cover Design: Brandon Hill
Interior Design: Sharon Page

Library of Congress Cataloging-in-Publication Data

Leclerc, Diane, 1963-
    Discovering Christian holiness : the heart of Wesleyan-Holiness theology / Diane Leclerc.
        p. cm.
    Includes bibliographical references (p.   ).
    ISBN 978-0-8341-2469-1 (hardcover)
    1. Holiness—Christianity. 2. Holiness churches—Doctrines. 3. Methodist Church—Doctrines. 4. Wesley, John, 1703-1791. I. Title.
    BT767.L38 2010
    234'.8—dc22

                                                                    2010035264

10 9 8 7 6 5 4 3

For Lacey

CONTENTS

ACKNOWLEDGMENTS

Serendipitously, I write the final words of this book on the one hundredth anniversary of my denomination, the Church of the Nazarene. I am thankful for being raised and nurtured in its arms. I am thankful for my call, my ordination, and my place to serve, first as a pastor and now as a professor. I am thankful for its leaders, such as Dr. Jesse Middendorf and Dr. Nina Gunter, who have encouraged me in significant ways. I am thankful for its rich history in spreading holiness throughout the land. I hope this book will make a small contribution to its mission.

As this project comes to a close, reflection on all the persons who have encouraged and strengthened me inspires a deep gratitude within. First, I'd like to thank my editors, Alex Varughese, for his support and affirmation as each chapter was written, and Richard Buckner, for all of his fine-tuning. Gratitude is also due to my teacher and friend Rob Staples, who served as my primary reader. His insights have been extremely helpful. While writing I became deeply aware of the many teachers through the years who influenced my own theology of Holiness. A few I mention here: Henry Spaulding III, Rob L. Staples, Paul M. Bassett, Al Truesdale, J. Kenneth Grider, Virginia Burrus, and especially Randy Maddox, who has mentored me in considerable and lasting ways, although never in a formal classroom. Also, the work of Mildred Bangs Wynkoop continually inspires me as I walk in her footsteps.

It is also fitting that I thank my students at Northwest Nazarene University (NNU), especially those who have taken the courses Christian Holiness and Theology of Holiness from me in the last two years. They have patiently allowed me to express the content of this book to them and have helped me process the material with their very postmodern eyes.

I would also like to thank my colleagues in the School of Theology and Christian Ministries at NNU, including Jay Akkerman, Joe Bankard, Wendell Bowes, Rhonda Carrim, Ed Crawford, Mike Kipp, Thomas Oord, Brent Peterson, Jim Rotz, and my dean, Mark Maddix. And special thanks to George Lyons and Richard Thompson who provided invaluable input at certain junctures in this project. The collegial encouragement and love I receive from these friends and their spouses are simply unmatchable. Thanks also go to Tiffany Triplett, who helped significantly with the glossary, Malloree Norris and Andrew Schwartz, my teaching assistants, who aided in some final editing.

I express my very deepest gratitude to my husband, Paul, for his innumerable sacrifices and unrivaled support, and to my son, Ethan, who gave up countless hours so that "Mom could write her book." Thanks also to my mother and my siblings, Janice Elder and Floyd Cunningham (a church historian and a valuable resource). Thanks also go to some of my close friends who have offered timely and strong support along the way, including Glena Andrews, Rob Thompson, Susan Armstrong, Whitney Van Brocklin, Ben and Melodie Turner, and my Five Mile Church family. And finally, this book is dedicated to my closest friend, Lacey Kilgore, who literally prayed me through the writing of this book, from the first word to the last, and who has loved me with such a Christlike love that my own pursuit of the life of holiness has changed in deeply significant ways.

FOREWORD

More than half a century ago, in a study of Wesley's doctrine of Christian perfection, John L. Peters wrote about a "watershed" in the development of Wesley's doctrine during the years after Wesley. He said:

> Down one slope would move the absolutist interpreters until Christian perfection would come to mean an almost exclusive emphasis upon a single climactic experience. Down the other slope would move the accommodative interpreters until Christian perfection would come to mean little more than a dimly remembered tradition. And both in mutual reaction would abandon the synthesis Wesley had labored to establish.[1]

To interpret Wesleyan-Holiness doctrine for one's own age is still to be confronted with the need to maintain the balance, or what Peters called the "synthesis," found in Wesley's thought, thus avoiding the two extremes to which it sometimes has been taken. This need applies to the whole scope of Wesleyan theology, not merely to the specific issue dealt with by Peters.[2]

At the same time, it is not sufficient to woodenly repeat Wesley. Instead, one must work backward by continually evaluating Wesleyan-Holiness doctrine in the light of the biblical witness and then work forward by responsibly applying it to the contemporary situation. Diane Leclerc's book *Discovering Christian Holiness* steers a middle course between the Scylla of absolutism and the Charybdis of accommodationism. This book is "absolutist" enough to remain faithful to the Wesleyan-Holiness tradition and its doctrine of entire sanctification and "accommodative" enough to endeavor placing Wesleyan-Holiness doctrine within the current 21st-century context. The doctrine is thus freed from some of the outmoded and misleading categories that have clung to it in the past, making it more up-to-date than any of the Holiness textbooks previously available.

Yet the author steers clear of the more adventuresome accommodative tendencies to cast Holiness doctrine only in popular postmodern categories. While postmodernism is addressed, it by no means becomes the only lens through which Holiness is examined. This is a thoroughly historical work, based on the theology of Holiness in the early church and throughout the Christian centuries. But it is also a theological work, based on biblical and historical foundations. Here again, while it might be tempting to move directly to contemporary theology in order to find a contemporary voice for Holiness, Leclerc resists this as well. The reader will not find here a theology of Holiness from the perspective of process theology, postliberal theology, deconstruction-ism, radical orthodoxy, or any of today's other theological options, believing them to be inadequate vehicles for communicating all the important elements of Wesleyan thought. The closest Leclerc comes to a particular slant is in her attempts to *correlate* theological construction (a la Paul Tillich's existential-ism) to real life—in order to bridge the "credibility gap" that the late Mildred Bangs Wynkoop highlighted nearly forty years ago.

While a student at Nazarene Theological Seminary, Diane Leclerc en-rolled in my seminar in Theological Anthropology. During that course she came to the conclusion that the predominant Protestant understanding of sin (as pride or egocentricity) was only half correct, that it was a mostly male understanding that did not really work for most women. I can take no credit for giving her the idea; in fact, I tried to argue her out of it. But during that semester-long interchange I thought I saw the making of a keen theological mind. In that, I was correct. She eventually convinced me that she was on to something. She kept working with her concept of sin until it eventuated in her doctoral dissertation, published under the title *Singleness of Heart: Gender, Sin, and Holiness in Historical Perspective,*[3] which won the Timothy Smith/Mildred Bangs Wynkoop Award given by the Wesleyan Theological Society for its unique contribution to Wesleyan theology in 2002.

And now, in this book, Leclerc turns her attention to the opposite of sin, namely, holiness of heart and life. Like one of her theological heroes, Wynkoop, Leclerc understands that some of the older categories and images in which Holiness doctrine was expressed in 19th- and early 20th-century teaching and preaching did not always communicate well, especially in non-American cultures. Again reminiscent of Wynkoop's work, Leclerc in her final chapter affirms that at its very center the Wesleyan-Holiness tradition is a "theology of love."

But this is not a mere replication of Wynkoop's theology. Leclerc does her own thinking. She has her own style and her own vision of the holy life and of what such a life should mean today. This vision is articulated with clar-ity in this volume. In discussing the biblical basis of Holiness doctrine, Leclerc elaborates a "Wesleyan way to read Scripture," acknowledging that everyone comes to the Bible with presuppositions and that Wesleyans, being no differ-ent in that regard, have definite presuppositional tools with which to approach Scripture. In her historical treatment of Holiness thought, she carefully seeks to contextualize Holiness teaching to an extent not done in many of the previ-ous works on the subject. This same contextualizing is evident in her exposi-tion of the theological implications of holiness, as she carefully relates it to the doctrines of God, sin, and salvation. In the final section, Holiness doctrine is turned over and examined in its various practicable and concrete facets, making the book a practical one for holy living in this present world. This book deserves a prominent place among the major studies that have been made of the Wesleyan understanding of holiness.

—Rob L. Staples, PhD
Professor of Theology Emeritus
Nazarene Theological Seminary

INTRODUCTION

Wesleyan-Holiness Theology in the 21st Century

This book is about holiness from the perspective of Wesleyan-Holiness theology. While other traditions are certainly not mute on the subject of holiness, Wesleyan-Holiness theology does offer a distinctive perspective that has arisen out of a rich history—a history that has placed those denominations known as Holiness denominations in a unique position in the church universal. As expected, such denominations place the theology of Holiness and the doctrine of sanctification at the center of their theological identity. These denominations have a distinct historical foundation. But each generation must not only claim this rich historical theology but also make it come alive in new ways. Thus this book is written from the perspective of Wesleyan-Holiness theology to and for the generations that find themselves in today's postmodern age.

The Holiness Movement began in the mid-19th century, and over a hundred years have passed since the formation of most Holiness denominations. This immediately raises the question, is Wesleyan-Holiness theology (so tied to its historic roots) still relevant for the 21st century? And yet this question implicitly presupposes that people in Holiness denominations know their heritage and their distinctive theology. Perhaps this should not be presupposed at all. Does Wesleyan-Holiness theology, as a vital, experiential, living and breathing theology, still exist?

I had the privilege of serving as a representative of my denomination for three years on a committee/consultation known as the Wesleyan Holiness Study Project. We were commissioned to strategize ways to promote the message of holiness in the 21st century. As we gathered (theologians and ecclesiastical leaders of a number of Holiness denominations), we soon realized that we shared a common anxiety about the future of Holiness, which some named a crisis. But instead of a crisis over the different ways of communicating holiness (as mentioned above), the crisis we were expressing was one of silence. Perhaps the confusion that comes from having more than one way to articulate holiness roused our anxiety, but whatever the reason might be, the danger we saw was the *lack* of articulation of holiness. The concern was not about holiness being preached this way or that way, but whether it was being preached at all.

The result of the Study Project was the publication and distribution of a short essay titled "Holiness Manifesto," released in February 2006. (A full-length book by the same title was published in 2008.[1]) In his introduction to the document, Kevin Mannoia (the project's leader) states, "There has never been a time in greater need of a compelling articulation of the message of holiness."[2] Mannoia is concerned that the pressing demands of a changing culture have driven pastors and leaders to focus on the "latest method" at the expense of the "holiness message." He recognizes that churches in North America are losing ground as membership is dropping, not only in mainline churches but in Holiness denominations as well. "In the process of trying to find the magic method for growing healthy vibrant churches, our people have . . . fallen prey to a generic Christianity that results in congregations that are indistinguishable from the culture around them. Churches need a clear, compelling message that will replace the 'holy grail' of methods as the focus of our mission. Our message is our mission!"[3]

I share the concern about the deafening silence of the message. I have been teaching classes on holiness (offered to both general education students and students studying for the ministry) for over ten years. When I ask the students from Holiness denominations about the doctrine of Holiness and entire sanctification, they plainly demonstrate that they have not "heard" the message. This does not necessarily imply that they did not hear it from the pulpit or in the Sunday School class but rather that they have not retained such teaching in any meaningful way. Out of a class of fifty students, I might have one or two who have some grasp of the doctrine. Also, possibly, as the work of the Wesleyan Holiness Study Project presupposes, the message of holiness is not being communicated or, at the least, not being communicated effectively. I have a theory why. I believe we have a whole generation of pastors who were deeply affected by a time in the history of the Wesleyan-Holiness tradition when the idea of perfectionism, rather than vital piety, dominated.

Understandably, during the post-World War II period society reflected a desire for stability and "normality." There was great emphasis, especially in the Protestant church, on morality, decency, and conformity. Likewise, Holiness denominations tended to emphasize "rules" more than the vitality of the life of holiness. Then in the 1960s the world underwent a dramatic shift.

As much as the Holiness Movement might have wanted to isolate itself from the surrounding social upheaval of this new period[4] and disapprove of any theological affinity with such radical cultural change, for an emerging generation with new eyes, theology as usual was not enough. I believe that possibly the generation of pastors either going through this shift or being born in it failed to find healthier ways to express the Holiness message. They certainly did not want to continue to preach perfectionism. And so they either ceased to preach the doctrine of Holiness or chose words and metaphors so different from traditional Holiness language that my students failed to recognize anything unique or distinct about what they heard. I find this especially true for the idea of sin. In this case the pendulum seems to have swung from legalism to pessimism about victory over sin. Many of my students believe that sin is inevitable, pervasive, and enduring in a Christian's life. Sadly, they seem to be unaware of a different way to live.

Possibly, Holiness churches have tried so hard to keep up with generic evangelicalism for the sake of numerical growth that they sacrificed their distinctive call to preach holiness "throughout the land." Indeed, in a culture of consumerism, preaching what people want to hear is easier than preaching the cost of discipleship. Unfortunately, generic evangelicalism often has a Calvinist slant. Possibly, in this kind of milieu, the optimism inherent in the Wesleyan-Holiness message has been muffled.

The epoch shift from a modernist to a postmodernist perspective is another contributing influence to the crisis of silence. This shift may have given to younger generations new ears that are unable to hear the old message of holiness. Understanding postmodernism may provide a clue about what these new ears are like and what it will take to reach them with the Holiness message.

The word "postmodernism" currently has two related but distinct meanings. While it is beyond our scope here to give an in-depth analysis of each, some attention will be beneficial. One definition of postmodernism is related to multiple fields of academic study such as literary theory, philosophy, architecture, art, cultural studies, and even theology. Postmodernism in this sense is a reaction to the premises of "modernism" (which appeared during the Enlightenment, in the 18th century, and found an intensified expression in the 19th century). Premises of postmodernism (that emerge mid-20th century) evidence a rejection of organizing principles, universals, and coherences. It embraces or, more technically, embodies complexity, ambiguity, and diversity. This type of postmodernism has also been termed **poststructuralism** because it is a rejection of the ways moderns have "structured" reality. For example, modernism seeks commonalities and generalizations even while focusing on the (idealized) individual, but postmodernism rejects the notion of generalizing anything. It can evidence an ethos of relativism and is criticized most for becoming, in its most extreme form, nonsensical because some of its adherents try to disrupt even the system of word meanings themselves.

Even though some theologians have embraced a postmodern/poststructural philosophical underpinning to do postmodern theology, postmodernism's basic rejection of any notion of absolutes, even religious absolutes, has made embracing it as a whole untenable for most, if not all, evangelicals. And yet, while the criticisms are often valid, a call to return to modernism is certainly not a practical answer. There is another option, and this brings us to our second definition of postmodernism used today and found in many Christian and even evangelical circles.

According to Jay Akkerman, postmodern Christians emphasize the "organic" over the "mechanistic" by preferring religious authenticity and spontaneity "over carefully airbrushed, compartmentalized, and rote cookie-cutter religious experiences; they prefer the whole rather than the part by understanding their faith as something that encompasses all of their lives." Directly countering the intense rationalism of modernism, "they are more open to ambiguity and mystery instead of being tied strictly to tight systems of rules of thinking and believing."[5] Henry Knight has offered key comparisons between this postmodern Christian consciousness—particularly as it is expressed in what is now known as the emerging church movement—and Wesleyan theology. He writes, "Wesleyans should support this new movement because the purposes and values emerging churches seek to embody—their vision of discipleship, church, and mission—is highly congruent with those of the Wesleyan tradition."[6]

Knight lists seven resonances between the beliefs and practices of the emerging church and those of John Wesley. He explains how these themes were present in Wesley's attempts to address his own cultural shift and how they are presently being expressed by the emerging church, and he convincingly shows how such resonances reveal the continuing relevance of Wesleyan theology in today's postmodern world.

PARALLELS OF WESLEYAN AND POSTMODERN THEOLOGY

1. A transformational model of discipleship
2. The missional emphasis of Christ's church
3. An incarnational model of ministry
4. The emphasis on community
5. The preeminence of proclamation through narrative forms
6. Innovation of practices of worship that maintain "primitive Christianity"
7. A "generous orthodoxy" ("catholic spirit") that emphasizes essentials of Christian life *more* than propositional, doctrinal correctness (though Wesley, of course, knew what he believed about every doctrine)[7]

Knight's analysis should be taken seriously. Indeed, "emerging churches are not responding to a passing fad but to deep, permanent, and pervasive cultural change. Subsequent generations will be shaped to an even greater extent by postmodern culture."[8]

In light of all this, a prudent question to ask is, how does "holiness" fare under a postmodern frame of reference? Is it a concept that has reached the end of its usefulness, indeed relevance? As Knight and countless others have suggested, the world has permanently changed. Returning to a modernist approach to "save" the Holiness doctrine would certainly prove futile. It would be equivalent to putting our theological heads in the sand. Constructing a theology based on modernist principles[9] is not only a lost cause but also dangerous. Such an endeavor would drastically lessen the relevance of "holiness" to the contemporary culture. Certainly, "holiness" lives and breathes wherever it finds itself, for it transcends any particular philosophical underpinning. And yet this transcendent and vital message must be "translated" into whatever cultural context we are addressing. The truth of holiness remains constant, but this truth must be made meaningful in differing contexts so that it is communicated effectively.

This "translation" is crucial in passing not only from one philosophical or historical era to the next but also from one global culture to another. Recently, there has been a rising sensitivity to the theological colonialism that has transpired through the decades. In some cases an Americanized articulation of the Holiness message was imposed on non-American cultures, and only now do we understand the repercussions of such an imprudent strategy. We are just beginning to see an openness to the truth of the Holiness message as appropriately expressed through, for example, African, Asian, and Latino vernacular, metaphors, and idioms. One trait of postmodernism is the recognition of globalization. The churches of the Holiness Movement have appropriately begun envisioning themselves as part of the global church. This must include the welcoming of theological cross-pollination. A one-way delivery system can no longer be accepted. Does this mean we are changing the spiritual reality of God's sanctifying grace? Absolutely not. We are broadening our understanding of how it can penetrate every culture by allowing it to do so!

▶ KEY ELEMENTS OF WESLEYAN THEOLOGY

With this firmly said, we can still identify elements of Wesleyan theology (understood from a Holiness perspective) that transcend time and place. The reader must be introduced to these elements in order to fully understand the rest of the book. And yet while the key elements of Wesleyan theology presented below are brief descriptions only, the book as a whole will deepen the reader's understanding of these introductory comments.

1. *Wesleyan theology arises out of the biography of John Wesley*

John Wesley was born on June 17, 1703, to Samuel and Susanna Wesley. Both Samuel's and Susanna's families had been part of the Puritan dissenters that had separated from the Church of England. However, John's mother and father both decided to rejoin the Anglican Church and did so with great zeal. Samuel was an Anglican priest, responsible for the church in Epworth, England. Biographers have been correct in seeing John's upbringing in this family as significant to his own spiritual formation. Samuel, an educated pastor who highly valued learning, wrote and published. Susanna also valued education, for her daughters as well as her sons. She is well-known for the Christian teaching she provided her children. She also served as an early model of a woman in ministry for John; for all practical purposes, she served as a copastor to the flock at Epworth.

Perhaps significant for later Methodism were the "house meetings" the Wesleys led in the rectory, where congregants would share openly about their spiritual journeys. They met regularly for prayer, scripture reading, and edifying conversation. Susanna often led these meetings. John seems to have had a special place in his mother's heart. She believed that God had spared him (from a fire) and called him for some very special purpose.

At age eleven, John entered the famous Charterhouse School in London. His older brother, Samuel, attended Westminster School nearby (where Charles, John's famous younger brother, was also a pupil later). Charterhouse provided John with a type of prep school education and also with an opportunity to begin his teenage reflection on his spiritual life. Through it all, John's tie to his mother remained substantial and influential. In 1720, John attended Christ Church (college) at Oxford University and began preparing for the priesthood.

Oxford provided a place for John Wesley to mature spiritually, as well as excel academically. Christ Church was one of the more prestigious colleges and, along with other professional disciplines, prepared young scholars for work in the church. Following his graduation at Christ Church in 1724, Wesley became a tutor and fellow at Lincoln College (also at Oxford), which meant he was supported financially throughout his years there. Training for ministry in the Church of England required the following: a bachelor of arts degree; examination by the bishop; ordination as a deacon, which acted as a two-year probationary period to prove the candidate possessed gifts for ministry and allow time to finish the master of arts degree; another examination by the bishop; and then another ordination as priest.

To prepare for his ordination as a deacon, Wesley began to read from the Pietist tradition, which focused on holy living. Three authors are extremely significant to Wesley's theological development. Thomas à Kempis (1380-1471), a German mystic, wrote *The Imitation of Christ*. Jeremy Taylor (1613-67) wrote *The Rules and Exercises of Holy Living* and *The Rules and Exercises of Holy Dying*. William Law (1686-1761), a contemporary of Wesley, wrote two significant works: *A Practical Treatise upon Christian Perfection* and *A Serious Call to a Devout and Holy Life*. From these three authors Wesley gained three primary ideas that related to his doctrine of Holiness. Holiness involves (1) a purity of intentions, (2) the imitation of Christ as the model for holy living, and (3) love for God and neighbor as definitive and normative of Christian perfection.

These ideas began to take shape at Oxford through Wesley's reading of these three authors. Entries in his diary at this time indicate a seriousness about his own holiness. Another highly significant development at Oxford was the formation of Wesley's Holy Club in 1729. The Holy Club was a study group that developed over time into what some believe to be the model of Wesley's "band" meetings. (He would later place all converts to Methodism into small groups for the purpose of spiritual accountability and encouragement; for a further description see p. 23.) The Holy Club was also where Wesley came to highly value what we might call social service ministry. Members would weekly visit those in prison or an orphanage, or the sick. These types of activities were a vital part of Wesley's understanding of spiritual discipline. By 1733, the Holy Club, now known as the Oxford Methodists, was strong and growing. Wesley, on the other hand, began to have doubts about his own salvation. He wrestled to find some kind of *assurance* that he in fact was a child of God. When an opportunity to go to Georgia as a missionary arose, Wesley went. As he said, "My chief motive . . . is the hope of saving my own soul."[10]

Three months after his father's death in 1735, a trustee of the organization the Society for the Propagation of the Gospel (SPG) invited John Wesley to Georgia. He, along with his brother Charles and one other member of the Holy Club, sailed in January 1736. For all practical purposes, the time they spent in Georgia was a pastoral, relational, and spiritual failure. Part of John's plan was to convert the "Indians." Entries in his journal show that far from being thirsty for the gospel (as John had imagined because of his strong belief in prevenient grace), the Native Americans offended his sense of order and discipline. He also had little tolerance for the colonists. Albert Outler calls John's practices as pastor "tactless" and his ministry in Georgia a "fiasco."[11] Things were further complicated with a messy romance for John. John fell in love with Sophie Hopkey but was perpetually noncommittal. She finally married someone else. John then barred her and her new husband from Holy Communion and was in turn sued for defamation of the new husband's character. Events escalated until John was to appear for a formal grand jury. Finally, John decided to leave for England to escape any further embarrassment.

Out of the Georgia debacle, one positive benefit emerged: John's acquaintance with the Moravians. He first encountered them on the trip to Georgia and was impressed with their assurance of their own salvation. He met with them on occasion while there, and upon returning to England he actually visited the Moravian settlement in Germany. They strongly supported the Lutheran doctrine of sola fide: salvation by faith alone. Wesley's more than ten-year quest for holiness had missed the power of this vital doctrine, and at this point in his life Wesley needed to know that he was a child of God, apart from his own efforts, or "works-righteousness." Peter Bohler, a Moravian who counseled Wesley on several occasions, challenged Wesley to "preach faith till you have it, and then because you have it, you will preach faith."[12] Wesley did exactly that. In doing so, Wesley offended Anglican sensibilities. He defended himself by stating that the *Book of Homilies* and the *Book of Common Prayer* both strongly affirmed the doctrine of salvation by faith. Rather than being discouraged, Wesley saw the controversy with his Anglican brothers in a positive light and stated that God's special blessing was on the sermons that gave the most offense. On May 24, 1738, John went to a Moravian meeting on Aldersgate Street and claimed for himself the assurance of salvation that he had sought. He felt his heart "strangely warmed" and wrote later in his diary, "I felt I did trust in Christ, Christ alone for salvation, and an assurance was given me that he had taken away *my* sins, even *mine*, and saved *me* from the law of sin and death."[13]

There is no consensus among scholars as to what happened to Wesley that night. Some call it his true conversion, others his evangelical conversion, others one spiritual step among many, some an entire sanctification experience. Wesley himself does not help us define the moment. He does reference 1738 as significant, but he could have meant the date of the first society meeting or the beginning of the evangelical revival in England. He does reprint his diary entry five times in other writings, but with no comment. What is sure is that Aldersgate turned Wesley in a new direction. Most scholars agree that Wesley experienced a new level of "assurance" of his salvation, based on grace and not on works; this "witness of the Spirit" (as Wesley also called it) will become a key doctrine in Methodism. From Aldersgate on, Wesley preached sola fide so strongly in Anglican pulpits that he was barred from preaching further in many such churches. Following the lead of his friend George Whitefield, Wesley decided that if he could not preach in the pulpits he would "preach in the fields."

The middle phase of Wesley's life was consumed by the rise and organization of the Methodist Revival in England and his need to clarify Methodist theology. The very first theological move that Wesley made was to reject the extremes of Moravianism. Although Wesley deeply appreciated their influence on his own life, and their doctrine of sola fide, Wesley began to be uncomfortable with their "quietism." Wesley saw that an overemphasis on the doctrine of grace could lead to a type of antinomianism—the belief that since grace is all, works are not only unnecessary but also harmful to Christians' dependence on God only for salvation; thus they should remain "quiet" before God. Wesley, from 1725 on, never wavered in his belief that a Christian expressed his or her Christianity through good works, particularly works of love and mercy to the most needy. Wesley, like the book of James, demanded that faith be shown and legitimized by such work.

The 1740s and 1750s saw the "rise of the people called Methodists." With the organization of societies, bands, and class meetings, Wesley provided his converts with a disciplined program of spiritual formation, in the context of fellowship with other Christians and focused pastoral care. Societies were larger groups, which would parallel the size of an average congregation. Band and class meetings were small accountability groups that were very intense. Most scholars see the formation of these smaller groups as crucial in the growth of Methodism, when other periodic revivals had initial success, but no long-term harvest. Wesley also initiated a large network of lay preachers. These preachers would travel to different societies to preach and to make sure Wesley's plan and theological vision were being carried out. Annual conferences to help govern the societies, first initiated in 1744, were also crucial in developing the distinctives of Methodism. The Methodist relationship with the Anglican Church was questioned early, both by Methodists and Anglicans. Wesley saw his movement as a renewal or an evangelistic order within the Church of England. Through the early years, Wesley steadfastly repudiated any hint of separatism.

In the context of the bands and societies, influenced by Wesley's own vision, Methodists began to testify to the experience of entire sanctification. "Holiness of heart and life" had always been one of Wesley's cherished phrases. As people began to profess the experience, Wesley began to see the benefit in preaching its attainability. John's brother Charles disagreed with his new preaching. Charles believed that an experience of entire sanctification is rare, and if it does occur, it will be very near a person's death. John would be forced to clarify his own position in the coming decade.

The years following 1760 until his death in 1791 will represent for us the "late Wesley" period. During these decades, Wesley faced major theological issues that would help define Methodism. Personal problems were also interspersed amid more theological concerns. What has come to be known as the "perfectionist controversy" began in the early 1760s. During his middle years, Wesley had begun to stress the attainability of Christian perfection and to advise his followers to "seek it now." Two of his followers, Thomas Maxfield and George Bell, took the doctrine to extremes. They were the leaders of the society in London. They emphasized that such perfection was "absolute" and claimed that a perfected Christian could not sin and would persist in an angelic-like state. They downplayed the gradual process that Wesley had always emphasized as equally important. The controversy led to much debate and aggression over the doctrine of sanctification. Wesley called a conference to settle the issue, and he clarified his own positions in such publications as *On Perfection* (1761), *On Sin in Believers* (1763), and perhaps most comprehensively in *A Plain Account of Christian Perfection* (first issued in 1766 and again in 1777).

Although Wesley had dealt with Methodists who deemed themselves Calvinists from the very beginning of the movement, the 1770s brought the issue to a head. The death of George Whitefield in 1770 can be seen as a catalyst for the reemergence of the debate. Whitefield had been a member of the Holy Club and became a very successful evangelist in both North America and England. Although closely associated with Wesley for many years, Whitefield disagreed with Wesley over the doctrine of predestination. Wesley was accused of not adequately representing Whitefield's views in the funeral sermon he delivered. In response to the controversy, Wesley published several works: *On Predestination* (1773), *Thoughts Upon Necessity* (1774), and *On Working Out Your Own Salvation* (1785). Wesley never wavered from his position on election. Ultimately, Methodism would stand resolutely in the Arminian camp—that is, all persons are elected by God for salvation, conditioned upon their acceptance of God's grace. In contrast, the Calvinist position held that only certain individuals are elected to salvation and that salvation is conditioned upon nothing; grace is "irresistible." Wesley's main argument against the doctrine of predestination, that is, the Calvinist understanding of election, was that it distorts our image of God and places God's sovereignty over God's love.

Also during the late period of Wesley's life, the issue of Methodism's separation from the Church of England reached a climax. Up to this time, Wesley had been resolutely against separation. He wanted to see Methodism as a renewal movement within the church. Charles was even stronger in his sentiments that separation should not occur under any circumstances. But an unexpected situation in America forced John's hand. In the 1770s, the rise of political issues in the American colonies resulted in the Revolutionary War. In the midst of the conflict, the Anglican Church retreated back to England.

This left the pastoral and practical problem of the administration of the sacraments to Methodists in America.

While Methodists had always met for preaching services and for society meetings, Wesley demanded that Methodists in England and America receive the sacrament of Holy Communion in Anglican churches. Wesley was deeply concerned that with the absence of Anglican priests, American Methodists would have no opportunity to receive the sacrament. Holy Communion was so important to Wesley that he decided to approve a Methodist ordination of Francis Asbury and Thomas Coke, and commissioned them as general superintendents of the Methodist Church in 1784 at a conference in Baltimore (known as the Christmas Conference). In essence, this initiated a series of events that gave American Methodists independence. English Methodists would become a separate denomination from Anglicanism after Wesley died.

Wesley's decision hurt his relationship with Charles. Things between them were never the same. Other personal difficulties arose. John Wesley had married against Charles's advice. The marriage was a complete failure; Molly Wesley finally left John for good in 1771. When she died in 1781, Wesley only heard about it much later. But despite all of these controversies and difficulties, Wesley remained a strong leader. He continued to publish, preach, and correspond with his Methodist people until his death.

Wesley was and is recognized as an exceptionally influential man—an evaluation that cannot be refuted, despite the difficulty historians and biographers may have had in sifting through all the evidence. Many traditions recognize him as their spiritual and theological father. The Holiness Movement—which arose during the 19th century and continues today—certainly does.

2. Wesleyan theology is soteriologically focused

Soteriology, or the theology of salvation, is at the center of the theology of John Wesley. Technically, God is certainly at the center, and Wesley would have argued that point to the end. And yet, with this established, Wesley believed that God's love and God's desire for a renewed relationship with humanity is the very message of the Bible, as witnessed to throughout the Christian tradition. Put most simply, the relationship between God and human beings is at the heart of Christianity and all Christian doctrine for Wesley. Understanding this divine-human relationship (especially how it is established and maintained) should be the purpose of all theological inquiry. And all theological inquiry should aid the actual living out of this relationship. Thus all Wesleyan theology is based in soteriology, is thoroughly optimistic, and perpetually practical in orientation.

In a sense, all other doctrines must arrange themselves around the question: "What must we do to be saved?" Most of Wesley's theology then is fo-

cused on what is known as the *ordo salutis,* or "order of salvation." By this
theologians are referring to how God and the human being are relating at any
particular point in the human being's Christian journey. Some Wesleyan theologians prefer to use the phrase *via salutis,* or "way of salvation,"[14] to indicate
that the Christian journey is a fluid, day-by-day experience and not a series of
isolated steps. Whichever phrase is employed to describe this divine-human
relationship, there are phases that can be identified and described.[15] But Wesley's theology never remains in the abstract. His belief that real persons can
experience the various dimensions of salvation makes his theology thoroughly
optimistic and practical.[16]

3. Wesleyan theology is thoroughly optimistic

Wesleyan theology is often known as an optimistic theology. Wesley
fully recognized the effects of sin on the human race and strongly affirmed a
doctrine of original sin. Without it, Wesley said, all of Christianity would fall.
We must recognize that human beings are broken and in need of salvation.
But as strongly as Wesley declared our sinful condition, he even more strongly
proclaimed the power of grace. Much of Wesley's theology is undergirded by
his understanding of prevenient grace. Prevenient grace is that grace that God
gives at our birth. This grace, which is the powerful work of the Holy Spirit, is
the grace that draws us, or "woos" us, to a relationship with God. We are not
on our own in our attempt to find God. God first seeks us. Once we have responded to prevenient grace and accepted justifying grace, Wesley's optimism
of grace shines most brightly. Wesley believed that we are not only saved by
grace but also sanctified by grace, which results in a real inner transformation
that expresses itself in outward change. One passage from Theodore Runyon
will be helpful here:

> Wesley was convinced that when the re-creative Spirit is at work real
> changes occur. Not only are we granted a new status in Christ through
> justification but God does not leave us where we were; God inaugurates a
> new creation, restoring the relation to which we are called, to mirror God
> in the world. . . . [There is real as well as relative change, says Wesley]. The
> relative change is that change in the way of being related [to God] brought
> about through our acceptance by God and is absolutely essential to every-
> thing that follows. But what follows, the real change, is the beginning of
> the new creaturehood, the *telos* toward which salvation is directed.[17]

It is for this reason (the belief in real change beginning at regeneration)
that Wesley so highly valued the experience of new birth. He complained
against those who would minimize its power to change inward and outward
sin. New birth, then, begins a new life to be lived in sanctifying grace. And
this sanctifying grace, received in a significantly deeper way when entire sanc-

tification occurs, is what encouraged Wesley to be so optimistic. Sin need no longer reign in the heart. An outpouring of God's love into the heart "excludes sin." We can live truly holy lives. As Wesley would say, to deny such optimism would make the power of sin greater than the power of grace—an option that should be unthinkable for a Wesleyan-Holiness theology.

4. Wesleyan theology is practical theology

Almost all Wesley scholars agree that John Wesley's theology is best expressed as *practical theology*. Wesley's theology always applies directly to real-life situations. He did not write a systematic theology in the same way John Calvin did. He never sat down and wrote out what he believed about all the Christian doctrines in one place. While referencing the Bible and Christian orthodoxy, Wesley's theological methodology is inductive. Out of Wesley's own practical life experiences he developed his theological "conclusions." Scholars must look at Wesley's more practical works—such as his sermons, journals, and letters—in order to weave together what Wesley believed about each traditional systematic doctrine. Wesley has thus been called a practical theologian. Many different sources influenced Wesley's theological conclusions. He is also thus known as an eclectic theologian—he takes the best he can find from a variety of origins and synthesizes it all into a creative theological vision.

Partly because of his inductive style and partly because of his own spiritual development, John Wesley pursued the task of articulating Christian truth from what could be called a deep dedication to theological humility. He delicately at times, and boldly at others, advocated for a careful and a decidedly humble differentiation of Christian essentials from nonessentials. He gained this perspective from the *via media* position of the Church of England. But he did claim as essentials those beliefs on which he staked his life, so to speak. Interestingly, the essentials he often claimed had to do with living the Christian life, rather than theological speculation. In his sermon "Catholic Spirit," Wesley offered a list of questions that he claimed were essential for Christians to answer in order to test whether they were "right-hearted" before God.[18] Wesley offered this test in a setting where he affirmed the inevitable reality of Christian diversity on theological and ecclesial matters. What Wesley offered in this list of questions are the "non-negotiables" for a true Christian, and he was not shy about proclaiming them. Again, interestingly, few of the questions he asked are centered on doctrine. The majority have to do with a living faith expressed through holiness as evidenced in the attitudes and actions of a person "filled with the energy of love."[19] In a sense we could say that Wesleyan theology is not just a set of doctrines but also an *ethos* out of which theology is "done"—always for the purpose of practical Christian living and love. Thus doctrine is foundational to love and not the final goal of religion.

FROM WESLEY'S "CATHOLIC SPIRIT"

The first thing implied is this: Is thy heart right with God? Dost thou believe his being and his perfections? his eternity, immensity, wisdom, power? his justice, mercy, and truth? Dost thou believe that he now "upholdeth all things by the word of his power"? and that he governs even the most minute, even the most noxious, to his own glory, and the good of them that love him? hast thou a divine evidence, a supernatural conviction, of the things of God? Dost thou "walk by faith not by sight"? looking not at temporal things, but things eternal? Dost thou believe in the Lord Jesus Christ, "God over all, blessed for ever"? Is he revealed in thy soul? Dost thou know Jesus Christ and him crucified? Does he dwell in thee, and thou in him? Is he formed in thy heart by faith? having absolutely disclaimed all thy own works, thy own righteousness, hast thou "submitted thyself unto the righteousness of God, which is by faith in Christ Jesus"? Art thou "found in him, not having thy own righteousness, but the righteousness which is by faith"? And art thou, through him, "fighting the good fight of faith, and laying hold of eternal life"? Is thy faith [energoumenē di' agapēs], —*filled with the energy of love?* Dost thou love God (I do not say "above all things," for it is both an unscriptural and an ambiguous expression, but) "with all thy heart, and with all thy mind, and with all thy soul, and with all thy strength"? Dost thou seek all thy happiness in him alone? And dost thou find what thou seekest? Does thy soul continually "magnify the Lord, and thy spirit rejoice in God thy Saviour"? having learned "in everything to give thanks," dost thou find "it is a joyful and a pleasant thing to be thankful"? Is God the centre of thy soul, the sum of all thy desires? Art thou accordingly laying up thy treasure in heaven, and counting all things else dung and dross? hath the love of God cast the love of the world out of thy soul? Then thou art "crucified to the world"; thou art dead to all below; and thy "life is hid with Christ in God." Art thou employed in doing, "not thy own will, but the will of him that sent thee"—of him that sent thee down to sojourn here awhile, to spend a few days in a strange land, till, having finished the work he hath given thee to do, thou return to thy Father's house? Is it thy meat and drink "to do the will of thy Father which is in heaven"? Is thine eye single in all things? always fixed on him? always looking unto Jesus? Dost thou point at him in whatsoever thou doest? in all thy labour, thy business, thy conversation? aiming only at the glory of God in all, "whatsoever thou doest, either in word or deed, doing it all in the name of the Lord Jesus; giving thanks unto God, even the Father, through him"? Does the love of God constrain thee to serve him with fear, to "rejoice unto him with reverence"? Art thou more afraid of displeasing God, than either of death or hell? Is nothing so terrible to thee as the thought of offending the eyes of his glory? Upon this ground, dost thou "hate all evil ways," every transgression of his holy and perfect law; and herein "exercise thyself, to have a conscience void of offence toward God, and toward man"? Is thy heart right toward thy neighbour? Dost thou love as thyself, all mankind, without exception? "If you love those only that love you, what thank have ye?" Do you "love your enemies"? Is your soul full of good-will, of tender affection, toward them? Do you love even the enemies of God, the unthankful and unholy? Do your bowels yearn over them? Could you "wish yourself" temporally "accursed" for their sake? And do you show this by "blessing them that curse you, and praying for those that despitefully use you, and persecute you"? Do you show your love by your works? While you have time as you have opportunity, do you in fact "do good to all men," neighbours or strangers, friends or enemies, good or bad? Do you do them all the good you can; endeavouring to supply all their wants; assisting them both in body and soul, to the uttermost of your power? —If thou art thus minded, may every Christian say, yea, if thou art but sincerely desirous of it, and following on till thou attain, then "thy heart is right, as my heart is with thy heart."[20]

5. Wesleyan theology is foundational to Holiness theology

Throughout this book the term "Wesleyan-Holiness theology" is used. This needs some explanation. The term certainly references a particular period in religious history. When John Wesley's Methodism was transferred to its American context in the 19th century, some of its original theology—birthed and nurtured in 18th-century Britain—changed. This should be seen as an expected occurrence. The doctrine of Christian perfection, which had been the "grand depositum" of Methodism, had put on new skin. American Methodists eventually took sides on the doctrine of entire sanctification. Divisions occurred in the latter half of the 19th century, and although the breaks were not precisely along the lines of Holiness theology, generally speaking those who held on to entire sanctification as a decisive moment with radical effects left mainline Methodism and formed several new denominations.

Some of these new denominations were characterized with certain theological anomalies, as was also the case with Methodism. On the one hand, some Holiness thinkers and preachers were not Wesleyan theologically. On the other hand, Methodism now represented Wesleyan theology without embracing the method and means of holiness set forth by these new denominations. Thus there was Holiness theology that was not Wesleyan and Wesleyan theology that was not Holiness-oriented. But most of the denominations that formed were in fact strongly Wesleyan in foundation while affirming Holiness theology. But again, the term "Wesleyan-Holiness theology" implies more than its historical context, and more than the present-day denominations that began at that time.

This book is written with the presupposition that Wesleyan-Holiness theology represents more than a historical development with ecclesiastical results. This book is written with the conviction that Wesleyan-Holiness theology is a distinctive type of theology among other theologies in the world today and that it has a unique voice and important place in current theological dialogue. Yet even more than this, this book is written in the hope that persons reading it will be formed as well as informed by its Wesleyan-Holiness theology. The theology presented throughout is vital and living and should call each of us, the writer included, to self-examination and spiritual deepening. In this sense, may the Spirit make the sum here more than the parts combined; in other words, may it be a means of grace.

▶ A NOTE TO THE READER

The parts and chapters of this book follow a basic pattern, loosely based on the Wesleyan quadrilateral. The foundational biblical and historical chapters represent Scripture and tradition. The remaining chapters accord with addressing the doctrine of Holiness from the perspectives of reason and experience. After important theological foundations are laid—namely, chapters on God, humanity, sin, salvation, and sanctification—the book will examine holiness from the following paradigms: perfection, purity, power, character, and love. Love, for Wesley and his successors, should permeate every fiber of holiness and thus should be understood as the overarching theme of the entire book and not just as a concluding chapter. Entire devotion to God is perhaps the best expression of our love for God and should also be seen as a thematic thread.

To aid the reader, objectives and vocabulary words begin every chapter. Each vocabulary word draws attention to a theological concept, and on the word's first appearance in the chapter, it is highlighted in bold. The vocabulary words are also found in the glossary at the end of the book. Each chapter ends with study questions and a few suggestions for further reading. These aids will hopefully be beneficial when the book is used as a textbook.

PART I

BIBLICAL HOLINESS

ONE

HOW TO READ THE BIBLE
AS A WESLEYAN

LEARNER OBJECTIVES

Your study of this chapter will help you to:

1. Define biblical interpretation
2. Identify Wesley's explicit methods of biblical exegesis
3. Describe the Wesleyan-Holiness theology of inspiration and understanding of biblical authority
4. Define the Wesleyan quadrilateral
5. Describe what is meant by the "wholeness of Scripture"
6. Identify the four elements of Wesley's "analogy of faith"

KEY WORDS

Biblical interpretation	Double inspiration
Biblical criticism	Subjective interpretation
Exegesis	Analogy of faith
Sola scriptura	Midrash
Hermeneutics	Eisegesis
Inductive (interpretation)	Dispensations
Soteriology	Original sin
Wesleyan quadrilateral	Justification
Tradition	New birth
Reason	Sanctification
Experience	

Holiness is a thoroughly biblical concept, divinely revealed through the biblical writers and relevant for every new generation. Any adequate definition of holiness is based on God's holiness and on God's call that we be "perfect" (or, holy) "as your heavenly Father is perfect" (Matt. 5:48). We know the character of God only through God's self-revelation in Jesus Christ and through the Bible's witnesses to him. And we know the holy life to which we are called as Christians only because God has revealed it to us in the life of Christ and through the Scriptures.

These simple statements are foundational, but we cannot stay with them long. As the title of this chapter implies, multiple ways to read the Bible exist, and the Wesleyan way—which is the perspective from which this chapter is written—is one among many. We must first acknowledge that even seeing holiness as a central theme in the Bible is an *interpretative* move. We must concede that other theological traditions do not come to the same conclusions about holiness and its corollary, sanctification. Even the words themselves in the original languages must be translated, which implies interpretative decisions by the translators. From individual words to the major themes of the Bible, we interpret.

Biblical interpretation is a complex activity that "hides" just under the surface every time we try to understand any portion of Scripture, especially when we try to apply it to our lives today. Even those traditions that affirm "the plain meaning of Scripture" must recognize that every reader comes to the text with presuppositions—the learned and the naive alike. Claiming to be *just* a Bible Christian is simply impossible. All people and traditions have methods for making sense of the Bible and applying it to their lives. Finding an application to life is the purpose of biblical interpretation.

Many questions suggest themselves at this point. How did different ecclesiastical traditions come to their differing theological conclusions about what the Bible says? What do these traditions affirm about Scripture's place in the life of the church? What does each tradition believe about the Bible's authority over against other authorities? Do different traditions have different methods of interpretation? Is it a given that good interpretation seeks to be completely objective? What is the history of biblical interpretation? What methods of interpretation are used today? Do individual persons have the right to interpret as they see fit, or do they need to be faithful to their community's interpretation? What is the very purpose of the Bible?

All of these questions and more like them raise methodological issues. Although methodological inquiry might be thorny at times, we must attempt it, even at the outset of a book on holiness. We cannot just turn, however tempting, to conclusions about what the Bible says about holiness without first being honest about how any conclusion is reached.

▶ METHODOLOGICAL QUESTIONS

As mentioned earlier, this chapter is written with the understanding that there is a Wesleyan way to read Scripture. For those of the Wesleyan-Holiness tradition, this approach to Scripture is foundational not only to a theology of Holiness but to a continuing self-identity as well. Confusion, tension, and conflict can arise when those in a community read and interpret scriptural texts in ways inconsistent with their tradition. Reading Scripture in accord with a community's tradition goes hand in hand with understanding that community's theology and history.

Before we go much further in our discussion of Wesleyan biblical interpretation, we must give attention to three clarifications.[1] First, reading the Bible as a Wesleyan does not imply that we read the Bible exactly as John Wesley did. Second, reading the Bible as a Wesleyan does imply certain understandings about biblical inspiration and the Bible's authority. And third, reading the Bible as a Wesleyan implies that the interpreter is spiritually (not just objectively) invested in the Bible and seeks to be submissive to its message. Framed as methodological questions, the importance of these three clarifications becomes increasingly evident as we examine them in greater detail.

1. To "read or not to read" like Wesley?

Generally speaking, John Wesley belonged to the "precritical" era of biblical interpretation. The "modern" period of higher and lower **biblical criticism** developed during the century Wesley lived. He was aware of some of the developments happening around him, and he even employed some aspects of modern **exegesis** in his work. But a more precise statement about Wesley would be that he belonged to the Reformation era of biblical interpretation. The key assertion for the Reformation was that of *sola scriptura* ("Scripture alone"), which countered the idea that church (Catholic) tradition was authoritatively on par with Scripture. Wesley modified *sola scriptura* as many of his Anglican contemporaries did. But the interpretative moves of Reformation **hermeneutics** significantly influenced Wesley's approach to the Bible.

Wesley did establish his own methods of exegesis. Scott Jones arranged these methods into seven different ideas:

1. Scriptural language should be used to explain or describe scriptural ideas; it should become dominant in our use of language.
2. The literal meaning of the text should be used first, unless it seems to contradict other texts or implies an absurdity. "In cases where two bibli-

cal texts appeared to contradict each other, [Wesley] stressed that the more obscure text should be understood in light of the clearer one."[2]

3. A text should be interpreted in light of its context.

4. Scripture interprets itself, and each individual text should be interpreted in light of the whole.

5. Commandments should always be seen as covered promises. In other words, whatever we are commanded to do God will enable us to do through grace.

6. Biblical writers employ literary devices at times that need to be discerned if an appropriate meaning of the text is to be ascertained.

7. The earliest text available should be sought, as well as the best translation.[3]

Although these suggestions may remain beneficial for us today, the question still remains: Does reading the Bible as a Wesleyan imply that we use, and only use, Wesley's methods and techniques? Most present-day Wesleyan biblical scholars say no. Advances in biblical exegesis and criticism need not be ignored. Joel Green is representative of this position. He states the following:

> To read the Bible as Wesleyans is not to adopt a precritical stance with respect to the nature and interpretation of Scripture. . . . Those who lament Wesley's precritical approach to Scripture, and who might imagine that recovering Wesley for Biblical Studies entails our embracing precritical assumptions and practices are mistaken.[4]

Green goes on to suggest that Wesley would have embraced many developments in biblical criticism and used them where appropriate.

So we should employ other methods besides Wesley's. But along with this understanding we should still take Wesley's guiding principles (as discussed below) very seriously.

2. What does a Wesleyan paradigm assume about biblical inspiration and authority?

The authority of the Bible was a given for John Wesley. Only further along in the Enlightenment era (18th century) did scholars question biblical authority and regard the Bible more as an object of investigation. For Wesley, the Bible was authoritative simply because it was inspired by God as a special revelation to humanity. Thus authority and inspiration are inseparably connected in his theology and his approach to biblical interpretation. "While recognizing that there are both divine and human elements in the process, he minimizes the human element and emphasizes the faithfulness with which the message is transcribed."[5]

Clearly, asking Wesley to prove the Bible's authority is somewhat anachronistic. The Bible is authoritative because it is true. The Bible is true because it reveals the message that God inspired the writers to convey. The message of the Bible, then, being inspired by God to such a degree that God is its "author," is fully reliable in its guidance regarding faith and practice.

The purpose of the Bible was also a given for Wesley. He followed the Anglican article of faith that affirms the sufficiency and reliability of the Bible in all things *pertaining to salvation*. Wesleyan-Holiness denominations also follow this position in their different articles of faith.

Like the question about proving biblical authority, asking whether Wesley was an inerrantist is also anachronistic. His position allowed him to be open to the developments in the areas of history and scientific discovery in his lifetime. He did not have to defend the truth of the Scriptures in areas they were never meant to address. The Anglican article on this point closely resembles the view of Scripture as set forth by the Protestant Reformation. Wesley, in accord with the early Reformers, would never have implied that the Bible is true in all forms of knowledge. It was Protestant scholasticism that shifted the focus of Scripture from revealing how to be in relationship with God to the belief that it reveals every doctrinal proposition in full.[6] As Robert Wall asserts:

> The Wesleyan tradition naturally inclines its biblical interpreters toward viewing their task as "open-ended and conversational." Meanings made of Scripture are more fluid and contextual. . . . This is so because Arminius (whom Wesley follows at this point) understood Scripture's authority in functional terms, whether to confirm the actual experience of conversion or to interpret the holiness of life for a particular setting. . . . Those of [later] Calvinist traditions, on the other hand, tend to press for a uniform interpretation of Scripture and its single meaning that justifies creedal and uniform "orthodoxy"—one book, one faith. Scripture's authority is viewed in propositional terms."[7]

Wesley's approach is much more **inductive** in nature. While the Bible certainly reveals all that is needed to formulate doctrine and theology, the biblical interpreter must go to the text without preformed and highly structured doctrinal assertions. Wesley came to believe that the primary theology revealed in the Bible is **soteriology**. But he would resist the idea that he predetermined Scripture's meaning by taking creed or doctrine to the Bible with him. Likewise, we should not take Wesleyan theological conclusions to the Bible. Biblical hermeneutics and biblical theology should always remain prior to more systematic theological foundations. But Wesley did not go to the Bible alone. Wesley took with him the other three components of what is known as the **Wesleyan quadrilateral**.

While Wesley did affirm the Reformation idea of *sola scriptura* and placed the authority of Scripture above all else, he did not follow all the implications of this doctrine without modification. When Wesley read "Scripture alone," he believed that the Bible is the primary source of authority, not necessarily the only religious authority. As Donald Thorsen says on this point,

> John Wesley's most enduring contribution to theological method stems from his . . . [inclusion] of experience along with Scripture, tradition, and reason as genuine sources of religious authority. While maintaining the primacy of Scripture, Wesley functioned with a dynamic interplay of sources in interpreting, illuminating, enriching, and communicating biblical truths.[8]

This is not to imply that **tradition, reason,** or **experience** can stand alone as authorities. The Bible stands alone above these three handmaids. Tradition, particularly the patristic period and the Church of England for Wesley, should be given serious consideration. Knowing how the church has interpreted the Bible through the centuries and how it has expressed these interpretations in its liturgical life is important. This is especially so when examining the development of orthodox beliefs and creeds such as those about the Trinity and Jesus Christ. Also, only through the exercise of reason is the biblical message discerned, formulated, and communicated. However, Wesley did not suggest that we can reason our way to God.

Experience serves in confirming the truth of Scripture. If Christians are not experiencing the scriptural message, then they should question their interpretation of the message. Wesley is known to have reexamined and subsequently reinterpreted Scripture in light of some of the experiences of his Methodist people.[9]

An exhaustive study of the Wesleyan quadrilateral and its interplay is beyond our scope. For our purposes here we note that the quadrilateral is one way that Wesley remained humble before the Bible; this humility is an important part of a Wesleyan ethos. The quadrilateral serves as a check and balance for assessing the reliability of any interpretation of Scripture.

Finally, returning to the topic of biblical inspiration, we must mention that Wesley believed in what could be called **double inspiration**. Not only did the Holy Spirit inspire the original writers as they wrote particular books of the Bible, but the Holy Spirit also inspires us now to both hear and apply the biblical message to our own hearts and lives. As Wesley himself said, "All Scripture is inspired of God—The Spirit of God not only once inspired those who wrote it, but continually inspires, supernaturally assists, those that read it with earnest prayer."[10]

3. What is *subjective interpretation?*

Biblical interpretation coming out of the modern period might first appear to be noble. Biblical interpreters studied the Bible using many of the scientific methods of the Enlightenment to reach a more objective understanding of its meaning. The Bible was examined as any literary text would be examined. This movement toward objective examination came to be called biblical criticism, which was subdivided into higher and lower criticism. Higher criticism asks questions about the authorship of each book, when it was written, how it fits into the canon, and so on. It seeks to give a historical context for each passage. Lower criticism (also known as textual criticism) examines all the intricacies of the texts themselves.

The development of biblical criticism since the Enlightenment shows a marked increase in biblical expertise. As mentioned earlier, Wesley himself would have made use of all the biblical resources that became available in the 19th and 20th centuries. Similarly today, Wesleyan biblical scholars should have a prominent voice in the sanctuary.[11]

But some Wesleyan scholars also offer an appropriate word of caution. Joel Green and others fear that the biblical interpretation of the modern period, particularly in "the academy," can lead to seeing the Bible too "objectively" and not as the Book of the Church.[12] This raises the question, Who can interpret the Bible best? Those outside the circle of Christian subjectivity? Or those inside the Christian circle? Asking this kind of question reveals a dichotomy that Wesley would never have anticipated.

Reading the Bible as a Wesleyan means that a person must acknowledge that he or she is always subjectively involved in the text he or she seeks to interpret. A person must have faith to affirm that God's holy character and humanity's appropriate response is fully revealed through Scripture. A person must have faith in the meaning and purpose of the Bible itself and enough faith to believe that what it shows is true. But faith is also needed to believe that the "goal of biblical interpretation" is "for the church [and is for] praxis."[13] Faith is needed to believe that any interpretation fails if it fails to ask the question, What are we to *do* in light of God's revelation in this particular community?

Having this faith does not mean ignoring all the data and insight that biblical criticism offers. It does not mean a person can be a sloppy or "romantic" interpreter of Scripture, completely unconcerned about what a passage meant when it was written. But it does mean acknowledging that while a more objective knowledge of Scripture can (and should) aid in good interpretation, a good interpreter is always subjectively engaged with the text on behalf of the faith community. A Wesleyan believes that the best interpreter of Scripture, then, not only comes to the texts with biblical tools but also and always with a confessional trust in God and with faith that the Holy Spirit is intricately involved in the task of discerning the Bible's life-giving meaning. Using the words of Charles Wesley, we could say that what John Wesley aimed for in biblical study is what he aimed for more generally: to "unite the pair so long disjoined—knowledge and vital piety."[14]

▶ GUIDING PRINCIPLES OF A WESLEYAN WAY TO READ SCRIPTURE

Biblical interpretation in the Wesleyan tradition is certainly interested in precise and thorough biblical exegesis. But such is not an end in itself. The following discussion explores interpretation as a means of grace, which is made more available when attention is given to the "whole tenor of Scripture" through the lens of what is called the analogy of faith.

1. *Biblical interpretation and the means of grace*[15]

Wesley believed that the Bible is the primary source for inducing theology and doctrine, but he stressed even more strongly the "devotional" purpose of the Bible. The Bible is one of the primary "means of grace" for Wesley. Its purpose is to reveal God's grace to humanity. Robert Wall offers a helpful summary:

> The revivalist ethos shaped by Wesley's [evangelistic] ministry shifted emphasis from "the faith which is believed" to the faith which believes. . . . Wesley viewed Scripture as the privileged medium of God's self-disclosure. The reading and hearing of the biblical word in evangelistic preaching and pastoral teaching create the context wherein the word of God is heard and understood as the instrument of prevenient grace, thereby restoring human freedom and enabling the Spirit to bring people freely to saving faith in and fervent love for God. This is the primary role that Scripture performs, then, and on this basis its authority depends. God "authors" Scripture not to warrant some grand system of theological ideas to guide people in orthodox confession, but rather to lead sinful people into thankful worship of a forgiving Lord.[16]

The Holy Spirit enlivens Scripture, often through preaching, to penetrate the hearts of people. It is a means through which God's prevenient grace is active. Prevenient grace draws people to the points of awakening, conviction, repentance, and new birth. The focus for a Wesleyan is not that the Bible is right and true (although it is) but that the Bible is effective in changing people's lives.

For the Christian, Scripture continues to be a crucial source of daily grace, resulting in an ever-increasing change often called growth in grace. Reading and searching the Scriptures then are the food of the Christian life that gives nourishment and energy in order for us to become all that God has created us to be. Put most simply, reading the Bible as a Wesleyan is always intended to aid in our progressive sanctification. Even the careful study of

Scripture in more technical hermeneutics has the potential to change the in-terpreter (if of course, the interpreter consents). Thus we return to the claim already made: The study of Scripture is most effective when we admit that we are subjectively engaged with it.

In this more devotional sense we can claim that the Bible is sacramen-tal—that it is a medium of connecting us with God and a means of opening our hearts to participate in God's gracious activity in our lives. "Since Scripture bears witness to a God who invites assent by loving concern and not by power plays, its [purpose] as a sacrament of divine revelation is understood finally in a profoundly relational way: Scripture discloses God by inviting faith in a God-for-us, who is then confirmed by our concrete experience of God's grace."[17]

Wesley advised his people to study and search the Scriptures in a de-voted and meditative way. He believed that the Holy Spirit would inspire their hearts, provide nourishment, and be present in the very reading of the Bible so that they could receive whatever grace they needed. At the end of his preface to his *Notes upon the Old Testament* Wesley gives specific instructions for reading the Bible devotionally:

> If you desire to read the Scriptures in such a manner as may most effec-tually answer this end (to understand the things of God), would it not be advisable 1. to set apart a little time, if you can, every morning and evening for this purpose? 2. At each time, if you have leisure, to read a chapter out of the Old, and one out of the New Testament; if you cannot do this, to take a single chapter, or a part of one? 3. to read this with a single eye to know the whole will of God, and a fixed resolution to do it? In order to know His will, you should 4. have a constant eye to the **analogy of faith** . . . 5. Serious and earnest prayer should be constantly used before we consult the oracles of God, seeing Scripture can only be understood through the same Spirit whereby it was given. 6. It might also be of use, if while we read we were frequently to pause and examine ourselves by what we read.[18]

Elsewhere, Wesley suggests the reader of Scripture pray a prayer taken from the *Book of Common Prayer* (1662 edition).

> I advise every one, before he reads the Scripture, to use this or the like prayer: "Blessed Lord, who hast caused all holy Scriptures to be writ-ten for our learning, grant that we may in such wise hear them, read, mark, learn, and inwardly digest them, that by patience and comfort of thy holy word, we may embrace, and ever hold fast, the blessed hope of everlasting life, which thou has given us in our Saviour Jesus Christ."[19]

Wesley's deep conviction about the purpose of Scripture—namely, to reveal God's character as love and God's desire to save humanity—is "proven" when real persons experience God in their lives. Scripture fulfills its purpose when God fulfills God's purpose in us.

Proclaiming that the Bible is a sacramental means of grace could imply a very private use of Scripture as it aids in the salvation and progressive sanctification of each individual. But Wesley would never approve any type of solitary or exclusive form of Christianity. While the Bible certainly aids us in our individual lives, it is a book addressed to the whole people of God. This led Wesley to stress the importance of preaching in the movement known as Methodism.

According to Rob Wall, one of the primary functions of Scripture is to inform the preacher, who then informs the people of its meaning. Wall argues that Wesley's "real (not rhetorical) conception of Scripture emerges [through] preaching."[20] Wall sees important parallels between the Jewish exegesis (called **midrash**) of the biblical writers and Wesleyan exegesis. "Homiletical midrash is a contemporizing hermeneutic, suitable for a sacramental view of Scripture, which supposes that interpreters mediate between God's Word and their own worlds. . . . The goal of biblical commentary is never simply to clarify the meaning of the biblical text per se, but rather to clarify how the text [de]ciphers the messiness of the readers' own context in order to liberate them from it."[21] Thus along with reading and meditating on Scripture, preaching also becomes an incredibly important means of grace (although Wesley never specifically labels it as such). Wesley (the Protestant) would have seen preaching as a sacred act that complements the official sacraments. Preaching is certainly sacramental in a more general sense. The responsibility of the preacher cannot be underestimated.

Certainly then, the Bible was never meant to be interpreted apart from the community of faith.[22] While Wesley obviously had a strong faith in the Holy Spirit to inspire and reveal, not only through the writers of Scripture but also through our reading of Scripture, we do not interpret in isolation. We are always accountable to the community of faith, especially as we interpret Scripture. Wesley explicitly denies that God would give only one person a new revelation about the Bible's meaning. Along with the quadrilateral, the Christian community acts as an appropriate check and balance of any one individual's interpretation of a text. The Christian community also extends across the centuries historically, and thus each community is also accountable to orthodox biblical interpretation that has come before it.

2. Biblical interpretation and the wholeness of Scripture[23]

Just as no one individual can interpret the Bible in isolation from the whole community, no single verse, or even passage, is to be interpreted in isolation from the whole Bible. This is one of Wesley's most pronounced principles of biblical interpretation. When Wesley spoke of biblical authority, he meant authority that is seen when the Bible is taken as a whole. He thus placed the Holy Spirit's inspiration not only with each biblical writer but also with those groups that determined the canon. "The Scripture therefore of the Old and New Testament, is a most solid and precious system of Divine truth. Every part thereof is worthy of God; and all together are one entire body, wherein is no defect, no excess."[24] He often spoke of "the general [or whole] tenor of Scripture" when considering its primary role in faith and practice. For him, every verse needs to be interpreted not only in light of its place in its passage and in its book but also in light of its place in the canon. In a sense every text is interdependent with all others.[25]

> Many biblical texts are intertexts, composed with other biblical texts in mind and heart, and still other texts, unknown or unintended by the author, that come to the interpreter's mind in canonical context. The talented interpreter listens for echoes of other biblical texts, however low their volume, and looks for allusions, however dim their reflection, that link biblical texts together, the one glossing and thickening the meaning of the other.[26]

Wesley's approach to Scripture avoids the contemporary notion of proof-text-ing, or **eisegesis**. Picking various verses out of context to prove a presupposed point blatantly contradicts one of Wesley's most important interpretative prin-ciples, that of interpreting the parts in light of the whole.

The question can be rightly asked whether Wesley viewed every part of Scripture as equal in value. Or more specifically, what did Wesley believe about the relationship between the Old and New Testaments? According to Scott Jones, the answer to this question is multifaceted. In general,

> Wesley's views on the relation of the Old Testament and the New Testa-ment reflect a type of dispensational understanding that allows for both continuity and change in God's relationship with humankind. . . . On one hand, Wesley emphasizes that the Old Testament is sacred Scripture and therefore binding on all human beings. On the other hand, he em-phasizes that there are aspects of the gospel available only in the New Testament which supersede portions of the Old.[27]

Wesley severely cautioned those who would quickly skip over the Old Testament and neglect its principles. But several quotes are offered here to illustrate how Wesley also believed that the Old and New Testaments are different. He uses the idea of different biblical **dispensations**[28] (eras) to explain these differences.

> The Jews and we are under different dispensations. The glory of the whole Mosaic dispensation was chiefly visible and external; whereas the glory of the Christian dispensation is of an invisible and spiritual nature.[29]

[The New Testament] is a far more perfect dispensation than that which He delivered in Hebrew.[30]

For there is no comparison between the state of the Old Testament believers, and that which ye now enjoy: the darkness of that dispensation is passed away; and Christ the true light now shineth in your hearts.[31]

Overall, Wesley believed the entire Bible should be seen as a whole, even though he viewed God's revelation as progressing from the Old Testament to the New. The Bible's continuity is maintained because Wesley affirmed its uniform theological message. But the question remains, what did Wesley believe about the meaning of the whole? This is where we very self-consciously and boldly move to proclaiming what Wesley called the "grand themes of Scripture." For Wesley, and for the Wesleyan-Holiness tradition, the Bible reveals the *salvation* that we find in the grace of God alone. So it is biblical theology that informs all systematic formulations. Biblical theology is soteriological.

3. *Biblical interpretation and the hermeneutic of love*[32]

The whole purpose of Scripture is to reveal God as a God of love, who out of love saves the world. Wesley specifically names the message of the "whole tenor of Scripture" as the "analogy of faith." The meaning of the word "analogy" has shifted from its use in the 16th to 18th centuries, when it specifically referred to the great themes of Scripture. Although Wesley followed many of his predecessors and contemporaries in this usage, he differed in the *content* of the analogy of faith. Not all traditions would put soteriology as the primary purpose of Scripture.

To read the Bible as a Wesleyan necessarily means that we adopt this interpretative lens of soteriology. We may still read the Bible as a Wesleyan and not use Wesley's specific methods. We may even read the Bible as a Wesleyan and hold to other beliefs about the Bible's inspiration and authority. But we cannot read the Bible as a Wesleyan and ignore Wesley's view of the analogy of faith. That Wesley sees the very revelation of God as soteriological affects every other aspect of theology and of pastoral advice—indeed Wesley's whole "system." The content of the analogy of faith is that important.

Paradoxically, the analogy of faith is both Wesley's most powerful proclamation and his point of greatest weakness. This is because no objective proof exists to guarantee that Wesley is right in his assessment of the biblical message. Wesley's interpretation of Scripture as a whole stands alongside other options. For example, Wesley believed that God's primary characteristic, as revealed in Scripture, is love. But Calvin believed that God's primary characteristic, as revealed in Scripture, is God's sovereignty. Love will take Wesley to a soteriology that affirms free grace and sanctification. Sovereignty will lead the Reformed tradition to emphasize God's control in the world and to the doctrines of irresistible grace and predestination. Other traditions will likewise place different Christian beliefs at the center of their hermeneutics and theological conclusions.

From his "hermeneutic of love" Wesley affirmed four related themes as central and necessary to understanding the Bible. They are original sin, justification by faith, new birth, and inward and outward holiness.[33] Our discussion of these four themes in what follows will also serve as a basic introduction to Wesley's theology. Each of these themes will be examined in greater detail in subsequent chapters.

▶ WESLEY'S ANALOGY OF FAITH

ORIGINAL SIN

Foundational to Wesley's focus on salvation is that humanity is in a broken condition from which it needs to be delivered. He sees this as a thoroughly biblical concept, spread throughout the Bible as a whole. This brokenness was not God's original design but came only after humanity "fell" through its first representatives, Adam and Eve. There was not much debate in the first centuries of Christianity about what this meant, or specifically about how our first parents' actions affected each of their descendants, including us. But in the late fourth century, the great theologian Augustine began to develop a theory about what became known as **original sin**. One of Augustine's opponents, Pelagius, believed that the primary effect of the Fall was that humanity become mortal. But Augustine believed more. He asserted that original sin is inherited and passed down to every human being. Though Wesley does not follow all of Augustine's theory, he does affirm that original sin affects all persons to their detriment.

Original sin influences our inclinations, and we end up committing actual personal sins. We are not guilty before God for original sin, but when original sin is actualized through our own choices, we are then guilty. These personal sins separate us from God. Foundational for Wesley is that we cannot bridge this separation on our own. We are helpless apart from God's grace and God's initiative toward us. Important for the Wesleyan-Holiness tradition is that original sin can be cleansed *in this life*; some other traditions believe that original sin can never be overcome until after we die.

Wesley believed, then, that one of the primary themes of Scripture, Old and New Testament alike, is that humanity is broken and sinful and helpless on its own. Many Old Testament stories and characters reveal this tendency toward sin and failure. The Old Testament is radically honest about the pro-clivity of people to fall away from God's plan, even if God's plan is ultimately for their good. The New Testament further illuminates the sinful human condition throughout its contents—from Gospels to Epistles. As Paul states clearly, "All have sinned and fall short of the glory of God" (Rom. 3:23). So following the analogy of faith, the question we should ask of each individual passage is how it might broaden our understanding of original sin.

JUSTIFICATION BY FAITH

Wesley came to understand this aspect of the analogy of faith after his biographically and theologically important encounters with a group of Mora-vians just before 1738. The Moravians were a group of Lutherans that helped Wesley understand experientially Martin Luther's famous declaration of sola fide: We are saved by grace alone through faith in Jesus Christ. Martin Luther, a Catholic biblical scholar, came to this conclusion when studying the book of Romans. His proclamation of this biblical theme helped initiate the Protestant Reformation.

Theologically, salvation by faith alone directly correlates with the doc-trine of **justification**. This is also known sometimes as "forensic" salvation. In brief, we stand before God guilty for the sins we have committed. When we place our faith in Jesus Christ and his sacrifice on our behalf on the cross, our guilt is taken away. And so our "legal" status (using the forensic analogy) changes from guilty to not guilty. God forgives all our sins because, according to some interpretations, Jesus has taken our sin and our rightful punishment on himself.

In a sense, Wesley's personal experience allowed him to see Scripture in a new light. In 1738 he became *assured* of his salvation and understood for him-self this verse: "The Spirit you received does not make you slaves, so that you live in fear again; rather, the Spirit you received brought about your adoption to sonship. And by him we cry, '*Abba*, Father.' The Spirit himself testifies with our spirit that we are God's children" (Rom. 8:15-16 TNIV). "From that time on, he insisted that faith alone was necessary for salvation."[34] If original sin is the condition that separates us from God, justification by faith alone is God's means for overcoming that estrangement. Wesley believed that Jesus Christ came to be the means of this justification.

Like Paul, Wesley believed that the Old Testament also depicts a God of mercy. God's covenant with Abraham was a covenant of faith. And as Paul explains in Galatians, faith was established even before the law. What the law does is show us as guilty before God in need of justification. Justification is by faith alone. This is foundational to the way all of Protestant theology in-terprets Scripture. God forgives sin, through faith, so that we can enter into a relationship with God. Yet, while Wesley strongly affirms this biblical theology, he goes even further.

NEW BIRTH

There is a key difference between justification and **new birth** in Wesley's theology. Not only does God forgive us for past sins when we accept Jesus Christ as our Savior, but he also regenerates us and gives us a new life. "Therefore, if anyone is in Christ, he is a new creation; the old has gone, the new has come! All this is from God, who reconciled us to himself through Christ" (2 Cor. 5:17). By separating justification and regeneration, although they transpire simultaneously, Wesley began to separate himself from the Reformed tradition.

In Wesley's scheme, new birth is the beginning of the holy life, the beginning of sanctification. When Jesus told Nicodemus that he must be born again, he was also calling us to the hope of truly living a brand-new life. The call includes living this new life in a brand-new way. God not only forgives sin but also cleanses us from all unrighteousness, and (most important for Wesley) actually enables us to live a holy life. New birth relates to what we call imparted righteousness.

The Reformed tradition emphasizes what is known as imputed righteousness. In other words, Christ's own righteousness is imputed, or given to us. God then sees us as righteous because we are covered over by Christ's actual righteousness. In actuality, however, we are still sinful behind Christ's "screen." Imparted righteousness, however, means that God not only sees us as righteous because of Christ but actually makes us righteous. This begins at new birth. Therefore salvation is not just a legal action in which we are proclaimed not guilty by way of Christ's sacrifice. Salvation for Wesleyans includes God's cleansing work within our hearts. This cleansing work is closely related to our theology of Holiness and sanctification.

HOLINESS AND SANCTIFICATION

John Wesley believed that God had raised the Methodist people for the very purpose of proclaiming the message of holiness. He saw it as the most important theme in Scripture and thus as the most important theme in Christianity and in the Christian's life. Since this entire book is about holiness and **sanctification**, we offer only the briefest of descriptions here.

Sanctification begins at new birth and continues throughout our lifetime. We therefore speak of initial sanctification, progressive sanctification, and entire sanctification as important steps in a journey of holy living. Through God's sanctifying work in our hearts we experience a deep inner transformation, through the indwelling of the Holy Spirit. This initiates the progressive restoration of the image of God in us; this transformation frees us both from the guilt and power of sin and moves us into a growing, holy, loving relationship with God and others. We walk in love as Christ walked. Christ-like love is then the best definition of holiness.

Sanctification, more precisely, refers to the *how* of holiness. How are we made holy by God? The word "holiness" refers to the content of our life—the *what* of the holy life. What does it mean to be holy? We affirm that all holy acts come out of a holy heart and that God changes our desires and motivations from within when we fully devote ourselves to following Christ in faith and discipleship. We depend on God's enabling grace every day in our Christian walk. Holiness means much more than sinlessness. To be holy, we must love. And love is never finished because there are always new opportunities to practice love for God and neighbor. This is the heart of the Wesleyan message.

SUMMARY STATEMENTS

1. A Wesleyan interpretation of Scripture makes use of the best exegetical tools available.

2. A Wesleyan interpretation of Scripture is focused on soteriology and follows the "analogy of faith."

3. A Wesleyan interpretation of Scripture affirms the "whole tenor of Scripture" and that all texts are interdependent. Any one text is to be interpreted in light of the whole.

4. A Wesleyan interpretation of Scripture makes use of the Wesleyan quadrilateral.

5. A Wesleyan interpretation of Scripture confesses the subjectivity of faith and the need for community in properly interpreting Scripture.

6. Practical holiness is the ultimate goal of a Wesleyan interpretation of Scripture.

QUESTIONS FOR REFLECTION

1. What is the purpose of biblical interpretation?

2. How might Wesleyan interpretation differ from other interpretative traditions?

3. Evaluate Wesley's position on scriptural authority. Is it adequate?

4. How has the Bible helped you grow spiritually?

FURTHER READING

Callen, Barry L., and Richard P. Thompson. *Reading the Bible in Wesleyan Ways: Some Constructive Proposals*. Kansas City: Beacon Hill Press of Kansas City, 2004.

Gunter, Stephen, et al. *Wesley and the Quadrilateral*. Nashville: Abingdon Press, 1997.

Jones, Scott. *John Wesley's Conception and Use of Scripture*. Nashville: Abingdon Press, 1995.

T W O

THE WHOLE HOLY TENOR
OF SCRIPTURE

LEARNER OBJECTIVES

Your study of this chapter will help you to:

1. Define biblical theology and its relationship to exegesis and systematic theology
2. Recognize that holiness is a major theme in both the Old and New Testaments
3. Describe how the Old Testament portrays God's holiness and humanity's call to holiness
4. Describe how the New Testament portrays God's holiness and humanity's call to holiness

KEY WORDS

Biblical theology	Positional holiness
Thematization	Consecration
Hermeneutic of love	Covenant
"Wholly Other"	Pentecost
Apophatic theology	Modalism
God's incomparability	Baptism with the Holy Spirit
Imago Dei	

Holiness is a biblical theme.[1] It is part of Wesley's fourfold "analogy of faith" as examined in the last chapter. Wesley saw himself and the Methodist people as advocates for "Scriptural holiness."[2] He believed biblical preaching about holiness was the reason why God had raised the Methodists. There was no doubt in Wesley's mind that the written Word of God calls us to be holy as God is holy and that this call is possible through grace.

As we begin this chapter, we must keep in mind what we established earlier, that a certain amount of subjectivity is inherent for every interpreter. There are specifically "Wesleyan" ways to read the Bible, and a person who is Wesleyan should do so (see previous chapter, pp. 40-45). But we must also not forget that recognition of subjectivity never justifies the imposition of a doctrine on a text that was clearly never meant to be interpreted as such. Biblical support for the doctrine of Holiness must be collected with great hermeneutical integrity.

The measure of any sound biblical interpretation is its attention to the "whole tenor of Scripture" when exegeting a passage or verse. Again, Wesley believed that inward and outward holiness is deeply embedded in the entire Bible and that every verse is dependent on every other verse in its meaning. But exactly how does one interpret the entire biblical message about holiness and sanctification? With hundreds of references, surely one person cannot exegete them all. And even if one person could do so, only looking for the words "holiness" or "perfection" or "sanctification" found in a concordance would miss extremely relevant passages that describe the life of holiness without using the words! With this said, this chapter will necessarily depend on the work of biblical scholars, specifically on various biblical theologies of holiness that have been written.

We will examine the **biblical theology** of Holiness from the perspective of Old Testament theology and New Testament theology, in much the same way as many biblical theologies are written more broadly, separated by the Old and the New. But again, the goal is to establish what Scripture *as a whole* teaches about holiness and sanctification.

▶ OLD TESTAMENT IMAGES OF HOLINESS

Before we begin an investigation of specifics, we must consider some broader interpretative questions necessary for the development of an Old Testament theology of Holiness from a Wesleyan-Holiness perspective.

INTERPRETATIVE QUESTIONS

1. What is the goal of biblical theology? What is its relationship to both exegesis and systematic theology? According to Walter Brueggemann, the goal of biblical theology is to "construe a rendering of God" and to offer a type of

thematization of biblical material.[3] This is not the same thing as commenting on one text at a time. Nor is it the same as offering a constructive systematization. Biblical theology is always the crucial link between biblical exegesis and "regular" theology as it is most often understood. Biblical theology must play a huge role in doctrinal development if we are to ever claim that a particular theological construction is scriptural. But the work of doing biblical theology itself is difficult, even hazardous, because there are a myriad of hermeneutical choices that must be made. By nature, biblical theology is the generalization of an immeasurable amount of details. Even the decision of what to include or exclude is a rather subjective enterprise. One necessarily wonders if the subjective choices he or she makes are adequate representations of the whole. It is easier to exegete individual passages and to do theology unhinged from biblical texts. Biblical theology requires a most exacting type of work.[4]

There is no real alternative, however. Israel's witness to Yahweh is developed text by text. But at some point these individual texts must be interpreted as a whole. Thus Wesley's "analogy of faith" is a biblical theology because it views the whole tenor of Scripture as emphasizing God's holiness and human holiness of heart and life. So the task of this chapter demands choices of emphasis in light of hundreds of potential texts.

2. What is the theological relationship between the Old Testament and New Testament? To what degree should we presume Christ in the Old Testament story, if at all? An important issue in doing biblical theology, and particularly Old Testament theology, concerns how Christians approach a clearly Jewish sacred text. For the most part, Christians increasingly cut themselves off from Jewish conversation partners throughout the centuries due to their imposition of Christian themes onto the Old Testament. Because of this, according to Brueggemann, different Christian scholars have taken different options. On the one hand, some have simply appropriated the Old Testament as a Christian book with Christian themes and have purposely neglected any type of Jewish reading. On the other hand, there have been Christian scholars, usually deeply immersed in the biblical criticism that dominated Enlightenment and, until recently, post-Enlightenment thought, who have attempted to set all Christian presuppositions aside in order to read the Old Testament objectively as a Jewish text.[5]

Is there a middle way? Again, according to Brueggemann, this middle way must be careful to make a distinction between interpretations skewed by misguided Christian polemics and interpretations that legitimately anticipate that the Old Testament will be fulfilled in the New.[6] There is a difference between anticipating Christ and seeing Christ in every Old Testament text. For example, we might state confidently that "fidelity dominates the vision of Israel." But we can also legitimately add that "this conclusion is as unambiguous in the faith of Israel as it is in the Easter affirmations of the Church."[7] William Greathouse, a Wesleyan-Holiness biblical theologian, quotes Augustine on this point. "The New is in the Old concealed; the Old is in the New revealed."[8]

3. Are there radical differences in the theology of God when those from other traditions interpret the Old Testament? Is a Wesleyan-Holiness theology of the Old Testament unique? Should it be? At the heart of these questions is not only how the Wesleyan-Holiness tradition is different from other traditions but also what it has to contribute to biblical theology as a whole. There is no doubt that God's holiness is a central theme of the Old Testament. We will explore this further in a moment. But is there a particular hermeneutic of God's holiness in the Wesleyan-Holiness tradition that influences a broader perception of God?

Yes, such a hermeneutic does indeed exist. God's holiness is interpreted through the **hermeneutic of love**. Other traditions might interpret God's holiness in light of God's power or God's sovereignty or God's justice. The Wesleyan-Holiness interpreter does not ignore these themes about God. But by interpreting God's holiness in light of God's love, he or she may reach different conclusions about God's character than those reached by others. Is this a doctrinal imposition upon the Old Testament texts? Yes and no. Yes, in that a theological statement about God becomes dominant in this interpretation. God is love. But no, in that Wesley and the Wesleyan-Holiness tradition believe that God's love not only is found in the whole tenor of Scripture but is its primary truth. This may sound like a circular argument. Indeed, this is where Wesley's analogy of faith in general is open to the most criticism. But as shown in the last chapter, reading the Bible in Wesleyan ways requires subjective choices based on the whole that then inform the interpretation of passages in particular. If the interpretative lens is incorrect, this manner of exegesis is at least consistent.

Adopting a hermeneutic of love is not without its difficulties, however, especially when reading the Old Testament. There are many passages where God seems anything but loving; consider the commands of God that condone genocide. There are also passages of Scripture where God seems self-contradictory; take for example God's command to Jonah to preach the impending destruction of the Ninevites without any mention of hope through repentance, but then God "relents" and spares the city (Jon. 4:2). Wrestling through difficult passages such as these can be challenging but not impossible. We will examine several such passages below, as we now turn our attention to an Old Testament theology of God and a theology of the holiness to which God calls us.

THE HOLINESS OF GOD

That holiness is a, if not *the,* dominant theme of the Old Testament is supported by the sheer number of occurrences of the Hebrew word for holy, or holiness, *qds.* The root occurs almost 850 times. In Leviticus, 152 times; Exodus, 102 times; Numbers, 80 times; Ezekiel, 105 times; Isaiah, 73 times; and in the Psalms, 65 times. Different scholars emphasize different nuances of the word's meaning, but all agree that holiness implies separation or otherness. Its root can mean "to be cut away"; it can also mean "bright" or "clear." Its opposite meaning is the profane or common. Old English suggests that holiness is about being "whole" or "healthy." The Latin suggests sanctification means to "make sacred" or to "set apart" for a sacred purpose.

Other variations in meaning of the Hebrew word *qds* in light of different contexts include the following:

a. Holiness is associated with fire in the Old Testament (Exod. 3:2-3; 19:18; 24:17; Deut. 4:12, 24; 5:22-27; 9:3; Ps. 18:8-14; Ezek. 1:4-28).

b. Holiness implies wrath against that which would threaten holiness (Ezek. 7; Zeph. 1:14-18).

c. Holiness inspires fear, awe, and reverence (Exod. 15:11; Pss. 64:9; 66:3, 5; 89:7; 99:3; 111:9; 145:6).

d. Holiness is remote, and unapproachable (Exod. 3:5; 19:12-13, 20-24; Josh. 5:15).

e. Holiness implies cleanness or purity (Lev. 10:10; Ezek. 22:26; 44:23).

f. Holiness carries with it the sense of majesty, honor, and splendor (Exod. 15:11; 1 Chron. 16:27; Pss. 8:1; 93:1; 96:6; 111:3).

g. Holiness is portrayed as unsearchable, incomprehensible, and incomparable (Ps. 77:13; Isa. 40:13-14, 18-20, 25-26).

h. Holiness is shown to be wonderful, in the sense that wonders appear when one least expects them (Gen. 28:17; Exod. 15:11; Deut. 26:8; Judg. 6:22-23; Pss. 9:1; 77:13-14; 105:2; 106:7; 107:8, 15, 21, 31).

i. Holiness is great, in the sense of being extraordinary (Pss. 77:13; 95:3; 104:1; Ezek. 38:23).

j. Holiness denotes supremacy and is responded to with exaltation (Pss. 47:7-8; 91:9; Isa. 6:1; Dan. 4:2, 17, 25, 32).

k. Holiness in God is often portrayed as jealousy (Exod. 20:3, 5; 34:14; Deut. 4:24; Josh. 24:19).

l. Holiness in God always implies life and vibrancy (Deut. 32:39-40; Josh. 3:10; Pss. 42:2; 84:2-4; Jer. 10:10).

Some of the above themes are more dominant than others; this does not represent an all-inclusive list. Interpreters differ in what they emphasize when speaking of God's holiness. Walter Brueggemann highlights God's otherness,

God's glory, and God's jealousy as quintessential. William Greathouse lists separation, glory, and purity as the most important connotations of the word "holy" or "holiness" in relation to God. W. T. Purkiser underscores God's holiness as majesty, radiance, and purity. Dennis Kinlaw focuses on God's otherness and God's jealousy. John Huntzinger emphasizes God's redemptive works (such as the Exodus) as displaying holiness and speaks of God's holiness in the context of Israel's worship. George Lyons emphasizes that God is unique and uniquely just and loving; "that is, [God] is holy in being and behavior."[9] These interpretations are only representative of potentially countless others, but they will direct our discussion. We will focus on God's incomparability, God's glory, and God's jealousy.

God's Incomparability. In contemporary theology God is often described as **"Wholly Other."** This means that God is transcendent—above the world (as in distant) and distinct from the world (as its Creator). Some scriptural passages imply that such otherness is so intense that seeing God is dangerous, if not deadly. God is one who "may not be easily approached, who may not be confused with anyone or anything else, and who lives alone in a prohibitive zone where Israel can enter only guardedly, intentionally, and at great risk."[10] God is great, majestic, wonderful, and supreme, is worthy of honor and worship, and is to be feared. God's otherness is also expressed in passages that speak of God as incomprehensible and ineffable. God is beyond human understanding and beyond description.

God cannot be compared to any other. This affirmation is the source of what is known as **apophatic theology**[11]: God can only be defined by what God is not. There are no adequate analogies to capture and express God's character positively according to this type of theology. And yet we do not have to restrict ourselves to apophatic descriptions of God as we affirm **God's incomparability.** God's self-revelation is apparent in God's relationship with Israel and in the writings of the Old Testament. Thus God has given us the positive content of God's holiness. One aspect of this self-revelation illumines God's holiness as glory.

God's Glory. God's holiness understood as glory has two different connotations. First of all, God's glory relates to God's right to govern Israel. We find God asserting authority over against rivals, whether human or divine. God emerges as more powerful and therefore is worthy of being glorified. To be glorified is to be exalted as the one worthy of worship and loyalty. But God's glory also has a second important connotation.

God's glory is also expressed in terms of God's presence. God's glory fills the temple. God's glory is manifested; it is near. When Moses asks to see God face-to-face, he is shown God's glory, which is a safe way to make God visible without harming Moses. Promising to be with Israel in the tabernacle, God said, "I will meet with the Israelites there, and it shall be sanctified by my glory" (Exod. 29:43 NRSV). God's glory also denotes God's protection and provision, as the people are fed manna and quail in the desert. God's glory is not the exact opposite of God's transcendence in the Old Testament. God's glory does not exclude God's transcendence. God remains wholly other. But by revealing glory as a type of presence, God does come near to Israel. God accommodated to their situation through various incarnations of glory, which would culminate with the actual presence of God in the incarnation—the person of Jesus Christ.

God's Jealousy. There is much discussion in Old Testament theology about God's seemingly contradictory acts. On the one hand, we find a God who is quickly wrathful when Israel is disobedient or participates in "unclean" acts that represent faithlessness. On the other hand, we find a God who is merciful, slow to anger, and abounding in love and who extends mercy even when Israel has been led astray. We find a God who seems insistent on maintaining power and authority. And we find a God who stands in solidarity with the people and who sets aside all self-regard for the sake of these people. Further, how do we reconcile the following images?

One viewpoint gives us these impressions:

- God is envisioned as the potter thoroughly engaged with what he or she creates (Gen. 2:7; Isa. 45:18; Jer. 18:3-6).
- God is seen as a gardener, who plants, cares, and is attentive to the flourishing of the garden (Isa. 5:1-2).
- God is a shepherd who attentively watches, protects, and cares for the sheep (Ps. 23).
- God is a mother who feeds and comforts (Num. 11:12; Isa. 66:13).
- God is a physician who actively intervenes for life and healing (Jer. 30:17).

And yet we also find the following:

- The potter smashes an ill-shaped pot (Jer. 19:11).
- The gardener is disappointed with the produce of vineyard and "plucks up" and "tears down (Isa. 5:5-7).
- The shepherd may scatter the sheep (Jer. 31:10).
- The mother can be neglectful and inattentive to the child (Num. 11:12; Isa. 49:14-15).
- The doctor may come too late, when the situation is beyond healing (Jer. 30:12-13).[12]

This is where the hermeneutic of love eases the discomfort that comes from such disjunctive activities of God. This hermeneutic aids us as we interpret the concept of God's holiness as expressed in God's jealousy. Some scholars interpret God's jealousy as an expression of God's need to maintain and demand exclusive worship. Rivals threaten God's self-identity. "[God] cannot tolerate worship . . . that is in defiance of [God's] essential and innermost nature."[13] God then punishes those who worship others or who worship inadequately. The suggestion in this type of interpretation is that God must maintain and protect God's own authority, sovereignty, justice, and supremacy.

If, however, we interpret God's jealousy from the perspective of love, the focus is not on God's self-identity but on the relationship with humanity that God desires. Defiance or faithlessness is not so much an affront to God but an aberration of the *imago Dei* that God created. We could say that even God's justice, then, must be interpreted soteriologically. It is out of love that God calls humanity to enact its original design. Only a relationship with God can enable the full expression of humanity's own holiness. The potter, gardener, shepherd, mother, and doctor do not discipline their subjects only because they are inadequate or because the subjects show their caregivers in a poor light. Or putting it bluntly, God does not discipline the people because they make God look bad! God's more negative activities are always redemptive in the larger picture. This may seem the easy way out of the conundrum of God's more "destructive" side. But such a rendering, with divine love as its guide, can be seen clearly in the Old Testament. And such a rendering surely anticipates the redemption of God in Christ, who was sent first to the lost sheep of Israel.

HOLINESS IN HUMANITY

According to George Allen Turner, "While the terms associated with 'holiness' stress the contrast between Jehovah and [humanity], which can be bridged by an act of cleansing, those associated with 'perfection' point to humanity's kinship with God and the possibility of fellowship."[14] Strictly put, only God is holy. Yet God commands, "Be holy as I am holy." This command pervades Old Testament theology, and when the New Testament turns to this theme, the writers quote the Old Testament. We could say that the *means* of human holiness, or perfection, changes in the New Testament, but this is not wholly accurate. Faith and grace permeate the Old Testament as well.[15] The Old Testament has a soteriology that is, yes, fulfilled in Christ and aided by the Holy Spirit. But Israel's call to holiness is also accomplished by faith. In a sense, we do not need Paul to point out that Abraham believed, and it was credited to him as righteousness (Rom. 4). We also do not need James to show us that Abraham's faith worked itself out in true righteousness and love (James 2). These themes are strongly and independently evident in the Old Testament (Gen. 15:6; 22:1-19).

Significantly, objects or places can be considered holy. This ritualistic sense of the holiness of the inanimate comes by way of the word "sanctification." Something is made holy when it is set aside for a sacred purpose. This can be easily translated to human holiness. A person is "sanctified" when he or she fulfills a holy purpose. This concept is certainly to be interpreted for the present day. The purpose of humanity (as we will see in later chapters) is to love God and others. When this purpose is fulfilled, a person is "holy." But too often the popular understanding of holiness stops there. The Old Testament can deeply enrich our understanding of human holiness today. We will examine five helpful aspects of the call to be holy.

1. **Derived Holiness.** Human beings derive their holiness from the unique holiness of God. "I am the LORD, who makes you holy" (Exod. 31:13; Lev. 22:32). "I am the LORD your God; consecrate yourselves and be holy, because I am holy. . . . I am the LORD who brought you up out of Egypt to be your God; therefore be holy, because I am holy" (Lev. 11:44-45). "Consecrate yourselves and be holy, because I am the LORD your God" (20:7). "You are to be holy to me because I, the LORD, am holy, and I have set you apart from the nations to be my own" (v. 26). There is a connection between God's holiness and our holiness that must not be forgotten. Our holiness is derived from our relationship with God. The holy in the Old Testament is often described as the "clean" and the unholy as the "unclean" or as the "profane" or "common." According to David Thompson, each of these terms refers not to a state of being but to a quality of relationship with God. "Thus, in these contexts clean and unclean do not substantially describe the condition of the person or thing, but characterize it with respect to its relationship to the divine."[16] To be unclean is to be unfit for relating to God; to be clean is to be in, and to be worthy of, a relationship with God.

This understanding of derived holiness has strong implications for the doctrines of imputed and imparted righteousness. Derived holiness does not need to imply **positional holiness** that only supports imputed righteousness in human beings. In Wesleyan thought, God not only sees us as righteous but also makes us righteous. But as William Greathouse expresses, our holiness is always "relative."[17] Yet what is too often forgotten is that this imparted righteousness is always dependent on a connection with God. It is not as if we relate to God, are made holy, and can continue to be holy apart from God, as if holiness is accomplished once and for all. To be out of relationship with God is to necessarily lose one's holiness. We become holy because God's holiness is "contagious" and "communicable"[18] only when the relationship is maintained. We can understand this better if we properly grasp the importance of **consecration** in Old Testament theology.

2. Consecrated Holiness. Holiness in the Old Testament is deeply connected to the concept of consecration. "To be holy is to be God's, effected by consecration."[19] When something (or someone) is entirely devoted to God, it is holy. Feast days are said to be holy because they are God's. The firstborn is consecrated to God and is thus God's holy possession. The people are called to consecrate themselves to God, for this God is their God uniquely—as evidenced, for example, by their redemption in the Exodus. This consecration is often expressed ritualistically. In the priestly context, for example, holiness necessitates that everything that is profane, common, or unclean be cleansed. This is often through a ritual act. This ritual act (which can be termed sanctification as well as consecration) then leads the person or thing to truly be available for divine service. "Persons who come into the presence of the Holy One must carefully prepare themselves by ritual washings and other means, since to present oneself with any degree of impurity is to invite disaster."[20]

And yet, something unclean can be made holy by its ritualistic contact with the "altar" of God. Exodus 29:37 has been used by early Methodists and the Wesleyan-Holiness Movement to show the connection between consecration (also known as entire devotion) and holiness or purity: "For seven days make atonement for the altar and consecrate it. Then the altar will be most holy, and whatever touches it will be holy." Consecration becomes extremely important to the doctrine of entire sanctification based on this Old Testament image. According to Adam Clarke, and then Phoebe Palmer (see chap. 4), Christ becomes the altar. When a person places "all" on the altar through the act of complete consecration, the "altar sanctifies the gift." This should imply a continual need to remain consecrated to God throughout the Christian journey. The point is that a person is holy when wholly God's, when fully in God's possession. This then implies that there are no rivals who might separate us from this entire devotion.

3. Unrivaled Holiness. A strong theme in Old Testament theology is that Israel is uniquely God's—God's people and God's nation. As observed earlier, God is jealous and possessive. Biblical writers often used possessive pronouns when talking about what is God's—whether it be Sabbaths, inanimate objects, or commands. Keeping God's commands, then, was a sign of the people's entire devotion to the one true God; there was no room for divided loyalty to other gods. "No wonder, then, that relationships which rivaled the people's consecration to God were both a breach of covenant (Lev. 25:55-26:2, 14-15; cf. Ezek. 23:39) and a profanation of the holy—of God's holy name (Lev. 22:32; Ezek. 20:30; 43:7-8)."[21]

The first two commandments of the Decalogue are foundational to God's relationship with Israel. "You shall have no other gods before me. You shall not make for yourself an idol in the form of anything in heaven above or on the earth beneath or in the waters below. You shall not bow down to them or worship them; for I, the LORD your God, am a jealous God" (Exod. 20:3-5). Wesley interpreted idolatry as the underlying sin beneath all others. The Wesleyan-Holiness Movement made idolatry the primary problem overcome by entire sanctification, and the key detractor from the life of holiness.[22] The Old Testament, like the New, calls persons to a single eye, an undivided heart, and worship of God alone. This prohibition against idolatry comes out of Israel's covenantal relationship with the Holy One.

4. **Covenantal Holiness.** God established a **covenant** with Abraham. "I will be your God, and you will be my people." This theme is repeated throughout the Old Testament (Gen. 17:7-8; Exod. 6:7; Lev. 26:12; Jer. 7:23). But God's covenant with Abraham is also anticipated, even in God's initial creative act. Adam and Eve were in a type of covenant with God, as they walked and talked with the divine (Gen. 1:28-31; 2:16-17). A covenantal relationship is also implied in the assertion that they were created in the image of God (1:26-27). In fact, according to Wesleyan theology, the *imago Dei* consists of right relationships as God intended, unpolluted by sin. Even in the garden we hear the implicit call, "Love the Lord your God with all your heart, soul, and mind, and love your neighbor as yourself" (see Matt. 22:37-40). And according to Wesleyan theology, when Adam and Eve sinned, they were deprived of this primary divine-human relationship that had defined their holiness. And yet we see even here that God remains true to them, faithful to this covenant despite their act of faithlessness.

Over and over again in the Old Testament we find God's faithfulness to the covenant even when Israel is faithless, stubborn, and disobedient, and even when the covenant is broken. The covenant at Sinai stipulated that Israel must listen to God and obey God's commandments as a prerequisite for Israel's holiness (Exod. 19:5-6). This reinforces the idea that Israel's holiness is dependent on its obedient relationship with the Holy God. This also means that Israel ceases to be a holy people the moment it ceases to listen to God and obey God's commandments. However, as the Old Testament history of God's relationship with Israel illustrates, Israel's failure to keep the covenant, most precisely seen in their failure to keep the law, does not force God's hand to forever abandon them. Israel's covenant God, who is holy, punishes the unfaithful covenant partners who have become unholy, but God does not reject them. The book of Hosea is a good illustration of this. God who is holy and faithful retains the relationship because faithfulness is an essential quality of covenantal holiness. As Paul says in 2 Timothy, "If we are faithless, he will remain faithful, for he cannot disown himself" (2:13). Does this mean that we can be careless and faithless without damaging effects?

5. Obedient Holiness. God may call us holy people and be wholly faithful to us. But according to the Wesleyan-Holiness position , such a pronouncement requires our response. As anticipated by Paul, God calls us holy and calls us to be holy; we are to become what we are. David Thompson states clearly: "The covenant further defines the holy as a relationship in which the will of God is done. Here holiness and righteousness are wed. Even in the Old Testament, understanding holiness as proper relation to God in no way renders the holy void of moral and ethical content."[23] So a relationship with God defines Israel as holy. God's holiness is contagious and communicable to those to whom God claims ownership. But this holiness of God does more than offer "positional" holiness. The holiness of God enables obedience and righteousness in those whom God claims. God's sanctification accomplishes this enablement. Put simply, we respond to purifying grace in true obedience. This raises an important question: Was personal holiness as consistent obedience possible for people of the Old Testament?

Sometimes Christians too easily assume that such obedience to God was impossible before Christ. This assessment is certainly contradicted by the presence of genuinely holy and obedient people in Israel's history. But we also find consistent and persistent calls for Israel's return to obedience throughout the prophets. In these same prophets we find hope and foreshadowing of something more—fulfilled, as we know, through Christ. According to Dennis Kinlaw, Wesley himself saw the New Testament as the new covenant in which the longings of those under the old covenant are finally realized. Kinlaw shows that Wesley often used Ezek. 36:25-29 when referring to the relationship between the new and the old. The prophet anticipates a time when God will bring this to pass:

> I will sprinkle clean water on you, and you will be clean; I will cleanse you from all your impurities and from all your idols. I will give you a new heart and put a new spirit in you; I will remove from you your heart of stone and give you a heart of flesh. And I will put my Spirit in you and move you to follow my decrees and be careful to keep my laws. You will live in the land I gave your forefathers; you will be my people, and I will be your God. I will save you from all your uncleanness. I will call for the grain and make it plentiful and will not bring famine upon you.

This passage *follows* a passage of God's rebuke:

> Again the word of the LORD came to me: "Son of man, when the people of Israel were living in their own land, they defiled it by their conduct and their actions. Their conduct was like a woman's monthly unclean-

ness in my sight. So I poured out my wrath on them because they had shed blood in the land and because they had defiled it with their idols. I dispersed them among the nations, and they were scattered through the countries; I judged them according to their conduct and their actions. And wherever they went among the nations they profaned my holy name, for it was said of them, 'These are the LORD's people, and yet they had to leave his land.' I had concern for my holy name, which the house of Israel profaned among the nations where they had gone. (Vv. 16-21)

Thus God's rebuke is followed by God's promise. In one sense, this promise is for the very people God addresses. God is calling for a pervasive repentance from these people and to a restoration of their righteousness.

But we can also read these words in a prophetic sense. A day will come when all things will be made new, when dry bones will live. Other prophets join the chorus. There will be a day when the law will be written on human hearts. There will be a day when a new power will further enable true obedience. There will be a day when God's own holiness will be revealed through the radiance of the Son of Man and when he will also say, be holy as God is holy.

▶ New Testament Images of Holiness

In keeping with the format of our review of an Old Testament theology of Holiness, we begin with some broader interpretative questions for the development of a New Testament theology of Holiness from a Wesleyan-Holiness perspective.

1. Is the New Testament consistent in its presentation of holiness? Are there significant differences of perspective between, say, the Gospels and the writings of Paul?

2. How is holiness in the New Testament new (different from the Old Testament)? What do the biblical theologies of Christ and the Holy Spirit add to the Old Testament images of holiness?

3. Are there any passages that have been pushed beyond their limits in an attempt to support a specific theology of sanctification? If so, what is the Wesleyan-Holiness tradition left with?

HOLINESS IN GREEK

Overall, the Greek New Testament affirms the Old Testament's various uses of *qds*. The primary word in Greek is *hagios*. This word, most often associated with the holiness of God, can also imply that something or someone has been set apart for a sacred purpose and entirely devoted to a holy God. The word for "clean," *katharos*, and the word *teleios*, which can be translated as "perfection," come into clearer focus in the New Testament. We also find *katartizo* in association with holiness. This word means to fix something that is broken in order for it to once again fulfill its potential and its purpose. There are other cognates for these words that further delineate their meanings. Contextual work is also crucial.

The following are some brief summary statements about holiness in the Greek New Testament:

1. Holiness implies purity of heart (sometimes expressed as purity of mind). A person who is pure in heart is undivided in loyalty and devotion. The heart represents the very center or essence of a person's being; it is purified only through association with God, and thus only truly derived from God. But this concept also implies a legitimate "cleansing" that leaves the heart pure, as in undefiled.

2. This purity is an inner quality with outward expression. It is something with which the person cooperates; there are many references to the admonition to "purify ourselves" (2 Cor. 7:1). This implies that the inner work of God is maintained synergistically. According to Kenneth Waters, purity is an "inward quality [that is] outwardly manifested in the pattern of human response and behavior, lifestyle, relationships, missional activity and vocational commitments. Holiness and outward righteousness are parallel in the Christian Scriptures."[24]

3. Holiness in the New Testament is "holistic." It is not a quality among others but the overarching good, "the sum and source of all other virtues."[25] In kind, holiness is holistic because it requires the presenting of the whole self "as a living sacrifice, holy and acceptable to God" (Rom. 12:1 NRSV). Holiness is also holistic in the sense that it involves both negative and positive *moral* content. That is, holiness is not just the absence of sin but also the presence of the good. The holy person, then, acts in love and does not simply avoid the unholy.

4. Holiness in the New Testament is both an individual and corporate calling. Each individual is called to holiness (Matt. 5:48; 1 Thess. 4:3-8; 1 Pet. 1:15-16). But the body of Christ as a united organism is also called "holy" and called to live out its corporate life and worship in holiness (1 Cor. 1:2; 12:12-26).

5. According to a Wesleyan-Holiness interpretation, the Greek New Testament implies an understanding of holiness that is threefold: a final holiness that will one day be revealed (1 John 3:2), a progressive growing in holiness throughout one's life (Phil. 1:6-11), and what has been termed "entire sanctification" and described as "crisic" in nature (1 Thess. 5:23-24).[26]

HOLINESS IN MATTHEW AND MARK

According to David Kendall, the Wesleyan-Holiness tradition has generally overlooked the Gospels in their search for biblical support for the theology of holiness and sanctification. He believes this is perhaps because "Jesus has very little to say on the subject of holiness." Apparently, "the standard terms are seldom found."[27] This does not, however, mean at all that Jesus has no theology of Holiness! He clearly speaks of holiness, though in different contexts and with a different vocabulary than the other writings in the New Testament.[28]

George Lyons suggests that few "ordinary" Jews would have taken a call to holy living as a call to them personally. Rather, groups such as the Sadducees, Essenes, Zealots, and Pharisees took special care to avoid the defilement characteristic of the world. All of these groups, some more than others, defined holiness as actual physical separation from those who might make them unclean. If they were "contaminated," they performed rituals to restore their own purity.[29] The Pharisees in particular attempted to obey the law (the 613 presented in the Hebrew Scriptures) as a means of avoiding impurity. It is incorrect to see them as insincere legalists. Jesus, however, did challenge their understanding that the term "holiness" only implied physical separation. David Kendall points out that Jesus cautioned the Pharisees strongly:

> Jesus argued that people contract the worst forms of defilement not from contaminated externals but from inner corruption. Not from food that goes in, but from the wellspring of the heart "come evil thoughts, murder, adultery, sexual immorality, theft, false testimony, slander. These are what make a man 'unclean'; but eating with unwashed hands does not make him 'unclean'" (Matthew 15:19-20). He pronounced woe upon those who cared most about purity; they had become whitewashed tombstones outwardly, but rotting corpses inwardly.[30]

Holiness then, according to Jesus, is more than a situated position in relationship with the world or with God; holiness is *more than* derived. It involves a pure heart. Jesus focused on an inner moral change that expresses itself as love. "Love the Lord your God with all your heart and with all your soul and with all your mind and with all your strength. . . . Love your neighbor as yourself" (Mark 12:30-31) is the essence of holiness according to Jesus Christ.

Also important for our construction of holiness in the first two Gospels is the Sermon on the Mount. Many of the Beatitudes break the traditional notion that only the professionally religious have any hope of finding themselves in the kingdom of God. The lowly and humble are those who will receive God's blessed responses. In Matthew and Mark, and certainly also in Luke, we see Jesus ministering to the least likely in the kingdom of this world. The kingdom of God is not offered only to some, but to all. Jesus' message reorders the status quo. Potential holiness is extended to the least, and when they respond, often their lives are radically transformed. Possibly part of the contribution of the Wesleyan-Holiness tradition to the church is its emphasis that *all* are called to holiness—literally all.

The Gospel of Mark paints holiness as dependent on a continuing relationship with God. We find the theme of discipleship prominent. According to Kent Brower, discipleship is entered through commitment and maintained through obedience. It is progressive and "unremitting." It allows for failure but calls for the very highest fidelity to the life of love.[31]

HOLINESS IN LUKE AND ACTS

Because the Gospel of Luke and the Acts of the Apostles are usually considered to be two parts of the same story by Luke, we will deal with them here as a unit. The overarching theme of both is the work of the Holy Spirit. Jesus is represented in Luke as the premier example of a life walked in the Spirit. Luke directly says that the Holy Spirit was with Jesus from birth; indeed the Holy Spirit was involved in his conception. Likewise, reference to the Holy Spirit in Acts becomes the major way of describing the newness of life the apostles and the growing number of disciples experienced.

The Gospel of Luke focuses on the Holy Spirit in the life of Jesus. Beyond his very birth, we find the Spirit at Jesus' baptism leading Jesus into the desert of temptation and out again, and then Jesus reveals his mission by quoting Isaiah:

> When he came to the village of Nazareth, his boyhood home, he went as usual to the synagogue on the Sabbath and stood up to read the Scriptures. The scroll of Isaiah the prophet was handed to him. He unrolled the scroll and found the place where this was written:
>
> "The Spirit of the LORD is upon me,
>
> for he has anointed me to bring Good News to the poor.
>
> He has sent me to proclaim that captives will be released,
>
> that the blind will see,
>
> that the oppressed will be set free,
>
> and that the time of the LORD's favor has come."
>
> (Luke 4:16-19 NLT)

One of Luke's major themes is that Jesus comes to those who need him most. But this sense of mission is clearly connected to the Spirit of God and the Spirit's enabling and empowering for Jesus to fulfill this mission. There is also the sense that the Spirit is involved in Jesus' mission to reveal God and the nature of God to humanity.[32] And what is God like? Luke 15 provides insight into the searching, saving, loving nature of the holy God. In sum, "according to Luke . . . Jesus is conceived by the power of the Spirit, commissioned by the Spirit, led by the Spirit, anointed by the Spirit, full of the Holy Spirit, and filled with the power of the Holy Spirit. His entire ministry is conducted in the Spirit."[33]

In Acts, Luke continues the emphasis on the Spirit and seeks to show that as the Spirit worked in Jesus' life, the Spirit will also work in the church following **Pentecost,** by empowering the disciples, commissioning them, leading them, anointing them, and filling them so that they can fulfill their missional purpose (Acts 1:8). Robert Wall reflects on this point:

> According to the final form of the NT, the shift from fourfold Gospel to Acts envisages a shift in narrative thematic and theological interest from Jesus (Gospel) to Spirit (Acts). Messiah, who is empowered by the Spirit for his earthly mission, becomes the heavenly baptizer by whose Spirit his successors on earth are now empowered to continue his ministry. This crucial shift marks out the programmatic historical problem facing the community of Christ's disciples: will they be able to survive his physical departure from them? The theological problem that Acts considers is this: what form of life does Israel take in its post-Jesus era? The succession from a messianic movement to an apostolic community and the continuity of Messiah's role to what he began is the central thematic of the entire narrative. Sharply put, the succession of eras in the history of God's salvation from messianic to apostolic . . . [is] marked off and facilitated by the Spirit of God.[34]

The demarcation between one era to the next is laid out in the first two chapters of Acts. At his ascension Jesus again reassures his disciples that another is coming; this is fulfilled at Pentecost. In Luke, John the Baptist foretells of one who will extend water baptism to include a baptism with fire. John states that "he will baptize you with the Holy Spirit" (Luke 3:16). This baptism, then, that transpires on Pentecost is a baptism of Jesus Christ using the Holy Spirit. We do not, therefore, technically move from the age of the Messiah to the age of the Spirit in a way that might imply some heretical form of **modalism.** The Spirit is the agent of God in Christ, not an independent force (Acts 2:32-39). Why is this important? Because the work of God in salvation and sanctification is always Trinitarian; it is wrong to state that Jesus saves, and the Spirit sanctifies. God (as Trinity) saves, God (as Trinity) sanctifies. Lukan texts do not support heretical modalism, which reduced God to one person who performs different functions when in different modes.

Still, it is clear that Pentecost is the fulfillment of the promise of this baptism, when the Holy Spirit comes in fullness. There is no doubt that what happened to the disciples was their **baptism with the Holy Spirit**. The question in the recent history of the Wesleyan-Holiness tradition is whether this apostolic experience should be seen as equivalent to entire sanctification and thus the pattern for all Christians.

More articles on the baptism with the Holy Spirit have been published in the primary theological journal of the Wesleyan-Holiness tradition, the *Wesleyan Theological Journal*, than on any other single subject. There is no consensus, however. For years this subject has been a matter of major debate in the tradition. Even today it divides two interpretative positions. Nevertheless, Pentecost marked a new beginning in the community and a transformation within individuals.

> It is by the Spirit that the faith community is healed and transformed (or re-created) into a suffering people faithful to God in an anti-God world. . . . It is by the Spirit that the suffering Jesus is "present" within the community and it is the Spirit who is empowered to bear witness to Jesus. In this sense, the baptism of the Spirit is a rite of initiation into a cruciform life.[35]

Significantly, Acts further implies that the Spirit brings not only power for the community to be missional witnesses to Christ but also purity and cleansing. The God of Luke 15 is manifested in the lives of new believers. The newness of life being offered is not just forgiveness for guilt but also reconciliation, regeneration and, in Acts, "Spirit baptism," which is often associated with sanctification.

HOLINESS IN JOHN AND JOHN'S LETTERS

Clearly the Gospel of John had a different purpose than the first three canonical Gospels written. Clement of Alexandria, a church father of the second and third centuries and one of the church's earliest theologians, asserts that John purposely intended to supplement the narratives of the other Gospels. John's agenda is plainly stated near the end of his book. As the plain text says, he has written it so that persons will believe that Jesus is the Christ and that they will have life in his name (20:31). This purpose is mirrored in the first chapter of John's first letter: "We proclaim to you what we have seen and heard, so that you also may have fellowship with us. And our fellowship is with the Father and with his Son, Jesus Christ" (1 John 1:3). What we find then in John is more than narrative. We find theological reflection meant to "strengthen faith and thereby produce life."[36] In John, Jesus moves from the Christ of history to the Christ of faith.

On the subject of holiness in John, we must again start with God. According to Kent Brower, John's Gospel moves us in the direction of the Trinity.[37] But unlike the depiction of the Holy God in the Old Testament as remote and transcendent, John portrays God as One of intimacy and love. Clark Pinnock writes, "As a circle of loving relationships, God is dynamically alive.

There is only one God, but this one God is not solitary but a loving communion that is distinguished by overflowing life."[38] Johannine scholar Moody Smith states, "The unity of the Father and the Son is expressed in terms of love and mission. . . . This unity and love is then extended to include Jesus' disciples, that is, the church (cf. 14:21; 15:9; 20:21), and mutual love becomes the ground and basis of the church's existence."[39] In Jesus' prayer in John 17, he invites us into an intimacy with God that is not some sort of mystical union[40] but an abiding (chap. 15) in the love of God. (Paul uses the phrase "in Christ"; Peter uses "participants in the divine nature.") The New Testament breaks through God's transcendence and speaks of a oneness with Christ and a oneness with others who are in Christ. The incarnation itself brings God near as "the Word became flesh." And so when Jesus prays "sanctify" them, images beyond purity emerge. Sanctification cannot be separated from love—a love derived from God's presence.

John's letters pick up this theme. Here John goes so far as to say that love can be perfect. First John had a profound impact on Wesley's understanding of Christian perfection. How does this book aid us? Only a few suggestions follow:

1. John acknowledges sin as a danger for Christians; but he in no way suggests that continual sin is to be characteristic of a Christian's life (1 John 1:5-10).

2. John promises forgiveness and a cleansing of "all unrighteousness" for all who repent (v. 9).

3. God's love is to dominate the Christian's life. The love of God "lavished on us" enables us to "set our hearts at rest in his presences whenever our hearts condemn us" (3:19-20).

4. As ones loved by God—"God first loved us"—we are to love our brothers and sisters. This love is active and seeks to meet the needs of the other person (vv. 16-18).

5. There is a sense that love is "complete" among us and that this perfect love drives out fear (4:17-18). This perfect love keeps the commandments and thus has ethical as well as relational content.

HOLINESS IN PAUL'S EPISTLES

Instead of striving for a general Pauline perspective on holiness, we will seek a more specific understanding by concentrating on two books—the epistle to the Romans and the first epistle to the Thessalonians.

The Roman epistle is Paul's most extensive theological argument. It has an important place in the development of the church. Martin Luther began the Reformation mainly because of his interpretation of Romans. John Wesley's life was dramatically changed as he listened to the reading of Luther's comments on Romans. The book of Romans holds a dominant place in Prot-estant theology. It also holds a prominent place in the theology of the Wesley-an-Holiness tradition. Not only does Paul speak of "salvation by faith alone," but he also speaks of sanctification as the appropriate corollary to the salvation we receive in Christ. We find both atonement and holiness in this important Pauline book (see all of Rom. 6 and 8, specifically 8:3-4). One could organize the book into sections: Chapters 1—4 clearly set forth Paul's doctrine of sal-vation. William Greathouse places the shift to sanctification proper at 5:12, with 5:1-11 as Paul's transition.[41] Chapters 5—8 and 12 are specifically about sanctification. The remaining chapters discuss the relationship between Israel and the church.

Chapter 5 contributes a unique discussion to the New Testament theol-ogy of the relationship between Adam, Adam's descendants, and Jesus as the "New Adam." Paul's discussion here hints at a doctrine of original sin, passed down to each successive generation. Adam's fall was an act of disobedience, but the New Adam obeys God completely and thus restores the potential for obedience to those who are in Christ. We find what is called the doctrine of re-capitulation here. What Adam took away from humanity through his harmful actions, Christ recapitulates through his restorative actions. If we look closely, however, Christ offers *all the more* exceedingly above simply an equalizing grace. "For if, by the trespass of the one man, death reigned through that one man, how much more will those who receive God's abundant provision of grace and of the gift of righteousness reign in life through the one man, Jesus Christ" (5:17). Where sin increased, grace increased all the more. Wesley will pick up Paul's wording here when he speaks of righteousness (or love) reigning in the heart instead of sin reigning there.

In chapters 6—7, Paul further elaborates on what life in Christ can really look like. He states, "Thanks be to God that, though you used to be slaves to sin, you wholeheartedly obeyed the form of teaching to which you were en-trusted. You have been set free from sin and have become slaves to righteous-ness" (6:17-18). Paul encourages the Romans in light of this freedom to pursue a life of holiness. Of note, while Paul speaks of them as slaves of righteousness and slaves to God in chapter 6, in chapter 8 he extends the discussion and proclaims that as sons (and daughters) of God, we move beyond any sense of slavery that brings fear and know ourselves to be children of God with a trust and intimacy that cries *Abba*, or "daddy." What accounts for this transition? Paul's elaborate discussion of the law in chapters 7 and 8.

If we examine the history of the interpretation of the latter half of Rom. 7 in the Wesleyan-Holiness Movement, we discover a shift that radically changes its meaning. Put simply, Wesley believed that the person Paul describes in the first person was someone pre-Christ, someone attempting to be saved through the law, an unregenerate. Calvinist writers (of Wesley's day and since), on the other hand, have tended to interpret this person's situation as the life of one already in Christ. Wesley's immediate successors affirmed Wesley's position. But some later successors in America in the 19th century began interpreting this person's situation as a regenerate Christian who was not yet entirely sanctified. Apparently W. B. Godbey was one of the first to suggest this position. We find support for this interpretation in the works of Beverly Carradine, Henry Clay Morrison, Charles Ewing Brown, and A. M. Hills (late 19th- and early 20th-century figures). In the 20th century, biblical scholars and theologians in the Wesleyan-Holiness tradition returned to Wesley's interpretation and saw these verses as describing an unregenerate person.

From the perspective of the Wesleyan-Holiness tradition, the plight of the person Paul describes in chapter 7 is conquered in chapter 8. The heart of the Holiness message springs from this description of life in the Spirit. Paul says that through Christ "the righteous requirements of the law [can] be fully met in us, who do not live according to the sinful nature but according to the Spirit" (8:4). This is possible only because of what "God did" (v. 3) by sending Jesus to us. Thus Paul is thoroughly optimistic about life in the Spirit. As we walk in step with the Spirit, we are given life, made God's children, filled with hope, guaranteed of God's love, and made more than conquerors over sin and whatever else might separate us from God. Paul follows these strong and optimistic statements by admonishing the Romans to "offer [their] bodies" to God as "living sacrifices," which will transform them (12:1-2) and enable them to love (vv. 9-21). Thus consecration, or entire devotion, is an important concept in the New Testament as well as the Old.

George Lyons writes, "Christian pastors and teachers find [themselves] increasingly in the position of the first-century apostles. [Their] task is not simply to convert pagans or to indoctrinate converts. It is to Christianize the Church."[42] Lyons specifically looks to the first epistle of Paul to the Thessalonians for guidance on this point. He argues that Christianizing Christians is exactly Paul's purpose in this letter and that the sheer number of references to holiness in this short book is noteworthy.[43] First Thessalonians is historically an extremely important book for the Wesleyan-Holiness tradition. If one were to pick a verse that represents the tradition, it would most likely be 1 Thess. 5:23-24. One might say that a biblical theology of Holiness would be incomplete without this epistle.

While reflecting on 1 Thessalonians, Lyons also writes, "For those of us who take seriously our Wesleyan-Holiness heritage, orthodoxy is not enough. We cannot justify our theological existence unless we actively promote 'holiness of heart and life."[44] This is what Paul does in this letter. He clearly shows that holiness is a call to everyone, not just an elite few. For Paul a "sinful" Christian life is an oxymoron! Holiness is not some abstraction; it is lived out through the grace of God. We can proclaim, based on Paul's words in this epistle and elsewhere, that holiness is more powerful than sin. The means to this power and purification is human consecration to the Holy One. It is a life totally given over, surrendered, and entirely devoted to God. As such, it is a life totally transformed by grace.

The last chapter of 1 Thessalonians gives specific and explicit attention to entire sanctification: "May God himself, the God of peace, sanctify you through and through. May your whole spirit, soul and body be kept blameless at the coming of our Lord Jesus Christ. The one who calls you is faithful and he will do it" (5:23-24). For the words "through and through," the Wesleyan-Holiness tradition has substituted the word "entire." Unfortunately, we often forget this holistic emphasis. "Entire" has taken on different connotations today. We might think of cooking a turkey, for example, and say that the turkey is entirely cooked. Yes, hopefully the whole turkey is cooked. But we tend to mean that the turkey has been cooked for the entire time needed and that it is done. We might say that cooking the turkey any more would ruin it! Unfortunately, some people have interpreted the word "entire" to mean "done" in this sense, and that no growth is required beyond this experience.

What Paul means in these verses is that we are sanctified throughout our whole being. There is not a part of us that God's sanctifying work does not touch. Paul does imply that this sanctification comes before the "coming of our Lord" but that it must be maintained. We are to be kept blameless. The only way this can be accomplished is to continue in holiness of heart and life. But thanks be to God, this continuation is not something we must do on our own. God is invested in our holiness. God's grace will continue to sanctify, in the sense that our holiness will go on and even grow as we remain wholly devoted.

HOLINESS IN HEBREWS AND JAMES

Unlike many of the writings of Paul, which were addressed to Gentile or mixed congregations, what we find in the books of Hebrews and James is the message of holiness preached to New Testament Jews. According to F. F. Bruce, the purpose of Hebrews is

to establish the finality of the gospel by contrast with all that went before it (more particularly, by contrast with the Levitical cultus), as the way of perfection, the way which alone leads [people] to God without any interruption of access. He [the writer] establishes the finality of Christianity by establishing the supremacy of Christ, in His person and in His work.[45]

Jesus is indeed contrasted with the old covenant as a better and more perfect way. He is wholly God and wholly human. His salvation is of another kind, better than before. But although the atonement is a prominent theme in Hebrews, so is sanctification. David Peterson writes, "Purification is the basis of sanctification. . . . By his sovereign action in Christ, God sets apart and binds to himself those who have been purified from the defilement of sin. This objective, consecrating work of God has profound implications for the attitude and behavior of those who believe."[46] Thus purity is now embodied and internal, not just ascribed to a person or an object on the basis of its use. Old Testament figures, as highlighted in Heb. 11, anticipated the fullness of this holiness now available.

The book of James is important in its portrayal of this embodied holiness in very practical ways. Holiness, or the "religion that God our Father accepts as pure and faultless is this: to look after orphans and widows in their distress and to keep oneself from being polluted by the world" (James 1:27). This type of loving and pure life is to be maintained even through trials and persecutions. Love perseveres. This love shows no favoritism, is merciful, is full of wisdom, and is always submissive to God. Faith works in righteousness, particularly in the community of faith.

An exhaustive treatment of holiness in the Bible is beyond the scope of what we can provide in this chapter. But hopefully these focal points can lay a foundation for further theological considerations in later chapters. The following summary statements highlight what has been presented in this chapter. In "Holiness History," the next part of our study, we will turn to the historical development of the theology of Holiness from the first century to the twentieth.

SUMMARY STATEMENTS

1. The Old Testament portrays God's holiness in terms that include God's incomparability, glory, and jealousy.

2. The "hermeneutic of love" helps Wesleyans interpret difficult Old Testament texts.

3. In the Old Testament, human beings are holy in the following ways: when they are in relationship with God; when they have consecrated themselves to God's service; when they have no other gods before the one true God; when they remain in covenant with God; and when they express their relationship with God through obedience.

4. The Greek used in the New Testament adds several new connotations to the meaning of holiness.

5. New Testament themes of holiness include the following: the work of the Holy Spirit (including "baptism with the Holy Spirit") is strongly emphasized as the means to fulfilling God's purposes in the Christian's life; love for God and neighbor continues to be normative of holiness; entire sanctification is a possibility in this life; the law "written on the heart" prophesied in the Old Testament becomes a reality; life in step with the Spirit brings freedom and genuine Christian growth in holiness and love.

6. Part of Paul's message includes the idea of "Christianizing Christians"—admonishing them to leave sin behind and live righteously.

7. The epistles of Hebrews and James were written for Jewish audiences and excel in their ability to apply the rich heritage of Judaism to the work of Jesus Christ, as the source for holiness. Hebrews offers a christological analysis of the narrative and theology of the Hebrew text; James gives a very practical guide to holiness, specifically as it relates to how we treat others.

QUESTIONS FOR REFLECTION

1. What is the relationship between the Old Testament and New Testament?

2. Is there a uniform understanding of holiness in the New Testament?

3. What is the Holiness message we receive from say, John? Acts? Paul? James?

4. What might it mean to Christianize Christians?

5. How have some texts been pushed too far to support holiness and sanctification?

FURTHER READING

Brower, Kent. *Holiness in the Gospels*. Kansas City: Beacon Hill Press of Kansas City, 2005.

Greathouse, William M., and George Lyons. *Romans 9-16: A Commentary in the Wesleyan Tradition*. Kansas City: Beacon Hill Press of Kansas City, 2008.

Lyons, George. *More Holiness in Everyday Life*. Kansas City: Beacon Hill Press of Kansas City, 1997.

Turner, George Allen. *The Vision Which Transforms*. Kansas City: Beacon Hill Press, 1964.

PART II

HOLINESS HISTORY

THREE

HOLINESS IN HISTORY:
LATE ANTIQUITY TO 1700

LEARNER OBJECTIVES

Your study of this chapter will help you to:

1. Identify holiness themes in the writings of the early church
2. Identify holiness themes in the medieval period
3. Identify holiness themes in the Catholic mystics and Anglican writers
4. Identify holiness themes in pre-Wesleyan Pietism

KEY WORDS

Late antiquity

Patristic

Apology

Asceticism

Eremetic monastics

Cenobitic monasticism

Heresy

Apostolic fathers

Gnosticism

Recapitulation

Theosis

Christian Platonist

Stoicism

Apokatastasis

Divinization

Hagiography

Origenism

Pelagianism

Quietism

Knowing that holiness is a biblical doctrine is extremely important. It is no less important to understand that it is also a historical doctrine, sewn securely into the fabric of Christianity from the beginning. Particularly important for the Wesleyan-Holiness tradition is the knowledge that Wesley did not develop his doctrine without any basis. The heart of the Holiness message surfaced very early in Christianity. Holiness themes continued in the Middle Ages, the Reformation period, and in Wesley's immediate theological predecessor, Anglicanism. With this in mind, an overview of significant periods and persons will follow in this chapter and the next, with emphasis on their contributions to the development of holiness thinking, or their significance in the Holiness Movement and the proclamation of Holiness theology.

▶ THE PATRISTIC PERIOD

As we saw in the last chapter, the concept of holiness is not an invention of the New Testament writers. The theology of the Hebrew people in the Old Testament certainly included the call to live holy and righteous lives. But the concept of holiness is not limited to biblical writers. There was also an extra-Christian emphasis on holiness, particularly expressed in the identification of the "holy man" in the culture of **late antiquity.**[1]

On the edges of society there were persons who stood apart from the common life of the typical Roman. They were seen as mediators between common humanity and the divine (the gods). Their separation included an economic separation—they were homeless and nomadic and had to scrounge for food. But this only added to their "holy" status in the minds of the Roman people, since the gods took care of them. They were separate enough to be considered wise sages. Often they were the ministers of the community, in the sense that they served the people when they were in need. This idea of the holy man in Roman society offers a secondary backdrop to the Bible in the development of the conception of holiness in early Christianity—the **patristic** period. This is particularly true during and after the time of severe persecution of Christians by the Roman Empire.

In the centuries following the apostolic period, Christianity developed in dramatic ways. One important development was the church's own self-identity in relation to the empire. Early on, Christianity was perceived as a Jewish sect. This gave Christianity a type of immunity or toleration from the Roman Empire, for it was granted the same liberties as Israel. But as Christianity slowly began to see itself, and to be seen, as a new religion, the empire took notice.

Persecutions began early in Christian history. At first they were sporadic and localized. Later, the persecutions were empire-wide, aggressive attacks upon Christianity as a whole. Justin Martyr (ca. 100-165 C.E.) argued in his

First Apology that Christians should not be punished solely for their name. Instead, they should be investigated individually for their character. Surely, he believed, such an investigation would reveal the Christians' love and purity and thus their guiltlessness before the state. Justin himself was martyred.

Martyrdom developed its own intriguing theology. Many Christians yearned to be martyred. It was the highest sign of holiness. The martyr was the "holy man" (in the Roman sense; there were just as many women martyred). The martyr stood as mediator between the common Christian and God. The martyr was the one who walked in the footsteps of Christ and took on his suffering. Interestingly, during this period, the church did not shrink under persecutions but grew significantly. One early church writer, Tertullian, said, "The blood of the Martyr is the seed of the Church."[2]

"Martyr" literally means "witness." Witnessing for Christ to the point of literally dying with him was the highest honor. Martyrs were honored above all others, even above ecclesiastical leaders or teachers. To speak of the "cult" of martyrdom is not inappropriate when consideration is given to how highly martyrs were exalted and admired. The martyr was the best personification of holiness. The persecuted church, then, serves as an important background for the development of "Holiness theology" in late antiquity. This period lasted from the apostolic period until 313. Holiness was alive and well during these years.

An extremely important event in the history of Christianity was the conversion of Constantine (ca. 272-337). When Constantine was vying for power and a singular hold on the Roman emperorship, he went into battle and supposedly heard a voice that said, "By this sign you will conquer." He looked into the sky and saw the cross that signified the Christian Christ. He won the battle. As a result of this experience, Constantine issued the edict of Milan in 313 and legalized Christianity. Constantine also promoted Christianity as the preferred Roman religion. There is much debate about the genuineness of Constantine's "conversion." At the very least, Constantine used this religious shift to his political advantage.

The results of such a turnaround are ambiguous. On the one hand, persecutions ceased, certainly for the betterment of the Christians themselves. On the other hand, masses of persons from the Roman populace were baptized as Christians immediately. Certainly this watered down the faith. The question quickly arose: how are we to perceive who is truly holy? No longer were there martyrs to hold the highest place of holy honor. Who would? It is no coincidence, it is theorized,[3] that just after Constantine's edict of toleration, a new martyrdom developed, particularly in the East.

This new martyrdom was the rise of **asceticism**. If a person could no longer be literally crucified with Christ, there was at least the option of metaphorical self-crucifixion, or self-mortification. Persons began to practice rigorous physical disciplines as means of spiritual purification. Severe fasting, poverty, chastity, and even self-mutilation were commonplace among ascetics. This further developed into the practice of hermitages. Men, and a few women, headed for the Egyptian desert in particular, where they lived primarily in solitude, with few interactions with each other. These, from then on, were known as the Desert Fathers.[4] Eventually these hermits or **eremitic monastics** formed communities that gave rise to what is known as **cenobitic monasticism**. These communities would be similar to what we know as monasteries or convents. In either case, the ascetics were identified by other Christians as the new holy ones who replaced the martyrs as Christian heroes.

Another important development in the cult or culture of the holy was the development of holy or right doctrine. The church began to recognize persons and ideas that misrepresented the gospel. Irenaeus of Lyons was one of the first to use the word "**heresy**" in a technical sense (ca. 175). He was opposed to the teaching of Valentinus, a Gnostic who was leading Christians astray. This is not exactly accurate, however, because the Gnostics considered themselves Christians. It was really Irenaeus who drew a line in the sand and declared that Gnostics stood outside the Christian circle. This led to the obvious, but thus far little-acknowledged need to articulate thoroughly Christian, or orthodox beliefs. Why were Gnostics heretics? What constituted true Christian faith? Since the Gnostics were also using what was yet to be canonized Scripture, on what basis could Christians claim to know the truth? Irenaeus and others began to speak of an "apostolic succession" as a way of legitimizing Christian doctrine.[5] Teachers who stood in this succession were the "holy ones."

Eventually it became necessary to call councils in order to firmly establish orthodox beliefs and doctrines. The first ecumenical council was called over the issue of Christ's relationship to God. It convened in 325 and was known as the Council of Nicaea. Three other councils followed that also dealt with christological issues. They further fine-tuned the orthodox position on the nature and person of Christ. They are the Council of Constantinople in 381, the Council of Ephesus in 431, and the Council of Chalcedon in 451. These three councils together with the Council of Nicaea are now known as the first four Ecumenical Councils (out of seven). This means that all of orthodox Christianity holds to their decisions.

Persecution and martyrdom, radical asceticism, and the growth of orthodoxy were important elements in the development of an early theology of the holy. We will give these elements further attention as we trace the development of Holiness theology throughout the history of the early church.

THE APOSTOLIC FATHERS

When historians refer to the **apostolic fathers** of the early church, they are referring to a specific set of writers who penned their works in the first century, or early in the second. They include Clement of Rome (30-100), Ignatius of Antioch (30-107), the authors of the *Didache* (100-150), the author of the *Epistle of Barnabas* (130-138), Polycarp (65-155), and the author of *The Shepherd of Hermas* (96-150). Christopher Bounds has offered a study that investigates each of these authors or writings on the theme of Christian perfection.[6] He summarizes his findings under the categories: "What Christian Perfection Entails," "The Possibility of Christian Perfection in the Present Life," and "The Means of Christian Perfection."

According to the apostolic fathers as interpreted by Bounds, Christian perfection first entails "a perfection of love, explicitly and implicitly summarized in the two great commandments. . . . Christian love is the dominant rubric by which perfection is understood."[7] Second, Bounds suggests that Christian perfection entails freedom from sin. "Negatively, this means that Christians are free from deliberate sin; positively, they live lives of complete obedience to the commandments of God."[8] Most of the apostolic fathers refer to an inward change that makes this possible.

Bounds also strongly asserts that the apostolic fathers clearly believed that Christian perfection is possible in this life. "Each of the Fathers teaches that Christians can be perfected in love, fulfill the two great commandments of Jesus, be freed from deliberate sin, and have their hearts oriented in love and purity."[9] This optimism about the possibility of Christian perfection, or holiness, continues throughout the ante-Nicene period. Not until over fifty years after Nicaea did Western thinkers become more pessimistic about sanctifying grace.

The means of Christian perfection as experienced in this life is simply the work of God "made possible through the redemptive life of Christ and the sanctifying presence of the Holy Spirit."[10] But this work of God is synergistic for the apostolic fathers. Persons must participate willingly with the grace of God in order to grow in holiness. This synergistic theme also extends into the later ante-Nicene period.

LATER ANTE-NICENE THEOLOGIANS

Justin Martyr (ca. 100-165)

Justin Martyr's writings represent a type of literature known as apologetics. But besides accomplishing their apologetic purpose, we also see elements of an acute optimism about the possibility of living without sin. Justin's concept of holiness should not be seen as a formalized doctrine in some wider theological *summa* that he had systematically developed, but rather as contextually influenced by his apologetic purposes in a time of persecution and martyrdom. His primary purpose was to defend Christians against false accusations of atheism and immorality. In both his *First* and *Second Apology*, he goes to great lengths to show that Christians, rather than engaging in practices that even pagans would find indefensible (such as cannibalism and sexual misconduct toward children), were in fact living lives that exceeded the virtuous life exalted by the Romans. One can find an underlying assumption in Justin that the professing Christian simply does not sin but is in fact blameless:

> Wherefore we demand that the deeds of all those who are accused to you be judged, in order that each one who is convicted may be punished as an evil-doer, and not as a Christian; and if it is clear that any one is blameless, that he may be acquitted, since by the mere fact of his being a Christian he does no wrong. (*First Apology*, VII)[11]

He also implies that if a person's life is found to be sinful, then this negates a Christian's profession of faith. "And let those who are not found living as He taught, be understood to be no Christians, even though they profess with the lips the precepts of Christ; for not those who make profession, but those who do the works, shall be saved" (*First Apology*, XVI).[12]

Justin is interested in defending individual responsibility for sin and in emphasizing free choice against more fatalistic cosmologies:

> We have learned from the prophets, and we hold it to be true, that punishments, and chastisements, and good rewards, are rendered according to the merit of each man's actions. Since if it is not so, but all things happen by fate, neither is anything at all in our own power. For if it be fated that this man be good, and this other evil, neither is the former meritorious nor the latter to be blamed. And again, unless the human race has the power of avoiding evil and choosing good by free choice, they are not accountable for their actions, of whatever kind they be. (*First Apology*, XLIII)[13]

Perpetua (d. 203)

Perpetua was a revered heroine of the early church, and the day of her execution was recognized and celebrated liturgically. The text itself (*The Martyrdom of Perpetua and Felicitas*)[14] portrays Perpetua as an "honorary man" for her virile bravery, an association that was common in martyrdom literature. Perpetua and Felicitas, her slave, died like men. Central to the original martyrdom account is Perpetua's relationship with her family. She had an infant son with her in prison while she awaited death. Similarly, Felicitas was about to give birth. Perpetua's pagan father tried, unsuccessfully, to convince her to deny her faith so that she could raise her child as she ought. She refused his pleas, and subsequently he had the child taken from her. How did Perpetua hold such resolve, one so strong that it caused her to deny her responsibilities as a parent and to defy her place as a daughter? She exhibited a singleness of heart that allowed her to devote herself entirely to God's will. The original text itself offers explicit approval for Perpetua's release from the cares and anxieties of motherhood, attributing such to divine intervention. While it could be argued that the prevalent perception of female martyrs and virgins as "virile" and "manly" is male-centered, such a perception at least allows women ascetics to obtain a certain level of autonomy. This theme will continue throughout the patristic period. Women like Perpetua are models of a single-hearted holiness.

Irenaeus (d. 202)

Irenaeus of Lyon was also persecuted and eventually martyred. While the circumstances of martyrdom were no less important for Irenaeus than for Justin, Irenaeus shaped his theology in conflict with those he deemed heretical, those who would consider themselves to be within the Christian camp. He is known more for his distinction between orthodoxy and heresy than for his martyrdom. Because of his clear demarcation of boundaries, he became one of the first Christian thinkers to formalize the concept of orthodoxy. His *Against Heresies* is a strong critique of the errors of Valentinian **Gnosticism**. And yet Irenaeus was also theologically creative in his refutation of heresy. Most notably, he furthered the early church's understanding of Christology and soteriology. He is most known for his **recapitulation** theology and his elaboration of Jesus Christ as the New Adam. He asserts that Jesus Christ obeyed where Adam disobeyed and that through this obedience Jesus opens the door for us to also fully obey God and thereby return to Adam's original state in this life. Recapitulation soteriology was utilized by Wesley and his successors, as were aspects of Irenaeus's theological anthropology.

Irenaeus's theological anthropology is also born in this setting of conflict. His debate with Gnostics, particularly their interpretation of the Fall, formed his understanding of human nature. Irenaeus was interested in defending the goodness of creation against the Gnostic tendency to call the material world evil.

In a highly original move, he envisioned Adam and Eve to be "like children," innocent and immature. This leads us to consider Irenaeus's teaching on sin to be "the antithesis, or rather the corrective, of that of St. Augustine."[15] Although Irenaeus held Adam and Eve responsible for their disobedience, he did not understand it to be as disruptive and universe changing as Augustine implied centuries later. Rather, sin is a result of immaturity and an opportunity for illuminating the mercy of God that will ultimately be expressed by a recapitulating Christ.

> So, from the beginning God had the power to give perfection to man, but man, newly created was unable to receive it, or to retain it if he had received it. That is why the Word of God, while perfect, became a little child with man, not for his own sake but because of man's state of infancy, in order that he might be received by man insofar as man was capable of receiving him. It was not, then, that there was impotence or lack on God's part; it was on the part of newly-created man. . . . Such then is the sequence, the rhythm, the tempo in which man, created and formed, is turned into the image and likeness of God. The Father decides and commands, the Son carries out and forms, the Spirit nourishes and gives life; little by little, man ascends toward perfection. (*Against Heresies*, 38.1-3)[16]

Irenaeus maintained a developmental understanding of human history. Concepts such as "stages of life" and "ascent toward perfection" make his system both compassionate toward human nature in history (recapitulated by a human Christ) and optimistic about humanity's ability to progress toward a perfect future (foreshadowed by an eschatological Christ). This has led some scholars to identify the burgeoning theme of **theosis** in the patristics as early as the work of Irenaeus.[17]

Irenaeus's classic statement of the doctrine of theosis is found in the preface to the fifth book of *Against Heresies*. Many scholars of the Wesleyan-Holiness tradition have associated the idea of theosis with the doctrine of sanctification. Irenaeus writes, "[We follow] the only true and steadfast Teacher, the Word of God, our Lord Jesus Christ, who did, through His transcendent love, become what we are, that He might bring us to be even what He is Himself."[18] Paul Bassett paraphrases this passage by stating, "Not only is there authentic divinity-becoming-flesh but there is also a flesh-becoming-divinity. In fact, the latter is the reason for the former. . . . The believer is actually transformed to deity in his [or her] essential character."[19] Clearly, Irenaeus believed that through Jesus Christ's recapitulating and saving work, humanity can be fully restored to its original design.

Clement of Alexandria (ca. 150—ca. 215)

Clement of Alexandria preceded the famous Origen as the leader of the catechetical and theological school in Alexandria. Clement was pursued during the great persecution of 202. He made the difficult decision to flee for a time and hide in order to avoid death. In light of this experience, he was even more determined to contribute to the budding orthodox literature, especially in his attempts to refute the Gnostics. Clement wrote not only in the ethos of persecution but also with enough theological clarity to contribute to the early formulation of doctrine.

Clement was a philosopher before he converted to Christianity, and he continued as a Christian philosopher following his conversion. He has long been considered a **Christian Platonist**. One of Clement's objectives was to reclaim the word "gnostic" from the Gnostics and assert that God does not give divine special knowledge only to an "elect" few. (Origen will pick up Clement's cause on this point.) Rather, Christ is the source of all true knowledge, and Christ's knowledge is available to all Christians. Clement's focus is on Christ as the true teacher.

Illumination or knowledge for Clement is not just intellectual knowledge but knowledge of Christ that enables true love. The perfect Christian, or the "true Gnostic," leads a life of morality but also specifically one without "passionate" immorality. Clement is undoubtedly influenced by **Stoicism** on this point—a philosophy that stressed the importance of keeping all emotion in check through reason. Clement does seem to identify Christian perfection with the ideal "stoic" who has deadened his or her "passion" altogether. It is unfortunate that Clement's Stoicism even interprets Christ as dispassionate; this will no doubt influence other interpretations of Christ's humanity in the early church. But if we can put the perplexing intricacies of his Stoicism aside for the purpose of a Holiness interpretation, we can see that Clement strongly believed in Christian perfection and affirmed that the perfect Christian leads a life of entire devotion to God, with a love in his or her heart that prompts holy living, even in the midst of suffering and persecution. Christ offers not only knowledge but also an example par excellence of right Christian living.

Clement seems to make a distinction between the faith of the ordinary Christian and the faith of "the perfect"; and yet he also clearly stated that "straightway, on our regeneration, we attained that perfection after which we aspired. For we were illuminated, which is to know God. He is not then imperfect who knows what is perfect."[20] But Clement also spoke of a growing perfection. "Being baptized, we were illuminated; illuminated, we became sons; being made sons, we are made perfect; being made perfect, we are made immortal. . . . This [progressive] work is variously called grace, illumination, and perfection."[21]

Further along in the Christian journey, the perfect Christian specifically has deeper insight into the nature of virtue. "Truly then, we are the children of God, who have put aside the old man, and stripped off the garment of wickedness, and put on the immortality of Christ, that we may become new, holy people."[22] The nature of this holiness is always love. As Clement says elsewhere, "The perfect man ought therefore to practice love, and thence to haste to the divine friendship, fulfilling the commandments from love."[23] In light of Clement's optimism (that held to perfection being possible in this life), he offers an elaborate system of Christian ethics that covers almost every situation imaginable. For Clement there was clearly a "Christian way" to do everything. It is noteworthy that John Wesley used Clement of Alexandria's ethical considerations as a model for his tract *The Character of a Methodist*.

Origen (ca. 165—ca. 254)

Origen was a brilliant writer who wrote what has been called Christianity's first systematic theology; he wrote in the early third century of Christianity. At a very early age he became the teacher of the Christian school in Alexandria. His one regret in life was that he had not been martyred beside his father as a teen. Although tortured at the end of his life, his wounds did not bring death or immediate martyrdom. It took him several years to die from the persecutions he suffered. Origen would be known more for his writings than his end.

Although Origen firmly established his essentials in his most important work, *On First Principles*, and although these essentials very much look like an early rendering of theological orthodoxy, Origen also wrote speculative theology on issues he believed were not addressed in Scripture. Thus Origen's complex speculative theology was suspect in his own lifetime and definitively rejected after his death. But despite such a condemnation, his value in history continues to be debated. While some scholarship has sought to rescue him back into the orthodox fold, others have taken a different tack and have questioned the validity of even speaking of pre-Nicene orthodoxy to begin with. In any case, "Origen's Christian commitment was unquestionable, but his theological conclusions stimulated passionate apologetic or repudiation; he was too right to be wrong, or too attractively wrong to be ignored."[24]

Unlike other patristic writers, Origen transcends his historical context with his creativity and originality. Peter Brown and Rebecca Lyman seem to appreciate this transcendent quality. Brown calls him "magnificently idiosyncratic."[25] Thematically, Brown gives his attention to Origen's concept of the body, and Lyman examines his "cosmology."[26] Both themes implicitly and at times explicitly relate to the doctrine of Holiness.

Brown (as well as Lyman) sees Origen's dialogue with the different Gnostics to be about the issue of the spiritual "diversity of humanity." At the very center of all of Origen's ideas is free will. Origen developed his famous doctrine of the Fall as an attempt to explain this human spiritual diversity. Rebecca Lyman examines Origen's theological anthropology and suggests that he was seeking to refute Gnostic determinism. Free will again becomes all-important to Origin's arguments.

While certain Gnostics explained the differences between individuals by stratifying them into three preordained categories, Origen strongly maintained a doctrine of individual freedom by saying that each soul has fallen according to his or her own choices, many falling into bodies. Although it may be tempting to see Origen as simply Platonic here (with the body being the prison house of the soul) Brown suggests that,

> For Origen, the fall of each individual spirit into a particular body had not been in any way a cataclysm; to be placed in a body was to experience a positive act of divine mercy. He distanced himself from many of his contemporaries by insisting that the body was necessary for the slow healing of the soul. It was only by pressing against the limitations imposed by a specific material environment that the spirit would learn to recover its earlier yearning to stretch beyond itself, to open itself ever more warmly to the love of God.[27]

Origen believed then in a more individualistic understanding of sin and consequently in a more individualistic understanding of salvation and holiness.

Origen's system is perhaps the most optimistic of all reviewed thus far, for not only was he certain that every soul has the potential to be transformed into the likeness of God and to return to perfect communion with God, but he also believed that every soul will make this ascent. Origen was condemned partly because this optimism led him to a doctrine of *apokatastasis* (universal salvation). It is certainly optimistic to believe that grace will even save Satan!

Brown's chapter on Origen is appropriately titled to reflect Origen's entire theological scheme, which is a call to "Be Transformed." It is this extreme optimism, as well as Origen's emphasis on human free will, his rejection of all determinism, and his interpretation of the Fall, that led Elizabeth Clark to place Origen and his followers in polar opposition to the theological anthropology of Augustine.[28]

Despite Origen's speculative and intellectual tendencies, his intense hope and optimism for humanity and his acute belief in the grace of God make his system profoundly personal and his soteriology highly synergistic. Or as Lyman expresses it,

> Although Origen was highly optimistic about the potential of human beings, he also recognized the need for constant divine assistance, the unassisted will being incapable of consistent obedience. This is due not merely to its changeable nature, but also because within Origen's theology the will itself is not merely an undetermined power, but the expres-

sion of piety and growth toward new life. One does not become perfect by will alone; **divinization** consists not in habit, but rather will and love directed toward God.[29]

And thus holiness is influenced by individual choice (not dependent on any inherited condition), a deep acceptance of grace as divine assistance, and ultimately a commitment to love and move progressively closer to union with God.

POST-NICENE PERSPECTIVES

The post-Nicene period of early Christianity is marked by the dramatic rise of asceticism and the quest for Christian consensus. It is also a time when subtle differences between Eastern (Greek) and Western (Latin) Christianity become more pronounced. Most of the figures explored in this section are Eastern. In fact, the Latin fathers discussed here were heavily influenced by Eastern themes. It is not that "holiness" is absent from Latin Christianity. In fact, an entire controversy known as the Donatist Controversy was over issues of high ethical standards and ecclesiastical purity. But the context and ethos that fed John Wesley himself was a clearly Eastern one.[30]

Antony (ca. 251—356) and Athanasius (ca. 293—373)

What we know about the life of Antony mainly comes from Anthanasius's **hagiography** (or biography of a holy person, in this case Antony). Antony was the first giant of the monastic movement who went to live in the Egyptian desert shortly after the Edict of Milan. Ironically, although Antony sought solitude, he was unable to flee civilization because it came to him. Making a pilgrimage into the desert to see this remarkable holy man became increasingly popular. The common Christian would seek Antony out for wisdom and direction.

According to Athanasius, Antony fought temptation in the desert and thus imitated for the people Christ's temptations in the wilderness. Temptations of the body—the need for adequate food or sex, the comforts of society on many fronts—were easily overcome by Antony. He was able to detach himself from usual human activities. His greatest temptations were matters of the spirit. Athanasius wrote about demons who wrestled with Antony constantly. But he was always the victor.

For the desert fathers in general, any concept of sin must be seen in relation to the telos, or goal, of humanity: perfected humanity expressed in purity and love. Whether the metaphor is a "return to Paradise," "the ladder of ascent," or the "pure contemplation of the divine Unity," sin is depicted in each as the greatest hindrance toward the telos of holiness. Asceticism is therefore a lifestyle intended to conquer the hindrances on a specific spiritual journey;

asceticism is a means to an end, not the end itself. The goal is described as the restoration of Adam and Eve's first state.

It is on this point that Anthanasius expressed Christ's role in this restoration. Athanasius, like Irenaeus before him, articulated a classic expression of the doctrine of theosis. In *De Incarnation* 54, Athanasius wrote: "He, indeed, assumed humanity that we might become God." This has also been translated as "God became man so that man might become God." A more literal translation from the Greek might read: "He became in-carnate (i.e., enfleshed) that we might become in-godded." Although debated by scholars,[31] the usual Wesleyan interpretation of this phrase is that we become like God, or like Christ, in our character, not that we share in God's *ousia*, or essence. Athanasius clearly believed that such an assent is possible in this life, though probably reserved for those willing to live "apart" from the world. Interestingly, Athanasius played an important role in the Council of Nicaea, where the Arians were defeated. The Arians argued that Christ was created by God at a point in time and that he did not share in God's divine essence but was only "like" God. The outcome of the council, which rejected these Arian premises, was important to Athanasius's ideas about theosis. If Christ had not been fully God, then God did not become incarnate in Christ and thus did not provide the means by which we become "in-godded."

Basil (ca. 330-79) and Macrina the Younger (324-79)

Basil was the older brother of Gregory of Nyssa. Along with their friend Gregory of Nazianzus, the three are known as the Cappadocian fathers. Each contributed much to the post-Nicene church. All were well-educated in philosophy and rhetoric. All were ordained and served as pastors or bishops. But it is Basil in particular who is known for his ascetic theory and practice. Interestingly, Basil said that all that he had learned of any spiritual worth came from his sister Macrina (called the Younger to distinguish her from her grandmother, also an ascetic, Macrina the Elder). Gregory of Nyssa is the one who wrote her biography, *The Life of Macrina*. But it is Basil who most closely took up her cause.

Macrina began a cloister for women on her family estate. Her disciples included her mother, as well as all their servants. They made vows to live an austere ascetic lifestyle. Gregory described Macrina as the premier example of holiness and compared her faith to the faith of Moses. For all intents and purposes, she represents a female model of theosis. Gregory of Nyssa, Basil, and Gregory of Nazianzus all spent time at Macrina's ascetic estate and recognized her for her devout holiness and deep spiritual maturity.

Basil's time at the family monastery inspired him to write one of the first "rules" of cenobitic monasticism. These rules were guidelines about how to live the ascetic life in community and included a schedule of how the members were to spend their days; they balanced work, private devotion, and corporate worship. There is no doubt that Basil was highly influenced by his sister's monastic routines. Basil's rules were guidelines for personal piety for centuries to come.

Gregory gave great attention to Macrina's death, as was the custom when writing hagiographies of remarkable persons. In his eyes, she had already become a saint before her death and died like the saint she was.

Gregory of Nyssa (ca. 335-ca. 394)

Gregory of Nyssa is considered the systematic theologian of this devout family and of the Cappadocian fathers. His work on the Trinity was influential at the Council at Constantinople in 381. He also wrote an important treatise titled *On Perfection*. Although it cannot be textually connected to John Wesley (Wesley never uses Nyssa's name), Gregory's themes are all about the concept of Christian perfection. Also Gregory's subject matter is representative of the Eastern position that so influenced Wesley's ideas on holiness.[32] Gregory offered an important insight on the nature of perfection. He reviewed thirty-two names of Christ. Those names that clearly exceed our human capacity, Gregory asserted, call us to worship. But most names describe an aspect of Christ that we are to imitate. Christlikeness, possible through participation in grace, is the goal of the Christian life.

This review of Christ's names enabled Gregory to declare that moral perfection is within our reach as we practice virtue. As with most Eastern thinkers, we find Gregory assuming that we need not sin. He wrote: "Perfection in the Christian life in my judgment (is) the participation of one's soul and speech and activities in all of the names by which Christ is signified, so that the perfect holiness, according to the eulogy of Paul, is taken upon oneself in 'the whole body and soul and spirit,' continuously safeguarded against being mixed with evil."[33]

Gregory also implied that virtue toward perfection continues to grow. It makes no sense to speak of arriving at perfection if perfection is defined in relation to the virtues. To stop growing in virtue necessarily makes a person less virtuous. Virtue must be active. Virtue cannot be contained within boundaries, even the boundaries of perfection, he said. "For this is truly perfection: never to stop growing towards what is better and never placing any limit on perfection."[34] On this point he countered a strict Platonism that change or mutability is a sign of imperfection.[35] Several other writings are indicative of

Gregory's theology of Holiness, including *De Professione Christiana*, which asks and answers what it truly means to be Christian. He again answers the question by calling for virtuous, Christlike living through divine grace.[36]

Pseudo-Macarius

After years of scholarship that assumed Macarius of Egypt was the writer of a very important early Christian work, *The Fifty Homilies*, we may now appropriately speak of the writer as "Pseudo-Macarius." We are left with theories about his possible identity. What we do know is that the place of writing was probably Syria, not Egypt. Some have associated the writer with Messalianism,[37] which was condemned as heresy at the Council of Ephesus in 431. But "a growing number of specialists are agreed, at any rate, on one point: when Messalian language appears in the Homilies, there is nothing specifically heretical about the way in which it is employed. . . . Today we continue to honor the Homilies as a classic of the spiritual life."[38]

Kallistos Ware clearly describes Pseudo-Macarius's three stages of spirituality: (1) The person not under grace is characterized as having a heart filled with evil that dominates the person's inward condition and outward behavior. (2) The next stage comes when a person receives saving grace through Jesus Christ. But this is a stage of spiritual struggle, as both sin and grace inhabit the heart. Principles of light and darkness are vying for dominance in the same heart. (3) Finally sin is cast from the heart through the power of the Holy Spirit as the person cooperates with this work. Pseudo-Macarius associates this final stage with perfection. "Such is the basic progression envisaged by Macarius: from a heart possessed by evil, to a heart indwelt by sin and grace, and then ultimately to a heart that belongs to God alone."[39] It is fascinating that this representation of the stages of the spiritual life matches so closely the paradigm that dominated 19th-century Holiness Movement language. Indeed, some of the Homilies read as if preached from a Holiness camp meeting pulpit! John Wesley himself, we know, read the Homilies and "sang" in response to them.[40]

Pseudo-Macarius is a writer who spoke of the transformation of the whole human person; this transformation enables the person to respond to God with loving obedience. Like Wesleyanism in general, the Homilies speak of a spirituality of the heart. They also reveal a strong pneumatology, or doctrine of the Holy Spirit: "The souls who seek sanctification of the Spirit, which is a thing that lies beyond natural power, are completely bound with their whole love to the Lord."[41] The Spirit is greater than sin as we seek the Spirit's sanctification.

> This [corruption] must be expelled again by that which is also foreign to our nature, namely, the heavenly gift of the Spirit, and so the original purity must be restored. And unless we will now receive the heavenly

love of the Spirit through ardent petition and asking by faith and prayer and a turning away from the world, and unless our nature will be joined in love, which is the Lord, and we are sanctified from the corrupting power of evil by means of that love of the Spirit, and unless we will persevere to the end unshaken, walking with diligence according to all of his commands, we will be unable to obtain the heavenly kingdom.[42]

A similar quote is found in Homily 44: "For if in this world a person would not receive the sanctification of the Spirit through much faith and imploring, and be 'made a participator of the divine nature' and permeated by grace by which he can fulfill every commandment without blame and purely, he would not be made for the King of Heaven."[43]

Pseudo-Macarius also makes the fascinating move of associating sanctification with the baptism of the Holy Spirit. "But here the people of God, being very special, receive the sign of circumcision inwardly in their heart. For the heavenly knife cuts away the excess portion of the mind, that is, the impure uncircumcision of sin. With them was a baptism sanctifying the flesh, but with us there is a baptism of the Holy Spirit and fire."[44]

Pseudo-Macarius also had a strong doctrine of theosis, or divinization. But rather than just being christological, it is also pneumatological. "The heavenly Spirit touched humanity and brought it to divinity."[45] He often spoke of sharing in the divine nature, through the work of the Spirit. He was completely optimistic that sin can be overcome in this life and that perfection expresses itself in virtue. "For this is purity of heart, that, when you see the sinners and the weak, you have compassion and show mercy toward them."[46] Later he affirmed:

Therefore, one who has found and possesses within himself the heavenly treasure of the Spirit fulfills all the commands justly and practices all the virtues without blame, purely without forcing and with a certain ease. Let us therefore, beg God, seeking and praying him to gift us with the treasure of the Spirit in order that we may be empowered to walk in all of his commands without blame and purely and to fulfill every justice asked of the Spirit with purity and perfection by means of the heavenly treasure which is Christ. . . . The person who has found the Lord, the true treasure, by seeking the Spirit by faith and great patience, brings forth the fruits of the Spirit.[47]

And so to summarize Pseudo-Macarius's contribution to an early understanding of sanctification, perfection, and theosis, we find (1) an optimism that grace can overcome sin; (2) a focus on the work of the Spirit in the heart that sanctifies and cleanses; (3) the need for a person to intentionally be single-minded and dependent on God; (4) a life of virtue and Christlikeness for the sanctified person; and (5) a purity of heart expressing itself as compassion, mercy, and love. For every quote offered above, there are dozens more on each point in *The Fifty Homilies*.[48] While it is extremely important to understand that Pseudo-Macarius is speaking to a community of ascetics and monastics, and his optimism is directed toward those who spend their lives pursuing holiness without distraction, much of his theology can be applied to any genuine Christian.

John Chrysostom (ca. 347—407)

At the beginning of his career, Chrysostom spent two years in monastic seclusion in the mountains outside Antioch. Ill health caused him to return to the city and to turn toward a very different life. He served as deacon and priest in Antioch (381-97) and as bishop of Constantinople (397—407) and became widely known for his homiletical skill. His early rhetorical education with the renowned Libanius was put to use in the pulpit, but Chrysostom's theology was clearly developed in an ascetic context. According to Peter Brown, it was Chrysostom's aim to bring the desert to the city, to make little ascetic communities out of households.[49] He was often characterized as a severe moralist by his Antiochian parishioners, requiring only slightly less of the average citizen than he did of monastics. Vigen Guroian states, "Primary for him was the nature of the Christian family as an ecclesiastical entity: the family as a vocation of the kingdom of God, obliging a discipline of spiritual and moral *askesis*. . . . The *askesis* [Greek for exercises of self-denial] serves not only the perfection of the individual but is directed toward communal perfection."[50] In the end "to be able to speak of Antioch as a totally Christian city" was only an ideal. It remained "the poignant, tragically unrealized wish of his life."[51] He found comfort in those who shared his ascetic rigor.

For Chrysostom, virginity was the means to the original creation. "[He] posits that virginity is the true human condition, not just the angelic one. . . . By adopting virginity, we not only become more godly, we are also recalled to our true human nature."[52] While some have argued that Chrysostom's high evaluation of virginity's potential lessened through his life, a more correct understanding may be to attribute his change of rhetoric to a change of audience. His early work, *On Virginity*, is addressed to fellow ascetics, while his later homilies were mainly addressed to married persons. And yet, in his homilies he expressed his desire that his "average" parishioners also search after holiness, even if he believed the most ideal situation for such a search is the ascetic life.

With this background in mind, we can now say something about John Chrysostom's understanding of Christian perfection. Following many of the Greek fathers, Chrysostom argued for a strong doctrine of free will. The individual is responsible for his or her own choices and sins. Although he did not exclude mentioning the effects of Adam's fall on his posterity, Chrysostom had a strong optimism for a person's capability and capacity for true virtue. If someone should fall, Chrysostom would strongly argue for personal responsibility, and he would exalt the human capacity for repentance. To him, the image of God can be restored and true progress can be made in the journey toward perfection. His later writings, as implied earlier, evidenced a shift in attitude. While he did not abandon his belief in monastic virtue, he did increasingly hold out the same standard of a virtuous life for everyone, monastic or not, married or not.

Against other scholarship that has seen Chrysostom's ethics as somewhat shallow and moralistic, F. X. Murphy maintains that Chrysostom's synthesis of the biblical message with Hellenism's rhetoric (content as well as technique) does offer a depth of ethical insights. Murphy states that Chrysostom's mature idea, that the quest for perfection and the truly virtuous life is for every Christian, is undergirded with a theology of love that almost calls the solitary life of his youth and his views on virginity into question.[53]

Thus Chrysostom believed that the capacity for true morality is universal, and he later declared that nonmonastics may be deserving of even greater admiration for their pursuit of perfection in the midst of worldly influences. Along with Chrysostom's optimism in the human capacity for moral choice, he held to a high standard of ethical behavior. He particularly admonished his clergy in Constantinople to live with pure integrity.

But even in his early writings Chrysostom's understanding of the virtuous life was not about asceticism for the sake of asceticism.[54] The goal was the imitation of Christ, not only in Chrysostom's prohibitions but also in his calls to action. Virtue is more than avoiding sin, although such avoidance is crucial, particularly when it comes to the lust for money or vainglory. Virtue's positive content is most importantly love.

John Chrysostom is clearly an Eastern father. There are two bridge figures between the East and the West in the latter part of the 4th century that are worth investigation—John Cassian and Jerome. Each will take a different tack in negotiating what had become two very different theological worlds.

John Cassian (ca. 360—ca. 435)

John Cassian was a monk who traveled the world. His birthplace is unknown. What we do know is that his native language was probably Latin; and yet his Greek is so proficient that he might have grown up in the bilingual area of Scythia Minor (present-day Romania). Around 380, when Cassian was only 20, he and his lifelong traveling companion Germanus went to Palestine to pursue the ascetic life. He settled in Bethlehem at a time when pilgrimages were popular and monasteries were flourishing. He and Germanus joined a cenobitic community there. After a few years they made the decision to follow Abba Pinufius to Egypt, where they experienced all the ascetic glory of the Egyptian desert. Cassian's experiences with the great desert fathers will be the source of his most influential writings, *The Institutes* and *The Conferences*.

After about fifteen years in the desert, Cassian and Germanus left Egypt when persecution of the Origenists began there. Long after Origen's death, there was a group that followed some of his more heretical theological ideas. Apart from these ideas, **Origenism** is most known for its mystical approach to the ascetic life. Origenists were extremely devout and devoted themselves to prayer in a manner that exceeded even the most dedicated orthodox monk. We might argue that their condemnation was more for their radical spirituality than their theology. However, as strong defenders of Origen's doctrine of human free will, the Origenists became suspect in a theological world moving increasingly toward the West and Western theological themes. Interestingly, many of them after leaving Egypt, including Cassian, headed north to Constantinople, during the time when Chrysostom was bishop.

Cassian and Germanus became Chrysostom's devoted disciples. Cassian seemed to gain a certain amount of ecclesiastical power while there. When Chrysostom was deposed toward the end of his life, Cassian was given the task of taking a letter to Rome and Pope Innocent on Chrysostom's behalf. Cassian remained involved in the ecclesial politics of Constantinople, and we will see him involved even in the controversy of Nestorius, which in turn led to the Council of Ephesus (which dealt with Jesus Christ's divinity).

But Cassian is most known for bringing Eastern monasticism to the West when he established monasteries in Gaul. It is here that his writings are most used. Each of the *Conferences* and *Institutes* is a record of conversations with the Egyptian monks. Their wisdom is brought westward. Cassian built his communities in Gaul on explicitly Eastern ascetic theory and practice. In his writings we see a dramatically clear connection with an Eastern understanding of Christian perfection, most specifically in his concepts of purity of heart and sanctification.

> The biblical anchor for Cassian's doctrine of purity of heart is "blessed are the pure in heart, for they shall see God" (Matt. 5:8). By linking purity of heart to the vision of God, the beatitude connects "goal" to "end." At the same time, Cassian's infrequent quotation of this particular text reminds us that his understanding of purity of heart does not depend on one biblical text alone but is rooted in a rich biblical and post-biblical tradition.[55]

Cassian's concept of purity of heart contains three major themes: purification, the theological equation of purity of heart with love, and the experience of liberation from sin that he calls tranquillity of heart. Cassian, like other Eastern figures, believed that the practices that aid in purity are not ends in themselves. He knew that the obsession with perfection can lead to despair, anger, or judgmentalism toward others. "Mistaking the means for the goal"[56] is dangerous. As Columba Stewart, one of Cassian's most recent biographers, suggests, "Cassian echoes Paul: not even total destitution can assure perfection unless there is also the love that 'consists of purity of heart alone' (*Conference* 1.6.3)."[57]

Jerome (ca. 347—420)

Jerome also stands as a bridge between East and West. But Jerome's path would take a turn very different from Cassian's. Like Cassian, Jerome was from the West. He also traveled and settled in Bethlehem. But certain controversies took him to a very different theological place when he returned home.

Jerome, especially interested in the development of female monasticism, gathered around himself certain benefactresses who became his ascetic disciples. Paula opened a convent in Bethlehem next to Jerome's monastery. He praised countless women for leaving husbands and children behind so that they could be entirely devoted to God.

Implicit in Jerome's ascetic theory, and in this reiteration of his desire that his virgins display an unwavering relational detachment, is his theology of marriage.[58] Such a theology is most explicitly seen in Jerome's involvement in a controversy with Jovinian (390s). After several years in Bethlehem he was given a copy of a writing by Jovinian that challenged one of Jerome's greatest convictions—namely, that the ascetic's life was higher and holier in the sight of God than the concession for sexual weakness called marriage. Jovinian's battle cry was that all women—virgins, widows, and matrons alike—are of "equal merit."[59] He was excommunicated for his efforts; despite this, some of the more prominent Christians in Rome supported Jovinian, and his influence continued.

Jerome's efforts to refute Jovinian's claims center on the first chapters of Genesis. Jerome assumes that "we must maintain that before the fall they [Adam and Eve] were virgins in Paradise; but after they sinned, and were cast out of Paradise, they were immediately married."[60] Thus, for Jerome, Adam and Eve's condition in the garden was virginal. God had not created them for marriage and sexual reproduction, but these were a direct result of the Fall. Virginity is "the preferred mode of human life."[61] Elaine Pagels assesses the situation by stressing that after Jerome's *Against Jovinian* reached Rome, "even those who agreed that virginity surpassed marriage were embarrassed by Jerome's vehemence."[62]

Another debate significantly shaped Jerome's theology, one that sealed his identity as a Western thinker. The Origenist controversy erupted in the early 380s and continued into the next century, finally mingling with yet another heresy, **Pelagianism**. Elizabeth Clark traces Jerome's increasing involvement in the controversy and shows that his concerns shift over time.[63]

According to Clark, as late as 396, Jerome still had made little effort to distance himself from Origen's thought. She attributes this to Jerome's inability to discern the theological intricacies and complexities of the debate.[64] Rather, a radical break from his long-trusted friend, Rufinus, is what intensified Jerome's involvement; the two used the controversy to air their mutual disregard. The "oft veiled but always breathtakingly savage attacks on his former friend"[65] litter Jerome's "orthodox" apologies. Rufinus had strong ties to Origenism and defended its cause. But to respond to Jerome's attacks, Rufinus charged Jerome with Origenism by marking Jerome's own dependence on Origen in many of his commentaries. Jerome, despite his arduous theological backpedaling, had "sown seeds for accusations of Origenism against himself."[66] When Jerome viciously charged Rufinus with heresy in turn, clearly he "espoused the anti-Origenist cause for personal rather than intellectual reasons."[67]

After many years, Jerome did finally begin to explicate the heretical aspects of Origenism in a systematic fashion. When he did so, he focused on the proposition that most infuriated him about Jovinian's declarations: Origenism refuted moral hierarchy. Jerome believed gradations of spiritual status between ascetics and married individuals must be preserved at all cost.

Peter Brown approaches Jerome's involvement in the Origenist controversy and its effects on his theology from a different angle. Rather than a gradual awakening, fluid and uncertain, as Clark implies, Brown portrays Jerome's stance against Origenism as a moment of decision. What Jerome was rejecting was the earlier, Eastern emphasis on the unlimited human potential for transformation. According to Brown, Jerome finally concluded that such "was irrevocably inapplicable to his own times";[68] and so, almost without knowing it, Jerome betrayed his own past. The glimmers of optimism in Jerome's thought began to fade.[69] While "writing against Pelagius in 415, Jerome went out of his way to destroy all hope of Christian perfection on earth."[70] He began to embrace a remarkably distinct anthropology. "To a new generation which had begun to listen to Augustine, sexual desire revealed the inescapable solidarity of all mankind in Adam's sin. . . . Jerome had lived into an age very different from that in which he had begun his career."[71]

Soon after Jerome's time, Rome fell, and the Dark Ages began in the West. We know that the church and Christian spirituality would continue to flourish in the East for centuries. The anthropological pessimism in theology that took hold of Western Christianity came true in the political realm as well. The savagery of humanity was revealed as Rome collapsed. Five hundred years would pass before the breath of life returned to Western Christianity, although there were certainly a few gasps along the way. The question is, can any sort of belief in Christian perfection be resurrected in the new millennium?

▶ THE MEDIEVAL PERIOD TO WESLEY

We have just intensely examined the theology of the early church period for two reasons. First, we had to establish that Holiness theology was deeply rooted in Christian tradition from its beginnings. Second, John Wesley studied patristic literature with an unmatched diligence. He developed the practice of reading the fathers (and mothers) early at Oxford. He continued to see them as an authority in Georgia and throughout his life as an evangelist and founder of a movement. He gave preference to those writers from the East and those who wrote during the pre-Nicene period.[72] Many themes found in the early church influenced his understanding of Christian perfection. He saw them as an important source of his own theological development. Certainly John Wesley was influenced by later writers as well. The following provides a brief overview of several of these more recent contributors to his thinking.

Bernard of Clairvaux (d. 1153)

As the West emerged from the Dark Ages, a rise in intellectual stimulation and accomplishment occurred. The theology of Scholasticism reinvigorated Christian reflection, particularly more technical theology. Monastic interest underwent a renewal. Even before the Franciscans and the Dominicans arose in the early medieval period, Bernard of Clairvaux established a new order, the Cistercians. He is known for other significant historical events, but it is his devotional works that display a deep spirituality with holiness overtones.

Unlike Jerome's last gasps to maintain a spiritual hierarchy based on vows of chastity, Bernard used marriage as a metaphor of the devout life. By portraying our relationship with God as a marriage, he extolled the depth of God's love for each individual. In the words of Paul Bassett, "The insistence by Bernard that God is the initiator, sustainer, and goal of Christian love is in no way new, of course. But what is new in Bernard (new insofar as it had been missing or mute since Augustine) is the expectation that through the action of divine love, our love can be perfect in this life."[73] Since Augustine, the concept of perfection had slowly been disassociated with love. "Bernard reunites the two."[74] Certainly the practice of such persons as Francis of Assisi, who made himself poor in order to love the poor, models a public, rather than cloistered love for neighbor.

Thomas Aquinas (ca. 1225-74)

One of Thomas's greatest contributions to Western Christianity is his application of Aristotle's philosophy to the task of theology. While his contributions to theology in general are vast, we will focus our attention on two aspects of Aristotle's teachings that Thomas Christianized.

First, Aristotle offered a definition of perfection very different from the one offered by Plato. For all intents and purposes, Plato believed that only the divine was perfect. Everything else, including humanity, is therefore by definition less than perfect, and without potential to be so. Similarly, what is real is not something material but only the form or idea to which the material inadequately points. So again, anything material, even the human being, is less than real and thus less than perfect. Aristotle, on the other hand, defined perfection as telos, or purpose. In other words, a chair, for example, is perfect if it accomplishes its purpose. If a person sits in the chair and is held up, the chair is fulfilling its purpose perfectly.

Second, Thomas elaborates on Aristotle's ethical theory. Aristotle emphasized the development of virtue as a goal of human life. Only the virtuous person can be truly happy. The way a person becomes virtuous is to practice and habituate virtuous actions. This in turn develops inclinations—he or she is inclined to do virtuous acts. Inclinations become character. As Thomas himself implied, our inclination toward virtue can never be fully destroyed, even by sin. What Thomas added to Aristotle's scheme is grace. This is crucial to Wesley's own understanding of sin and the image of God. From Thomas, Wesley also gained insights into the doctrine of prevenient grace, sin as a volitional act, and the meaning of perfection. These will be discussed at length in later chapters of this book.

PRE-REFORMATION CATHOLIC MYSTICISM

Julian of Norwich (1342—ca. 1416)

Julian of Norwich was an English mystic. She was an anchoress at the Church of Saint Julian in Norwich. We do not know her real name. Through a series of visions, Julian developed an intense belief in God as loving, compassionate, and merciful. Her work, *Sixteen Revelations of Divine Love*, is said to anticipate some of Martin Luther's theology of grace. Although she lived with great physical pain, Julian's theology was optimistic. She spoke of God's love in terms of joy as opposed to law and duty. For Julian, suffering was not a punishment from God. She believed that God loved everyone and would offer grace to any in need. Like Catherine of Siena, Julian's theology is unusually holistic. They both avoid a body-soul dualism common in other mystics of their day. Julian's theology of Holiness is centered on God's ineffable love.

Catherine of Siena (1347-80)

Catherine of Siena was known for her positive influence on the politics of the Catholic Church. After years of solitude, she decided to leave her cell and engage the world for Christ. She had the ears of the popes. She is also known for her theology. For our purposes here we will examine two aspects of her deep theological formations. First of all, Catherine seemed to have an intuitive grasp of truth that she attributed to the Holy Spirit. She believed that the Spirit alone leads women and men into "the depths of God." "When this happens the person so graced has a knowledge of God which, while in harmony with the knowledge arrived at by one's faith-enlightened intellect, is deeper and more perfect."[75] Second and similarly, Catherine demonstrated that the essential characteristic of mysticism is its affective dimension. Catherine described this affectual awareness as an ability "to taste and see the depths of the Trinity."[76] Like Catherine, Wesley will have a strong place in his theology for this affectual dimension of Christian truth and faith.

Thomas à Kempis (ca. 1379—1471)

From the well of the work of Thomas à Kempis we know that Wesley drew deeply. Thomas à Kempis was a German Catholic monk who wrote devotional material. He is most known for his book *The Imitation of Christ.* Wesley stated directly that at a very important time in his development he read this book. Wesley said it significantly shaped his understanding of holiness and Christian perfection. Previously he had not made the connection that the very essence of holiness is Christlikeness. Wesley would not sway from this essential definition for the rest of his life.

POST-REFORMATION CATHOLIC MYSTICISM

Francois de Sales (1567—1622), St. Teresa of Avila (1515-82), Francois Fenelon (1651—1715), and Madam Guyon (1648—1717)

From the post-Reformation mystics listed above, Wesley gained a deep appreciation for the transforming power of an inner life. The specific means of grace, most importantly prayer and solitude, were incorporated into his own understanding of progressive sanctification. He did hesitate, however, to embrace post-Reformation mysticism fully, for two primary reasons. First, he believed the pursuit of mystical union with God was not the primary goal of the Christian life. Second, and likewise, he rejected the tendency of the mystics toward what is known as **quietism**—an actual rejection of good works as counter to a dependence on the grace of God. He would reject some of the Moravians' teachings for this same reason. (Again, this will be explained in greater detail in later chapters.) Interestingly, some scholars are beginning to make connections between the mysticism of Madam Guyon and the 19th-century Holiness Movement. Phoebe Palmer is now being studied from the perspective of mysticism. We do know that Palmer read Guyon at the suggestion of her good friend Thomas Upham.

POST-REFORMATION PIETISM

Johann Arndt (1555—1621)

Pietism was mainly a movement within German Protestantism (Lutheranism). In reaction to the rigidifying of doctrine after the initial Reformers Martin Luther and John Calvin, there were those in Protestant circles who began concentrating on the practices of piety, which were rooted in the inner experiences of the religious life. Johann Arndt's writings were mainly mystical and devotional; they were inspired by such persons as Bernard of Clairvaux and Thomas à Kempis. His primary work, *Wahres Christentum,* influenced both Roman Catholic and Protestant piety. Arndt emphasized Christ's life *in* persons in order to challenge the more forensic side of Reformation theology that paid almost exclusive attention to Christ's work *for* persons.

Philipp Jakob Spener (1635—1705)

Philipp Spener wrote an important Pietist text, *Pia Desideria,* which proposed several ways to restore the fervency of true Christian faith. He also began to institute close circles of prayer and Bible reading; he emphasized the priesthood of all believers and the inner work of the Holy Spirit. One form of Pietism was the Moravianism that was extremely important in Wesley's own spiritual development. While Wesley will break with Moravianism eventually over some issues, we cannot overestimate their influence on his life.

ANGLICANISM

Wesley of course drew much of his theology from the Church of England. King Henry VIII separated the church from Roman Catholicism in 1532. The English Parliament established a form of government that placed the king as the head of both the church and the state of England. The first official statement of English theology came in the "Ten Articles of Religion." These articles showed that while Henry had separated from Catholicism politically, he did not support all the tenets of the Protestant Reformation. Important for the development of the English faith were two works: *The Book of Homilies* (1546) and *The Book of Common Prayer* (1549). Here we may note that theology is inextricably tied to liturgy, or worship.

After Henry died, his son Edward VI took the throne at a young age. During his reign, the church moved in the direction of the Reformers. But when Edward died, his sister, Queen Mary, took an aggressive stance back toward Catholicism. She is known as Bloody Mary because she used any means necessary to suppress any opposition to the Catholic position. Some on the opposing side were exiled. When Mary died, these (primarily Calvinist) exiles returned to England determined to rid the church of the excesses of English Catholicism. They came to be known as Puritans.

Elizabeth became queen after Mary. She was Edward and Mary's sister, but by a different mother. Elizabeth sought and fought hard for a united church; she wished to protect the church from Rome's designs to regain control, on the one hand, and the aggressive Calvinism of the Puritans, on the other. The Act of Uniformity (1559) helped to bring a middle position. Through it, Elizabeth established a church government separate from Catholicism and reestablished the *Book of Common Prayer* and the *Book of Homilies* as theological guides. Her resolution became known as the "Elizabethan Settlement." Although succeeding kings and church leaders would attempt to throw off the balance in one direction or the other, the settlement and its *via media* became the lasting paradigm of English theology and doctrine.

Wesley was an Anglican from birth to death. His loyalty was deep and unshaken by his practical need to ordain Methodist ministers in America. But beyond an outspoken loyalty, much of Wesley's theological vision was influenced greatly by Anglican thought. Directly from the Anglican theology of the 18th century, Wesley embraced certain theological understandings. For our purposes here, we will mention the following focuses of the Anglican theology of Wesley's day: the goodness of God; a rejection of a satisfaction theory of the atonement; conditional election; imparted righteousness; Christ as central to all theological conclusions; the Bible as the sole rule of faith; an inclination toward the *via media*; a belief that theology is best expressed practically and liturgically; the use of early church sources, and most importantly, an emphasis on holiness of heart and life.

We now move to the next chapter to discuss Wesley's own theology of Christian perfection, as well as the 19th- and 20th-century expressions of the theology of Holiness. We will examine several persons for their contributions to Holiness doctrine or their contributions to the movement that propagated it.

SUMMARY STATEMENTS

1. Early Holiness themes influenced John Wesley, especially pre-Nicene and Eastern sources.

2. Eastern Christian theology focused on asceticism and was very optimistic about advancing in holiness.

3. Christian mystics focused on prayer and immediate experiences of God as the way toward holiness.

4. Thomas Aquinas interpreted holiness and perfection from an Aristotelian perspective.

5. John Wesley was influenced by a type of Pietism known as Moravianism.

6. Anglicanism had a strong theology of Holiness that influenced Wesley.

QUESTIONS FOR REFLECTION

1. What did the apostolic fathers believe about holiness? The patristics? The mystics? The Pietists?

2. How do Western and Eastern Christian theologies contrast with each other?

3. Should all Christians be "ascetics"? Why or why not?

4. What did Anglicanism contribute to Wesley's overall theological vision?

FURTHER READING

Brown, Peter. *Body and Society.* New York: Columbia University Press, 1988.

Campbell, Ted. *John Wesley and Christian Antiquity.* Nashville: Kingswood Books, 1991.

Greathouse, William M. *From the Apostles to Wesley.* Kansas City: Beacon Hill Press of Kansas City, 1979.

FOUR

HOLINESS IN HISTORY: 1703—2000

LEARNER OBJECTIVES

Your study of this chapter will help you to:

1. Distinguish Wesley's ideas from later Methodism
2. Describe the relationship between American Methodism and the Holiness Movement
3. Identify many significant persons in the Holiness Movement's family tree
4. Describe the issues of the Holiness Movement in the 20th century

KEY WORDS

Postmillennialism

Premillennialism

We must acknowledge, as we approach this chapter on Holiness theology since John Wesley, that the Wesleyan-Holiness Movement is not the only tradition that emphasizes holiness. Surely the Orthodox, Catholic, and Protestant traditions do not suddenly go mute on this biblical and historic concept when Wesley appears on the scene. But we can say that after John Wesley, a distinctive understanding of holiness and of sanctification develops. For this reason we can legitimately speak of a Wesleyan-Holiness theological tradition. The following chapter will explore some of the tributaries that flow into this tradition. An assessment of other more outlying streams will also be important. The final goal is to reach a brief description of some representative Holiness denominations.

The context of this chapter is far less complex than the previous one. The overall context is Methodism: as founded by John Wesley; as carried on in Britain after his death; as transformed in the early American setting; and as split into "mainline" Methodism, on the one hand, and the Holiness Movement, on the other. Each of the persons examined below represents one thread of the larger tapestry started by Wesley himself. Each person will contribute something unique to the overall storytelling of Holiness theology in the 18th, 19th, and 20th centuries.

▶ JOHN WESLEY

In a very real way, each of the chapters in this book covers the theology of John Wesley; most do so explicitly. Because of this, his overall theological vision and his specific theology of Holiness can best be discovered by reading the entire book. For our purposes here, we will simply provide some very brief summary statements that will anticipate and aid in negotiating the chapters to come.

SUMMARY STATEMENTS[1]

1. Wesley maintained that love for God and neighbor is descriptive and normative of the Christian life. Love is not only present but also "ruling" in the heart of Wesley's mature or perfect Christian.

2. Wesley came to equate entire sanctification with a level of Christian maturity and was cautious about claiming it too soon in the Christian pilgrimage. But he also exhorted persons to seek the experience "now."

3. Holiness, or perfect love, is a work of grace that is both progressive and instantaneous. Wesley scholars speak of sanctification in four stages: (*a*) initial sanctification, which is equivalent to being born again; (*b*) progressive sanctification, which is the daily growth in Christ that happens both before and after entire sanctification; (*c*) entire sanctification, which cleanses the heart and

enables perfect love; and (*d*) final sanctification, also known as glorification, which transpires after we die.

4. Holiness, or perfect love, is synergistic; it is lived out in a dynamic relationship with God who provides the grace we need to be holy as we cooperate with such grace.

5. Wesley became suspicious of terms such as the "destruction" of sin, because this implied an impossibility of sin's return. But Wesley was highly optimistic about how love shed abroad in our hearts through faith can exclude sin. He tired of the debate over whether or not Christian perfection was sinless. His emphasis was on love, not sinlessness, as the goal of Christian maturity, although he certainly did believe that love conquers sin.

6. Wesley believed "that the Christian life did not have to remain a life of continual struggle" against the power of sin. For him, to deny this type of victorious transformation was "to deny the sufficiency of God's empowering grace—to make the power of sin greater than the power of grace," which was unthinkable for Wesley.

These summary statements certainly cannot encompass the whole of Wesley's theology, but they do encapsulate an ethos of Wesley's mature thought on the subject of holiness and sanctification. We now move to developments that follow Wesley himself. We will start with the post-Wesley British Methodism of the 18th and 19th centuries.

▶ POST-WESLEY BRITISH METHODISM

Wesley was born an Anglican and died an Anglican. He never wanted his Methodists to separate from their mother church. And yet he allowed the Methodists in the American colonies to ordain their own clergy. This happened for a very practical reason. The Americans were no longer able to take Holy Communion because most if not all of the Anglican priests fled the colonies during the Revolutionary War. He permitted the Methodist ordinations in 1784 so that his Methodists could receive the sacraments. This did not affect British Methodism, and thus they remained a part of the Anglican Church until after Wesley died. The official split in England happened in 1795.

For the most part, the British Methodists living during and after Wesley's life continued to emphasize Wesley's own Holiness themes. But there are differences that will influence later expressions of Methodism as well.

JOHN FLETCHER (1729-85)

John Fletcher was Wesley's chosen successor to lead Methodism. But Fletcher died before Wesley. Theologically, however, Fletcher did move Methodism forward. Fletcher's *Checks to Antinomianism* was key to the development of British Methodism's identity. During Wesley's lifetime, some Methodists followed aspects of Calvinism, particularly as expressed by Wesley's friend George Whitefield. Fletcher's *Checks* in effect ended the question and clearly marked Methodism as Arminian.

Another important contribution of Fletcher was his linking of entire sanctification with the baptism of the Holy Spirit. That Wesley never propagated Fletcher's theology on this point marks Fletcher as a unique contributor to later formulations. His thinking would influence Holiness doctrine a hundred years later in the work of persons such as Phoebe Palmer and Asa Mahan.

Fletcher clearly associated Pentecost with entire sanctification and thus made Pentecost an applicable experience for all Christians. There is a difference, however, between Fletcher's concept and the Holiness Movement's understanding of what Spirit baptism accomplishes. The linking of Pentecost with entire sanctification in the later American context is a linking of holiness with bold power, particularly the power to witness. Fletcher, on the other hand, links Pentecost with perfection and with love. We find in Fletcher, then, a very different tone.

> We must receive so much of the truth and Spirit of Christ by faith, as to have the pure love of God and man shed abroad in our hearts by the Holy Ghost given unto us, and to be filled with the meek and lowly mind which was in Christ. And if one outpouring of the Spirit, one bright manifestation of the sanctifying truth, so empties us of self, as to fill us with the mind of Christ, and with pure love, we are undoubtedly Christians in the full sense of the word.[2]

ADAM CLARKE (CA. 1760—1832)

Adam Clarke is most known for providing the Methodist people with an extensive biblical commentary, first published in 1826. According to William Greathouse's interpretation, Clarke's theology especially focused on sanctification as the enabling and fulfilling of God's original purpose. Clarke himself wrote,

> The whole design of God was to restore man to his image and raise him from the ruins of his fall; to make him perfect; to blot out all his sins, purify his soul, and fill him with holiness; so that no unholy temper, evil desire, or impure affection or passion shall either lodge, or have any being within him; this and this only is true religion, or Christian perfection.[3]

This is very much like Wesley. Where Clarke pushed Wesley's theology further was in his intense emphasis on entire sanctification as the most important means of this Christian perfection. While Wesley ideally wanted his Methodist preachers to teach a balanced emphasis on both the gradualness of progressive sanctification and the instantaneousness of entire sanctification, Clarke clearly emphasized the latter. Also, as seen in the quotation above, while Wesley saw Christian perfection as imperatively connected with love, Clarke tended to stress the purification from sin. While Clarke's doctrine was not in disagreement with Wesley's, the degree to which Clarke underscored cleansing from sin did push Christian perfection in a slightly different direction. As time went on, there was a widening between those who emphasized perfect love and those who emphasized sinlessness as definitive of heart holiness.

RICHARD WATSON (1781—1833)

Richard Watson was the first Methodist to write a systematic theology. He differed from Clarke in both theological emphasis and methodology. According to John Peters, Clarke wrote in the spirit of an evangelist, while Watson wrote as a scholar and teacher.[4] Perhaps the methodology is enough to explain the difference in content. The voice of an evangelist perhaps necessitates a call to decision, like the call to the instantaneous experience of entire sanctification. Being a theologian and scholar allowed Watson more deliberate rumination and perhaps more theological reflection on Wesley. For whatever reason, we find in Watson a greater emphasis on love, which parallels Wesley. We also find an emphasis on the various stages of sanctification, including initial sanctification. According to Greathouse, Watson, like Wesley, strongly affirmed the liberating effects of regeneration.[5] However, this does not mean that Watson is mute on the subject of entire sanctification.

Watson's *Theological Institutes* reads at times like an apologetic against those who held to the position that we are bound to the sinful nature until after we die. "The attainment of perfect freedom from sin is one to which believers are called during the present life; and is necessary to that completeness of 'holiness.'"[6] Watson went on to proclaim the many spiritual benefits received from God for those who have been entirely sanctified. He gave strong biblical support for his position. He also used early church fathers and the ideas of philosophers. His is a thorough and reasoned treatment of the doctrine of Holiness that particularly stresses the possibility of its present attainment.

WILLIAM BURT POPE (1822—1903)

William Burt Pope was a biblical scholar and a systematic theologian. Speaking of Pope, John Peters writes, "Here was Wesley in undistorted miniature."[7] Thomas Langford describes Pope as a catholic Christian and no sectarian when it came to Christian piety and doctrine. Langford goes on to say, however, that Pope rejected any syncretism with the developing modernism in England. Although he was an exact and precise biblical scholar, he remained precritical long after the development of biblical criticism.[8] Thus, Langford argues, there is little in his primary work, *A Compendium of Christian Theology*

(1877), that differs from Wesley, Clarke, or Watson. William Greathouse, on the other hand, carefully examines Pope's theology of sanctification and offers many points of contribution. One will be mentioned here.

Pope discussed entire sanctification at length and highlighted, as others have, the work of the Holy Spirit in the event. What Pope offered was a deeper connection between the work of the Spirit and the consecration of the believer. In some ways, Pope's understanding resembles the American emphasis on consecration as absolutely requisite if God is going to cleanse, purify, and sanctify a person's heart. What seems different, however, is that while the American formula of faith, consecration and testimony, places significance on the person's work,[9] Pope was careful to stress that the work of sanctification is done by God through the Holy Spirit's intervening agency. The Holy Spirit enables the person to consecrate himself or herself to God. This is similar to the faith of regeneration—faith is a gift of the Spirit to which a person then responds. Pope also referred to the work of the Spirit as the seal of this consecration; the Holy Spirit also is the "energy" that "worketh by love."[10] In the end for Pope, holiness is the unity of God's purification and our Spirit-enabled consecration.

THE BOOTHS, CATHERINE (1829-90) AND WILLIAM (1829—1912)

Cofounders of The Salvation Army, Catherine Booth and William Booth, were members of the Methodist Connection, but they were expelled from it because they favored a group interested in Methodist reform. Catherine Mumford was born to a Methodist family in England in the early 19th century. At an early age, the family moved to Boston, where they were heavily involved in the Temperance Movement. She returned to London at the age of fifteen, where she started attending Methodist class meetings. In 1851, favoring the aforementioned reform group, Catherine was expelled from the Methodist Connection. William Booth was a member of the group. Catherine married him at the age of thirty-six and had eight children. Influenced by Phoebe Palmer, Catherine published *Female Ministry* in 1859, where she called women to accept and seek all areas of Christian ministry, including preaching; she herself began to preach the following year.

William Booth was her cofounder and the first general of The Salvation Army. After marrying Catherine in 1855, William became a minister in association with the Methodist New Connexion Church. His passion was evangelism, and he believed his calling was to a wide itinerancy; when the Methodists wanted to restrict him, he resigned and left the church in 1861.

The ministry of the Booths first centered on areas of extreme poverty. A work in London, named The Christian Mission, expanded in its efforts to evangelize and also in its attempts to care for the bodily and social needs of the poor. The mission was reorganized as The Salvation Army in 1878. The doctrine of Christian perfection was central to the theology of The Salvation Army. From the army's understanding of the doctrine, the social imperative of reform became central to its religious practice. In the United States, The Salvation Army was quickly associated with the American "Holiness Movement," which provided a theological basis for the army's interest in reform. The year his wife died (1890), William published *In Darkest England—and the Way Out.* In it, Booth outlined specific programs that would ease the plight of the poor and offered a direct political and practical theology. At his death, the army was well established. Different children of William and Catherine took over leadership.

▶ 18TH- AND 19TH-CENTURY AMERICAN METHODISM

As mentioned earlier, Wesley allowed for an American split from Anglicanism because of the practical matter of administering Holy Communion. American Methodism was thus officially organized in December 1784 when Thomas Coke and Francis Asbury were then allowed to ordain preachers as Methodists apart from the Church of England.

As Methodism developed through the 19th century, it would become a powerful force in American religion. Some scholars would even call it "the Methodist century" because of its dominance in American culture and life.[11] The individuals and events reviewed here are only a very small representation of those that shaped Methodism's growing power in America.

RICHARD ALLEN (1760—1831)

In 1784, Methodism in America was still small. The life and work of such persons as Francis Asbury did take effect, however. One of the most important conversions out of this "Great Awakening" ethos (a great sense of revival that swept across America and Britain) was that of a slave, Richard Allen. According to one of Allen's biographers, Dennis Dickerson, "Allen proclaimed his allegiance to the Wesleyan way. 'I could not be anything else but a Methodist,' he declared, 'as I was born and awakened under them.'"[12] And yet, by the end of his life, Allen split away from the Methodist Episcopal Church.

Allen was nurtured early in a Methodism that displayed actively and passionately the kind of love that promoted egalitarianism. His slave master was also brought into the Methodist fold, and so Allen was able to purchase his own freedom in 1783. He began to preach across the mid-Atlantic region. Once when he preached in Pennsylvania, "the whites insisted that he extend his stay so as to preach additional sermons. . . . These easy interactions with Wesleyan whites, many of whom endorsed Methodist opposition to slavery, showed a religious body without distinctions of color and class and one devoted exclusively to salvation, spirituality, and piety."[13]

This type of color-blind acceptance, however, did not continue. According to Dickerson, the ordinations of 1784 did Methodist egalitarianism no favors. Some Methodists began to recognize "rank and hierarchical authority" as the measure of a preacher's worth. Even Asbury recognized the effects this would have on black preachers. After several difficult encounters with a prejudice new to Methodism, Allen decided to break from the Methodism he loved. He began African Methodism in America. He established the first African Methodist Episcopal congregation in 1794 and the denomination by the same name in 1816. Allen's aim was to try to recapture what Methodism had lost. Dickerson implies that it was African Methodism that truly became the "heirs" of the Wesleyan movement.[14]

Allen sought to preach what was essential to historic Christianity and Methodist theology. This included an emphasis on sanctification, but not sanctification for sanctification's sake. African Methodism expressed Wesley's concept of perfect love that, put most simply, fed the poor. Later, white Methodism would split over the very issue of slavery. It was only the African Methodist Episcopal Church that stayed united through the Civil War.

THOMAS RALSTON (1806-91)

With Thomas Ralston we begin really to see how Wesley's theology of Holiness was changed by its context. The American situation—its foundational principles, its culture, its freedoms—became the syncretistic melting pot where British Methodism blended, changed, and transformed. First among the reasons for this transformation was the blending of Wesley's already optimistic theology with the intense American optimism that dominated the 19th century. Second, Wesley's doctrine of Christian perfection met the unique brand of American revivalism. And third, Methodism became a religion of the populace to an even greater degree in America than it had been in Britain. All of these intersections had theological implications. Some Methodists clearly resisted the resulting syncretistic changes; others did not. Those who did accept and accentuate the changes would eventually move further into the ethos of the Holiness Movement.

American Methodist preachers and teachers like Ralston began to preach entire sanctification with a unique urgency. Wesley believed in entire sanctification and certainly urged his people to seek it. But in Wesley we see a willingness to wait for God's sanctifying action. In America the message was to seek entire sanctification and to actively seek it now. Ralston echoes many preachers voicing this message. "The great matter is, with each and all of us, that we lose no time, but arise at once, and 'press toward the mark for the prize of the high calling of God in Christ Jesus.'"[15]

Contributing to this repeated call to seek entire sanctification now was American revivalism, which gave persons a place to do exactly that. Wesley's followers sought entire sanctification in the setting of their small groups known as classes or bands. There were no "altar calls" to speak of in the fields where Wesley preached. It is a unique invention of American revivalism to call persons forward to make a decision in the moment. This chiefly applied to being "born again." But when American revivalism met John Wesley's doctrine of Christian perfection, the call to the "mourners' bench" also included a call to be entirely sanctified. In this context, stress on the instantaneousness of the experience only intensified.

In the American setting, we also see a boldness about what to expect from entire sanctification. Again, where Wesley was cautious about expectations, American preachers, with their American optimism, were more assured. Ralston, like others, can thus write:

> If, through grace, we forsake one sin, we may forsake all sin. If we may be cleansed from one sin, we may be cleansed from all sin. If we may keep one commandment, we may, through grace, "keep the whole law"—that is, the law of faith and love, under which we are placed by the gospel. . . . If we may advance to one degree of holiness or sanctification, which we attain when we are justified, why may we not, on the same principle, "go on to perfection?"[16]

While Wesley would not disagree with this statement in principle, it reveals a new tone. At least Ralston here keeps an appropriately strong emphasis on grace. This will not always be the case as Holiness theology in America continues to develop. An emphasis on grace and dependency on God would be difficult to maintain when the American dream meant being self-made and *earning* it all.

PHOEBE PALMER (1807-74)

Phoebe Worrall was born in a typical American Methodist home. Despite receiving only the equivalent of a grammar school education, she nurtured a literary ability that would be invaluable in later years, when her writing— books, tracts, articles, and poetry—made her known to countless readers. At nineteen years of age, Phoebe Worrall married Walter C. Palmer, a physician who was able and quite willing to support her religious vision.

A series of personal tragedies (the deaths of three children) led to a religious experience in 1837 (entire sanctification) that impelled Phoebe Palmer to enter a religious vocation that included preaching and teaching laity. Through this vocation, she influenced the lives of thousands, began the Holiness Movement (in the estimation of many)[17], and birthed several denominations that today count her their matriarch. Yet Palmer remained a firm Methodist.

Phoebe Palmer, with her sister Sarah Lankford, led the famous Tuesday Meetings held in her home, often considered the birthplace of the Holiness Movement. One of Palmer's most important contributions was the publication of *The Way of Holiness*. This book made entire sanctification understandable to the public. She herself had struggled with the doctrine because, in her estimation, preachers made it so difficult to understand. Some have criticized her simplification of the Holiness message. What it accomplished, however, was to make the experience of entire sanctification accessible to a whole generation of ordinary people.

Palmer's teaching about the doctrine offered the burgeoning Holiness Movement a response to the question, "How is one entirely sanctified?" She developed a three-step formula that guided persons seeking the instantaneous experience. Consecration—the giving over of everything to God—is followed by a faith that believes God truly wants to sanctify the heart. Once this sanctification occurs, the person must testify to the experience. This is known as Palmer's "altar covenant," which was based on exegesis done by Adam Clarke. Consecrating everything to God is in effect placing all on the altar, which is Christ. The altar then sanctifies the gift. Palmer also influenced the movement by emphasizing, as Wesley did before her, the social dimension of holiness— she called persons out of their comfort zones and into the streets and missions to meet the needs of the less fortunate.

RANDOLPH FOSTER (1820—1903)

Randolph Foster was born in Williamsburg, Ohio, in 1820. Though he abandoned education at the age of seventeen, he later became professor of systematic theology at Drew Theological Seminary and eventually became its president. He was elected as bishop in the Methodist church in 1872.

What we find in Foster's theology is a strong defense of entire sanctification as a subsequent event to regeneration. While Wesley himself and many of his theological successors had to argue that entire sanctification could occur *before* death, Foster finds himself in a position of needing to argue that there is more to anticipate *after* regeneration. Some Methodists had begun to imply a type of completeness in perfection at a person's new birth. "But it may be asked with earnestness, 'Is not the work of God perfect in regeneration?' And we answer, it is a perfect regeneration. But a perfect regeneration is not a perfect sanctification, no more than perfect penitence is perfect regeneration. The soul is perfectly born anew, but it is not perfectly made holy."[18]

According to Greathouse, Foster represents those Methodists who remained faithful to Wesley's teaching on Christian perfection. "Christian Purity, as the work came to be known, was clearly intended to keep the Methodist Episcopal Church on the solid foundation of its original Wesleyan position. . . . [Foster offered] a clear and urgent call to scriptural holiness as it had been understood within Methodism from its beginnings."[19] Greathouse's suggestion is supported by Foster's affiliation with Northwestern and Drew Seminary when these schools were being influenced toward maintaining entire sanctification as a subsequent and definite work of grace. But what Greathouse does not make clear is that even in the early decades in America, Methodism lacked a single voice on the topic. Foster and others may have called for an emphasis on "scriptural holiness as it had been understood from its beginnings," but early in the century "Wesley's position" began to be blurred. Later in the 19th century, Methodism moved away from what would become the "Holiness" interpretation of Wesley. John Miley represents the steps in Methodism's de-emphasis of entire sanctification.

JOHN MILEY (1813-95)

John Miley assumed Randolph Foster's position as chair of systematic theology at Drew when Foster (his brother-in-law) left to become bishop. While some Methodists, such as William Burt Pope, resisted the "advances" of modernism, John Miley explicitly sought to update Wesleyanism for the modern world. This is clearly evident in his *Systematic Theology*, published in 1892.

Langford calls Miley a "natural" as well as dogmatic theologian.[20] This is due to his attempts to put science and theology in dialogue. Miley believed that he served the tradition by "directing it in new ways."[21] Where we see this most clearly is in Miley's strong emphasis on religious experience—not unlike others near the turn of the century and after. Miley made important moves regarding the Bible. First, he suggested that Scripture is important in offering knowledge of Christian faith and doctrine but that it cannot produce a direct experience with God. "The experience of God is immediate; the Scriptures clarify and give normative expression to the source meaning of that experience."[22] Second, Miley advanced the dynamic theory of biblical inspiration and firmly moved Methodism away from any "mechanistic" or "dictation" tendencies. This would influence such persons as H. Orton Wiley as he described the Church of the Nazarene's position on biblical inspiration.

On the doctrine of sanctification, Miley cleared the way for the Methodist interpretation that states that sanctification may or may *not* include a "second blessing." While his aim may have been to encourage the toleration of different understandings of sanctification, what resulted was a widening between mainline Methodism and the denominations that made up the Holiness Movement. This is not to imply that the holiness interpretation disappeared from Methodism after this ideological split. For example, Asbury

College, and later Asbury Theological Seminary, under the leadership of such persons as Henry Clay Morrison (1857—1942), avoided the move toward a more liberal Methodism. Daniel Steele and John Wood would also be considered holiness Methodists.

DANIEL STEELE (1824—1914)

Daniel Steele was a Methodist minister who served as a pastor and an evangelist before teaching New Testament and theology at Boston University. Steele closely followed Fletcher in linking entire sanctification with the baptism of the Holy Spirit. As a New Testament scholar, he closely associated the book of Acts with the experience. He also states directly that Jesus himself experienced "two receptions" of the Holy Spirit, first at his baptism and second at his ascension. This exegesis gave Steele the boldness to speak of our "two receptions" of the Spirit: at regeneration and at entire sanctification. On Steele's interpretation of Acts, Greathouse states that "subsequently this became standard holiness teaching."[23] Steele is also representative of those who speak of the "entire eradication" of sin. Where Steele aligns with Wesley is when he speaks of love as central to the experience of entire sanctification.

JOHN A. WOOD (1828—1905)

John Allen Wood, who began his career as a pastor in the Methodist Episcopal Church, was one of the founders of the National Camp Meeting Association for the Promotion of Holiness, which soon became an important means of spreading the Holiness message across America.

Wood's book *Perfect Love,* which quickly became a classic of Holiness theology, follows a common pattern for those proclaiming holiness toward the end of 19th century. He distinguished entire sanctification from regeneration; he emphasized that holiness is attainable; he warned of the results of not seeking entire sanctification; he argued with those who might object to the doctrine; and he offered steps for obtaining the experience. Similar to Phoebe Palmer, he advised that persons seeking holiness must (1) understand what they are seeking, namely, the "destruction or removal of inbred sin"; (2) come to a firm and decided resolution to obtain the experience; (3) make an entire consecration to God and place "every item upon the altar"; and (4) have faith.[24] The following is a list of admonishments about faith for entire sanctification:

1. Believe that God has promised it in the Holy Scripture.
2. Believe what God has promised God is able to perform.
3. Believe that God is willing to do it.
4. Believe that God has done it.

Are you now committing all, and trusting in Christ? If you are, it is done.[25]

Later theologians would question the wisdom of this type of "claim it" theology.[26] Preaching and publications advocating for this approach were dominant in the emerging Holiness ethos. We now briefly turn to a type of Holiness optimism that, perhaps surprisingly, managed to sidestep Methodism.

▶ 19TH-CENTURY HOLINESS MOVEMENT: A NEW KIND OF CALVINISM

The revivalistic Calvinism of the 19th century met the traditionally Wesleyan doctrine of Christian perfection at Oberlin College in Ohio. Oberlin was established in 1834 with an explicit reform agenda and a belief in human equality. The college was founded at the conjunction of several events. Abolitionism was a growing concern across the States, often directly connected to religious fervor. Lane Theological Seminary in Cincinnati became a place of deep controversy over the issue of slavery. Students, including Theodore Weld, pushed for more radical abolitionist action. They acted on their beliefs by treating blacks as equals, associating with them outside the seminary. A decision was made to forbid students from living out their abolitionist sentiments and to quiet all classroom or faculty discussions of slavery. Forty students withdrew in protest.

In the meantime, a school had begun known as the Oberlin Institute. It was explicit about its reform agenda and its belief in human equality. They contacted Asa Mahan, a trustee of Lane who supported the students. He agreed to come as the first president. The Lane students followed along with nearly three hundred others the first year. Astonishing for that time, Oberlin admitted both blacks and women.

Oberlin theology was not disconnected from its social agenda. Charles Finney (1792—1875), the great revivalist and professor of systematic theology at Oberlin, and Asa Mahan (1799—1889), the college president, were attentive to entire sanctification, a new revivalist theme spreading across America, Canada, and Great Britain. Calvinists such as Finney and Mahan rejected a necessary connection between the doctrine of Christian perfection and Methodism. They began preaching a new synthesis of Calvinism and sanctification that became known as New Theology or New Calvinism. Their approach received great criticism from more traditional Calvinistic denominations. This New Theology was thoroughly optimistic about the personal and social change that can come through sanctification.

Asa Mahan is most known for his rekindling of John Fletcher's connection of entire sanctification with the baptism of the Holy Spirit. Entire sanctification was thus linked to power and Spirit-initiated ability. He believed people were enabled to do even more than humanly possible because of this Spirit baptism.

This opened new horizons, particularly for the women of the Holiness Movement. It is perhaps no coincidence then that Antoinette Brown, the first woman in America ordained to preach, was a graduate of Oberlin College.

Oberlin's radicalism waned after Finney and Mahan. This decline may be directly related to the college's return to a more traditional Calvinistic theology—a theology lacking the 19th-century understanding of Christian perfection.

HANNAH WHITALL SMITH (1832—1911)

Hannah Whitall, born as a Quaker in Philadelphia, experienced entire sanctification, which she named the "secret" of happiness. This belief resulted in a book that has become a religious classic, *The Christian's Secret of a Happy Life.* Hannah became involved in organizations interested in women's concerns such as the Women's Christian Temperance Union and the Suffrage movement. These social concerns were connected to the social optimism of Holiness theology.

Hannah and her husband, Robert, traveled to England on a speaking tour. Her first conference in England advocating her theological stance was held in 1873. In 1875, this conference was invited to Keswick by its Anglican curate. Becoming an annual event at Keswick, the conference came to be known as the Keswick Convention.

The conference is historically and theologically significant because of its relationship to, and reinterpretation of, the doctrine of entire sanctification (as held by Methodist-related churches). Keswickianism—as this reinterpretation came to be known—was started and maintained by non-Wesleyan figures, such as Smith and W. E. Boardman (a Presbyterian), who emphasized "the higher Christian life." Calvinistic Keswickians, like Wesleyans, emphasized a distinct moment of full consecration; however, unlike Wesleyans, Keswickians believed that the power of the "old nature" is *countered* by the presence of the Holy Spirit, rather than *cleansed away.* This is a subtle, but clear distinction. The movement was associated with the revivalism of D. L. Moody (the Smiths followed in Moody's tracks on their tour of England), and later Billy Graham; it was also associated with institutions such as Moody Bible Institute, Wheaton College, and Dallas Theological Seminary.

Early attempts at cooperation between the Wesleyans and Keswickians took place, but when Keswickian theology gravitated toward a premillennial eschatology, the distance grew. The Keswick Convention continues to meet annually and attracts visitors from all parts of the world. Keswickian theology is considered a close cousin of the more Wesleyan-Holiness Movement.

▶ THE AMERICAN HOLINESS MOVEMENT: THE METHODIST "COME-OUTERS" OF THE LATER 19TH CENTURY[27]

An emphasis on entire sanctification was clearly a common trait of the Wesleyan-Holiness Movement. But most of the new denominations forming from those persons who had come out of official Methodism had a strong *reforming* impulse as well. Many persons broke away from the Methodism they loved for reasons that were not solely theological. Holiness theology as interpreted by the "come-outers" led to an involvement in egalitarian-based social action. Pentecostal holiness, named for its association with the power of the first Pentecost (not with speaking in tongues), made all things new and thus demanded the overturning of oppressive social structures. Holiness theology was intricately intertwined with such causes as abolitionism, the rights of women (particularly to preach), care for the poor, temperance, and many other services directed to the most needy of society.

It is no coincidence then that the people described in the following profiles are known more for their reforms than for their theological formulations. Early Holiness denominations attempted to reclaim Wesley's teaching on Christian perfection *and* the social agenda that arose out of it. "Primitive Methodism," as it was called, also included care for the poor, arguments against slavery, and several activities requisite of the early British Methodists.

ORANGE SCOTT (1800-1847) AND LUTHER LEE (1800-1889)

One of the first denominations to split from the Methodist Episcopal Church was the Wesleyan Methodist Connection, co-founded by Orange Scott and Luther Lee. Orange Scott was born into a very poor family. Despite this and an almost complete lack of education, he became an accomplished pastor and strong abolitionist. He brought the matter of slavery to the General Conference of the Methodist Episcopal Church as a delegate in 1836. His vehemence led to disapproval from many, and he was removed from his leadership role on the district. He then joined the American Anti-Slavery Society and traveled and spoke for their cause. He finally decided to leave the Methodist Church. Along with Luther Lee, a group seceded in 1842. They organized the Wesleyan Methodist Connection.

Luther Lee was born in the famous "burnt-over" district in upstate New York. This phrase was used because the fire of revival had swept this part of the country in a dramatic way. He became a pastor for the Methodist Episcopal Church in the same region. In 1839 Lee became a leader in the Massachusetts Anti-Slavery Society. After the new denomination had begun, it elected Luther Lee as its first president. Interestingly, he preached the ordination service of Antoinette Brown, the first woman ordained in America. For the rest of his life he served as pastor of several new Wesleyan churches and as professor of some of its early colleges.

B. T. ROBERTS (1823-93)

B. T. Roberts was the founder of the Free Methodist Church. He was raised in a firmly Methodist culture and was dramatically called into the ministry. Roberts began his shift out of Methodism through the publication of his article "New School Methodism." He was concerned about the upward mobility of the Methodist people who were progressively accommodating themselves to the culture around them. Symbolic for Roberts was the pew rental system in many Methodist Episcopal churches. The wealthier members of a congregation could pick a pew that they then basically owned. This of course went against Scripture, in Roberts' mind, and against the mission to the poor that was so central to "primitive" Methodism. Roberts was also deeply committed to the abolition of slavery. Thus the name that was chosen for his "come out" denomination has two connotations. The "free" of the Free Methodist Church referred to free pews and free people. Roberts, in particular, took up an intensified ministry to the poor. According to Douglas Cullum,

> From Roberts' perspective, the upwardly-mobile, progressive "New School Methodism" of his day had forsaken Methodism's original mission of spreading "scriptural holiness over these lands." The publication of his article was the single most decisive factor that led to Roberts' expulsion from the Methodist Episcopal Church in 1858.[28]

The denomination was founded when a group following Roberts and another group following John Wesley Redfield (who had also been expelled) united in 1860. The early Free Methodists lived simply in order to best minister and preach to the poor. Free Methodism was thus as much a type of practical piety as it was a theological branch of the Wesleyan-Holiness Movement.

AMANDA BERRY SMITH (1837—1915)

The life of Amanda Berry Smith, born a slave in 1837, represents a life affected by the egalitarian impulse of Holiness theology. She became an evangelist, missionary, and social reformer. She early attended the Methodist Episcopal Church but found herself in an entirely white class meeting. Apparently, the leaders were only willing to teach her at the end of the meeting, but she had to report for work before the meeting ended. She stopped attending and drifted away.

Earlier in her life Amanda had experienced a vision in which she saw herself preaching. After the death of her husband, James Smith, she experienced entire sanctification under the ministry of John Inskip, who had been highly influenced by Phoebe Palmer. There is some evidence that Amanda

Berry Smith attended Palmer's Tuesday Meetings, which were extraordinarily important in the development of the Wesleyan-Holiness Movement. Palmer's stance on the issue of slavery is questionable.[29] Nevertheless, Smith's encounters with Palmer seemed to have aided her in associating spiritual empowerment with the elimination of prejudice.

In 1879, Smith became a missionary, first to India, where she stayed two years, and then to Africa (Liberia and Sierra Leone) for another eight. Although she was officially a member of the African Methodist Episcopal Church, they did not support her ministry efforts. She spent most of her ministry career associating with the white Holiness churches and associations. She also became heavily involved in organizations that emphasized abolition and temperance. She became a wide speaker for the Women's Christian Temperance Union under the leadership of Frances Willard. This placed Smith on the scene as a nationally recognized evangelist. One of the greatest gifts Smith left behind was her autobiography, published first in 1893. She revealed that she never fully felt accepted in either white or black circles. Insightfully she writes, "I think some people would understand the quintessence of sanctifying grace if they could be black about twenty-four hours."[30] Interestingly, she also wrote that part of her entire sanctification experience involved her acceptance and gratitude for her blackness.

DANIEL WARNER (1842-95)

Even while new denominations were coming out of the Methodist Episcopal Church, there were close associations across denominational lines. National associations of various sorts became prominent in the Holiness Movement. However, there were some persons who suspected denominational distinctiveness to be potentially divisive, even within these broader associations. And yet these persons did not possess a call to nondenominationalism per se. Rather, they worked toward what might be called a transcendent denominationalism—based on the belief that Christ's call to perfect unity within his church should transcend denominational affiliations.

Daniel Warner was raised in a German Church of God that followed the theology of John Winebrenner. Winebrenner broke off from the German Reformed Church over two points that became central to the theological position of the denomination he founded: first, the Bible is the only authoritative rule for faith and practice; and second, every Christian needs to have a personal conversion experience or new birth. Winebrenner also affirmed free will and rejected strict creedal affirmations and church membership—principles with which Daniel Warner agreed. But after Warner had an entire sanctification experience, the German group rescinded his minister's license. A Church of God splinter group relicensed him, and he continued as a pastor, evangelist, and an editor of one of the many important Holiness papers of the late 19th century, the *Gospel Trumpet*.

Warner participated in national associations with the aim to promote the Holiness message. But he eventually left these associations. He felt strongly that God had revealed to him that any hint of sectarianism was against Scripture. One of Warner's biographers, Barry Callen, states:

> Warner's come-outism was inspired by a vision of the church outside all denominations, enabled by dynamic holiness. He cared deeply about the unity of believers, saw holiness as the way to it, and judged the continuing existence of multiple and often competitive denominational structures to be an evil among God's people that God intended to end.[31]

Warner advised people to leave all systems and structures and welcomed many into a movement simply known as the Church of God. It later identified itself by the extension "Anderson" (Indiana) in order to distinguish itself from other denominations that took the name Church of God. Years later the movement (as they prefer to be called) faced the need for organization. Having an official church membership, however, was deemed unnecessary.

This movement is considered to be a strong sibling in the Wesleyan-Holiness Movement's family of denominations. Like others, the Church of God began with an inclination to minister to the marginalized. But unlike some other denominations in the movement, the Church of God has managed to maintain a high population of African-Americans. It has also held a good percentage of women preachers and ministers. Although the Holiness Movement has been called a sect by historians looking at the movement from the outside, the ecclesiology of such groups as the Church of God reveals a legitimate ecumenical impulse.

MARTIN WELLS KNAPP (1853—1901)

Another example of this unity-directed ideology can be seen in the life and work of Martin Wells Knapp and the establishment of the International Revival Prayer League (which became the Pilgrim Holiness Church) and the opening of God's Bible School. Knapp was influential in launching radical holiness or sweet radical holiness groups. These groups were characterized by a rejection of cultural vices and the espousal of radical (monetary) simplicity as a means to reach the poor and establish traits of the communal church in Acts. Radical holiness is misunderstood if it is seen pejoratively as a form of legalism.

PHINEAS BRESEE (1838—1915)

Phineas Bresee was born and educated in New York State. Deciding to enter the ministry, he moved his family to Iowa and joined the conference of the Methodist Episcopal Church. In 1864 he was appointed as presiding elder in the Methodist Conference of West Des Moines. He did not enjoy his role as an administrator, so he went back to circuit preaching. Later in his life, he moved to Los Angeles, where he had become known as an effective and powerful evangelist, and pastored many prominent Methodist churches in Southern California.

Bresee had experienced entire sanctification in 1867 and was not shy about preaching it. He was also intensely interested in inner-city mission work. He withdrew from the Methodist Episcopal Church in 1894 and associated with the Peniel Mission in Los Angeles. In 1895 Bresee and the University of Southern California president, J. P. Widney, organized a local church he called the Church of the Nazarene. Bresee was its pastor. He also started a Holiness magazine known as the *Nazarene Messenger*. His work blossomed into a small denomination.

The Church of the Nazarene grew numerically not only through conversions but also through mergers. Important historically were the mergers with the New England Association of Pentecostal Holiness Churches in 1907, with the Holiness Churches of Christ in Texas in 1908, and with a group from Tennessee, the Pentecostal Mission, in 1914. The name was briefly changed to the Pentecostal Church of the Nazarene (it was changed back in 1919).

Bresee was known as a keen mediator. For the sake of unity, he compromised on issues he thought were "non-essential." For this reason, the Church of the Nazarene does not take a particular stand on eschatology, for example. Bresee also blended the Methodist tradition of infant baptism with the more Anabaptist emphasis on believer's baptism—parents could choose either.

The name Church of the Nazarene was a means of associating the denomination with *the* lowly Nazarene and spoke of its particular interest in the poor and marginalized. The denomination quickly organized overseas mission work that has remained strong. Theologically, the denomination is thoroughly Wesleyan (often taking a *via media*, or mediating position, on many issues) and is soteriologically focused. Entire sanctification is emphasized, and the denomination clearly associates itself with the tradition of the Wesleyan-Holiness Movement. It is considered to be the largest Holiness denomination.

▶ THE HOLINESS MOVEMENT IN OTHER PARTS OF THE WORLD

Before we proceed to the Wesleyan-Holiness tradition of the 20th century, we must pause to ask how the Holiness Movement developed in other parts of the world during the latter half of the 19th century. We will use Great Britain and Asia as only two examples of the worldwide spread of the Holiness message.

There were many prominent Holiness preachers who went to Great Britain in order to preach entire sanctification. The Keswickian sympathizers and the more strictly Holiness evangelists, such as Phoebe Palmer, made an impact there. Holiness theology was alive and well in Great Britain. According to Floyd Cunningham, "One could find little difference between the preaching of British Holiness leaders such as William Arthur, Samuel Chadwick, W. D. Drysdale, and Oswald Chambers, and their American counterparts. Great Britain and America shared a common Holiness language and literature."[32] George Sharpe from Scotland spent many years in America and associated with those in the National Holiness Association. When he returned home, he found that "a number of people in Scotland and England taught and believed the doctrine just as he."[33] Many persons, such as Francis Crossley, William McDonald, George Grubb, and the Booths, were influential in the development of the British Holiness identity.[34]

The Wesleyan-Holiness Movement of the 19th century spread throughout the world, not just in North America and Europe. It spread throughout Asia, even China. One brief example will be offered here.

The Oriental Missionary Society (OMS, now OMS International), although officially nondenominational, was thoroughly Holiness in its theology and preaching. It was long supported by God's Bible School and Martin Wells Knapp. It began with a Bible school in Japan and quickly expanded with a mission strategy developed by founder Charles Cowman. It distributed millions of Bibles and tracts. OMS's greatest success came in the mission field of Korea. Two students trained at the Bible school in Japan began the work. They helped open a Bible school. Later Robert Nam Soo Chung, a graduate of God's Bible School and of Asbury College, and Sung Bong Li energized the OMS's work through their revivalist preaching. Eventually a denomination developed independent from any American denomination. Korea Evangelical Holiness Church was in close connection with the Bible school begun years earlier. MyungJik Lee was director and professor at the school and became the principal Holiness theologian in Korea in the early 20th century. Of note, this Bible school eventually became Seoul Theological Seminary, which grew to be the largest Wesleyan seminary in the world. Wars would of course divide Korea and cause the denomination to struggle. But by 1995 it had nearly one million members. Christianity in Korea has exploded. Along with other denominations, the Wesleyan-Holiness Movement still has a very strong presence there.

▶ 20TH-CENTURY HOLINESS THEOLOGY

In the 20th century one of the Wesleyan-Holiness Movement's greatest challenges was how to transform a movement into a cluster of denominations.

Thus, much energy in the earlier part of the 20th century was spent on organization and in writing new systematic theologies for the new denominational contexts. As the century progressed, Wesleyan-Holiness theology was strengthened and shaped. Each of the persons profiled below made significant contributions to its development.

A. M. HILLS (1848—1935)

Aaron Merritt Hills, who began his ministry in the Congregational Church, later became associated with a number of Holiness institutions of higher education.

Hills's style was polemical and at times antagonistic. His writings include criticisms of certain behaviors, such as the use of tobacco and alcohol, because he believed that the social crises of the late 19th century were spiritual in nature. As a strong **postmillennialist,** he believed that the doctrine of Christian perfection would solve social problems. His criticisms were also directed toward doctrine. He blatantly criticized Keswickian theology, higher biblical criticism, and **premillennialism.** His stances against Darwin certainly paint him as a conservative. But interestingly, he also criticized the theory of verbal dictation and the absolute inerrancy of the Bible.

His most important work, *Holiness and Power,* published in 1897, was highly circulated. His systematic theology, *Fundamentals of Christian Theology,* placed free-agency as its central hermeneutic and "tended to root faith and sanctification in the acts of the human will."[35] *Holiness and Power* is an interesting read for a historian. Throughout the book he quotes the important figures of the 19th-century Holiness Movement and brings their theology forward into the 20th century, including Daniel Steele, Phoebe Palmer, Catherine Booth, Hannah Whitall Smith, and Charles Finney. His intent was to offer evidence for entire sanctification by offering personal testimonies and biblical support for the doctrine of Holiness. This testimonial approach was common in Holiness literature.

SAMUEL LOGAN BRENGLE (1860—1936)

Samuel Logan Brengle began his ministry as a Methodist Episcopal Church circuit preacher. The Salvation Army's agenda appealed to him, and he traveled to London and met the Booths. Brengle was more of a theologian than the Booths, and after years of service he began a writing career. His books sealed the Holiness message in the denomination's theological consciousness in new ways.

Brengle brought back into the Holiness Movement Wesley's attitude toward entire sanctification. Specifically, Brengle maintained that God's assurance, or the witness of the Spirit, is needed to claim the experience. This counters those who had stressed a more naked faith (faith without any witness), such as Ralston and Palmer. Interestingly, he published a book titled *The Way of Holiness* in 1902, using the exact title of Palmer's classic on the subject. Brengle was an early call back to the Holiness theology of John Wesley (stressing entire *and* progressive sanctification), although the 19th-century Holiness Movement believed it was doing exactly that in light of the drift away from entire sanctification in mainline Methodism. Brengle's message of the need for balance (between the "moment" and the process) would find strong supporters in the latter part of the 20th century.

H. ORTON WILEY (1877—1961)

Henry Orton Wiley, a pastor, educator, and college president in the Church of the Nazarene, completed his three-volume *Christian Theology* in 1941, which soon became the most important theological work in the Holiness Movement for several decades. What Wiley brought into 20th century Holiness thought was a synthesis of Wesleyan theology with the modern emphases on the personal, on theological anthropology, and on faith as a personal relationship with God, through the Son, and nourished by the Holy Spirit. God is a personal God. Christian experience is an important source for theology in Wiley's thought, as it was for Wesley and broader theologians such as Friedrich Schleiermacher. Wiley remained true to Wesleyanism's optimism of grace without collapsing his theology in the Protestant liberalism of the era. He also managed to avoid the new pessimism of "new orthodox" theologians such as Barth, Brunner, and Niebuhr.[36] Wiley was highly dependent on Pope and Miley and less dependent on Holiness literature than might be expected. Wiley's tone is similar in ways to Brengle's, because Wiley also moved the tradition toward reclaiming a more balanced Wesley than was presented by 19th-century figures who strongly followed Fletcher's emphasis on baptism with the Holy Spirit.

MILDRED BANGS WYNKOOP (1905-97)

Mildred Bangs grew up under the influence of some of the great early preachers of the Church of the Nazarene, and H. Orton Wiley was her theological mentor. She had the rare privilege of typing Wiley's *Christian Theology* for publication.

Mildred and her husband, Ralph, began their life together as evangelists. They both preached and were in high demand in California, Oregon, and Washington. They would also pastor together through the years. After receiving her doctorate in theology, Mildred taught at Western Evangelical Seminary and later served as president and professor at Japan Christian Junior College and Japanese Nazarene Theological Seminary (from 1960 to 1965).

While in Asia, she studied the culture intensely, attempting to understand not only how relationships worked but also how she might best articulate Holiness theology to the Asian mind. It is clear that this experience expanded her own theological vocabulary that later had such a profound effect on those who read her holistic understanding of holiness.

After returning from Japan, Wynkoop taught at Trevecca Nazarene College and later at Nazarene Theological Seminary (the first woman ever to be elected to the seminary's faculty). She was also the first woman elected president of the Wesleyan Theological Society. As a theologian, Wynkoop was well known and a much sought-after speaker, both inside and outside the Church of the Nazarene. According to many scholars, Wynkoop's *A Theology of Love: The Dynamic of Wesleyanism*, published in 1972, revolutionized the way the doctrine of Holiness was articulated in the Wesleyan-Holiness tradition. This work presents her interpretation of John Wesley's theology of perfect love.

Like Wesley, she was eclectic in her thought, creative, synthetic, and thus unique. Her book challenged models that had represented the only perspective on entire sanctification. This was controversial, and for many, Wynkoop was deemed too radical. However, now over thirty years later her book continues to be influential and is still used in Wesleyan-Holiness higher education.

What made Wynkoop's theology so significant? It was her intense focus on human experience and human relationships. Her understanding of sin and her understanding of holiness are articulated in terms of relationality. Our capacity for relationships, for *loving* relationships, is our God-given purpose and destiny. There is a God-designed holy manner for relating to God, to others, and even to ourselves. Sin distorts these relationships. God-derived love restores them. Holiness, then, is found most clearly when we love as God first loved us. Thus, sin is not simply reduced to a set of broken rules and laws, which can easily deteriorate into stagnant legalism. Sin is anti-relationship, anti-love. Holiness as love, as defined by Wynkoop's interpretation of John Wesley's theology, is dynamic and alive. Most of all, it is *relevant* to the life we live day in, day out. Holiness must be "credible" in real life.[37]

GEORGE ALLEN TURNER (1908-98)

George Allen Turner was an important biblical scholar in the Holiness tradition of the 20th century. His ministry included pastorates in the Congregational Christian Church and the Free Methodist Church and a long career of teaching at Asbury College. Part of his legacy there was his emphasis on the Wesleyan imperative toward the needs of the poor and oppressed. Turner's doctoral dissertation, published as *The More Excellent Way* (1952), was later revised and published in 1964 as *The Vision Which Transforms*. This served as one of the strongest biblical defenses of the theology of Holiness in the 20th century.

In a later debate in the Wesleyan Theological Society, Turner defended the mid-19th-century position of associating entire sanctification with the baptism with the Holy Spirit. This debate would serve as a watershed in the development of Holiness theology in the 20th century. Other important figures in the debate were Donald Dayton and Larry Wood. The debate revealed a marked difference between those who wanted to stress the Wesleyan side of the Wesleyan-Holiness Movement and those who wanted to stress the Holiness side. From that point on there has been a tendency to identify Holiness theologians by the side of this issue on which they stand. It is probably fair to say that present-day theologians are still identified in this manner.[38]

RICHARD S. TAYLOR (1912—2006)

Richard S. Taylor clearly stood in the Holiness part of the Wesleyan-Holiness tradition. Richard Taylor was a minister and educator in the Church of the Nazarene. He was one of the most prolific Wesleyan-Holiness writers of the 20th century. "Taylor's ministry has been characterized by vigorous polemics against Calvinism and extended defenses of the traditional doctrinal formulations of the Holiness Movement."[39] He was one of the strongest proponents of the 19th-century Holiness understanding of entire sanctification. His most important works were *The Right Conception of Sin* (1939), *The Disciplined Life* (1962), and *Exploring Christian Holiness, Vol. 3: Theological Foundations* (1985).

WILLIAM GREATHOUSE (1919—)

William Greathouse represents those calling for a return to more classic Wesleyanism. Greathouse has served the Church of the Nazarene as a professor, president of both Trevecca Nazarene College and Nazarene Theological Seminary, and as general superintendent of the denomination. Also important in the development of 20th-century Wesleyan-Holiness theology have been his assorted publications. He has numerous publications in the areas of historical theology and biblical theology as they pertain to the doctrine of Holiness, including most recently a two-volume commentary on Romans, coauthored by George Lyons.

Greathouse represents the aforementioned balance between a strong emphasis on entire sanctification as a decisive moment and the need for progressive growth in grace. He has been particularly interested in rearticulating the importance of the means of grace, including the Lord's Supper, as vital catalysts in one's growth in holiness.

J. KENNETH GRIDER (1921—2006)

Joseph Kenneth Grider, who received his PhD from Glasgow University, was a prominent theologian and educator in the Church of the Nazarene. He was professor of theology at Nazarene Theological Seminary from 1953 to 1992. Grider offered many theological works to the Wesleyan-Holiness Movement. His most important work was *Entire Sanctification: The Distinctive Doctrine of Wesleyanism* (1980), which strongly defends the 19th-century Holiness model and the baptism with the Holy Spirit. He also published *A Wesleyan-Holiness Theology* in 1994, which many consider his magnum opus, a work aimed to offer an alternative to H. Ray Dunning's *Grace, Faith, and Holiness*. Grider viewed Dunning as one of the relational theologians (with Mildred Bangs Wynkoop, William Greathouse, and Rob Staples) who, he believed, were lessening the strong and distinctive emphasis on entire sanctification that dominated 19th-century Holiness thought. In a sense, Grider believed that the 19th century had improved on Wesley himself; the relational theologians were calling for a reclamation of a more classical interpretation of Wesleyan theology, which for Grider threatened the urgency of the Holiness message of entire sanctification.

ROB L. STAPLES (1929—)

Relational theologians, like Rob L. Staples, did not abandon the doctrine of entire sanctification. Rather, they believed that Wesley's balanced emphasis on regeneration, progressive sanctification, and entire sanctification had been largely forgotten and that the 19th-century understanding of entire sanctification had overshadowed God's grace throughout the Christian journey. Before his retirement, Rob Staples was professor of theology at Bethany Nazarene College (now Southern Nazarene University) and at Nazarene Theological Seminary. Grider's time and Staples's overlapped at NTS. Staples became involved in the Wesleyan Theological Society debate over the baptism with the Holy Spirit in the 1970s, by writing a summary of the issues.[40]

Staples's greatest contribution to Wesleyan-Holiness theology came from his publication of *Outward Sign and Inward Grace: The Place of Sacraments in Wesleyan Spirituality,* published in 1991. Staples emphasized the important place of the means of grace and the sacrament of Holy Communion in particular in spiritual development. He calls Communion the sacrament of sanctification and thus ties sacramental spirituality with Wesley's doctrine of Christian perfection.

JAMES EARL MASSEY (1930—)

James Earl Massey has been a minister, preacher, and educator in the Church of God (Anderson). He served for many years at Anderson College as campus pastor, professor of preaching and New Testament, and as dean of the School of Theology. He also served as university professor and dean of the chapel at Tuskegee University.

Massey was a highly important African-American preacher and scholar in the Holiness tradition of the 20th century. Reconciliation has been a consistent theological theme for him; he practiced it during the civil rights movement as a pastor and friend of Martin Luther King Jr., and he has developed it through sermons and biblical commentaries that he has edited or authored. Three of his books have been on the art of preaching as a means to reconcile people to God.

Unusually ecumenical, Massey has served church councils, lectured on dozens of college and seminary campuses, and received honors as one of the great preachers of recent generations. He is respected in the larger evangelical community and also by mainline denominations. He is a life trustee of Asbury Theological Seminary and holder of the Lifetime Achievement Award of the Wesleyan Theological Society.[41]

HOWARD SNYDER (1940—)

Howard Snyder was born in the Dominican Republic in 1940. He has served the Free Methodist Church as pastor, missionary (to Brazil), and professor. He has taught at United Theological Seminary in Dayton, Ohio, and has been a faculty member at Asbury Theological Seminary since 1996. "Snyder has long urged Wesleyans to affirm a radical believer's church ecclesiology while working for racial, economic, and environmental justice."[42] He has just completed an extensive biography on B. T. Roberts. Snyder has been and continues to be a prominent theological voice in the Wesleyan-Holiness tradition.

SUSIE STANLEY (1948—)

Susie Stanley is mentioned here for her founding of an extremely important organization, the Wesleyan-Holiness Women's Clergy Association. She received her PhD in American Religion and Culture from Iliff School of Theology in 1987. She has taught historical theology at Western Evangelical Seminary and at Messiah College. In 1993, she represented the Holiness Movement at the World Conference on Faith and Order of the World Council of Churches. Stanley is an ordained elder in the Church of God (Anderson).

In the early 1990s Stanley recognized an important need in the lives of many Wesleyan-Holiness women pastors and worked to find ways for them to connect. Over one hundred women attended the first Come to the Water conference in Glorietta, New Mexico. The conference reconvened every two years. Nearly six hundred women attended the conference in Nashville in 2008. Besides the conference, Stanley has led the organization in publishing and curriculum development on the topic of women in ministry. Also significant are her two books, *Feminist Pillar of Fire: The Life of Alma White* (1993) and *Holy Boldness: Women Preachers' Autobiographies and the Sanctified Self* (2002); both are important sketches of women leaders and preachers in the 19th century.

Now that we have completed the biblical and historical reviews of Holiness theology found in the first chapters of this book, we will explore what Holiness theology should look like today. To do this, our dialogue with Scripture and history will continue, with the hope of communicating a theology of Holiness relevant to both the present and the future.

SUMMARY STATEMENTS

1. John Fletcher and other early British Methodists modified some of Wesley's teachings on Christian perfection.

2. Methodism's understanding of Christian perfection in America was influenced by American principles and culture.

3. Revivalism was an important mechanism for preaching Christian perfection.

4. The Holiness Movement was deeply connected to social reform and egalitarianism.

5. The Holiness Movement stressed the instantaneousness of entire sanctification.

6. Holiness theologians of the 20th century differed on their emphasis—either on classical Wesleyanism or on the Holiness Movement's modifications of Wesley's teachings.

QUESTIONS FOR REFLECTION:

1. Is the Holiness Movement today concerned with social reform?

2. How did the Holiness Movement differ from Methodism at the end of the 19th century?

3. Is theological fidelity to Wesley important? Why or why not?

4. What are some present-day issues as the Holiness Movement operates in a postmodern world?

FURTHER READING

Chiles, Robert. *Theological Transition in American Methodism*. Lanham, MD: University Press of America, 1983.

Dieter, Melvin. *The Holiness Revival of the Nineteenth Century.* Metuchen, NJ: Scarecrow Press, 1996.

Peters, John. *Christian Perfection and American Methodism.* New York: Abingdon Press, 1956.

Smith, Timothy. *Revivalism and Social Reform.* New York: Abingdon Press, 1957.

PART III

HOLINESS THEOLOGY FOR TODAY

FIVE

THE HOLY GOD

LEARNER OBJECTIVES
Your study of this chapter will help you to:

1. Understand some of the historical and contemporary debates about the nature of God

2. Identify the various roles of Jesus Christ as Servant

3. Identify the work of the Holy Spirit in regeneration and sanctification

4. Recognize how crucial it is to the Wesleyan-Holiness tradition to emphasize God's love

KEY WORDS

Trinity	Natural theology
Theodicy	Marcionism
Transcendence	*Imago Dei*
Synergism	Recapitulation
Moral attributes	Prevenient grace
Natural attributes	Spiritual senses
I-Thou	Rationalism
Immanence	Empiricism
Omnipresent	Epistemology
Patripassionism	Inclusivism
Modalism	Exclusivism
Impassibility	Pluralism
Panenthesism	Regeneration
Aseity	*Ordo salutis*
Soteriology	*Via salutis*
Deism	Awakening
Condescension	Paraclete

God is holy, and God calls us to be holy. Understanding more about God is thus essential to our study of holiness. Although we cannot explore everything the Bible and Christian tradition say about God, we can give our attention to those areas that are especially relevant to a Holiness theology. To do this, certain qualifications will be helpful to keep in mind as we begin.

Although we intend to be faithfully Trinitarian, we will not pursue an examination of the deeper facets of the doctrine of the **Trinity**. A study of the Trinity could encompass an exploration of both God's unified life inside the Trinity and God's Trinitarian interaction with us. God's relationship(s) within God's self is a matter of speculation, but God's self in relation to us is something we can know about, because God chose to relate to us. This chapter will thus emphasize God's activity toward humanity, with special consideration given to God's salvation offered to us. *God is the God who saves.* This says something definite about God's holy nature. God's holiness affects God's relationship with us.

This chapter and the chapters that follow it overlap in many ways. The chapters that follow cover the topics of humanity, sin, and salvation. An intended distinction is observable between the chapters. While this chapter is about God's activity toward us, the next chapters are about our response to that activity.

SALVATION

"Salvation" in its Wesleyan sense is not just a term that is synonymous with justification, or being forgiven of one's sins. It implies the whole Christian life, and necessarily includes sanctification, Christian growth, and transformation throughout a person's life until he or she dies. Salvation, then, is much more that just getting to heaven.

▸ THE HOLINESS OF GOD

Theology as God-talk is complex. The vast variety of available theologies can read like a menu at a smorgasbord. Besides the many nuances of more classical traditions (Catholic, Orthodox, Lutheran, Calvinist, Wesleyan, etc.) the addition of the contextualized theologies of the mid to late 20th century makes our options countless. Even more recent attempts to return to tradition (e.g., radical orthodoxy) are reactions to earlier reactions against a supposedly outdated understanding of God. Why did "God" inevitably change in the 20th century? Why did God "die"? Why was God resurrected in so many different forms? These are certainly complex issues. Explanations are modestly offered here.

"DEATH OF GOD" THEOLOGY

> The "God is dead" idea flourished to such a degree that it is considered its own theology, decades after Nietzsche's declaration. The "death of God" movement developed in the 1960s with such proponents as Harvey Cox.

First of all, "God," under the sheer weight of the evidence of abject evil, collapses. Understandably perhaps, the problem of evil becomes a primary preoccupation of theology after the Holocaust. **Theodicy** takes on more precedence than it had ever received throughout the history of Christianity. The God of love who would allow such suffering is put on trial. To counter the arguments that theodicy raises, some assert the traditional view of God as monergisticly coercive (a view that sees God as willing to override our free will and act independent of our responses). It is understandable that many are tempted to reassert strongly God's control in a world that seems so out of control. But this kind of sovereignty is seen by many as incompatible both with a loving God and with the enormity of suffering in the world. Particularly for Wesleyans, it seems misguided to put forth God's control in an effort to save God from the questions that arise in the midst of tragedy. But there is also the temptation to swing to the other side and reduce God and God's ability to act in the world. Namely, we are tempted to give in to the tendency to make God in our own image.

Maintaining God's holiness is one way to avoid our tendency to anthropomorphize God (i.e., describe God by only using human characteristics). There has always been the temptation in theology to make God into a type of co-creature.[1] (In a sense, it is this humanized God that Feuerbach, Nietzche, Freud, and Marx perhaps rightly killed.) Yet even when this anthropomorphizing is avoided, there is still the danger of restricting God's being to our own assertions. In this sense, all attempts to define God—especially all metaphysical attempts—possess the temptation to idolize our own ideas about God. But properly understanding God's holiness leads to a confession of God's mystery. Any attempt to redefine God that removes God's mystery is misguided.

One of the benefits of passing from a modernist outlook, with its confidence that reason can provide comprehensive conclusions about God, to a postmodernist one is the revitalization of God's mysterious nature. In a way, it is a revitalization of God's holiness. It is a reaffirmation that God is transcendent.

GOD AS TRANSCENDENT

God is transcendent. A crucial aspect of God's holiness is found in this otherness. God is "wholly other," different from all God created. It is this otherness that allows us to make the paradoxical statement that *only* God is holy, and as such, God calls us to be holy. Important in maintaining that God is transcendent and that God is holy is the following statement: *God is necessarily independent from all that is not God.* Again paradoxically, God is necessarily free.

While this viewpoint is basically a classical understanding of God, it is not always affirmed today, even in Wesleyan circles. At issue is the belief that God is intimately involved with us, suffers with us, and is truly immanent in the world. But God's *independence* does not nullify this essential belief. **Transcendence** and independence do not imply that God is indifferent or without empathy toward creation. Rather, it says the opposite. It is God's "otherness" that allows God to freely engage with creation, especially in the expression of love.

Some theologies, reacting to certain theories of transcendence, have suggested a type of panentheistic *interdependence* in the relationship between God and humanity, where God is almost reduced to a human level. But instead of taking this route, Wesleyan theology has maintained that a divine-human dynamic and synergistic relationship is more than sufficient to uphold God's loving interactions with us. This **synergism** does not need to limit God's freedom in order to affirm our own.

DIVINE VOLITION

For centuries (beginning in the Scholastic period—ca. 1100-1400 CE) theologians have argued over whether or not God is a *volitional* God. The debate goes something like this: On the one hand, if God is something by nature, then God cannot act otherwise; but on the other hand, to limit God's ability to be or act by appealing to God's nature necessarily implies God's "natural" limitation, and God's essential freedom is lost. The debate arises when theology attempts to discern and distinguish the natural attributes from the **moral attributes** of God. The **natural attributes** are those qualities of God that are necessary attributes. In other words, if God ceases to be x, then God ceases to be God. Often the quality of love is considered to be a natural attribute. If God ceases to love, God ceases to be God.

God's freedom raises interesting questions. Does God have a necessary relation to what God has created? Some present-day theologians maintain that there is a *need* in God to be related to something external to God's own self.[2] The issue raised here has implications for God's self-sufficiency and thus God's holiness.

If God needs humanity, God could potentially misuse humanity for God's own ends, so to speak. Yet, God did not love us, indeed, did not even create us in the beginning, because God had some void that needed to be filled. This would be similar to saying a parent procreates a child to meet his or her own needs. We would consider such a parent to have missed what it truly means to be a parent and to be potentially dangerous to the child![3] There is a giftedness associated with the life that a child receives from his or her parents. When parents no longer view this life as a gift, children can suffer. If we believe parents holding such a view are dangerous, why would we think that a God who thinks similarly is tolerable or worthy of worship? A God like this would use the world for God's own gain. But even if we say God needs to be related to God's children in some gentler way, we would reduce God's independence, then God's essential freedom, then God's holiness, and then God's ability to love as a God loves. God's creation must be maintained as a *gift*.[4]

God can only love with *agape* when God is essentially free from need or dependence upon the creation. If we affirm that God intends us as human beings to love with *agape* love, then that *agape* love requires a freedom from our own needs in any and all loving acts. Like God's transcendence, it is only in a type of self-transcendence that love is truly possible. If we seek to meet our needs through another person, love necessarily becomes *philio* or *eros*. Self-sacrifice is necessary to *agape* love.[5] If this is true for us, it is certainly true for God, the source of all love. Any type of necessary interdependence between God and God's creation can be a challenge to God's unconditional love. It objectifies the needed person(s). The now classical argument of Martin Buber on the difference between I-Thou and I-It must certainly apply to God's relationship with the creation. Put simply, Martin Buber believed that all relationships should be based on treating persons as persons, as thous. The opposite, an I-It relationship, would be where one or both parties treat the other as an object, only in terms of what that other person can do for the first; an I-It relationship is inherently selfish. So again, God must be seen as one who established and certainly maintains the **I-Thou** relationship toward humanity. If this line of thinking is affirmed, it is hard to envision God as needy in any sense of the word. God is holy in God's independence. It is in this vein that we affirm that God is transcendent.

GOD AS IMMANENT

God's holiness as God's essential freedom, otherness, and transcendence is a reasoned abstraction. But when we affirm God's holiness as God's **immanence** and as God's immanent involvement in the world, we speak of both revelation and our experience of God. God's holiness in immanence, expressed as *agape* love, moves God to a love that is "wide and long and high and deep"—a love we can "know" even though it "surpasses knowledge." Indeed this love is what fills us "to the measure of all the fullness of God" (Eph. 3:18-19). Could there be a better statement of God's immanence than here expressed by Paul? This love is anything but indifferent or impassible.

Although God is independent God is engaged with the world. God has freely chosen not only to create all things but also to be intimately involved ever since. Indeed, God is the sustainer of the universe. Important to this sustenance is the affirmation that God is both **omnipresent** and ever-present. God's omnipresence, through the Spirit, is a declaration that God is in all places. God as ever-present affirms God's eternal nature and that God always is. But more than that, God's ever-presence affirms that God has never ceased to be with creation throughout its history. Further, God's omnipresent and ever-present character is not just a theological assertion but also a soteriological one, with implications for the Christian life. Through God's presence we see a glimpse of God's infinite devotion to us, God's dedication to our salvation—to our renewal in the image of God—as we directly experience God's holiness. In light of this, we would do well to address a notion of God's holiness that has had a negative practical effect.

A misunderstanding about both God's transcendence and immanence has led to the idea that because God is holy, God is unable to co-habitate with sin. This type of thinking began as an appropriate effort to maintain God's holiness and God's otherness. Unfortunately, the idea has extended too far. For some persons, the statement that God cannot be where sin is has left them despairing of God's presence in their lives. The idea that God leaves every time we sin runs counter to numerous verses in Scripture that proclaim God's abiding presence.[6] Indeed, it is a misunderstanding of the atonement to suggest that God, despite Jesus' existential feelings of forsakenness, actually left him on the cross. Such an idea threatens an important quality of God—that God is unified in purpose. We must maintain the mystery that God experienced death.

In our case, the Holy Spirit surely does not abandon us whenever we commit a sin. We might even say the Holy Spirit must be "present to sin" in order to cleanse it away. God's love for us compelled Christ to take on the sin of the world so that we might be free of it. We must keep in mind that God is angered by sin because of its disintegrating effect on us. God hates sin because God loves the sinner. God seeks to conquer sin but not because God is too pure to be in its presence. After all, God is omnipresent. God seeks to conquer sin because God is for us.

Thus a deep understanding of God's immanence guards against any hint of indifference in God. God's love for humanity not only moved God to send "his only begotten Son" (KJV) but (as Jesus himself promised) also did not, and does not, leave us as orphans. The Holy Spirit has come to be all- and ever-present in the world and in our lives. It is an empathetic and passionate presence.

This leads us to another related danger when considering the immanent character of God. It is one that has been debated throughout the history of the church. Succinctly stated, is God impassible? That is, can we influence God to the point that God "changes"? The belief, called **patripassionism** (which literally means "the father suffers"), was condemned as heresy. Its censure, however, resulted in a pendulum swing that denied any passion in God at all.

The original heresy stated that God the *Father* became incarnate and died on the cross, which suggested a type of **modalism** (i.e., God the Father became God the Son, and then God the Spirit, thus denying the essential Trinity). Unfortunately, the denunciation of the heresy led some orthodox thinkers to move toward propagating the idea that the Father possessed stoic-like qualities. However, this is a misunderstanding of the character of God, especially for those whose tradition emphasizes that God is love. God is moved. God is empathetic. God suffers with us. God is anything but stoic.

Related to the question of God's **impassibility** is the question, Does God change? Unquestionably there is evidence in the Old Testament that God changes God's "mind," even changes plans. In light of this, the verses "Jesus Christ is the same yesterday and today and forever" (Heb. 13:8) or "God is not a man, that he should lie, nor a son of man, that he should change his mind" (Num. 23:19) should not be interpreted too rigidly (unless by it we mean God's essential nature does not change). However, we do not need to move toward a panentheistic understanding of God to accept the biblical evidence of God's change of heart or mind. **Panentheism** holds that, metaphorically and metaphysically, the world is "in" God; thus whenever the world changes, God changes with it. It is not necessary to embrace this understanding in order to affirm God's more empathetic qualities. It is more than possible to hold to God's independence and God's passionate relationality at the same time.

GOD AS LOVE

God's relationality is a natural attribute. God is by nature relational. But further explanation is necessary or we will find ourselves returning to the debate about God's independence. As Augustine affirmed, God as Trinity is composed of the innerrelations of that Trinity.[7] And as Eastern theologians emphasize, the love internal to the essential Trinity mitigates any subordinating of one person to another. That is, *agape* love expressed by God is first expressed in God. There is love shared between the three persons of the Trinity. Thus we can say God is love without needing to suggest that we are the only objects of that love—as if God needs us in order to be who God is, as love.

But does God's relationality stop at the borders of God's own essence? As a natural attribute of God, yes. This is what theologians mean by God's **aseity**—that God is sufficient in and of God's self, and that God comes from nothing but God; God is underived. And so God's relationality is first a statement about the Trinity. But God, who is love in God's self and between God's persons, chooses to extend that love to creation. The stories of God's interaction with humanity in Genesis clearly show that God intends to be in relationship with what God has created, especially and uniquely with human beings. Does God "need" this relationship? In light of all that has been suggested above, no. But desire is different from need. It is accurate and appropriate to say that God desires a relationship with humanity. God as love expresses love. God is able to love because of God's Trinitarian nature. But God, who chooses to create in order to extend God's love beyond God's self, desires to be lovingly related to all.

An understanding of God as holy, as transcendent, as immanent, and as relational finally brings us to the supreme affirmation that God is love. And this love is what most exactly defines God's holiness and most precisely modifies God's transcendent and immanent relationship with the world. God's holiness as love is not only the height but also the very depth of all that Wesleyan theology affirms. The love of God expands both far and wide into all that it believes. This does not contradict the suggestion that at the heart of Wesleyan theology is **soteriology**, for God's love is a love that reaches infinitely toward us in order to save. The ultimate expression of this love comes to us in the incarnation. Christ is love personified. As such, he reveals that the nature of love is an embodied servanthood willing to carry a cross.

▶ THE SERVANTHOOD OF THE SON

Any deistic tendencies (**deism**) that arise from affirming the transcendence of God are countered not only by a strong understanding of God's relational immanence and love but also by affirming that "God so loved the world that he gave his one and only Son" (John 3:16). As Martin Luther would say, this divine **condescension** in the Son is truly among the most loving (and thus saving) acts of God toward us.[8] Relevant to God's giving of the Son are the many important ramifications of this gift. The incarnation reveals God's character to us; Jesus recapitulates humanity for us; he lives a life of love as a model before us; the Son is God's means for saving us and the whole world; the Son is our hope for the resurrection; the Son takes on the role of priest for us; and in all these acts, he shows us that even divine love is best expressed as servanthood. To each of these Christological expressions of holy love, we now turn our attention.

THE SON AS THE REVELATION OF GOD

If we want to know what God is like, we look at Jesus. In the very act of sending the Son, we see God as self-giving love. But even more so, the person of the Son reveals the Father perfectly (although not exhaustively) and reveals God as holy, perfect love. Jesus Christ is the full and final revelation of God. **Natural theology** fades into the background as the light of God's revelation bursts forth in the incarnation. In the proclamation of the mystery of the Christian faith, we declare that Christ was born. The *logos* of God became flesh and dwelt among us. This "scandal of particularity," this "concrete universal," this incarnated God is the "foolishness" on which the gospel is founded. Although the church took more than 450 years to fully describe the paradoxical significance of God's incarnation (in the Chalcedon Creed), it is a simple biblical proclamation that changed and continues to change the world.

What we were unable to do for ourselves, "God did" (Rom. 8:3) by sending the Son. The church is clear. Jesus was not just like God in characteristics but fully God (in essence) and thus fully able to reveal God.

We could assemble a long list of Christlike dispositions and actions based on Christ's ministry portrayed for us in the Gospels. The very heart of Christ

OLD AND NEW TESTAMENTS

Throughout the history of the church, particularly in the history of biblical interpretation, there has been a debate about God's "consistency" between the Old and New Testaments. The ultimate expression of discontinuity is found in **Marcionism**, which was declared heretical. And yet what Marcion was attempting to do is perhaps more noble than it first appears. He was attempting to deal seriously with a God portrayed in the Old Testament as wrathful, even "homicidal" (even genocidal) toward individuals or groups. Other attempts have been made to find God's graciousness in the Old Testament. One Christian adage is to interpret the Old Testament in light of the New. The question then arises, Does Jesus Christ stand as a type of corrective for how we view God?

reveals God as holy love. But not only so, Jesus Christ also reveals to us God's intentions for humanity.

THE SON AS THE RECAPITULATION OF HUMANITY

Writing in the second century, Irenaeus of Lyon worked out a preliminary, but robust, Christology that influenced the later church (see previous discussion in chap. 3). One of the most profound ideas he offered was the idea that Jesus Christ recapitulates humanity. Irenaeus elaborated on Paul's understanding of Christ as the second Adam (see Rom. 5). That is, what was lost because of Adam's disobedient fall is restored in the obedience of Christ.

The incarnational life of Jesus Christ (and not just his death) reveals for us true humanity as it was meant to be. Jesus is both fully God and fully human. As such, he is able to show clearly who God is and who God originally created us to be—not only in God's image but also as fully human. In Jesus we see our potentiality. Sin is an aberration to true human life and creation as a whole. But we see the fully human, the perfect human, in the person of Jesus Christ. In Christ we see who we are meant to be as human beings. Through Christ we can be restored, renewed in this humanity.

Unlike other traditions, Wesleyan theology is thoroughly optimistic about such a restoration, indeed, transformation of human life. In Christ we have the hope that our potentiality to be truly human can be actualized. This transformation is at the heart of our understanding of sanctification. The Fall distorted the image of God in humanity; Christ's obedience (even to death on a cross) enables the progressive restoration or renewal of that same image. And what is the *imago Dei* in Wesleyan theology? It is the capacity to love and be loved in divine and human relationships, as well as loving the creation. Thus we may appropriately claim that the sanctified life is a life where the ability to love as God loves is enabled in us. That is, in light of the doctrine of **recapitulation**, we may claim that through grace we become more and more human, hence renewed in the image of God. (We will investigate this further in the following chapters.)

In Christ we see our call to be more like Christ; we also see the call to be more and more ourselves—who God originally created us to be. Any hope for such transforming grace comes from the sacrificial life of Christ—expressed through his death on a cross—but also vitally revealed in his continual attitude of servanthood while he lived.

THE SON AS SERVANT AND MODEL

Deep within the Christian tradition is the view that Christ is our teacher. Clement of Alexandria stands out as one who emphasized the didactic nature of Christ's ministry on earth. Not only does Jesus Christ reveal God to us, not only does he personify humanity as it was originally created, but he also shows us how to live our human lives *in God*. He taught his disciples. He taught specifically through his sermons, his parables, and his illustrations. But he also taught through example. In this sense, Jesus represents for us the actualization of God's call to holiness. Jesus Christ showed his disciples a life of full obedience to God and of the fullest expression of love to others. But this call to holiness is not intended only for Jesus. Through his lips we hear the words "be perfect [or holy], therefore, as your heavenly Father is perfect" (Matt. 5:48) directed at the church. And what is the content of this holiness? Jesus made clear that it is not the strict observance of the law. But it is not a vanquishing of the law either. Rather, the law will be fulfilled when the two greatest commandments are enacted. Love for God and love for neighbor are at the very heart of Christ's teaching and way of living.

Often Jesus countered the world's order of things. In many respects, he turned it upside down. We hear from him that the first will be last and the last will be first (Matt. 19:30); that if we want to find life, we must lose it (Matt. 10:39); that discipleship is about denying oneself and carrying crosses (Luke 9:23); that the kingdom of heaven cannot be found where we might be tempted to look (Luke 17:20-21); that the Messiah will not lead an earthly rebellion, but will suffer and die (John 18:36; Luke 17:25). But beyond his verbal teaching, we know also that he took a towel and wrapped it around his waist, took water from an ordinary basin, and washed his disciples' feet (John 13). As teacher and model he revealed that life in God is about servanthood. One might say that servanthood is the ethic of God's love.

THE SON AS SAVIOR OF THE WORLD

Christ's incarnation, recapitulating work, and teaching model of servanthood are salvific, but his cross is what most expresses God's saving love. Wesleyans are thoroughly and appropriately christological. Numerous theories of the atonement exist, and all have important soteriological features and perhaps equal viability. But Wesleyans, following tradition as a whole, appropriately focus on the cross as the greatest expression of God's self-giving, self-sacrificing, self-emptying love. There are many places in Scripture that interpret the meaning of the cross, but possibly none are more eloquent than the hymn Paul "sings" to the church in Philippi:

Your attitude should be the same as that of Christ Jesus:

Who, being in very nature God,

    did not consider equality with God something to be grasped,

but made himself nothing *[kenosis]*,

    taking the very nature of a servant,

    being made in human likeness.

And being found in appearance as a man,
    he humbled himself
and became obedient to death—
    even death on a cross! (Phil. 2:5-8)

According to biblical scholar George Lyons, the traditional interpretation of sections of this passage could lead the reader to believe that Jesus was acting "out of" God's character in his self-emptying work on the cross. "But in light of biblical theology, it seems to me that a *causal* interpretation is more appropriate." That is, "Christ's willingness to surrender his prerogatives as God, to become a human, to become a servant, to accept the cross is not *despite his prior status as God, but* **because** *of it*: '*Because* Christ was in the form of God, . . . he emptied himself.'"[9]

If Christ reveals the nature of God to us, fully and finally, then we must conclude that God's nature is holy love, as demonstrated and thus defined by Christ's sacrificial act on the cross. It is this type of kenotic love that God fully expressed in the sending of the Son to be the Savior of the world.

THE SON AS THE RESURRECTED ONE

How the cross relates to the Resurrection in matters of salvation is a complex question. Although it is appropriate to say that all grace comes from the death of Christ on the cross, this is still an incomplete account of God's saving act without reference to Christ's resurrection. Only in the light of his resurrection from the dead does his death gain the unique saving significance that could not have been achieved otherwise, no matter how holy the life Jesus lived. Paul puts it clearly and strongly: "If Christ has not been raised, our preaching is useless and so is your faith. . . . If Christ has not been raised, your faith is futile; you are still in your sins" (1 Cor. 15:14, 17). We do not have faith in the Resurrection, even as we do not place our faith in the cross. We have faith in the crucified one who was resurrected.

The meaning of the Resurrection is found in its theological significance and in its ethical ramifications. Theologically, the Resurrection is the dialectical partner of the cross of the crucified Christ and is thus crucial for an appropriate understanding of both Christology and soteriology. But it also goes beyond sheer doctrine in its significance. The Resurrection must be viewed not only as a historical event but also through the eyes of faith—or more precisely—through the eyes of a person who has faith. Only then does the rigidity of dogma and creed come to life and vitality. But we have more than faith in a historical event, or even more than hope of our coming resurrection. There is an aspect of resurrection in which we presently participate.

In a sense, not only is Jesus Christ the resurrected one, but he should also be seen as the resurrected one throughout his entire life. This keeps us from seeing him only as a holy or moral man who was willing to die. While hard to wrap our minds around, Jesus as human continually participated in resurrection power. His whole life anticipated the cross, as the cross anticipated the Resurrection. This need not lessen the reality of Christ's death or the actuality of his suffering. We place our faith in the crucified Lord. But that faith is confirmed and empowered by the Resurrection. In the same way, we now participate in resurrection life and power in Christ, even though we can only anticipate our own final resurrection. Through participation in this resurrection life and power, we live differently.

THE SON AS THE HIGH PRIEST AND MEDIATOR

Even as the one who was resurrected, who is exalted, and who ascended into heaven and is at the right hand of God Almighty, Christ remains our servant. The New Testament alludes to Christ's continuing work. John calls Jesus Christ our advocate and implies that Christ is always *for* us. The writer of Hebrews clearly depicts Jesus' role as our high priest. He is a priest who is able to sympathize with our weaknesses because of what he suffered on earth. As fully human, Jesus represents us to God. As God, Jesus mediates God's love to us. Therefore, "let us then approach the throne of grace with confidence, so that we may receive mercy and find grace to help us in our time of need" (Heb. 4:16).

Paul explicitly states in Rom. 8:34 that "Christ Jesus, who died—more than that, who was raised to life—is at the right hand of God and is also interceding for us." In the same chapter of Romans, Paul had already declared that the "Spirit himself intercedes for us with groans that words cannot express" (v. 26). But lest we imagine the second and third persons of the Trinity as trying desperately to appease the first (as if we are "sinners in the hands of an angry God"[10]), Paul interjects that indeed "God is for us" (v. 31). "He who did not spare his own Son, but gave him up for us all—how will he not also, along with him, graciously give us all things?" (v. 32). As stated earlier, God is unified in purpose, to save all that will be saved.

Christ reveals that God's love toward us is a gift—self-giving in nature and soteriological in purpose. And it is this same love that is expressed in Christ's attitude of servanthood toward his disciples; it is this love that led him to reassure his disciples in the Upper Room that he would not leave them alone. The Holy Spirit was coming.

▶ THE PRESENCE OF THE SPIRIT

Influenced by a Wesleyan paradigm, Holiness denominations emphasize the full personality of the Holy Spirit, rather than subordinating and depersonalizing the Spirit under language such as "the Spirit of Christ." Keeping this in mind, we will continue our considerations by exploring the primary soteriological activities of the Holy Spirit as they reveal to us the holy God. Once again, the theme of servanthood should be in the forefront of our thoughts, because the Holy Spirit not only serves the purposes of the Father and the Son but also expresses God's holy kenotic love toward us and thus *serves* us.

THE HOLY SPIRIT AND PREVENIENT GRACE

Foundational to a Wesleyan paradigm is the doctrine of **prevenient grace**. Indeed, God's prevenient work is synonymous with the Spirit's activity. Technically for Wesley, the way of salvation begins with God's free gift of prevenient grace, that which always "comes before," seeking to woo and draw us to God. Prevenient grace *is* the presence and work of the Holy Spirit; and this pneumatological emphasis is what keeps prevenient grace vital and personal and keeps it from merely being an abstract concept. We will consider three functions of the Holy Spirit as expressed in prevenient grace: its purpose in conferring "knowledge" about God, its "extra-Christian" role, and its awakening task.

Wesleyan theology is inductive by nature. It is experientially informed. As such, any declarative statements we might make come from life in God, not from dogmatic propositions about God to which we then attempt to conform. Truth is not defined in a "modernist" fashion, objectively attained, analyzed, and asserted. Truth is found in persons and through experiential "knowledge" of persons (and is thus dynamically relational). For example, for Wesley a person could hold to any or all creedal affirmations and still not be "right-hearted" or related to the source of truth for such affirmations. This is not to say that the creeds are irrelevant. Indeed the creeds can be seen as the collective experiences of early believers. But ultimately belief is not simply an intellectual assent to an agreed upon truth but deep, courageous trust in the God who saves. And thus, when the Spirit guides us in truth, we are guided by our experiences of grace, as we entrust ourselves to God. Another way of saying this is that our **spiritual senses** inform our theology.

Wesley mediated a path between his contemporaries—between the Cambridge Platonists, on the one hand, and the popular empiricists, on the other. He developed the idea of the spiritual senses. Similar to the Platonists who utilized a classical form of **rationalism**, Wesley held to divine initiative in the giving of divine ideas. But Wesley was anything but a pure rationalist. Shaped by his age, he strongly held to the empiricists' method of obtaining truth. A strict **empiricism**, however, usually led to the conclusion that any knowledge about God is impossible, for it cannot be perceived through the five senses. Wesley's **epistemology**, not surprisingly, reflects his tendency toward *via media* (a middle way). He conceived of a "spiritual sense" given by God through which we perceive God.

PLENARY INSPIRATION

Wesleyans believe that the Holy Spirit sufficiently inspired the original writers of the canon. Most Wesleyans believe in the plenary inspiration of Scripture, which entails a rejection of a mechanical or verbal doctrine and absolute inerrancy, and which explicitly states that the Bible is perfect in its intention to "reveal God's will concerning us in things necessary to our salvation" (see pp. 36-38). This position has implications for the way in which we interpret Scripture. Soteriology once again guides our interpretive moves.

Technically speaking, prevenient grace gives all persons this spiritual sense; the Holy Spirit draws all persons to God through this sense.

Wesleyans affirm that God wants all persons to be saved. But the meaning of salvation must be clarified. Wesleyan theology sees salvation broadly: we have been saved, we are being saved, we will be saved. That is, heaven is not the only goal. A spiritually abundant life here on earth is also important. This precludes the denigrating of human life in any way. It also guards against Christianity's temptation toward dualism or neo-Gnosticism, which implies that the goal of life is the spirit's escape from the body. Evangelism takes on new meaning in this context of affirming human life. We are not just trying to "get people to heaven." We believe that being Christian is the very best way for a person to live life here and now.

This opens up the question on what Wesleyans believe about persons from other religions. Wesleyan theology is a form of **inclusivism**. This differs from **exclusivism,** on the one side, and **pluralism** (see glossary for definitions) on the other. Wesleyans draw directly from Paul's discussion in the early chapters of Romans. Paul states that there are those who are living apart from the law of Judaism who will be judged apart from the law. They will be judged on how well they live up to the light they have been given. Paul alludes to a sense of conscience given to all humanity. So possibly, someone could reach eternal salvation without having had an opportunity to know Christ's gospel. This is a function of prevenient grace. An exclusivist, in contrast, would reject this idea. Only those who have expressly confessed Christ as Lord have any hope of heaven.

For Wesleyans, prevenient grace is a profound expression of God's infinite love for the world. This love excludes no one. Because of a strong belief in prevenient grace, Wesleyans maintain the possibility of eternal life for those who have not heard of Jesus.

In the same way, those who have not appropriated the gospel personally because of their "infirmities"[11] are also saved by God's prevenient grace. This would include infants and children still incapable of making a personal decision for Christ, as well as mentally or emotionally diminished or damaged individuals.

At the very heart of the belief in prevenient grace is the belief that God is drawing all persons into a relationship. From birth, God calls all persons to God's self. This call is constant and unrelenting. God woos us to seek and follow. God not only woos but also awakens. This aspect of prevenient grace will be covered in the next section on **regeneration,** since they are tightly connected in the *ordo salutis (via salutis)* or order (or way) of salvation.

THE HOLY SPIRIT AND REGENERATION

It is prevenient grace—the Holy Spirit—that draws us, awakening our souls to the need for God. This grace, as with all grace, can be resisted. But if it is allowed to do its work, prevenient grace and the presence of the Holy Spirit will bring a person to the place of **awakening.** This is the place where we are convicted and convinced of our own sinfulness and helplessness apart from God. But this convincing work of God does not lead us to despair, for we are also convinced of the hope of our redemption. Conviction and hope, then, are not merely human responses to the Spirit's prior work, but rather expressions of the Spirit's work in our hearts as we cooperate with the ever-available grace of God.

Personal awakening is closely connected to repentance in Wesley's scheme; and awakening, if responded to, leads to repentance, faith, and regeneration. Repentance can be equated with godly sorrow—sorrow in the sense that we are convinced of our condition; it is godly in the sense that it does not lead to despair but rather to trust in the sufficiency of God (2 Cor. 7:10). A second meaning of repentance is the actual relinquishing of sin and amending our ways toward God.[12] It is also crucial to invoke the Spirit when speaking of faith itself, for faith is a gift of God and not a human work. Synergistically enacted, Spirit-aided repentance and faith lead to regeneration.

It is the work of Jesus Christ that makes regeneration possible. The Holy Spirit is active in this regeneration. We are made new creations through the work of the Holy Spirit. Regeneration implies more than justification's forensic meaning (formally wrought by the atonement) and the familial language of adoption as sons and daughters, and coheirs with Christ. Regeneration implies not only an actual change in relation to guilt or in our relation to the family of God but also an actual change in being. We are new again.

Regeneration can be correctly linked to initial sanctification. Holiness is imparted to the regenerated, not just imputed. This work is thus effective through the Spirit's transformative activity, which begins at new birth. This is why Wesley cautioned his preachers against proclaiming sanctification in such a way that the power of the new birth is minimized. Holiness begins at regeneration. Sanctification begins at our new birth in Jesus Christ.

Further, the Spirit bears witness to our spirit about this transformation in nature and relationship. While Wesley himself adapted the doctrine of assurance through his life (finally suggesting that one could lose the witness without losing his or her salvation), in most instances assurance is the subsequent gift given by the Holy Spirit for the purpose of spiritual confidence before God or before one's own self-doubt. The Spirit enables the heartfelt acceptance of God's acceptance.[13]

THE HOLY SPIRIT AND SANCTIFICATION

God's will is that all be sanctified. We often refer to the Holy Spirit's work in sanctification. Some might argue that this designation—the Holy Spirit "sanctifies believers"—threatens an appropriate christological focus of God's sanctifying work. But this phrase can be interpreted as the *application* of christological grace through the Spirit's work. Sanctification is the work of God in Christ through the Holy Spirit.

The Holy Spirit enables the liberating work of God, which finds fulfillment in regeneration, sanctification, and holy living. The Holy Spirit sanctifies believers, initially, progressively, entirely, and finally. That is, it is more than possible to grow in our ability to love God with our whole being and to express the holy love of God to "neighbors as ourselves." Through the presence of the Holy Spirit, and as God pours out God's love into the heart, love "excludes sin."[14] This grace, which heals the *dis-ease* of sin and empowers us for sacrificial living, is again out of the heart of the holy triune God. The Holy Spirit can indeed make Christians' attitudes the same as Christ Jesus, who emptied himself (kenosis) "of all but love."[15]

The Spirit is at work continuously in God's sanctifying activity, specifically through the Spirit's indwelling and *cleansing* presence.[16] Further, the empowering work of the Holy Spirit is what enables a person toward life and godliness (2 Pet. 1:3-4), which includes "spiritual development and improvement in Christlikeness of character and personality."[17]

THE HOLY SPIRIT AS PARACLETE

As Christ and his disciples gathered in the Upper Room on the night he was betrayed, he began to speak plainly to them about the disturbing impending events. During his discourse, he described the coming of the Holy Spirit.

Among the many activities of the Spirit that Jesus mentioned, perhaps most needed and most pressing was Jesus' promise of God's continuing presence through the Holy Spirit, specifically as **Paraclete**. The root words in Greek are *para*, which means "alongside," and *kaleo*, which means "to call." The Holy Spirit, then, is the one called alongside Christians to help bear the load. It is often translated as "comforter."

The Comforter comes fully as Immanuel leaves. "God with us" in the Christ sends another to be present with his disciples, the Holy Spirit. As Christ has represented the Father, the Spirit will represent Christ. It is here that the designation "Spirit of Christ" makes most sense. While we want to maintain the Spirit as a definite person of the Trinity, the Spirit's unity with Father and Son, in character and in purpose, assures us of God's loving presence in our lives. And the presence of God through the Holy Spirit is the greatest comfort anyone would need.

Pentecost is truly a day that changed the world. While we must avoid any hint of modalism, we may still appropriately see the coming of the Holy Spirit as an unprecedented event in history. The Spirit was active in the history of the Hebrew people. But the Spirit appeared during extraordinary moments for very specific purposes. Not until Pentecost did an understanding of the indwelling presence of the Spirit, a presence that specifically brings power, arise.[18] Pentecost changed the disciples. The dramatic nature of the event led some Holiness Movement thinkers to equate Pentecost with the experience of entire sanctification.[19] This has certainly been debated—whether or not such an association is exegetically tenable. But at the very least, Pentecost must be seen as the beginning of a new age of God's work and presence in the world. It is certainly the new birth of the church. What was initiated there continues today. Indeed, we affirm not only that the Spirit is present and active within each individual but also the mystery that the Spirit is *in* the church.

THE HOLY SPIRIT AND THE CHURCH

The Holy Spirit is genuinely present and active in the church, continuously and effectively. It is the Holy Spirit that calls the church together as the body of Christ. The embodied marks of the church are spiritual marks, made true only by the presence and activity of the Spirit. It is the work of the Spirit that makes the church one, or unified. It is a mystery of grace how God can take the great diversity evident in this human institution and unite it in spirit and in purpose. The language of "body" life is an expression of the interdependence and equality of each participant, called forth and enabled by the gracious work of God.

Further, the church enjoys the fellowship of the Holy Spirit when the church expresses its essence and purpose in worship, preaching, sacramental ministry, obedience to Christ, and mutual accountability. The Holy Spirit is fully immersed in the practices and functions of church life. The worship of God is aided by the Spirit, and the Spirit's presence is assured to be amid those gathered in Christ. The whole act of preaching, from text to sermon and delivery, is done by the inspiration, guidance, and presence of the Holy Spirit. Any form of ministry in which the church invests finds fruit only as the Spirit brings it to fruition. Obedience to Christ is possible through the enabling work of the Spirit. Mutual accountability is more than a human endeavor. It is a means of grace. All means of grace are efficacious through the work of the Spirit, particularly the sacraments.[20] And when the church demonstrates the redemptive work of Christ in the world, it is done only through the power of the Holy Spirit.

The Holy Spirit, the third person of the Trinity whose essence is also holy kenotic love, truly is ever-present and efficiently active in and with the church of Christ; the Spirit truly is convincing the world of sin and regenerating those who repent and believe; and the Spirit genuinely sanctifies believers and guides them into all the truth as it is in Jesus.

SUMMARY STATEMENTS

1. It is love that most exactly defines God's holiness and modifies God's transcendent and immanent relationship with the world. God's holiness as love is the height and depth of all that Wesleyan theology affirms.

2. God's transcendence and immanence must be carefully balanced.

3. The incarnation reveals God's character; Jesus recapitulates humanity; he models a life of love; he is the means of our salvation; he is our hope for resurrection; he is our priest; and in all these acts, Jesus shows us that even divine love is best expressed as servanthood.

4. Kenosis is at the heart of God's character, as revealed to us in Jesus Christ.

5. The Holy Spirit is truly ever-present and efficiently active in the church; the Spirit convinces the world of sin, is active in regeneration and sanctification, and guides us into all truth as it is in Jesus.

6. God's desire for relationship with us includes the intimacy of indwelling through the Holy Spirit.

QUESTIONS FOR REFLECTION:

1. How does the Wesleyan-Holiness tradition's emphasis on God's love differ from other traditions? Does it lead us to different theological conclusions?

2. What does it mean to say God is holy? What does God's holiness entail?

3. Why is it important to say that Jesus Christ is fully human?

4. What role does the Holy Spirit play in bringing about our salvation?

FURTHER READING

Dunning, H. Ray. *Grace, Faith, and Holiness.* Kansas City: Beacon Hill Press of Kansas City, 1988.

Migliore, Daniel. *Faith Seeking Understanding.* Grand Rapids: Eerdmans Publishing, 1991.

Oden, Thomas. *Systematic Theology, Vol. 1: The Living God.* New York: Harper Collins, 1987.

Powell, Samuel. *Discovering Our Christian Faith.* Kansas City: Beacon Hill Press of Kansas City, 2008.

Stone, Brian P., and Thomas J. Oord. *Thy Nature and Thy Name Is Love: Wesleyan and Process Theologies in Dialogue.* Nashville: Kingswood Books, 1991.

SIX

CREATED AND FALLEN HUMANITY[1]

LEARNER OBJECTIVES

Your study of this chapter will help you to:

1. Recognize the most important aspects of humanity from a theological perspective

2. Define sin

3. Understand the doctrine of original sin from a Wesleyan perspective

4. Identify prevenient grace's effects on original sin

KEY WORDS

Theological anthropology

Natural image

Moral image

Deprivity

Depravity

Natural state

Legal state

Evangelical state

Affections

Tempers

Dispositions

Hamartiology

Idolatry

Forensic salvation

Pelagianism

Critical to any theology of Holiness is a reflection on what it means to be human as a creation of God and in relation to God. Just as critical is a proper understanding of sin and specifically how sin has affected humanity since the Fall. We can only speak of some sort of original or perfect humanity hypothetically—as the humanity experienced by Adam and Eve. We can speak more concretely about a perfect humanity seen in the person of Jesus Christ. But whenever our present human condition is considered, it should be understood as fallen. But what does this fallen state mean? What, if anything, remains of the original design? What can be rescued? And perhaps most importantly, what can be renewed? Such questions and countless others show that salvation and sanctification cannot be divorced from **theological anthropology** (i.e., the study of humanity in relation to God) and a doctrine of sin.

▶ HUMANITY

It is beyond our scope to offer a comprehensive discussion of humanity, especially when it comes to the doctrine of theological anthropology. To talk about humanity only from a theological perspective is not without its challenges. Humans cannot be separated from biology, sociology, psychology, and other areas of social and scientific study. Reflections on what it means to be human raise key issues of anthropology, theological or not. But there is much that can be said theologically and biblically about humanity that can stand independently from social and scientific research. We will attempt to state concisely what we can say about humanity as created *by God*.

There are two significant theological themes that arise out of the creation account given in Genesis.

First of all, according to both Jewish and Christian interpretation, it is extremely important to affirm that all that God created was good, especially human beings. This contrasts with other creation myths coming from other religions and philosophies.

Early in Christianity a movement known as Gnosticism began to threaten the church from within. One of the issues that finally resulted in Gnosticism being deemed heretical was its belief about how the world was created and its estimation of that creation. Although there were differences among the Gnostics themselves, the basic creation story had two deviant components. First, Gnosticism held that God was not the Creator; instead, a fallen demigod created the world. What follows logically is that what this demigod created is necessarily evil. Thus all of creation, including humanity, is inherently corrupt from the moment of its creation. Anything material is the enemy of the spirit or soul. This mimics one of Plato's ideas, that the "body is the prison house of the soul." According to Gnosticism, the goal of spirituality is to finally free the eternal element in humanity from its material, finite, and destructive body. It was against this backdrop of Gnosticism that the orthodox church strongly affirmed the incarnation and the "resurrection of the body" in its theology and creeds. It is vital for the Christian to affirm that God created us as good in all of our humanity, body and spirit alike. Some comments on the "parts" of the human are appropriate here.

There is a difference between the Hebrew and the Greek perspective on humanity. For the Hebrews in the Old Testament, the human being is seen holistically. That is, there is not a radical distinction between the body and the soul. It is not that the body has a soul or that the soul has a body but rather that the soul and body are so intertwined to be practically indistinguishable in real life. From Greek philosophy, however, we see the tendency to speak of distinct parts—body, soul, and spirit. Indeed, Paul himself employs such language. But the differentiation between the three has been taken to the extremes of trifurcating (or bifurcating in certain instances) each aspect as separate entities. Are we required to take Paul's model as the New Testament—and thus superior—anthropology? Or as some scholars say, is the Hebrew model the more pervasive biblical model, with Greek philosophy being superimposed over it?

Here we might well consider information gained outside a strictly theological framework. Recent research on the brain has raised the question in a different way. What is the difference between brain and mind? Is there something within us that transcends pure neurophysiology? Are we simply reduced to synapses and neurotransmitters because we can indeed be explained by such physical impulses? Is this all we are? This has led one confessionally *Wesleyan* neuropsychologist to advocate what he calls a "nonreductive physicalism."[2] That is, we are our bodies. This is true. But this does not mean we are only our bodies. There is something within us that transcends and thus counters the notion of humanity being reduced to pure biology. We might even call the Hebrew model a holistic anthropology of nonreductive physicalism! Mildred Wynkoop advocates that in the New Testament a unity of personality is everywhere assumed and dismisses what she calls "speculative trichotomy" as unhelpful Hellenism.[3]

The second crucial affirmation we receive from the Genesis account is that humans, both male and female, are created in the image of God. Various traditions have defined the image in various ways. An interpretation of the image in the early church period (which was ultimately deemed heretical) proposed that the image was an actual physical resemblance to God.[4] There do seem to be many anthropomorphized images in Scripture. But ultimately, orthodoxy claimed that these should be interpreted metaphorically.

Some Western interpreters of the image have declared that it resides in our human capacity to reason. This is the view of many classical theologians, including the great Catholic theologian Thomas Aquinas (d. 1275). Another interpretation is that humanity resembles God in its relationship to the rest of creation. Just as God stands in a hierarchical position over humanity, so too does humanity stand in a hierarchical position over the earth. Still another explanation of the image is that of human freedom. God created us free and self-determining. These differing conclusions about what the image of God actually is present a diversity of opinion that may seem uncomfortable. But Scripture does not offer its own explanation. Is there a specific interpretation avowed by the Wesleyan-Holiness tradition?

Foundational to Wesley's own understanding of humankind is that human beings are relational. We are created for relationship. We are created for love and created to love. Wesley was aware of the different interpretations of the *imago Dei*, but according to Mildred Bangs Wynkoop and others, he held strongly to the image as the capacity to love.[5] H. Ray Dunning has expanded on the definitive relationships of humanity as they were meant to be: we are created to love God, love others, and have an appropriate love for self and for the world.[6] Perhaps the scriptural passage that is most profoundly definitive of Wesleyan theology is Luke 10:27: "'Love the Lord your God with all your heart and with all your soul and with all your strength and with all your mind'; and, 'Love your neighbor as yourself'" (see Lev. 19:18; Deut. 6:5).

There are moments in Wesley's writing when he distinguishes between the natural and moral image in humanity. These parallel the natural and moral attributes of God. The **natural image** of God in humanity refers to those characteristics or faculties definitive of being human. The **moral image** in humanity refers to the character of holiness and love that God originally intended and now intends for humanity.

Key to understanding Wesley's view of humanity and salvation is the fact that after the Fall, the image remains. It is distorted but not obliterated. And thus salvation for Wesley (broadly defined to include sanctification) is the process of the restoration and renewal of the image of God in us. This idea that the image remains after the Fall has led some Wesley interpreters to speak of a doctrine of total **deprivity** instead of total **depravity** as Wesley's preferred way of referring to the Fall's effects.[7] Through the Fall, we are *deprived* of our primary relationship with God, and our other relationships are consequently distorted; but the capacity for love, and the hope of renewal remains. Prevenient grace enables this capacity to be actualized, and opens our senses to God. Since prevenient grace is given to all, humanity "without God" is a "logical abstraction."[8] The very strong Calvinist doctrine of total depravity, on the other hand, is not as optimistic.[9] Through the Fall, we are totally depraved, without God in the world, and corrupted beyond repair in this life. Calvin's idea of common grace aids in the effects of the Fall but not to the extent of Wesley's prevenient grace. These two very different understandings of the Fall and the effects on the *imago Dei* would produce very different doctrines of salvation in Wesley and Calvin.

Wesley also spoke of certain human states, the natural, legal, and evangelical states.[10] The **natural state** is only a hypothetical state before the Fall. It was the state in which God created Adam and Eve. Only Jesus, as the Christ, was born into a natural state, free from original sin (discussed below). By the **legal state** Wesley means our position before God prior to an experience of new birth. We live under the law, and if we allow the law to do its work, it will bring us to the place of recognizing our need for salvation. Prevenient grace assists us in being awakened to this need. The **evangelical state**, then, is subsequent to new birth in Christ; we are not under the law but now under grace. This new birth begins the process of the renewal of the image of God in us.

Another important aspect of Wesley's anthropology is his focus on what he calls religious **affections** and **tempers**. Although it is correct to interpret Wesley as advocating a more Hebraic and holistic view of the human being, for the purpose of explaining Christian growth in holiness, he does distinguish between certain facets of psychology within each person. Along with the human will and personal liberty, he identifies affections as those inner **dispositions** that integrate the rational and emotional dimensions of human life. When these dispositions are habituated, they become enduring affections that actually bring freedom for human action. For example, a person habituates acts of kindness to the extent that it can be said he or she is a kind person because kindness has become a part of who he or she is. In the next opportunity for kindness, then, that person is free to be kind, in the sense that choosing an unkind act is very unlikely. The person is inclined in a positive direction. His or her affections will be consistent with these habituated inclinations.

Wesley drew here on Aristotle (as communicated by Thomas Aquinas). The difference between Aristotle and Aquinas, and thus Wesley, is that a Christian view of Aristotle's virtue ethics (a model that focuses on character development by practicing certain virtues, i.e., honesty, goodness, courage) incorporates grace. All that has been said here can be said for developing the character of holiness. As God's sanctifying grace aids us, holiness can become what we are inclined to do, because our dispositions have become affections, which in turn produce, in this case, holy character. This will be further examined in chapter 11.

▶ SIN

What is sin? Perhaps surprisingly, this is not easily answered. Different traditions define sin differently. There are also different types of sin. Often sin is divided into three distinct categories: systemic evil, personal sin, and original sin. Systemic evil is best defined as a series of events that in the end hurt or oppress others. The products that we buy might be made by child or slave labor. While we certainly do not intend to participate in harm, the system in which we live is, in a sense, fallen. Perhaps we should boycott companies that buy from companies (and so on) that oppress. The problem is, it is almost impossible to buy anything that does not ultimately oppress someone. Just as there is no perfect economic system, there is no perfect political system either. Just being citizens in a certain country implicates us in injustices at times. The concept of systemic evil believes that there are societal sins. But we do not usually think of such sins as sins for which we are culpable.

Personal sins are the sins to which we usually attach guilt. Personal sins are usually seen as acts of disobedience against some law. But the laws, as found in Scripture, are not as arbitrary as they might appear. Even the hundreds of Jewish laws that we no longer follow all had very specific purposes. Most if not all were given by God for the purpose of protecting us. The Ten Commandments are not just ten laws God made up so that we would know God is boss and that when we break them, we are sinners. If we delve deeper, we will see that the Ten Commandments are all very purposeful. Keeping them is a means of loving God and others. Jesus clearly says that fulfilling the two commandments of love fulfill all of the law. Breaking a law, then, could be seen as anti-love. Indeed, one definition of sin could be any time we go against the law of love. But as different traditions attempt to define sin more precisely, different theologies of sin emerge.

As just observed, the Wesleyan and Calvinist positions on the effects of the Fall on the image of God make the respective theologies very different from each other. In turn, Wesleyans and Calvinists argue over the issue of sin. Their arguments are based on two very different understandings of what sin is. According to John Calvin, sin is falling short of the glory of God, or missing the mark. Thus *any* non-Godlike qualities or imperfections in humanity are considered sinful. Understandably then, a Calvinist could claim that we sin in thought, word, and deed daily. Most would simply say we are sinful because we are not God.

Wesleyans, on the other hand, have stressed the volitional element of sin. Sin, for Wesley, is a willful transgression of a known law of God. That is, sin is always a conscious act of rebellion against what God desires for us. This might also imply that not knowing the law is a legitimate excuse for our responsibility before the law. We are innocent if we are ignorant. However, Paul addresses this in Rom. 2. Paul introduces the concept of conscience and proposes that because all human beings have been given an inward sense of right and wrong, they have no excuse even if they do not have the Hebraic law. All stand responsible before God. And in a sense, this affirmation is vital to understanding a Holiness perspective on sanctification, since a Holiness perspective claims that this type of rebellion—whether it be rebellion against the law or against the conscience—is not *necessary*. There can be victory over sin (using this definition). However, Wesley did not offer this definition of a willful transgression as his only definition of sin.

SHEEP AND GOATS

"When the Son of Man comes in his glory, and all the angels with him, he will sit on his throne in heavenly glory. All the nations will be gathered before him, and he will separate the people one from another as a shepherd separates the sheep from the goats. He will put the sheep on his right and the goats on his left.

"Then the King will say to those on his right, 'Come, you who are blessed by my Father; take your inheritance, the kingdom prepared for you since the creation of the world. For I was hungry and you gave me something to eat, I was thirsty and you gave me something to drink, I was a stranger and you invited me in, I needed clothes and you clothed me, I was sick and you looked after me, I was in prison and you came to visit me.'

"Then the righteous will answer him, 'Lord, when did we see you hungry and feed you, or thirsty and give you something to drink? When did we see you a stranger and invite you in, or needing clothes and clothe you? When did we see you sick or in prison and go to visit you?'

"The King will reply, 'I tell you the truth, whatever you did for one of the least of these brothers of mine, you did for me.'

"Then he will say to those on his left, 'Depart from me, you who are cursed, into the eternal fire prepared for the devil and his angels. For I was hungry and you gave me nothing to eat, I was thirsty and you gave me nothing to drink, I was a stranger and you did not invite me in, I needed clothes and you did not clothe me, I was sick and in prison and you did not look after me.'

"They also will answer, 'Lord, when did we see you hungry or thirsty or a stranger or needing clothes or sick or in prison, and did not help you?'

"He will reply, 'I tell you the truth, whatever you did not do for one of the least of these, you did not do for me.'

> "Then they will go away to eternal punishment, but the righteous to eternal life." (Matt. 25:31-46)

For example, Wesley was quick to point out that there are sins of omission as well as commission. A sin of commission is when we commit an act forbidden to us. We break a law. But James is clear in his letter, that sin is also a correct label whenever we know the good we ought to do, and do not do it (omit doing it) (James 4:17). In a real sense, particularly in light of Matt. 25, we know that we should take care of the poor, visit the sick and imprisoned, and generate other acts of mercy. But most of us omit these on a daily basis. And thus, according to this definition, we sin. Does this cancel out our hope of a sanctified life? Not if we are clear about what we mean by sanctification. An unhealthy understanding of holiness—what we might call perfectionism—has wrongly held that confession is inappropriate for the sanctified Christian. This is certainly not true for Wesley.

The closer we draw to God, the deeper our need to live a confessional life, confessing our complete dependency on God at the very deepest level of our being. That is, the issue of breaking an obvious law or even omitting a good deed may become less and less the issue as we grow in grace. But then the Holy Spirit, in molding and shaping us, can go deeper into our heart; our response should be godly sorrow whenever we grieve the heart of God.

Wesley tired of the debate over whether sanctification led to sinlessness.[11] His deeper concern was living a life filled with the love of God and growing in our discernment of how we can best express this love to each other and a needy world. Sometimes our concern over sin is, as 1 John says, out of a fear of punishment (4:18). Wesley, following this verse in 1 John, wanted to stress that perfect love casts out fear. When we grow beyond such fear, our motivation changes. We do not seek holiness for our own sakes so that we can declare ourselves holy and sinless and place our security there. Holiness is normative for and definitive of loving God with our whole being and loving our neighbor as ourselves. Holiness is always for the sake of the other. When we do this, we are being who God created us to be. As Wesley stated, love will exclude sin. This applies not only to the personal sins we commit but also to the doctrine known as original sin.

The recent shift from a modernist to a postmodernist theoretical framework has all sorts of connections to real life. This presents the theologian with the task of correlation—communicating religious truth to a new context. We must perform this task to speak the truth without losing its dynamic character. All language about sin is metaphorical. But the use of metaphor—perhaps new metaphors for a new generation—does not discount that sin is real. Experience does not permit us to ignore it. Postmodern theology—despite the changes it brings—need not take sin lightly.

ORIGINAL SIN

In a serious attempt to make "adequate provision for the human element in life"[12] and to avoid speaking of the most experiential of all doctrines only in the abstract, we will turn to the Bible and then Wesley, with his understanding of "inbred" sin or original sin. Through Wesley's emphasis on experiential life and faith and on the nature of sin, we can find language that also communicates and resonates with the postmodern "needs" for relationality, the search for meaning, and the quest for an experientially based spirituality. But before we begin any historical or systematic review of sin, we must begin with Scripture as foundational to all we know about fallen humanity.

We must first acknowledge that Scripture does not satisfy all our curiosity about original sin. It does not explain the cause of sin. Interestingly, the familiar theological terms describing sin are not biblical expressions. Such terms as "original sin," "inherited sin," "carnality," "depravity," and "inbred sin" are not found directly in the Bible. All of these are generalizations or abstract words, and abstract words are seldom if ever found in the Bible. Not even "the Fall" is a biblical term.

Aside from a couple of references to Adam in Paul's writings, the Bible is silent about the transmission of the Fall. There is nothing to suggest that people inevitably sin because of that historical experience. In 2 Cor. 11:3, Paul expresses a fear that the believers might be drawn away from the simplicity of single-heartedness that is in Christ, and he references Eve. But in this passage nothing is said about the influence of her sin on the human race. Rather, the assumption is obvious that we need *not* sin. Paul's reference to Adam's sin in Rom. 5 and 1 Cor. 15 is not a theory of sin but an occasion to magnify the victory of Christ over the effects of sin. Paul says that death came into the world by one man's sin, but more importantly, life came through Christ.

The closest Paul comes to relating human sin to Adam is in Rom. 5:19, "For as by one man's disobedience many were made sinners, so by the obedience of one shall many be made righteous" (KJV). But in this passage, the counterbalancing reference to Christ makes a detailed theory of original sin (which will only come over three hundred years later) impossible to hold as biblical. What Paul does do is to show that all persons do sin. In this he is intensely realistic. Even in Rom. 3:23, Paul says that in sinning, humans have fallen short. He does not say, having fallen short, humans sin. Scripture is clear that for sin to be sin a real measure of personal responsibility is presupposed. This does not discredit all theologizing about the connection between Adam and us. But what the Bible is most interested in conveying is that each individual is, in an essential way, the real cause for the sins he or she commits. However the universal human impulse to reject God is explained (and the Bible does not explain it), the fact remains that each person is personally liable for that rejection.

Again, strangely enough, the Bible says nothing to us about how sin is transmitted. Certainly the influence of sin is far-reaching, but the method is not explained. In fact, we are not given speculative answers to any of the intellectual problems we might have with a theory of sin. Only the damaging effects of our own personally chosen sins are discussed, and that seems to be all that is needed. Whatever we may say, then, beyond the express teaching of Scripture must be identified as human tradition—as sacred as such is. Unfortunately, tradition (as a source of truth in the Wesleyan quadrilateral) has no uniform expression of transmission theory, nor is it consistent about other aspects of the theology of sin. Humility around the issues of **hamartiology** will help guard against a distortion of the scriptural theme of salvation.

The Bible is also silent about an interpretation of the "essence" of Adam's sin and how this essence or root of sin manifests itself in us. Augustine was the first to make his interpretation "doctrinal" for the church.

Augustine and Pelagius were contemporaries in the late third to early fourth centuries. Pelagius held that not only did human beings not inherit guilt from Adam but they also did not inherit any corruption. And thus each person has the same choice that Adam and Eve had in the garden. He affirmed that we are born with *natural freedom*. Augustine, on the other hand, pushed hard for a strong doctrine of original sin, total depravity, inherited guilt, and thus a very strong doctrine of grace (ultimately leading to his theory of predestination). The conclusion of the debate was that Pelagius was deemed heretical by orthodox Christianity. But Augustine did not attain a complete victory. While the Council of Orange (529) confirmed his doctrine of original sin, the council did not affirm Augustine's doctrine of double predestination.

Wesley rejected Pelagius (although he showed some sympathy for him).[13] And yet he does not parallel Augustine's doctrine either. For Augustine, the essence or root of original sin was best defined as pride. While most interpreters of Wesley have followed the traditional version of original sin as pride, a different reading of Wesley has been offered.[14] While Wesley used the word "pride" often, it was never used as the overarching paradigm of original sin, according to this analysis. Wesley's most direct sermon on the topic, "Original Sin" (1854), shows this lack of dominance of the word "pride." Here, **idolatry** is unmistakably classified as the primary definition of original sin, with "pride," "self-will," and "love of the world" listed under it.[15] Wesley said, "all pride is idolatry"[16] as is "love of the world." That is, there are two forms of original sin: inordinate love of self (pride) and inordinate love of others, here described as "love of the world." Wesley further explains this phrase: "What is more natural to us than to seek happiness in the creature, instead of the Creator?"[17] Wesley also wrote a sermon titled "Spiritual Idolatry," which he penned near the end of his life. In this sermon, idolatry is clearly his primary way of talking about the essence of original sin.

FROM WESLEY'S SERMON "SPIRITUAL IDOLATRY"

Undoubtedly it is the will of God that we should all love one another. It is his will that we should love our relations and our Christian brethren with a peculiar love; and those in particular, whom he has made particularly profitable to our souls. These we are commanded to "love fervently;" yet still "with a pure heart." But is not this "impossible with man?" to retain the strength and tenderness of affection, and yet, without any stain to the soul, with unspotted purity? I do not mean only unspotted by lust. I know this is possible. I know a person may have an unutterable affection for another without any desire of this kind. But is it without idolatry? Is it not loving the creature more than the Creator? Is it not putting a man or woman in the place of God? giving them your heart? Let this be carefully considered, even by those whom God has joined together; by husbands and wives, parents and children. It cannot be denied, that these ought to love one another tenderly: they are commanded so to do. But they are neither commanded nor permitted to love one another idolatrously. Yet how common is this! How frequently is a husband, a wife, a child, put in the place of God. How many that are accounted good Christians fix their affections on each other, so as to leave no place for God! They seek their happiness in the creature, not in the Creator. One may truly say to the other, I view thee, lord and end of my desires. That is, "I desire nothing more but thee! Thou art the thing that I long for! All my desire is unto thee, and unto the remembrance of thy name." Now, if this is not flat idolatry, I cannot tell what is.[18]

Original sin as idolatry was also a key issue in the development of Holiness theology in America. Phoebe Palmer developed doctrines of sin and holiness that had significant implications for the Holiness Movement of the 19th century. For our purposes here, Palmer followed Wesley in his discussion of spiritual idolatry and yet spoke from a woman's perspective. Rather than reciting the traditional litany of those things that interfered with the spiritual life—selfishness, lack of faith, betrayals of the flesh—Palmer, with striking frankness, admitted that the primary obstacle to her spiritual growth had been "a large house involving proportionate cares." Her own experience of entire sanctification entailed her relinquishing of the "idols" of husband and children. It is crucial to note that while Palmer's experience of sanctification involved a kind of liberation from earthly affections and domestic obligations, such liberation did not develop out of a discontent with family ties. The first commandment, then, enables the second: Loving God with *all* one's being (unrivaled) enables love for others. Thus Wesley's own preferred definition of holiness, love, is made possible not only through an overturning of the traditional idolatry of *self* but also through an overturning of an idolatry of others.

Why is this important for us? Much Holiness preaching has emphasized the sin of pride as the root of a person's sin. It would make sense, then, that such a person would be admonished to think less of himself or herself. But low self-esteem is a rampant problem even in Christian communities. Perhaps preaching that presupposes pride even worsens the situation. While one form of sin is an inappropriate egocentricity, the opposite is also inappropriate. The overarching metaphor of idolatry can address both forms of sin. Idolatry of others is intricately connected to low self-esteem. Persons who are encouraged to find themselves in Christ alone can find a healthy and balanced view of how they see themselves.

Whatever sin is practically, it can only be recognized fully for what it really is by seeing it against its opposite—namely holiness. Any definition of sin attempted prior to the proclamation of the provision of grace misunderstands the scriptural priority of holiness. But also true is the observation that a clear understanding of sin is necessary in order to understand the breadth and depth of human redemption.

Underlying Wesley's understanding of sin we find one of his strongest metaphors for salvation: salvation as healing. This necessarily led Wesley to an understanding of sin as "disease." Salvation is "therapeutic." We find deep resonances between Wesley and the Eastern fathers on this point. This way of conceptualizing sin as disease correlates with Wesley's optimism about (sanctifying) grace, envisioned as a deep (progressive) cure. The metaphor offers great benefit. And yet, this more Eastern perspective can be criticized for being light on sin, so to speak, even to the point of interpreting the Fall as a rather understandable consequence of Adam and Eve's immaturity. Similarly, overly emphasizing the restoration of the image of God in humanity can lead to under-stressing the distortion. Since some postmodern theology can be criticized also for being light on sin, the discussion here is still highly relevant.

We must not overlook the insights on sin of "Western" thinkers (such as Augustine, Luther, Calvin, Søren Kierkegaard, Karl Barth, and Reinhold Niebuhr). Although admittedly the West has perhaps too closely connected

forensic salvation with such views of sin (salvation as forgiveness tends to be emphasized more than inner transformation), grappling with the depth of human sinfulness offered by such views would serve us well. In doing this, Wesleyanism's optimism about an actual transformation of nature can only gain in strength. One such Western view is offered here in order to apply a Wesleyan analysis to it.

According to some interpreters (Søren Kierkegaard and those who have adapted his ideas), humanity is born into an existentially anxious reality, one that arises out of creation, even before the Fall. This reality is prototypically found in Eden, but it is in every individual. While Adam is unlike us in that he was the first (the first always being different from his progeny), this difference has a quantitative character rather than qualitative.

> [A person] belongs to nature, but not to nature alone, for he is poised between nature and some other realm, and he is subject to imperatives which neither realm can explain of itself. He is material, yet spiritual; he is determined, yet free; he is derived like the rest of nature from what came before him, and yet, unlike anything else in nature, he alone is responsible for creating himself.[19]

This causes anxiety. But the human is really "anxious about nothing." That is, the anxiety is not a result of some immediate situation, but about being able to fulfill one's potential in a limiting world. In this scheme, anxiety is defined as a disposition that results from this broad situation.

When a person tries to deal with this anxiety apart from God, anxiety results in sin. The person is aware of the freedom of potentiality; he or she is able. But the person is also aware of his or her destiny and fixedness. And awareness of ability *and* limitation causes anxiety. It is the place where the finite touches the infinite, where the temporal touches eternity, where necessity touches freedom. This state of ambiguity gives rise to the temptation to fall to one side of these opposing tensions or the other. If the person falls toward the side of finitude and fixedness, he or she will sin by failing to choose to actualize his or her full potential. If the person falls toward the side of infinitude and freedom, he or she will sin by trying to actualize himself or herself apart from God.

Out of the predicament, Adam and Eve first sinned and estranged themselves from God. But all humanity after them has also fallen by sinning. That is, the original sin of Adam and Eve can be found in every person. It is this original sin that affects us. But it is always our choice to make sin actual by choosing sin.

What we gain from this Western model is a sense of the depth of sin and the intricacies of how it affects our entire being, particularly in our ability to relate. Sin, as an intentional act of the will, brings about estrangement in all of our relationships, even in our relationship with ourselves. For example, even in the offer of mercy, despair discounts the self to itself as too far gone. This deep estrangement fragments the self from itself; it severs our intended relationships with others, but most importantly, it keeps us from God, even if we glimpse God's reconciling call. It is our sin that keeps us from believing that anything can conquer sin.

Long seen as foundational to Wesley's entire theology, the concept of prevenient grace has largely been assumed rather than appropriately emphasized. Its significance can be seen when overlaid on the West's pervasive concept of depravity. Wesley's understanding of prevenient grace helps us envision the potentiality for something different. Fundamental to any doctrine of original sin is the belief that humanity is unable to rectify the situation in which it finds itself. God is the only means by which a fractured self is given any potentiality for change. But by what means are we saved? How are we rescued out of absolute depravity?

Augustine and the Reformed tradition's emphasis on such depravity necessarily led them to the doctrine of predestination. Only God can save. Salvation must come through election, because a person is utterly incapable of doing anything—even enacting faith—to participate in or aid in God's salvation. It is only in his arguments with Pelagius that Augustine was finally led to this extreme position.

But while Wesleyans have never embraced any notion of predestination, at times they have gone the other way to a practical **Pelagianism**. Void of an understanding of prevenient grace, we find no way of explaining how the steps of faith are possible except as an act of the human will. It is we who must move ourselves toward reconciliation and faith. While we can find a Christ who suffered for us, we really do not find the mechanism by which we have faith to begin with, nor to explain how faith overcomes estrangement. If it is the presence of God that effectively vanquishes the power of sin, is it we who must find our way into that presence, or is there a movement toward us, even in our estrangement, that does not override our will? It is here that the power of the concept (and certainly the reality) of prevenient grace solves the problem of deciding between predestination and our hidden Pelagianism.

As suggested earlier, the best way to understand prevenient grace is pneumatologically. That is, this grace is not a substance any more than sin is a substance. We are better served to envision prevenient grace as the activity, even presence of the Holy Spirit. Unlike Reformed Western thinkers, Wesleyan theology believes that the sinful predicament into which we are born is not the only factor in our human situation. If we are pulled by an original sin that has accumulated throughout history, there is a counter balancing pull toward life and away from self-destruction. The presence of God, through the gracious activity of the Holy Spirit *enables* the will, not to save itself, but to move toward God who is moving toward us. This is different from Pelagius's conceptualization of the activity of the will. We have *free will* because we have been *graced* by the very presence of God. We have graced free will.

If we hold to a fractured self that is incapable of relating to others without great distortion, we can also hold to the Wesleyan concept of prevenient grace, which allows for a renewal in the *imago Dei*—for the possibility of genuine love for others, self, earth, and ultimately for God. But does this renewal only begin at the point of salvation? This is a difficult question, but Wesley had a rather surprising answer. First a quote from Kierkegaard is in order:

> [Our] basic condition makes ultimate self-improvement impossible. This is the force of the Greek phrase from Aristotle meaning "in terms of possibility," e.g. as the oak-tree is in the acorn, the chicken in the egg. . . . The self we desire to become *is not even potentially present,* and all efforts to develop it from the existing basis are futile, until the self is in "equilibrium." Then, and only then, does the self exist "in terms of possibility," present in itself an ideal basis for satisfactory development. . . . "Becoming" can now take place.[20]

Thus Kierkegaard and other Reformed thinkers believe that it is only after being in a saving (even predestined) relation to God that potentiality is even offered. There is no acorn at all before salvation. True humanity is not even potentially present in those who are in sin and who have actualized sin through choice. But rather than waiting for salvation for the potentiality to be restored, Wesleyan theology opens up the possibility of true human potential in those who have yet to find equilibrium and salvation. Prevenient grace, then, gives us our potential. Our very nature changes in its potentiality immediately from the moment of birth (life) because not only are we affected by original sin, but also such sin is counteracted by prevenient grace. Our potentiality is restored. Our potentiality begins to be actualized through saving faith.

To review, Pelagius held that not only did human beings not inherit guilt from Adam, but they also did not inherit any corruption. And thus each person has the same choice that Adam and Eve had in the garden. He affirmed that we are born with *natural freedom.* Augustine, on the other hand, pushed hard for a very strong doctrine of total depravity and inherited guilt and a strong doctrine of salvation as a gift of God in Christ through the Holy Spirit. The *via media* comes through Wesley's doctrine of prevenient grace. The grace that God gives to every human being born into the world gives that person *graced freedom.* Although a bent toward sin is inherited, grace is given so that sinning (actual sin) is maintained as a choice for which we can rightly be held accountable. Wesley's rejection of inherited guilt maintains God as truly just. It also keeps Wesley from being pressed into a position of affirming predestination. Augustine's doctrine of sin was so strong that only a predetermined, irresistible act of God could save us. Wesley avoided this logical conclusion through his affirmation of universal prevenient grace.

But Wesley also held that our potentiality is not simply that of the first humans. Wesley clearly states in his sermon "What Is Man?" that our potential is now even greater since Christ came to earth. We can become more than Adam or Eve ever could. While prevenient grace gives us "the acorn," our potential begins the process of actualization most acutely at the moment of our second birth. It is here that the process we have called healing truly begins. And to this the next chapter turns, with these words of Wynkoop providing an apt transition:

> Salvation has to do with the whole disrupted relationship. Being a disruption in the sight of God and in the hearts of [people], the central concern is to correct that relationship. Nothing less can be dignified by the term salvation. The alienation must end. Only God can do this. This we know, in Christ the estrangement ended. We must meet God with a single-hearted love. Any duplicity, or mixed motives, makes cleansing fellowship impossible. Christ's sacrifice of Himself on the cross not only made God's approval of us possible but makes a pure heart also possible. Sin is *in this life* possible of correction. Alienation is ended between God and [us]. The antithesis of loving God is not a *state*, nor is holiness a *state*, but an atmosphere daily, hourly, perhaps even momentarily, maintained in the presence and by the power of the Holy Spirit. This calls for the deepest measure of participation. But the participation is not a strained, unnatural, fear-inspired thing, but the whole person committed to God with abandon. This does not put an impossible burden on the human psyche, nor does it require any particular measure of maturity, ability, or knowledge. But it does ask for growth and nurture and a deepening spiritual sensitivity that never ends.[21]

SUMMARY STATEMENTS

1. It is important to hold to the goodness of God's creation, especially human beings.

2. The *imago Dei* is defined as the capacity for love and relationships according to Wesleyan-Holiness theology.

3. "The Fall" did not obliterate the *imago Dei* in humanity.

4. The definition of sin we use is intricately connected to how we understand salvation.

5. Original sin is defined as idolatry for Wesley.

6. Sin can be overcome in this life through the sanctifying grace of God.

QUESTIONS FOR REFLECTION

1. How might we explain good acts coming from those who do not yet believe?

2. What information gained from the sciences might inform our theological anthropology?

3. How is Wesley's position a middle position between Pelagius and Augustine?

4. Does original sin make us guilty before God in Wesleyan-Holiness theology? Why is this important?

FURTHER READING

Kierkegaard, Søren. *Sickness unto Death*. Princeton, NJ: Princeton University Press, 1941.

Leclerc, Diane. *Singleness of Heart: Gender, Sin and Holiness in Historical Perspective*. Lanham, MD: Scarecrow Press, 2001.

Maddox, Randy. "Holiness of Heart and Life: Lessons from North American Methodism" in *Asbury Theological Journal*, 50-51 (Fall 1995—Spring 1996), 151-72.

Wesley, John. Sermon, "Spiritual Idolatry." In *The Bicentennial Edition of the Works of John Wesley*. Vol. 3. Nashville: Abingdon Press, 1983—.

SEVEN

FULL SALVATION[1]

LEARNER OBJECTIVES

Your study of this chapter will help you to:

1. Identify key aspects of Christ's atonement
2. Understand the various concomitants of conversion
3. Consider many false ideas about entire sanctification
4. Plot the various forms of sanctification in the *ordo (via) salutis*

KEY WORDS

New birth

Justification

Regeneration

Adoption

Assurance

Witness of the Spirit

Redemption

Reconciliation

Initial sanctification

Imputed righteousness

Imparted righteousness

Entire sanctification

Initial sanctification

Progressive sanctification

Final sanctification

Ontological

Teleological

When "evangelicals"[2] invoke the metaphor of salvation, they are talking about being in a personal relationship with God through Jesus Christ. Usually a moment in time is identified when a person places his or her faith in Christ as the beginning of that relationship. A particular phrase has been borrowed from Jesus' discussion with Nicodemus in John 3: "You must be *born again*" (v. 7, emphasis added). There are other metaphors that one might use as well. But the primary metaphor we invoke theologically is that of salvation. It is from the Greek word for salvation, *sōtēria*, that we speak of the doctrine of *soteriology*.

We now may legitimately ask, what are we saved from? Certainly evangelicals and Holiness people alike believe that persons are saved from hell and saved from the guilt of our sins. But Holiness theology explicitly takes it a step further and affirms that persons can also be saved from the *power* of sin in this life. God "breaks the power of cancelled sin."[3] Here is where Wesleyan-Holiness theology moves beyond more Reformed forms of evangelicalism. For Wesley, salvation implies the entire Christian life, from **new birth** to death and eternal life.

Strictly speaking, we are not saved by following the law but only through what Christ accomplished on the cross. But there is more to salvation than receiving the gift of this act that was accomplished on our behalf. Full salvation involves such a genuine transformation (through God's grace) that, as Paul says, "the righteous requirements of the law might be fully met in us" (Rom. 8:4). In human life, then, **justification** (freedom from sin's guilt) and sanctification (freedom from sin's power) are strongly intertwined. It is only for the sake of discussion and clarity that we separate them here using salvation to speak of forgiveness gained from the atonement, and sanctification to speak of the inner transformation that comes from more fully participating in the life of God (through Christ's atonement and in step with the Spirit).

▶ SALVATION

It is correct to see the denominations in the Holiness Movement as Protestant—as ones who affirm Martin Luther's primary emphasis: We are saved by grace through *faith alone* (salvation by grace through faith *in Christ* alone). As Ephesians states, we are saved by grace through faith in Christ, and not by works, so that we cannot boast, or place confidence in our own achievements (see 2:8-9). This grace comes because Christ suffered on the cross.

Although it is beyond our scope to delve into the various theories about Christ's suffering—the different theories of the atonement that have developed since the early church—we will discuss key aspects of Jesus' death that we affirm to be essential to salvation and to a full understanding of what he did on our behalf.

First of all, we affirm that Jesus' death was *voluntary*—that he willingly died. He was not forced against his own will when people tried him, beat him, and killed him. He acted willingly. He also, perhaps more importantly, was not forced by God. As he wrestled and struggled in the Garden of Gethsemane, he could have refused to drink the cup of sorrow, pain, and anguish. God would not have forced him to go through with it. He had free will that God would not have overridden. But we know that Jesus submitted to God's will and spoke from his heart, "Not my will, but yours be done" (Luke 22:42). Jesus' death was voluntary. If it were not, it would not be effectual in our salvation.

Second, we affirm that Jesus' death was *purposeful*. That is, random events did not bring him to the cross, as if other random events would have led him to a different conclusion. Jesus Christ was born so that Jesus Christ would die. God intended for this to happen. Again, he would not have forced Jesus to go through with it, but we affirm that this was God's plan for the redemption of the world. "What the law was powerless to do . . . God did by sending his own Son" (Rom. 8:3). While the Jews, even Jesus' disciples, anticipated a different kind of Messiah (a political one), Jesus as the Messiah did come as prophesied. There is a genuine anticipation based on God's revealed purposes. And at the end of his life, when Jesus directly told his followers that he would die, their eyes finally saw (although not fully until after Pentecost) that this had been where his life had been headed all along.

Third, we also affirm that Jesus' death was *actual*. There were early Christian heresies that denied that Jesus died a fully human death. The Gnostics held the belief called Docetism (from the Greek word *dokein,* "to seem"). Following their myth of the creation and their belief that all things material are inherently evil, they believed that God could not have allowed Jesus to have a real human body. He only appeared (seemed) to have a human body, and he only appeared to die. Orthodox belief, however, has deemed an actual death crucial for Christ's death to be salvific. He bled real blood, suffered real wounds, experienced unspeakable pain, and died a true human death. If anything, his death was even more agonizing because he bore the weight of the sin of the whole world.

And fourth, we affirm that Jesus was *innocent*, and we deem that innocence as utterly essential to his ability to save us. The Old Testament speaks of the perfect sacrifice for sin as an unblemished lamb. Jesus is spoken of by John the Baptist as the Lamb of God. By implication, Jesus' sacrifice was perfect. Tradition has held that it was because Jesus never sinned that he was able to take on the sin of the world. If he himself was a sinner, he would have only been able to die for his own sin, for as Paul states, "All have sinned and fall short of the glory of God" (Rom. 3:23), and he implies that all sin deserves punishment. But we know that the New Testament clearly affirms that Jesus was in every way like us, except he did not sin. This innocence was needed for Jesus' death to save all of humanity, and not just himself.

What Jesus accomplished on the cross, the atonement, is what brings salvation, but it is only part of the whole span of the study of soteriology. One aspect gives attention to how Jesus' life and death atone for sin. Perhaps more importantly from a Wesleyan-Holiness perspective is the question of how his atonement affects us.

The first declaration we must make from our theology is that salvation is synergistic—the atonement is the source of salvation, but we must accept it. What this means is that we must participate in the grace available through Christ's work by cooperating in our salvation. This implies our activity in accepting the grace and even the faith God gives. This faith should not be seen as a work we accomplish, but as an intentional reception of the work Christ has done for us. When this faith is activated and grace is given, we are saved, both in our being saved from the guilt of sin and in our beginning the process whereby God breaks the power of sin. We call this sanctification. There are many metaphors for this initial saving event. Each of the following is a designation for a different aspect of the same moment of salvation.

JUSTIFICATION

To be justified by God implies that our sins are forgiven. The guilt of our sins is taken away. God no longer condemns us for our transgressions. This is at the heart of the theme of the Reformation. Again, Luther was separated from his Catholic counterparts by his declaration that we are saved by faith alone. We call this his doctrine of justification. It is sometimes called a forensic view of salvation. We are guilty. We deserve punishment. But Jesus Christ takes the punishment for our sins upon himself. Thus God as judge is able to say that we will no longer be held accountable for our past sins. The guilt is atoned for. Wesley also certainly believed in justification, just as Luther also believed in sanctification. However, Wesley particularly emphasized that salvation goes beyond justification to address the underlying problem or disease. Wesley's therapeutic model takes him further.

REGENERATION

Wesley's favorite term for salvation is "new birth." This concept means that we are regenerated, born again, and are new creations in Christ. Wesley never wanted his doctrine of sanctification to minimize the power and significance of new birth. Truly, "the old has gone, the new has come" (2 Cor. 5:17). Wesley went further to say that new birth is an event that plays a major role in breaking the power of sin in our lives and that we should expect significant change in a person from the moment he or she enacts faith. This is **regeneration**.

ADOPTION

Wesley strongly emphasized the importance of being a child of God and coheir with Christ. This aspect of salvation also implies that we are born into a family, a community of brothers and sisters in Christ. This prevents us from imagining salvation as a purely privatistic concept. We are adopted by God and adopted into the family of God. The verses that Wesley used on this point are Rom. 8:14-15.

Here, **adoption** was not the only point mentioned. Paul also emphasized what Wesley called the doctrine of **assurance**, also known as the **witness of the Spirit**. Not only are we adopted as God's children, but also the Spirit witnesses to our spirit that this is true. The Spirit gives a deep inner assurance that we have been accepted by God as God's own beloved children and that Jesus is closer than a brother.

REDEMPTION

Redemption implies liberation from sin. The Exodus acts as the primary biblical metaphor for redemption. It is certainly a significant metaphor in the Wesleyan-Holiness understanding of full salvation, or sanctification. Just as the people were in bondage to the Egyptians, we are in bondage to sin. Sin is our master, according to Rom. 7. But as Moses led his people out of Egypt, Jesus leads his brothers and sisters out of bondage and into the "promised land" where we are no longer held captive to anything, other than our willing obedience to God. We are no longer slaves to sin. Redemption also entails receiving a new purpose, namely, to love God with all our being, and our neighbor as ourselves. Just as a "redemption center" today recycles an old product into a new one, our lives are redeemed from sin and for love.

RECONCILIATION

We are reconciled to God. This is a theme we find in John Wesley's writings and also in Charles Wesley's hymns. This is the sense that the alienation and estrangement from God implicit in sin is overcome when we come into a new relationship with God. It is **reconciliation** that overturns what some Wesley scholars have called total deprivity, or relational privation. Total deprivity, as mentioned earlier (see p. 158), is a modified understanding of Calvin's concept of total depravity, which states that the Fall of Adam places all of his offspring (humanity as a whole) in complete and utter darkness. Deprivity, on the other hand, affirms that the image of God remains (although distorted) and that we are sinful primarily because we have been deprived of the initially intended intimacy with God. The moment of salvation overcomes the estrangement and initiates us back into a relationship with God that then grows in intimacy as we grow spiritually.

INITIAL SANCTIFICATION

Wesley never used the term **initial sanctification**. But it signifies his belief that the process of being made righteous begins at the moment of salvation. At the moment of salvation, the righteousness of Christ is *imputed* (**imputed righteousness**) to us. This means that God accounts us as holy because of Christ's holiness. But again, we part ways from the Reformed tradition because Wesleyans so strongly believe that at the moment of salvation, God begins to *impart* righteousness (**imparted righteousness**) to us. That is, God not only accounts us as righteous or holy but also makes us actually holy in a progressive way as we begin our journey as Christians. It is not that Luther and others do not affirm imparted righteousness. But Wesley made it central to his theology of Holiness. The moment of our salvation is also the moment of our initial sanctification. Initial sanctification quickly progresses into a growing sanctification. To sanctification as a whole, we now turn our attention.

▶ SANCTIFICATION

Let us begin our discussion of what sanctification is with a clear understanding about what sanctification is not. Wesley himself often used the rhetorical form of defining some aspect of theology by first showing what it is *not*. We will attempt to clarify our understanding of sanctification by countering several *myths*.

1. Holiness and entire sanctification are synonymous

This is a mistake that is easy to make. To be theologically precise, holiness and sanctification begin when a person is born again and continue throughout his or her life. Holiness should never be limited to one instantaneous event. Also, holiness is a way of being. **Entire sanctification** is one of the mechanisms that brings this way of being to fuller fruition or actualization.

The diagram below is a representative of the whole sanctifying work of God in our lives.

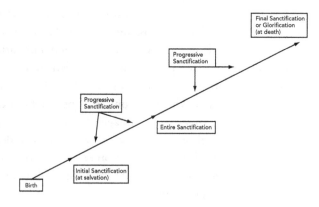

This represents what is sometimes called the *ordo salutis*, or the order of salvation. (Some Wesley scholars, like Randy Maddox, prefer *via salutis*, or way of salvation, to depict a more fluid, ongoing dynamic.) At birth, each person is given prevenient grace, which will draw him or her toward a relationship with God. If the person cooperates with this grace, a conversion or saving moment results, through an awakening, conviction, repentance, and faith. At this same moment, the process of sanctification begins with what is called **initial sanctification**. God bestows righteousness and begins to impart that righteousness in such a way that the person is then being made holy (a present-tense, active verb). This is not a completed event, however. **Progressive sanctification** follows. This can also be called gradual sanctification, growth in grace, or even spiritual formation. As growth occurs, the person will be drawn to a place where an even deeper commitment is possible. This is the moment of entire sanctification. *After* this deeper work of grace takes place, progressive sanctification again follows. Growth continues, through sustained entire devotion, until the person dies and then experiences **final sanctification**, also known as glorification. "We shall be like him, for we shall see him as he is" (1 John 3:2).

2. Entire sanctification is the destination of the Christian life

There are three dangerous implications that arise from this false assumption. First of all, it implies that the experience of entire sanctification is the end of Christian growth. It is just as important to emphasize growth in grace *after* the experience of entire sanctification as it is prior to the experience. Second, it implies that we have arrived at the pinnacle of the Christian experience and that God's grace has done all it can do, which is also false. God designed that we would continue to be renewed in the image of God throughout our lives. Entire sanctification is a significant point but certainly not the highest experience. Third, we must never imply that we are seeking after an *experience*. Entire sanctification is only possible when we are seeking first after God and the life lived in God. Entire sanctification has to do with our relationship with God; it is unfortunate if we disconnect the experience from its relational aspects.

3. Entire sanctification takes away our ability to sin

As we examined in the last chapter, sin is a complex issue when related to a Wesleyan-Holiness understanding of holiness. But what we can say for certain is that nothing will ever take away our *ability* to sin. Our free will is always in play. God does not take away from us our own choices, and thus we can always choose to sin. Grace provides us with a way out, but ultimately it is our choice to respond to the Holy Spirit or reject God's aid. The assumption that our ability to sin is taken away after entire sanctification is clearly an error.

It happened to be one that Wesley himself faced directly (the "perfectionist controversy").[4] He was quick to oppose and counteract it, strongly.

4. We do not receive the Holy Spirit fully until we are entirely sanctified

This idea is contrary to scriptural teaching and yet is a myth that has been perpetuated in folk theology. Paul says in Rom. 8 that if we are in Christ, we have received the Holy Spirit. It is the moment of our new birth when the Holy Spirit comes to abide in us. But even more precisely, the Holy Spirit is very active in our lives even *before* we ever know Christ, in the Spirit's ministry of prevenient grace. We believe that the Spirit is at work in the life of every individual from birth, drawing all persons to a relationship with God. We believe that the Holy Spirit awakens persons to their need for salvation, convicts them of sin, and applies the atonement of Christ to them when they respond in faith. The grace of God, appropriated by such faith, is what brings salvation. The Spirit *indwells* the believer from this moment on.

Another misunderstanding on this point is that we get a portion of the Spirit at salvation and all of the Spirit at entire sanctification, as if God were stingy with the Holy Spirit. It is our growing capacity to experience the fullness of God that may explain this sense that we get more of the Spirit later. But again, it is not God that withholds the Spirit. Our ability to experience the Spirit is what grows and expands.

5. Those not entirely sanctified are sinners and second-class citizens

As just stated, the relationship of sin and salvation is a complex one. Overemphasizing entire sanctification to the point of deemphasizing the new birth experience is dangerous. Christian life up to the point of entire sanctification has at times been portrayed as a life of horrific bondage to sin, with little or no victory. This is contrary to Wesley's thinking, as we will see in subsequent chapters. We should never view those who have been entirely sanctified as better than those who have not; nor should we view those on the road toward entire sanctification as lesser Christians. If we are in Christ, we are thoroughly Christian.

A corollary of this wrong thinking is the belief that the best candidates for entire sanctification are backsliders! There is certainly no prerequisite of falling away from God in order to make a deeper commitment. The language of some who express the experience of entire sanctification—namely, "I have *recommitted* my life to Christ"—could falsely imply that some sort of failure or straying is *necessary* for the experience to happen. This is completely false. The ideal is that we grow in Christ between the first and second works of grace without any regression.

6. Only those who are entirely sanctified go to heaven

This myth cropped up from a misinterpretation of Heb. 12:14, which says, "Without holiness no one will see the Lord." This misconception grows out of the error of collapsing holiness into the experience of entire sanctification. As we will see, holiness has a much broader meaning. God's sanctifying work is imparted to us, from the moment of our new birth until our glorification in heaven, with entire sanctification being a significant step in the spiritual journey. It is a perversion of the gospel itself to imply that only those who have reached this step are candidates for eternal life. An even more subtle implication can be made here as a part of this myth. It could suggest that it is our own righteousness that earns a way into heaven. This leads to the next issue.

7. Legalistic self-righteousness is what holiness looks like

If holiness is reduced to a list of dos and don'ts, legalism is quick to follow. This was the problem with the Pharisees Jesus confronted. They looked only at the externals and forgot the significance of the heart and inner life. They also forgot that all righteousness comes from God. Paul is clear in his letter to the Philippians that he was perfect when it came to obeying the law. But that was not enough. He needed Christ to clean him from the inside out. One of the dangers of emphasizing the need for personal holiness is that we can forget its purpose and make it an end in itself. This leads us to the next myth.

8. Sinlessness is the goal of the sanctified life

The interpretation of Wesley is correct that emphatically states that if we conceptualize holiness as the absence of something, namely sin, we not only have given holiness a weak and misleading definition but also are in danger of losing the very heart of the Christian life. Holiness is about the *presence* of something: love. And love is completely relational. We might be able to conceive a life that is sinless, if we define sin as a rebellious act against the law of God. But this life would not be truly holy unless it exhibited genuine love.

Jesus told a parable about an evil spirit that leaves a person. It goes out through arid places and seeks rest, but it does not find it. It decides, "'I will return to the house I left.' When it arrives, it finds the house swept clean and put in order. Then it goes and takes seven other spirits more wicked than itself, and they go in and live there. And the final condition of that man is worse than the first" (Luke 11:24-26). If we only speak of holiness as a clean house, with nothing else to fill the void, we are in danger of becoming even more sinful than when we started, Jesus implied. It is crucial to holiness identity to say that sinlessness is not the complete goal of holiness and sanctification. The void must be filled with love. "Love for God and neighbor" *is* Wesley's definition of holiness.

9. The entirely sanctified do not face temptation

Again, even though there is an immediate scriptural counteraction for this, it is still a myth that causes persons great confusion. The Scripture tells us that Jesus was tempted in the desert. It also explicitly tells us that he was tempted in every way, just like us, except that he did not yield to temptation (Heb. 4:15). And so, we believe that even though Jesus was without sin from birth, and holy in every way, he himself faced temptation. And yet, people often struggle under the belief that as they grow in their faith, temptation will lessen. If people who have experienced entire sanctification have this result as an expectation of the experience, and then find themselves tempted, great suffering in the form of spiritual self-doubt can occur for needless reasons.

10. It is impossible to live up to the expectations of the sanctified life

Generic evangelicalism has taught recent generations that they are sinners, saved by grace. And this *is* an important message. But what we mean when we sometimes employ the language of "full salvation" is that there is more. We are sinners saved by grace, but it is God's design to transform us from within to become something more. The Wesleyan message is that the Christian life is not doomed to a cycle of perpetual sin and failure, where the power of sin seems greater than the power of grace! But rather that God designed, before the very foundation of the world, that we be like Christ in heart and life. God is faithful in calling us to holy lives; if God has called us, then "he will do it" in us (1 Thess. 5:24).

We have now reviewed certain myths about entire sanctification—what entire sanctification is *not*. Our attention now turns to the positive affirmations that we can uphold.

1. Entire sanctification is subsequent to regeneration

This then implies there is a second experience in the Christian journey that takes a person beyond what is accomplished at the time he or she was saved. While progressive sanctification is also subsequent to regeneration, entire sanctification most often happens at a point of decision.

2. Entire sanctification breaks the power of sin

The Wesleyan-Holiness tradition believes that the power of sin can be effectively dealt with (broken, cleansed) so that we might live victoriously in this life.

3. Entire sanctification is characterized by entire devotion to God

Consecrating everything (ourselves, our possessions, our family and friends) to God and committing our whole being to God's service is the first requisite of the entirely sanctified life.

4. Entire sanctification results in obedience and love

When the power of sin is cleansed by grace, we are filled with a new power through grace to be obedient to God's deepest desires for us. Our intentions are purified, and our capacity to love grows into a true ability to love.

5. Entire sanctification has an element of both taking away and giving to

Our inner disposition to sin is "taken away," but immediately the abiding presence of the Spirit dwells within us in deeper and more pervasive ways than ever before. Wesley spoke of this when he said, "love [God's love] excludes sin" in the heart.[5]

6. Entire sanctification is through faith (by grace) alone

John Wesley took Martin Luther's doctrine of sola fide and applied it to the second work of grace.[6] Just as we can do nothing to deserve salvation, we can do nothing to deserve sanctification. We must always cooperate with the grace of God, but we cannot earn it.

7. Entire sanctification is (usually) followed by the witness of the Spirit

As mentioned earlier, one of Wesley's most important doctrines is the witness of the Spirit, also known as the doctrine of assurance. The Spirit testifies with our spirit that we are the children of God. We have applied this also to the experience of entire sanctification. God will assure us that we have allowed God to do the deeper work and that sanctifying grace has been given. (Of note, Wesley was aware later in his life that because of nonspiritual factors [such as perhaps mental illness, in today's terms] a person may conceivably be unable to experience this inner assurance.)

8. Several metaphorical phrases can be used to describe entire sanctification

This implies that there is no one linguistic statement that is better than another. Certain periods of history have preferred certain phrases over others, but none is normatively dominant. All language is metaphorical in a sense. New metaphors should arise for and from new generations.

9. Entire sanctification requires subsequent growth, which must be intentionally nurtured

Entire sanctification is far from the end. We do not arrive and wait it out after the experience! We are enabled by the experience of entire sanctification to grow without some previous encumbrances. There is a major difference between a pure heart and Christian maturity. To have the heart's intentions purified gives us new potential, but the maturing, growing process is still what realizes, more and more, this potential.

10. This growth is growth in Christlike character

We must always see the goal of the Christian journey to become more and more like Christ. This is definitive and normative of the sanctified life, with Christ's love at the forefront of our understanding of the character of God.

▶ THE STRUCTURE OF AN EXPERIENCE

The question still remains: How does entire sanctification happen? It is here that we see some differences between Wesley and the 19th-century paradigm. According to Wesley, entire sanctification could occur in this life. Many testimonies from his Methodist people confirmed this in Wesley's mind and heart. But his advice for those seeking after the experience was to "wait for it in the means God has ordained." This waiting did not imply a passivity (attending to the means of grace is a very active lifestyle). But it did reflect Wesley's deep reverence for God's timing to do the work; this timing is usually unknown to those who are waiting.

In the 19th-century model, however, persons were taught to seek after the experience, almost aggressively—to pursue it now and expect it now. A formula developed known as the altar covenant. It consisted of three distinct steps. First, the person seeking entire sanctification must consecrate all to God by placing it on the altar of Christ. Second, he or she must have faith that God is capable of sanctifying him or her wholly and that God wants to do it now. Persons who have exercised this faith can be absolutely sure that God has sanctified them. The third and final thing to do is to testify to the experience. Some have criticized this formula severely, believing that it leads to a type of "claim it," mind-over-matter, rationalistic, even austere version of "faith alone."[7] While this charge may have some credence in the abstract, persons who followed this pattern often displayed deep emotion, which is then also criticized. It is hard to see how the critics of this paradigm can charge 19th-century seekers with sober rationalism and exaggerated emotionalism at the same time. What is true is that the altar covenant made the experience of entire sanctification accessible to all persons.

Phoebe Palmer, for example (the first to articulate the altar covenant paradigm [see p. 114]), had struggled for years to find the experience, because the Methodist teaching on the subject in the first part of the century was too sophisticated and obtuse for average laity. She desired to help simple folk find a shorter way than she had, as she negotiated her way through a frustrated and thwarted longing for the experience. Her formula did help thousands and thousands of people find the second blessing. American optimism and revivalism gave this shorter way a context of rich soil in which to bear fruit.

Although this new revivalism of the 19th century—which preached that salvation *and* entire sanctification were available now "for the taking"—allowed many to find the experience, the danger exists of fixing and solidifying that model of the way of holiness as *the* truth. Whenever a spiritual experience (which always transcends any language used to explain it) is made into a formula, there is the danger of it becoming rigid. The assumption could thus arise that if a person's experience differs even in the minutest ways, his or her experience is illegitimate. We must be careful not to propagate the notion that anything outside of our defined parameters is suspect, especially since people experience entire sanctification in many different ways:

- For some it is as quiet as a whisper; for others as loud as thunder.
- For some it simply requires the next step of obedience; for others it is a wrenching of the soul.
- For some it can come early in the Christian life; for others after many years of seeking.
- For some it is a response to holiness preaching; for others it can be an experience to which they are drawn by God, having never heard it explained.

The experience of entire sanctification is as unique as each individual. Comparing and contrasting one experience with another is unhelpful, sometimes even damaging. Demanding that a person's testimony mimic others is only to set up a standard that allows us to judge and criticize what does not fit the mold.

We need to *balance* the interpretation of entire sanctification given by Wesley with that of his American successors. This balance can often guard against any excesses. And yet one area that truly deserves our attention remains.

The doctrine of entire sanctification clearly needs a renewed emphasis as we move into the 21st century. We need to use language and symbol in such a way that persons in this new millennium can find that significant deeper work of God for themselves. Because many perceive the doctrine as confusing or unrealistic, new ways of expressing it are needed. And yet, in an attempt to address these legitimate issues, some in the Wesleyan-Holiness tradition have suggested as a helpful option the de-emphasis of the second crisis aspect of the experience.

Many are sympathetic to these concerns. Defining the word "crisis" and what it actually implies is important. But abandoning the concept of secondness would call into question an important emphasis of the Wesleyan-Holiness tradition. While we must find ways to keep our expression of entire sanctification dynamic, relevant, and realistic, and to allow for differences from person to person, entire and progressive sanctification must be understood as distinct realities. We can address part of the problem that has led some to suggest the de-emphasis of a second crisis. We can do this by emphasizing even more the transformation possible to us through spiritual formation. Reemphasizing Wesley's understanding of the means of grace is absolutely crucial to a balanced and healthy proclamation of God's sanctifying work in the lives of God's people. We will discuss this topic extensively in chapter 11.

▶ THE EFFECTS OF ENTIRE SANCTIFICATION

What does entire sanctification do for us? Let's address this issue by invoking some theological words. Entire sanctification has **ontological, teleological,** and relational effects in our lives.

ONTOLOGICAL EFFECTS

When theologians talk about ontology, they are referring to the study of being. While this can take on a rather abstract meaning in theological explorations, it also has a very practical and relevant meaning, one that is relevant to our understanding of holiness. Ontology raises such questions as, What does it mean to be? What does it mean to be, in relation to God? In relation to others? In relation to ourselves? And what of our nature? What does it mean to be human? We have addressed some of these questions in previous chapters. Here it is important to note that we can conceive of sanctification in terms of how it affects our being or nature. The plain question is, Does sanctification change our very nature? If so, how?

Although differences exist between Wesley and the 19th-century Holiness Movement on this issue, Wesleyan-Holiness theology generally affirms that God does indeed transform our nature through sanctification—or more precisely, God renews our original nature. The popular adage that we sin because sin is "only human" or "I sin because I am human" is simply wrong theologically. And it has unfortunate practical implications. God's original design for humanity was inherently good. Only after the Fall did humans become sinful and come under the sway of this original sin in every succeeding generation. So, technically, sin is an aberration of the human condition—a great malformation. It is not "only human" to sin.

Sin takes us away from our humanity, not closer to it. To be renewed through sanctification (both in its entire and progressive form) is to be restored in nature to what God originally intended. Perhaps a helpful metaphor would be that of cancer. In our original state, we are healthy, cancer free. But as cancer invades a part of the body, the body becomes diseased. The body is still a body—its essence does not change—but it is an unhealthy body. Only as the disease is removed from the person does the body of that person return to its original state of health. By implication then, to become holy is to become truly human. To be truly human, through God's inner transformation and restoration of our nature, is to become all we were created to be: holy and wholly ourselves.

TELEOLOGICAL EFFECTS

If our ontology is changed (restored) by sanctification, then our telos or destiny changes as well. Some translations of the Bible use the word "perfect" when translating the Greek word "telos." What this literally means is complete, or full, in the sense of a culmination—maturity. It is sometimes translated as "end" and means the maturity of time, circumstances, or character. It can also mean that which has reached completion consistent with an intended end. It carries with it a sense of destiny—*not* in some predetermined way—but in the sense that those who allow themselves to be influenced by the sanctifying grace of God are in line with their intended destiny. We were created to live in communion with God, and that eternally. Although sin has entered the world, God will bring all things to completion so that we will live in communion with God forever. Thus our relationship with God now is not only a restoration of Eden but also a foretaste of the kingdom of God.

RELATIONAL EFFECTS

"Relationality" is not a creation of the postmodern era or church. It existed before the foundations of the world. God, in triune nature, and in self-expression through the creation, is essentially relational. And we, created in God's image, are also essentially relational. Theologically speaking (in a Wesleyan mode, specifically), this means that a human cannot be imagined without reference to relationships; to be human necessarily means being in relation—to God, others, self, and the world. To be holy means to be in proper and loving relationship with each of these. This is God's design and destiny for humanity. If sin is a distortion of these relationships through different forms of nonlove or existential estrangement, then holiness implies a restoration of not only our nature and our telos but also our very capacity for relationships as well. Love was never an abstraction for Wesley, and holiness is impossible without active participatory love. It is redundant to label a Wesleyan theologian as a relational theologian. Similarly, holiness and love, although distinct in definition, are synonymous in practical life.

By examining holiness from the three perspectives we have just discussed, some ongoing issues in Holiness theology are introduced. We will touch on some of these issues here:

Why is it significant to make the Holiness doctrine Trinitarian? The theological diversity in the church, so evident as we move further into the 21st century, has prompted many theologians to call for a return to the Trinity as the basis for all other theological rendering. And so to be appropriately in accord with the tradition of the Christian church of the last 1,700 years, it is important that Holiness theology also ground itself in a Trinitarian model. Why is this important?

It has been too easy in Holiness history to fall into the danger of bifurcating—or more precisely, trifurcating—the work of the first, second, and third persons of the Trinity. All too often people have said something to the effect that Jesus Christ saves and the Holy Spirit sanctifies or that when we are saved we receive Christ and when we are entirely sanctified we receive the Holy Spirit. This is one of the practical problems arising when "baptism with the Holy Spirit" language is used as a metaphor for entire sanctification. Such a metaphor can be useful but not if it sends the message that the unsanctified believer (which is actually a misnomer) does not have the Holy Spirit in his or her life.

This misuse of the metaphor also leaves the impression that sanctification is separate from the atonement of Christ. The more precise understanding is that both salvation and sanctification are possible through God's gift of God's only begotten Son, through the Son's obedience to death on a cross, and through the Holy Spirit applying what the Son did to our lives as we appropriate God's free gifts of forgiveness and cleansing. This is not to leave out the drawing (prevenient) grace enabling our response and the resulting assuring grace of the Holy Spirit. The whole work of God in the heart of a human is a work of the Trinitarian God.

Does a relational paradigm imply "positional" holiness? In the last quarter of the 20th century several theologians advocated a new paradigm for understanding the doctrine of Holiness. They attempted to reformulate the doctrine, believing that the mid-century paradigm had become sterile and irrelevant in light of massive cultural change. Proponents of this new paradigm believed that a return to Wesley was the very means of making holiness contemporary. They found Wesley himself to be, as stated earlier, a relational theologian. A rediscovery of Wesley, for these interpreters, meant a rediscovery of the relational dynamic of Holiness theology.

The call for rediscovery continues, as we move into the 21st century. There is a need to retradition ourselves to retain our Wesleyan-Holiness identity in an age when evangelicalism is increasingly synonymous with fundamentalism. When theologians began to express this new (yet old) relational paradigm in the 1970s and 1980s, they were met with great resistance. And the charge leveled against them was the danger of positional holiness.

Positional holiness is often used to describe a Calvinist or Keswickian understanding of sanctification. As stated earlier, for a Calvinist, we are only made righteous through the *imputation* of Christ's righteousness. Because of our position before God through the atonement of Christ, God *perceives* us as righteous, although we do not possess any righteousness ourselves. Keswickians take this understanding of justification and apply it to sanctification as well. There is no inner cleansing, other than the power of the Spirit to suppress our sinful nature. Wesleyan-Holiness thought, on the other hand, wants to stress that God imparts righteousness to us; that is, God makes us actually righteous through an inward work of grace, beginning at the moment of regeneration and particularly significant at the time of entire sanctification.

"Positional holiness" is a correct label for the Calvinistic or suppressionistic understandings of how God brings about holiness or righteousness to the believer. But the charge of positional holiness leveled against more relational theologians in the Wesleyan-Holiness tradition is unfounded. To emphasize the relational aspect of holiness, expressed through love, does not neglect the transformative work of God in our inner being. It certainly does not deny the ontological and teleological changes that come through the process and crisis of sanctification.

So far in this part of our study we have covered the theological foundations for a clear understanding of holiness. Holiness theology must reflect on the character of God before it begins to articulate any concept of the holiness of humanity. We are to be "perfect, therefore, as [our] heavenly Father is perfect" (Matt. 5:48). This makes knowing the perfection of God paramount in any knowledge of the holiness to which God calls us. We have also investigated the doctrines of theological anthropology and sin. A theological perspective on what it means to be created in the image of God as fully human is crucial for understanding holiness as a renewal of that image, and to guard against any notion that holiness requires us to be more than human. Holiness must also be defined only when a thorough examination of its opposite, sin, is considered. And the link between salvation and sanctification, with an *ordo* or *via salutis* fully fleshed out, will safeguard against many misconceptions about holiness, both theologically and in practical living.

Our attention now turns to Part 4 of this book and the *living out* of these biblical, historical, and theological foundations. Holiness will be connected to the following themes: holiness and purity, perfection, power, character, and love. Certainly each of these themes have biblical, historical, and theological underpinnings. This shift, however, comes in the emphasis on living holiness. If holiness is not lived, then certainly holiness is dead.

▶ EXCURSUS: "WHAT IF I'VE ALWAYS BEEN A CHRISTIAN?"

This chapter was written as a basic review of the topics of salvation and sanctification. The *ordo salutis* used is a prototypical evangelical one (sometimes also referred to as Pietistic). And yet this model represents only half of our theological heritage. It comes from the revivalistic and pioneering side of our roots, one that expanded into the American West and preached for sinners to repent and be baptized. While Wesley was also evangelical in his preaching, his Anglican heritage included the practice of baptizing infants, which led to the subsequent confirmation of a person's faith. Wesley was not ignorant of believer's baptism, but it was rarer than it is for us today because most everyone in England had already been baptized as babies.

Wesley himself never claimed an evangelical conversion experience as we know it today. While others want to consider his experience at Aldersgate in 1738 as his evangelical conversion, Wesley rarely refers to this experience later in life. He cites his experiences in 1725 as more influential (this is the year he read in preparation for ordination as a deacon). Probably most precisely stated according to what he experienced at Aldersgate is the interpretation that says he finally felt the witness of the Spirit of his already experienced salvation. How is this distinction helpful for us today?

The Holiness tradition is old enough to have four and even five generations of adherents. That is, thousands of people have been born into the tradition rather than being saved into it. They may not baptize their babies (although some Holiness denominations certainly allow for it), but they raise them in the tradition's theology and doctrines. Unfortunately, they often use language that fails to recognize this reality. They try to get their children saved as if they are adult sinners. But if we hold to a strong doctrine of prevenient grace as we should, such efforts make no theological sense.

We believe that prevenient grace covers the hearts of children until they reach an age of accountability (which is probably, in light of psychology and neurobiology, around the age of 12). If, then, they accept Jesus Christ personally before this age, they have never technically been sinners! Wesley believed that most Anglicans had sinned away the grace of their infant baptisms. But his Methodist revival and its goal of Anglican renewal was directed at adults. When it came to children, Wesley advocated strongly for Christian education, not childhood conversion experiences.

Does this mean that we should stop evangelizing our children? Yes and no. Yes, if we view them as out of God's grace. No, if what we mean by evangelizing is giving children an opportunity to appropriate and experience the love of God for themselves.

This proper understanding of theology should aid those who feel their testimonies are lacking somehow because they have always known themselves to be Christian. But if we think about it, what better testimony could there be to the grace of God? One does not need a horrible life in sin to be able to praise God for God's glorious grace! While Holiness theology does not want to de-emphasize its Pietistic roots and the doctrine of sola fide, it must leave room for those who experience what we might call the more Anglican model in its roots, even in Holiness denominations.

SUMMARY STATEMENTS

1. "Salvation" is a broad term for Wesley, encompassing the whole Christian life, which includes sanctification.

2. The atonement of Jesus Christ was voluntary, purposeful, actual, and innocent.

3. The salvation moment has several meanings: justification, regeneration, adoption, reconciliation, redemption, and initial sanctification.

4. Sanctification begins at conversion and ends at death. It is a misnomer to use the word "sanctification" when really meaning "entire" sanctification.

5. Entire sanctification has ontological, teleological, and relational effects on the person.

6. Sanctification is the renewal of the image of God; it also makes us more and more human.

QUESTIONS FOR REFLECTION

1. Why is it important to be Trinitarian in our theology of conversion and entire sanctification?

2. Why is it important to say that sanctifying grace is "humanizing" grace?

3. Does the "altar covenant" still communicate today? Why or why not?

4. Can you think of new metaphors for entire sanctification that better fit the 21st century?

5. Does your conversion experience match the Pietistic or Anglican model?

FURTHER READING

Grider, J. Kenneth. *Entire Sanctification*. Kansas City: Beacon Hill Press of Kansas City, 1980.

Lodahl, Michael, and Tom J. Oord. *Relational Holiness*. Kansas City: Beacon Hill Press of Kansas City, 2005.

Palmer, Phoebe. *The Way of Holiness*. New York: G. Lane and C. B. Tippett, 1845.

Ruth, C. W. *Entire Sanctification*. 1903.

Wynkoop, Mildred Bangs. *Foundations of Wesleyan-Arminian Theology*. Kansas City: Beacon Hill Press of Kansas City, 1967.

PART IV

HOLY LIVING FOR A
NEW CENTURY

EIGHT

HOLINESS AS PURITY

LEARNER OBJECTIVES

Your study of this chapter will help you to:

1. Define legalism and antinomianism and identify their dangers
2. Understand the importance of purifying grace to balance tradition
3. Distinguish between purity of intentions and purity of life
4. Identify obedience as a means of grace
5. Consider the topic of human sexuality in the context of purity

KEY WORDS

Covenant	Antinomianism
Legalism	Quietism

Several themes are at the very heart of Wesleyan-Holiness theology. Purity is one. We cannot define holiness fully unless we speak of a pure heart. Unfortunately, purity is one of those ideas that has often been misunderstood. Because of such misunderstanding, real people have been weighed down by a doctrine that should bring freedom. The word "purity" often invokes feelings of shame instead of a full confidence in the cleansing grace of God. This chapter will discuss the concepts of morality, cleansing, and obedience and how they relate to holiness and sin. The deeper aim here is to bring a healthy understanding of purity to the forefront of our reflections.

▶ DEFINING MORALITY

A distinction can be made between morality and ethics. For our purposes here, "morality" will be defined as an individual's personal choices to avoid certain actions, thoughts, and attitudes. "Ethics," on the other hand, will be defined as social morality—what we do, personally and communally, in the positive sense to help others. In this chapter, our attention will be on personal morals; social ethics will be emphasized in the next chapter on Christian perfection. Another way to look at this simply is that purity can be defined as an *absence* of sin. Perfection, on the other hand, denotes the *presence* of love.

Where do we get our sense of what is right and wrong? The obvious answer is the Bible. But the Bible itself seems to point to something deeper than knowledge. It implies there is a conscience within every human being—a moral center that seems inherent in what it means to be human. This conscience is a gift of God made active through prevenient grace. Paul speaks of an inner knowledge or conviction "apart from the law." God gives enough light so that those ignorant of the Jewish law—or by implication, laws in general—have no valid excuse for not taking responsibility for their own sins.

But certainly, the main emphasis in Scripture is on the law as the measure of what sin is. "I would not have known what sin was except through the law. . . . Once I was alive apart from law; but when the commandment came, sin sprang to life and I died. I found that the very commandment that was intended to bring life actually brought death" (Rom. 7:7, 9-10). The law itself is "holy, righteous and good" (v. 12), but it reminds us of our inability to keep the law apart from the grace of God. As discussed in chapter 6, laws were not arbitrarily given by God but were given for the purpose of protecting us and directing us toward loving God and others.

The foundation of Jewish law, the Ten Commandments, is based on the **covenant** first established with Abraham. In that covenant we see God initiating a synergistic relationship with humanity. On God's part, God will always be faithful. Abraham is to promise faithfulness as well. Indeed, he is to walk by faith. But even in Gen. 15, there is a foreshadowing of what God will ulti-mately do for us in sending Jesus Christ. At the ceremony when the covenant is to be confirmed ritually, Abraham is supposed to walk through a path of sacrificed animals, but he doesn't. And so God walks for him, in Abraham's place. What Abraham could not do for himself, God did. What we cannot do for ourselves, God did through the cross.

We see, then, throughout the Old Testament, the story of a people who do keep the covenant, but more often than not we see people who are faithless and disobedient. The giving of the law was a gracious act of God to help guide the people in living out their covenantal, divine-human relationship. Unfor-tunately, they failed over and over again. But God always remained faithful to them, offering enduring love and mercy. And ultimately, God made a new covenant through Jesus.

The writer of the letter to the Hebrews refers to the system of sacrifices that atoned for sin in the Old Testament. "The blood of goats and bulls and the ashes of a heifer sprinkled on those who are ceremonially unclean sanctify them so that they are outwardly clean. How much more, then, will the blood of Christ, who through the eternal Spirit offered himself unblemished to God, cleanse our consciences from acts that lead to death, so that we may serve the living God!" (Heb. 9:13-14). The new covenant is like the old because it is based on a relational faith. But the new covenant goes beyond the old because not only through Jesus Christ are sins atoned for outwardly, but also through Christ's *cleansing* blood our reason for sinning is addressed inwardly. The new is based on God's loving willingness to give God's own Son "once for all" (Heb. 7:27) so that the law could be inwardly "written on [our] hearts" (Rom. 2:15). Our works match our professions of faith, because something has hap-pened *in* us and not just *for* us.

This raises the question of the relationship between faith and works. This has been an issue throughout the history of the church. It is an issue that is not fully resolved, even in the New Testament. It is clear that Paul, reacting against his own background as a Pharisee, wants to emphasize faith. We find important discussions in Romans, Galatians, and Philippians on this point. In Philippians, Paul writes, "If anyone else thinks he has reasons to put con-fidence in the flesh, I have more: circumcised on the eighth day, of the people of Israel, of the tribe of Benjamin, a Hebrew of Hebrews; in regard to the law, a Pharisee; as for zeal, persecuting the church; as for legalistic righteousness, faultless" (Phil. 3:4-6). But he goes on to say that all of these externals he con-siders rubbish, "that I may gain Christ and be found in him, not having a righ-teousness of my own that comes from the law, but that which is through faith in Christ—the righteousness that comes from God and is by faith" (vv. 8-9).

Martin Luther became convinced of sola fide from reading the book of Romans, particularly chapter 4. Paul uses Abraham as the highest example of faith: "What then shall we say, that Abraham, our forefather, discovered in this matter? If, in fact, Abraham was justified by works, he had something to boast about—but not before God. What does the Scripture say? 'Abraham believed God, and it was credited to him as righteousness'" (vv. 1-3). The rest of the chapter affirms over and over again that God accounted Abraham as righteous because of his faith. This includes the faith that he displayed when offering up Isaac. If anything, Paul here nearly denigrates works as potentially dangerous. Yet this certainly does not mean Paul is unconcerned with Christian conduct. Most of his letters deal with morality and ethics to some degree. But contrast Paul's use of Abraham with James's:

> You foolish man, do you want evidence that faith without deeds is useless? Was not our ancestor Abraham considered righteous for what he did when he offered his son Isaac on the altar? You see that his faith and his actions were working together, and his faith was made complete by what he did. And the scripture was fulfilled that says, "Abraham believed God, and it was credited to him as righteousness," and he was called God's friend. You see that a person is justified by what he does and not by faith alone. (James 2:20-24)

No wonder it is rumored that Martin Luther wanted to cut James from the canon![1] It is actually on this point that John Wesley moved away from a sect of Luther's theological descendants, the Moravians. Wesley began to see that while the **legalism** that had bound him (until his Moravian "Aldersgate" experience of sola fide) must certainly be left behind, the potentiality of **antinomianism** (the **quietism**) of his Moravian friends must be avoided. Antinomianism is the premise that God's grace is so overarching and merciful that we can keep on sinning. James stands as an important corrective to the fanaticism to which Luther's position could lead. Wesley's emphasis on the *grace* that brings *holiness* (that grows in "ever-increasing glory"—2 Cor. 3:18) walks a crucial line between legalism on the one hand and antinomianism on the other. It is purifying grace that can maintain the balance and can cure the damage caused by either extreme.

Legalism has at times been one of the Wesleyan-Holiness tradition's greatest threats. It entered the tradition's history more by means that were sociological than theological. Wesley's early Methodists emerged from the first Great Awakening; the Holiness Movement from the second. Both arose out of revivalism, and so have been referred to as the Wesleyan Revival of the 18th century and the Holiness Revival of the 19th. Interestingly, the methods of each respective revival looked different; the results looked the same. Thousands upon thousands heard preaching about salvation and about sanctification, and thousands upon thousands responded. Wesley used his classes and bands to initiate people into a new birth or sanctification experience and to nurture their spiritual life. The Holiness Revival used the mourner's bench as the primary vehicle for calling people to a decision for Christ. Certainly each revival saw an extraordinary work of the Holy Spirit that swept across Britain (and other places in Europe) and the United States. Persons were indeed greatly awakened to a new spirituality.

One additional aspect of the Holiness Movement's revival was the development of camp meetings and the National Camp Meeting Association. People from various denominational backgrounds (Methodists in particular) set off for the ocean or the woods for many days, sometimes weeks, of holiness preaching and manifestations of the Spirit's working. A common testimony was that the Holy Spirit broke the desire for one vice or another. And thus, former behaviors fell away as a result of such an intense (and genuine) spiritual experience. But how do the next generations hold on to such spiritual experiences that resulted in changes in conduct?

Two such efforts presented themselves historically. First was the quest for more and more revivals. After the formation of denominations from the revival and camp meeting experiences, the push for new revivals was strong, even after the fire of the Awakenings had dimmed. Over a hundred years later, the place of revivals in Holiness churches is debated. Do these older methods have potential to reach the postmodern world, or is the Spirit calling the church to other means?

The second way subsequent generations attempted to hold on to the positive moral outcomes of the Second Great Awakening were the lists of rules for conduct that became central to the identity of almost all Holiness denominations. What had been a *consequence* of the Holy Spirit's work were now written down as *necessary evidence* of the Holy Spirit's work. What had been descriptive now became regulative. Previously, persons who experienced the power of the Holy Spirit were enabled to give up certain behaviors. For the generations to follow, this often came to mean that if certain behaviors are still present, then the Holy Spirit most certainly is not. Holy living, as a movement of the Spirit, became for some a list of rules. This set the stage for legalism and judgmentalism. Morality lived out of a vital relationship with God was sometimes reduced to moralism on which to evaluate our own and even others' perfection.

Does this mean that the rules or guidelines found in manuals and books of discipline should be rejected? Certainly not. "The law is good." It is the abuse of the law that threatens the law's credibility. Paul, champion of faith, still took the time to list what we should avoid. Three examples follow. In the first passage (Rom. 1:29-32), Paul writes about those outside the church. In the second passage (Gal. 5:16-21), Paul is contrasting life in the Spirit with the carnal nature as a way of admonishing the Galatians to remember they are no longer of the world. In the third passage (Col. 3:5-10), Paul directly states that the Colossians should rid themselves of sins, for new life in Christ certainly means new behavior.

Rom. 1:29-32

> They have become filled with every kind of wickedness, evil, greed and depravity. They are full of envy, murder, strife, deceit and malice. They are gossips, slanderers, God-haters, insolent, arrogant and boastful; they invent ways of doing evil; they disobey their parents; they have no understanding, no fidelity, no love, no mercy. Although they know God's righteous decree that those who do such things deserve death, they not only continue to do these very things but also approve of those who practice them. (TNIV)

Gal. 5:16-21

> So I say, live by the Spirit, and you will not gratify the desires of the sinful nature. For the sinful nature desires what is contrary to the Spirit, and the Spirit what is contrary to the sinful nature. They are in conflict with each other, so that you do not do what you want. But if you are led by the Spirit, you are not under law. The acts of the sinful nature are obvious: sexual immorality, impurity and debauchery; idolatry and witchcraft; hatred, discord, jealousy, fits of rage, selfish ambition, dissensions, factions and envy; drunkenness, orgies, and the like. I warn you, as I did before, that those who live like this will not inherit the kingdom of God. (NIV)

Col. 3:5-10

> Put to death, therefore, whatever belongs to your earthly nature: sexual immorality, impurity, lust, evil desires and greed, which is idolatry. Because of these, the wrath of God is coming. You used to walk in these ways, in the life you once lived. But now you must rid yourselves of all such things as these: anger, rage, malice, slander, and filthy language from your lips. Do not lie to each other, since you have taken off your old self with its practices and have put on the new self, which is being renewed in knowledge in the image of its Creator. (NIV)

All the behaviors listed represent the opposite of purity in some form or another. But it certainly can be argued that the lists of rules we find in Scripture are different from the lists we find in denominational statements. One difference is that the denominational lists change over time as culture changes. This does not need to mean that denominations are accommodating culture, although some church splits have occurred over this very charge. What it does mean is that what a denomination considers to be essential must be seen as dynamic when it comes to Christian conduct. If certain behaviors are not directly stated in Scripture as sin, then a certain amount of discernment is necessary. For example, the Bible is not silent about dress and jewelry and the like. But at one time appropriate dress meant long sleeves on black garments. The question is, what is appropriate and inappropriate dress today? There will always be arguments on points such as these. But on some issues we must be careful not to look back pejoratively and declare as old-fashioned and irrelevant everything our predecessors thought. Often they had better reasons for their calls to abstain from certain behavior than we may think.

The issue of alcohol is one such example. The Holiness Movement was at the forefront of a wider anti-alcohol stance from the very beginning. Organizations formed to propose banning alcohol altogether and worked hard toward prohibition. But their reasons were different from what we might suppose. In the 19th century, women had few rights. They rarely earned a paycheck and were in most cases dependent on their husbands' earnings for the survival of themselves and their children. An organization such as the Women's Christian Temperance Union was actually formed to protect women. Not only did husbands drink away their earnings, but they also sometimes became violent when drunk and abused their wives and children. This background reveals a very different reason why Holiness denominations have shunned alcohol than we might have expected. Is this stance still relevant today? The present existence of such organizations as M.A.D.D. (Mothers Against Drunk Driving) seems to point to a continuing relevancy.

The point of this discussion on denominational guidelines is twofold. On the one hand, when the letter of the law becomes more important than the spirit of the law, legalism can ensue. And determining our holiness on the basis of rule keeping is dangerous to a healthy spirituality. But on the other hand, "the law" itself can still be good and contain good reminders about our need for Christian integrity. While "everything is permissible, not everything is beneficial" (see 1 Cor. 10:23).

It is, then, the purifying grace of God that guards against both legalism and antinomianism. *Grace* keeps us from any hint of self-righteous legalism. *Purifying* grace continues to call us toward this real, transforming holiness and away from antinomianism. Although the temptation toward legalism may be stronger, Holiness churches are not free from the temptation to antinomian living. Paul also addressed this issue in Romans. Apparently there were persons who abused the doctrine of grace by proclaiming, let us "go on sinning so that grace may increase" (Rom. 6:1). And "if our unrighteousness brings out God's righteousness more clearly . . . [and] if my falsehood enhances God's truthfulness and so increases his glory, why am I still condemned as a sinner?" (3:5-7).

Although most people know better than to say such things today, there is still an incipient danger in some thinking. More common perhaps is the mind-set that says, "If I indulge myself in this sin today, I know God will forgive me tomorrow." This is a misunderstanding of the unconditional love of God and grows out of an attitude that cheapens grace. It forgets that our salvation cost Jesus Christ his very life. Indeed, as a familiar phrase says, grace is free, but it is not cheap. The grace that Jesus can offer because of his sacrifice includes purifying grace.

▶ PURIFYING GRACE

According to Wesleyan-Holiness theology, one of the primary themes of Scripture is God's call to pursue holiness in heart and life. As God purifies our hearts, and as we cooperate with grace and live in the Spirit, our internal holiness will manifest itself in outward action: we become persons of *integrity*; our outward and inward lives are integrated. But the opposite of integrity can be true as well. Jesus said to his disciples regarding the Pharisees, "The things that come out of the mouth come from the heart" (Matt. 15:18). And to the Pharisees themselves, Jesus warns, "Woe to you, teachers of the law and Pharisees, you hypocrites! You clean the outside of the cup and dish, but inside they are full of greed and self-indulgence. Blind Pharisee! First clean the inside of the cup and dish, and then the outside also will be clean" (23:25-26).

A Holiness morality implies that we will avoid certain behaviors, not out of our own will and discipline to conform to an external moral code, as necessary and practical as such a code is. We avoid certain behaviors because they are unloving and because we are being cleansed of all but love and are becoming loving people. We are motivated to live like Christ who is the epitome of self-emptying love. He, then, is our true motivation and model. As Jesus said, by fulfilling the law of love, we will fulfill all the law. According to Holiness theology, certain behaviors are simply inconsistent with our *inward* transformation and will fall away as we walk in the life of the Spirit.

It is in this sense that sanctification implies being set apart from the world. As the old adage based on John 17 goes, we are to be "in the world . . . but . . . not of the world" (vv. 11, 15). This clearly counters any interpretation that implies a literal separation from society for the purposes of keeping our-selves clean. We are to be fully engaged with culture in order for us to be salt and light and a positive influence. But we are not to be *of* the world in the sense of being influenced negatively by it. Scriptures warn of the double-mindedness that can result when we do not see ourselves as appropriately separate.

To be sanctified as "set apart" also means to be set apart for God's pur-poses. The word and image in the Old Testament was an image that reached even to inanimate objects. If something was used in the tabernacle or temple, it was duly sanctified especially when placed on the altar. We extend that im-age to humans to say that we are to be sanctified holy in order to be set apart for God's holy purposes in our lives. Phoebe Palmer, following Adam Clarke, developed the altar covenant by interpreting Christ as the altar. When we place ourselves "on" him fully, we are sanctified holy, set apart individually and communally as the holy people of God to accomplish what we are called by God to do in the world. Palmer was not implying any sort of positional holiness, as if we are holy only by being placed on Christ the altar. In this metaphor, Christ does more than set us apart. He also purifies us from within. We are cleansed through the purifying grace of God so that there is a real and not just relative inner change.

To be theologically precise, God's cleansing is the means to a pure heart. Purity is the result of God's cleansing grace. But purity should never be con-sidered a *state* that we have reached. In the words of Thomas Cook, "We teach, not a state of purity, but a maintained condition of purity, a moment-by-mo-ment obedience and trust. 'The blood of Jesus Christ cleanseth us from all sin' all the time by cleaning us every Now."[2]

The opposite position—namely, that we are purified once and for all as a completed act—has raised difficulties in past expressions of what might be called Holiness folk theology. The primary question is, What does it mean to say that original sin is cleansed at the moment of entire sanctification, if con-tinual cleansing is the more prevalent biblical concept? Continual cleansing is only a problem if original sin is considered or conceptualized as a substance.

Recently, the word "eradication" was removed from one Holiness de-nomination's official nomenclature. This word has a long history and was used specifically to distinguish Holiness theology from that of suppressionism, also known as Keswickianism, which held that original sin remains but is sup-pressed from being the dominant force. For a long time the word "eradication" was a part of a Holiness theological identity. The word has lost its power how-ever, if not its relevance in the present context.

Why was it removed in this one instance? The main problem with the word is its unfortunate implications. It is a metaphor, clearly. To eradicate something is to root it out, almost in the sense of a surgical procedure that cuts something detrimental out of the body. This led, regrettably, to a conceptualization of original sin as a substance, a thing that is removed from us.[3] A metaphor became concrete in folk theology. Yet if sin is envisioned as a substance, how do we make sense of the metaphor of eradication if we sin again? Is sin then surgically transplanted back into us? The metaphor becomes nonsensical. If, however, the metaphor of cleansing is used (perhaps still with a medical meaning as if a wound is cleaned out), it is not impossible for an infection to return.

This idea of original sin actually fits Wesley's understanding of sin as a disease very well. Metaphorically, original sin for Wesley is described as a disease, a wound in humanity and in each individual that needs to be healed. Medicinal cleansing is certainly an image embraced in the Scriptures. Then, there was no antiseptic at hand, and so instruments were cleansed or purified by either water or fire—which became religious symbols in the end.

Whatever metaphors are embraced, the most important aspect of entire sanctification is that original sin (as equated with Paul's concept of *sarx*) is effectively dealt with by the work of God so that it no longer reigns in our hearts, as Wesley would say. Yet in order to be Holiness theology and not Keswickian theology, we must venture to say a bit more. It is the cleansing, purifying grace of God that accomplishes this potential for victory and freedom. It brings about a single-heartedness that inclines us toward God's will. We can resist this work or cease to cooperate with it, but God is able to do the work of purifying our heart. "The one who calls you is faithful and he will do it" (1 Thess. 5:24).

We must further clarify Wesley's understanding of purity at this point. He made a distinction between purity of the intentions and purity of the heart and life by implying that while our intentions may be purified, maturity is needed for these intentions to be further and further actualized. There is a difference between Christian purity and Christian maturity according to Wesley and his followers. What does Wesley mean by *intentions*? A couple of quotes will be helpful here. They both come from Wesley's very important work, *A Plain Account of Christian Perfection*. The first quote is intended to answer the question, What is Christian perfection? The spiritual metaphors he uses include the idea of purity of intentions.

> Look at it again; survey it on every side, and that with the closest attention. In one view, it is purity of intention, dedicating all the life to God. It is the giving God all our heart; it is one desire and design ruling all our tempers. It is the devoting, not a part, but all our soul, body, and substance, to God. In another view, it is all the mind which was in Christ, enabling

us to walk as Christ walked. It is the circumcision of the heart from all filthiness, all inward as well as outward pollution. It is a renewal of the heart in the whole image of God, the full likeness of Him that created it. In yet another, it is the loving God with all our heart, and our neighbor as ourselves. Now, take it in which of these views you please (for there is no material difference), and this is the whole and sole perfection.[4]

Earlier in the document, Wesley more specifically defined purity of heart and life of the one wholly devoted to God:

For he is "pure in heart." Love has purified his heart from envy, malice, wrath, and every unkind temper. It has cleansed him from pride, whereof "only cometh contention"; and he hath now "put on bowels of mercies, kindness, humbleness of mind, meekness, long-suffering." And indeed all possible ground for contention, on his part, is cut off. For none can take from him what he desires, seeing he "loves not the world, nor any of the things of the world"; but "all his desire is unto God, and to the remembrance of his name."

Agreeable to this his one desire, is this one design of his life; namely, "to do, not his own will, but the will of Him that sent him." His one intention at all times and in all places is, not to please himself, but Him whom his soul loveth. He hath a single eye; and because his "eye is single, his whole body is full of light. The whole is light, as when the bright shining of a candle doth enlighten the house." God reigns alone; all that is in the soul is "holiness to the Lord." There is not a motion in his heart but is according to his will. Every thought that arises points to him, and is in "obedience to the law of Christ."[5]

What these quotes reveal is that God initially purifies our intentions. But as we continue to act out of these intentions, purity of life will grow toward greater and greater maturity. In other words, purity of intentions is crucial in activating our potential toward holiness. As God continues to work, this potential for purity becomes more and more actualized.

The saying goes, "The way to hell is paved with good intentions." This saying is a good reminder that if we only have intentions and no actions, we are in danger. But for Wesleyans, the saying does not exactly fit. Good intentions are crucial for us. The intentions of our hearts, purified by grace, set us *toward* God's will. Further grace enables us to *fulfill* it. As Kierkegaard said, "Purity of heart is to will one thing."[6] The willing of the one thing must take action, however. Sanctification must be followed by a growing maturity. The human's part in this sanctification is consecration, or devotement. God is the one who does the purifying, first of the intentions and then of the life lived out of these intentions. Out of Wesley's ideas, Holiness theology has affirmed that we can speak of a true purity (or perfection) of the heart, even if our lives do not yet completely reflect an absolute purity (or perfection) in action.

▶ OBEDIENCE

This raises an important question. What place does obedience play in the sanctified life? We have just affirmed that we are not contradicting ourselves to say that a nascent purity grows into developing and maturing purity. But sufficient emphasis must still be placed on the call to have our wills aligned with the will of God. This is only evidenced through our grace-enabled obedience.

Again, from Wesley: "God reigns alone; all that is in the soul is 'holiness to the Lord.' There is not a motion in his heart but is according to [God's] will. Every thought that arises points to him, and is in 'obedience to the law of Christ.'"[7] The law of Christ is the law of love. But this is not some wishy-washy sentimental law. The law of love demands the highest morality we can imagine. And obedience to this morality is to be of the highest quality. But how do we avoid making obedience into a new legalism?

On this point, Wesley shows his genius. When talking about obedience, Wesley did not place the emphasis on our own exercise of the will but on our willingness to participate in God's grace. Obedience is one of Wesley's means of grace. As all other means of grace, obedience to Christ gives us grace in order to obey Christ! As we are obedient, we receive more and more grace to be obedient. Yes, we must exercise our will. But it is not a solitary willing. It is a willing that is bathed in God's grace and accompanied by the purifying presence of the Holy Spirit. Obedience to Christ and his law is not something we must muster up, trying as we might to desire to be faithful and act faithfully. Grace is given so that we are empowered both to desire and to do the will of God. This keeps us from any legalistic self-righteousness. But there is a danger toward antinomianism as well when discussing obedience to younger generations.

An aspect of the postmodern mind is that it is highly suspicious of authority. Authority is not ascribed any longer to someone because of a title or an office. This may come off as blatant disrespect. But a deeper issue is at work here. Many in the postmodern world have suffered from the dysfunction and abuse of those in authority over them. These deep wounds perhaps legitimately cause a deep suspicion of those in authority in general. Even Christian postmodernists do not avoid some of this suspicion of anyone over them in the church. Holding the office of pastor, for example, is no longer enough of a reason to give a pastor respect. In general, for the postmodernist, all respect and any willingness to place oneself under the authority of another is based on the credibility and trustworthiness of the person. Trust is fostered only if one feels loved.

This can be applied to God as well, especially if God is only associated with law and judgment and imagined as a great magistrate in the sky. By implication, allowing God's will to be authoritative in one's life is based on whether or not God is credible and trustworthy. But so many today question whether or not God is even love. In an increasingly secular—even post-Christian—world, the love of God is no longer simply presumed. And in this post-Holocaust world, issues of theodicy (questions of God's justice and the existence of evil) still loom large.

But despite a generation tentative about God's trustworthiness and love, God still passes the test. According to Wesleyan-Holiness theology, the character of God is portrayed as love, and love as God's very essence. The Wesleyan-Holiness message can meet the needs of those in this new age. It affirms that God has always been faithful. It proclaims that we can be sure of God's goodness and deep concern for our good. When a person submits himself or herself in obedience to Christ, he or she finds God to be a solid rock. Based on what we know of God in Christ as revealed to us by the Holy Spirit, a person has good reason to place himself or herself under God's authority. This requires humble submission, yes. But for many, a lack of submission arises out of woundedness and a need for self-protection, not necessarily out of pride. As always, the gospel is good news for the wounded, the broken, and the dying. "For God did not send his Son into the world to condemn the world, but to save the world through him" (John 3:17). The church is called to be ministers of this reconciliation. And this fulfills the law of love.

Another question remains for us as we consider the concept of purifying grace. If we are being sanctified, and purity of intentions is manifesting itself in our lives, and our lives display the character Wesley described in his words quoted earlier, do we still sin? We have already established that Wesley never implied that the capacity to sin is taken from us. He strongly countered this heretical idea wherever he came across it. We will always have the ability to sin. But that said, is sin still a part of the Christian life?

Wesley wrote two sermons that are relevant for our discussion here: "On Sin in Believers" and "Repentance of Believers." His main objective in "On Sin in Believers" was to counter the idea (which he attributed to Count Zinzendorf, a Moravian) that when we are justified, we are entirely sanctified. There is no remaining sin in us, whatsoever, including no "inbred sin." Wesley argued that this was a new doctrine; it went against the ancient church, the Greek and Roman church, the Reformed churches, and the Church of England. All of Christianity has affirmed that sin remains in the life of one justified. As Article Nine states (of the Anglican Articles): "Original sin is the corruption of the nature of every man, whereby man is in his own nature inclined to evil, so that the flesh lusteth contrary to the Spirit. And this infection of nature doth remain, yea, in them that are regenerated."[8] Wesley countered every argument that Zinzendorf presented, and walked through passage after passage of Scripture to present a correct interpretation. The point is clear. Repentance is essential to the Christian life because Christians sin. But Wesley asserted that both the guilt and the power of sin are broken at justification—a statement we are not so ready to claim today. But Wesley argued his point well.

> We allow that the state of a justified person is inexpressibly great and glorious. He is born again, "not of blood, nor of the flesh, nor of the will of man, but of God." He is a child of God, a member of Christ, an heir of the kingdom of heaven. "The peace of God, which passeth all understanding, keepeth his heart and mind in Christ Jesus." His very body is a "temple of the Holy Ghost," and an "habitation of God through the Spirit." He is "created anew in Christ Jesus": He is washed, he is sanctified. His heart is purified by faith; he is cleansed "from the corruption that is in the world"; "the love of God is shed abroad in his heart by the Holy Ghost which is given unto him." And so long as he "walketh in love," (which he may always do,) he worships God in spirit and in truth. He keepeth the commandments of God, and doeth those things that are pleasing in his sight; so exercising himself as to "have a conscience void of offence, toward God and toward man": And he has power both over outward and inward sin, even from the moment he is justified. (II.4)[9]

Wesley continues, however, by saying, "Was he not then freed from all sin, so that there is *no* sin in his heart? I cannot say this; I cannot believe it. . . . The Apostle here directly affirms that the flesh, evil nature, opposes the Spirit, even in believers; that even in the regenerate there are two principles, 'contrary the one to the other'" (III.1).[10]

Wesley was concerned that Zinzendorf's idea would lead to a lackadaisical attitude about striving against the sin that so easily entangles us. Sin is no longer a threat to the soul for Zinzendorf, and thus watching and praying for protection is unneeded. Wesley makes no attempt in this particular sermon to talk about a correct interpretation of what sanctification does to inbred sin. His intention is only to set right the wrong idea that Christians do not sin after justification because they are wholly pure, and that continually.

In *Repentance in Believers*, on the other hand, Wesley is very clear about entire sanctification. We find in this sermon some of his most direct statements about this doctrine. He does not claim for entire sanctification what Zinzendorf does for justification—that entire sanctification makes us practically unable to sin. But Wesley does speak of a radical transformation as a result of this work of God's grace.

Indeed this is so evident a truth, that well nigh all the children of God, scattered abroad, however they differ in other points, yet generally agree in this;—that although we may "by the Spirit, mortify the deeds of the body," resist and conquer both outward and inward sin: although we may *weaken* our enemies day by day;— yet we cannot *drive them out.* By all the grace which is given at justification we cannot extirpate them. Though we watch and pray ever so much, we cannot wholly cleanse either our hearts or hands. Most sure we cannot, till it shall please our Lord to speak to our hearts again, to speak the second time, "Be clean": and then only the leprosy is cleansed. Then only, the evil root, the carnal mind, is destroyed; and inbred sin subsists no more. But if there be no such second change, if there be no instantaneous deliverance after justification, if there be *none but* a gradual work of God (that there is a gradual work none denies,) then we must be content, as well as we can, to remain full of sin till death. (I.20)[11]

Inbred sin can be cleansed. But even here, it is repentance that opens us up to such cleansing. He continues:

> Thus it is, that in the children of God, repentance and faith exactly answer each other. By repentance we feel the sin remaining in our hearts, and cleaving to our words and actions: by faith, we receive the power of God in Christ, purifying our hearts, and cleansing our hands. By repentance, we are still sensible that we deserve punishment for all our tempers, and words, and actions: by faith, we are conscious that our Advocate with the Father is continually pleading for us, and thereby continually turning aside all condemnation and punishment from us. By repentance we have an abiding conviction that there is no help in us: by faith we receive not only mercy, "but grace to help in" *every* "time of need." Repentance disclaims the very possibility of any other help; faith accepts all the help we stand in need of, from him that hath all power in heaven and earth. Repentance says, "Without him I can do nothing": Faith says, "I can do all things through Christ strengthening me." Through him I can not only overcome, but expel, all the enemies of my soul. Through him I can "love the Lord my God with all my heart, mind, soul, and strength"; yea, and "walk in holiness and righteousness before him all the days of my life."[12]

Thus entire sanctification is an act of God that comes through repentance and faith. Repentance as the deep conviction in our hearts that we are guilty and helpless apart from the grace in Christ; faith as the confidence in the work of God in us—indeed, we are purified by faith.

The question remains, however, Do we still sin after the "second change"? If we apply Wesley's narrow definition and define sin as a willful transgression of a known law of God, and thus as a rebellious and defiant act, we may appropriately say that such sin as a pattern can indeed be broken. If we consider his wider discussion, and view sin as consisting of anything that goes against love, including sins of omission, then even those entirely sanctified do indeed sin. Wesley himself was tired of the question of whether or not we could reach sinless perfection in this life. He was frustrated because it seemed the motivation for this question was to pin him in the corner of affirming an absolute perfection, which he vehemently denied.[13] What he wanted to maintain was that the love of God could so fill the heart of the person wholly devoted to God, that such love would exclude sin. This love of God is a purifying love, continuously filling up the heart of those who love God. Knowing, willful, rebellious disobedience is foreign to such a purified heart. Committing such sin is not impossible, but it would go against the nature that has developed from God's cleansing and empowering grace.

Wesley also wanted to stress that personal morality and purity is maintained and nurtured through the community of faith and not through our individual strivings alone. Wesley's classes and bands served as strong accountability groups for those who participated. They served the purpose of encouraging the good (works of mercy) and helping the members to avoid evil. As the sidebar illustrates, the accountability groups were scrupulous in examining the lives of their members.

WESLEY'S RULES[14]

The design of our meeting is, to obey that command of God, "Confess your faults one to another, and pray one for another, that ye may be healed."

To this end, we intend:
1. To meet once a week, at the least.
2. To come punctually at the hour appointed, without some extraordinary reason.
3. To begin (those of us who are present) exactly at the hour, with singing or prayer.
4. To speak each of us in order, freely and plainly, the true state of our souls, with the faults we have committed in thought, word, or deed, the temptations we have felt, since our last meeting.
5. To end every meeting with prayer, suited to the state of each person present.

6. To desire some person among us to speak his own state first, and then to ask the rest, in order, as many and as searching questions as may be, concerning their state, sins, and temptations.

Some of the questions proposed to every one before he is admitted among us may be to this effect:

1. Have you the forgiveness of your sins?
2. Have you peace with God, through our Lord Jesus Christ?
3. Have you the witness of God's Spirit with your spirit, that you are a child of God?
4. Is the love of God shed abroad in your heart?
5. Has no sin, inward or outward, dominion over you?
6. Do you desire to be told of your faults?
7. Do you desire to be told of all your faults, and that plain and home?
8. Do you desire that every one of us should tell you, from time to time, whatsoever is in his heart concerning you?
9. Consider! Do you desire we should tell you whatsoever we think, whatsoever we fear, whatsoever we hear, concerning you?
10. Do you desire that, in doing this, we should come as close as possible, that we should cut to the quick, and search your heart to the bottom?
11. Is it your desire and design to be on this, and all other occasions, entirely open, so as to speak everything that is in your heart without exception, without disguise, and without reserve?

Any of the preceding questions may be asked as often as occasion offers; the four following at every meeting:

1. What known sins have you committed since our last meeting?
2. What temptations have you met with?
3. How were you delivered?
4. What have you thought, said, or done, of which you doubt whether it be sin or not?

Such rigorous examination seems out of place in our contemporary context. But should it? We do not trust each other enough to allow such honesty and openness about our lives. But should we? Perhaps another aspect of the postmodern mind, that of seeking deep, authentic relationships especially in the church, will allow for this type of communal accountability once more. However it might express itself, we must fight against making our personal morality a private affair. The adage "there is no holiness but social holiness" should not simply mean that we seek societal change through compassionate ministry. It should also remind us that holiness is lived out and maintained in relationships and through community. Any conception of purity must also envision purity in the context of relationships.

▶ EXCURSUS: EMBODIED HOLINESS AND HOLY SEXUALITY

Christians sometimes unknowingly embrace a negative attitude toward sexuality—an anti-sexuality. Why this is so stems in part from misunderstandings about the biblical concept of the body and its relationship to sin and spirituality.

Through the pages of this book we have suggested in several places that the Gnosticism of late antiquity stood as a threat to early Christianity. Gnosticism represents a dangerous dualism between things corporeal (material) and incorporeal (spiritual). But although Christians in our present culture are wary of what has been identified as a new Gnostic spirituality, such Christians would never suspect that a similar dualism has incipiently found a place in different expressions of orthodox Christianity. Such ideas hide wherever and whenever we imply that the body is unspiritual and the soul is spiritual and whenever we imply that we are to fight against the body—including our sexuality—as a means of liberating our soul.

This type of subtle Gnosticism can come from a complete misreading of Paul's discussion of sin in Romans and elsewhere. Different translations have used different words for the Greek word *sarx*. Most literally, it means *flesh*. It is against the flesh that Paul says we struggle. But Paul is not speaking about the physical body. He refers, rather, to the spiritual condition we sometimes call the sinful nature, or carnality. Although we certainly have in Scripture what might be labeled "sins of the body" (including sexual sin), it is wrong to assume that these are somehow worse than sins of the mind or sins of the spirit. As suggested earlier, in chapter 6, even these distinctions are unhelpful. It is more fitting for us to use a Hebrew model when we consider theological anthropology—one that views the human much more holistically than the Greek tripartite theory. Either way, God created every part of us good.

Another source for anti-sexual attitudes among Christians comes from the theology of Augustine. The great Western theologian contributed an unprecedented amount of theological insight to the developing church during the early centuries of Christianity. But some of his ideas have affected us negatively, even down to the present day. They surface in his views on sexual sin. Augustine believed that the most prominent expression of human sin is concupiscence, also known as lust (for a variety of things). Because he maintained this firmly, the concupiscence of specifically *sexual sin* became the deadliest of all sins in the mind of Western Christianity.

For centuries we have struggled under this weight. As a result, sexuality itself (apart from any act) is often subjectively experienced as evil when God clearly created it as good. Even (or perhaps even *especially*) in Christian circles we find great ambiguity and confusion about sexuality. Augustine's position pushed him to saying that all sex is in some way sinful, for all sexual acts arise out of lust—even sex in marriage. For Augustine, sex was saved from its shamefulness only by its procreative purpose in marriage. Whenever a child is conceived, the sex act is redeemed.

We do not have to and we should not embrace this position. Our intention here, then, is to redeem sexuality itself from centuries of flawed theology. Let us state our point clearly. God does not want us to feel shame about our sexuality or our bodies. Too often we feel sinful and shameful when we should not. Experiencing ourselves as sexual beings means understanding ourselves as God created us—full of hormones and drives that help define us as being human.

But we must also acknowledge that we live in a sex-saturated society. While we would be wrong to assume that previous generations were purer generations, we must acknowledge that today sexual immorality is no longer hidden and is generally accepted. Sex outside marriage is no longer shunned by society. There is no longer an assumed societal code of sexual mores (except when it comes to pedophilia). The world is a very different place than the world of our great-grandparents. It is not likely that society is going to change back, and so the present and future generations will need great discernment in negotiating through the many choices more readily available and even encouraged by society.

While society has changed, the wisdom of God has not. We must see biblical warnings against sexual immorality, not as grand restrictions from a wrathful God, but as loving care for humanity. As all sin, sexual sin can be very damaging—damaging physically (e.g., if sexual diseases are transmitted), damaging psychologically, and certainly damaging relationally. God created our sexuality, and it is good. But outside the parameters God also created, the potential for harm to ourselves and to others is great. It is difficult, if not impossible, for sexuality expressed outside these parameters to not be dehumanizing.

God's call for us to remain sexually pure benefits us in ways we often don't understand until we fall. Innocence is underrated. The temptations are great, particularly now since most sexual sin is no longer considered sin and since the accessibility of sexual material is unprecedented. People are experiencing more and more sexual behavior at younger and younger ages, sometimes long before moral development has matured. As the church, is the advice "Just say no" all we have to offer? Is it simply a matter of the strength of one's own willpower?

We must be careful to walk a fine line in what follows. On one side is the danger of claiming too much from the doctrine of sanctification and purity of heart. We should never imply that God's ability to purify our intentions reduces sexual temptation. Christ was the purest of all human beings, but he was tempted in every way we are, probably *more* than we are, for Satan knew his strength. Sexual temptation is complicated because it often produces a strong physiological reaction. The physiological reaction itself is not sinful. It is only when we choose to act that sin is sin. And yet, on the other side, we do not want to claim too little, especially as Wesleyans. As has been shown throughout this book, we believe that the power of grace is greater than the power of sin. And we believe that God can purify us from guilt and shame and empower us to live righteously even during the greatest temptation. What do we claim then about temptation?

Following Scripture, we believe that the Holy Spirit will always provide a way out. If we cooperate with the Holy Spirit's power, we can know victory. At the same time, the idea of instantaneous victory over all temptation must be mediated by reality and by a needed discussion of sexual addiction.

Although God has the power to do anything, victory over addictions often comes through a step-by-step process to unhabituate the addictive behaviors. As we will explore in a later chapter about character development, we do not come to every new situation morally neutral. Our future choice may be influenced by past decisions that have become deeply ingrained and habitual. If these past decisions have been positive (and as such, always assisted by the grace of God), good character develops, which influences future decisions positively. But the opposite is true as well. When we consider addictions, which are even stronger than negative habits because they involve biochemical changes, overcoming them can be a slow and painful process. Spiritual victory in this case should be defined as the person's commitment to stick with the process. God's grace is not limited by the time it takes. We should rather reflect on the abundance of grace necessary to once again match purity of life with a person's purity of intentions. Unfortunately, however, the message we often send to persons with sexual addictions is one of impatience that charges them with faithlessness if their addictions are not overcome in whatever arbitrary timetable we set.

Wesley seemed to have great insight into the process required to change "tempers" and "affections." Unfortunately we have lost some of that through an overemphasis on entire sanctification as a cure-all for everything we struggle with. We also need to realize that addictions leave deep wounds. For most persons, the continuation of strong temptation throughout their lives is a natural consequence they must suffer. Compassion and support for such woundedness should be our reaction.

Another aspect of sexual purity must be raised here. The author remembers being a counselor at a teen camp in the early 1990s. Each morning the teens watched a video series on sexual purity, with the message "Just say no." But the author knew, based on statistics and the real-life experiences of persons with whom she pastored, that some of the teens there were not allowed to say no, because someone in a position of power over them was sexually abusing them.

Statistics say that one in four women and one in six men have been sexually abused as children.[15] The statistics are shamefully the same whether we are considering those outside or inside the church. And one of the most common tactics of abusers is to get the abused to assume emotional responsibility for what is happening.

So what can we say about such abuse? The Bible speaks of the millstone prepared for those who prey on children or the weak. An image of a horrific death by drowning is reserved for them (Matt. 18:6). The message of the gospel is one of mercy to all who repent, but this does not mean there is no justice. It is time for the church to speak on behalf of those taken advantage of in such a harmful manner. Is there a message of hope for those who have had their purity stolen from them in such a vile way?

Christ is the great Physician who attends our wounds. He does not leave us by the side of the road when others pass us by. He rescues us in our pain, binds up our wounds, and begins the process of mending our hearts. Abuse leaves deep emotional and psychological scars. Often he uses wise counselors as means of grace in our lives as we attempt to overcome what seemed like our very destruction. But God is always with us and will never leave us. In Christ, through the Holy Spirit, we find the balm that eases the sting and begins the healing. It is not an instantaneous cure but a long road toward restoration.

And restoration *is* possible, both for those who have lost their innocence through their own choices and for those who lost it against their will. On the one hand, there is forgiveness and cleansing; on the other, solidarity and presence. For both, there is healing and redemption even for our sexuality. For those who have sinned, their sin is cast "as far as the east is from the west" (Ps. 103:12). For those who have been sinned against, God is closer than our own breath. And our God is the God who makes everything new.

SUMMARY STATEMENTS

1. Purifying grace guards us from the extremes of dead legalism and dangerous antinomianism.

2. Personal morality is never a private affair but is lived out in the context of community.

3. Certain behaviors are inconsistent with our inward transformation and will fall away as we walk in the Spirit.

4. There is a difference between purity of intentions and maturity in action.

5. Obedience to God must be based on our view of God as loving and trustworthy, and seen as a means of grace.

6. Human sexuality is good and nothing to feel shame about. The context in which it is fully expressed is what makes it damaging or not.

QUESTIONS FOR REFLECTION

1. How does the concept of purifying grace guard us from extremes?

2. How should we view denominational codes of conduct?

3. Is "obedience" an oppressive or liberating term for you?

4. What does it really mean to be sexually pure?

FURTHER READING

Kierkegaard, Søren. *Purity of Heart Is to Will One Thing.* New York: Harper & Brothers, 1938.

Oden, Thomas C. *Doctrinal Standards in the Wesleyan Tradition.* Grand Rapids: Francis Asbury Press, 1988.

Wesley, John. Sermons: "On Sin in Believers" and "The Repentance of Believers." In *The Bicentennial Edition of the Works of John Wesley.* Vol. 1. Nashville: Abingdon Press, 1983—.

Winner, Lauren. *Real Sex: The Naked Truth About Chastity.* Grand Rapids: Brazos Press, 2005.

NINE

HOLINESS AS PERFECTION

LEARNER OBJECTIVES:

Your study of this chapter will help you to:

1. Describe what Christian perfection entails

2. Identify what Christian perfection does not mean

3. Define involuntary transgressions, imperfections, and infirmities and explain how they relate to Christian perfection

4. Reflect on the issues involved in developing social ethics (ethics of love)

KEY WORDS

Christian perfection

Platonic realism

Involuntary transgressions

Imperfections

Infirmities

Perfectionist controversy

Homeopathic

Social gospel movement

Liberation theologies

Why would a chapter on **Christian perfection** still have a place in a textbook meant for the 21st century? "Perfection" is historically the most misunderstood word in the Wesleyan-Holiness tradition, as well as in Methodism. Why not abandon the word altogether? Does it function in any positive way today? Is it worth maintaining in light of all the misconceptions that surround it? These are important questions. But ultimately, we need to address this matter for two reasons. First, "perfection" is a biblical word, and as such it needs to be interpreted correctly. "Be perfect, therefore, as your heavenly Father is perfect" (Matt. 5:48) cannot be simply brushed aside. Second, "perfection" is one of the primary words used in explaining sanctification in Holiness history.

In the end, we may choose a different word to translate the Greek and to make holiness vocabulary more relevant to today's church and culture. But for now, the aim of this chapter is to present Christian perfection in a way that reveals the misconceptions about it and explains, perhaps even rescues, its truth. Wesley himself faced steady opposition to the doctrine and even criticized his own preachers for failing to preach it enough. This led him to ask: "Shall we drop it, or make a point of it?"[1] He made a point of it. His question is still fitting for us today.

▶ CHRISTIAN PERFECTION CLEARLY DEFINED

The word "perfection" is not a strictly Christian or even religious word. Humans' ability to think transcendently and imagine something beyond their own experience led the early philosophers to ponder a hypothetically perfect being and later to assert "the divine" as that perfect being. Plato believed that perfection is found in the mind (the forms). Anything material was necessarily less than perfect for Plato, because the actual (physical) entity would be flawed in comparison to the mental image. Plato believed that the forms are real and that the world is less than real. Anything actual, then, is less than perfect. For Plato the idea of perfection also led to the conception of the absolute Good (or God). Anything less than absolute Good was imperfect by definition. It would thus be impossible for a human being to be perfect according to **Platonic realism**.

Aristotle, on the other hand, introduced the idea of perfection in this way: something (or someone) can be perfect if it is fulfilling the purpose for which it was created. A perfect chair is the chair that holds a person up who is sitting in it, even if the chair has scratches or flaws. Interestingly, Calvinists tend to rely heavily on Plato when defining perfection and its opposite, sin. While Wesley is Platonic in some respects, on the issue of perfection, he is Aristotelian. The vitally important question, then, is What is the purpose for which we are created? We need to delay any definitive statements about perfection without due consideration of this crucial question.

When the question of our purpose is asked, many persons quote the Westminster Shorter Catechism, which states, "Man's chief end is to glorify God and to enjoy Him forever."[2] The Westminster documents are from the Reformed perspective. Would Wesley disagree with this statement? Wesley often used the Westminster documents. But clearly from the whole of Wesley's writings we see our "chief end" as *loving* God, which has a different connotation than glorifying and enjoying. Love extends further. We might say as Wesleyans that our purpose is summed up in the two greatest commandments: We are to love God with our whole being, and our neighbors as ourselves.

SIN AS REFUSAL

In a word, sin is the refusal of God's will and of his love. It is not only a refusal to "do" this or that thing willed by God, or a determination to do what he forbids. It is more radically a refusal to be what we are, a rejection of our mysterious, contingent, spiritual reality hidden in the very mystery of God. Sin is our refusal to be what we were created to be—[children] of God, images of God.[3]

By implication then, we are perfect (in the Aristotelian sense) when we are fulfilling these commandments through the grace of God. Thus perfection is never accomplished as a state or condition, because opportunities to love are endless. There is within Wesleyanism a *dynamic* element of perfection. It is not static but can grow. Reuben Welch once gave this helpful example.[4] His daughter began piano lessons early in her life. She would practice and practice a piece until it was played, for all intents and purposes, *perfectly*. But as she got better, her ability to play harder and harder pieces grew. When she was older, she was able to sit down and play an extremely hard piece, also *perfectly*. In both instances, she was able to play perfectly. But obviously there was growth in her ability to do more.

We are created to love God with our whole being and our neighbors as ourselves. Holiness optimism believes that this is possible through God's grace. But the task is never done. We can never love enough, in the sense that we are done and as if a task is achieved or a level is reached. Love is as new as every new opportunity to love. Thus we can fulfill our purpose in love and yet also grow in our ability to do so as we progress before and *after* entire sanctification. Entire sanctification offers a significant point of the infilling of God's love and God's Spirit, but it is not the end of the journey.

With these introductory remarks in place, we now turn our attention to a more comprehensive treatment of Christian perfection in Wesley and his successors.

WESLEY

The amount of material that John Wesley wrote on the subject is rather astounding. He decided to collect some of his various writings and reprint them in the text *A Plain Account of Christian Perfection*, first published in 1766. Many of his thoughts there are presented in the form of questions that he answers. It is clear that many of his Methodist followers and his non-Methodist opponents were unclear about what Wesley meant by the term. Another important text is his sermon "On Perfection," written in 1784. This work can be seen as the summation of all his thoughts after years of attempting to explain himself. This work is also useful when contrasted with his 1741 sermon, "Christian Perfection."[5] As to an overarching theme, Wesley stated this: "Pure love reigning alone in the heart and life—this is the whole of Scriptural Perfection."[6] This statement would require countless explanations from him.

Wesley often returned to the year 1725 (and 1726) in his reflections of who influenced him and why. As mentioned earlier, it was the year he was reading in preparation for his deacon ordination. He wrote that in that year he read from three significant authors: Thomas à Kempis (*Imitation of Christ*), Jeremy Taylor (*Rules and Exercises of Holy Living and Dying*), and William Law (*Christian Perfection* and *A Serious Call to a Devout and Holy Life*). From these authors, Wesley gleaned three primary ways of describing Christian perfection: purity of intention, the imitation of Christ, and love to God and neighbor. Wesley used these definitions to describe both the second change experience of entire sanctification and the lifestyle lived out of that experience. Important to the whole of Wesley's thoughts is that such is a gift of God through grace, and never self-made.

As noted in the last chapter, by using the phrase "purity of intention" Wesley is speaking of an act of God's grace that displaces sin with love as the motivating factor in the heart. This type of purity is characteristic of those who possess a single eye or single-heartedness before God. The purified intention of such a person is to live at all times to please and honor God.

Both descriptive and normative of this purity of intention is the life that imitates the life of Christ. We have the mind of Christ and thus know God's will. Further, we are enabled to do the will of God, not just understand it. It is not just a goal to shoot for, but the true end of faith intended to be lived out in the here and now.[7] We are to walk as Christ walked. We are enabled to live as

Christ lived. Out of the pure heart, we do more than subsist. We actively live like Christ in the world. And the purest characteristic of Christ's life is perfect love. This is the most important factor in determining perfection. Do we love as God has loved us? When we do (or perhaps even more precisely, when we *intend to* in the fullest meaning of that word), we are perfect in fulfilling our original purpose.

In 1784[8] in his sermon "On Perfection," Wesley offered nine[9] definitive statements about Christian perfection. Written about seven years before his death, this sermon can be seen then as his most developed understanding of the doctrine, after years of clarifying and reclarifying an infinite number of finer points. Here they are:

1. Christian perfection means to love God with all one's heart and one's neighbor as oneself.

2. Christian perfection is to have the mind that is in Christ.

3. Christian perfection produces the fruits of the Spirit.

4. Christian perfection is the recovery of the image of God.

5. Christian perfection brings inward and outward righteousness, sanctity of life issuing from sanctity of heart.

6. Christian perfection is a work of God, sanctifying the person through and through (from 1 Thess. 5:23).

7. Christian perfection begins and is maintained through a person's perfect consecration to God.

8. Christian perfection consists of a person's thoughts, words, and actions directed to God in praise and thanksgiving.

9. Christian perfection is salvation from all sin.[10]

These characteristics are contrasted with Wesley's strong affirmations of what Christian perfection *is not*. These will be covered after the end of this section. We now move to a discussion of Christian perfection in the 19th century.

WYNKOOP ON CHRISTIAN PERFECTION

After extensive study about John Wesley on Christian perfection and after a thorough review of the biblical words for perfection, Mildred Bangs Wynkoop offers the following general observations:

1. Christian "perfection is teleological." It is the end and goal of humanity.

2. Christian "perfection, in the Bible, is an absolute requirement, in the sense that the Christian should always be in the quest for it."

3. Christian perfection is both purity of intentions and maturity in life.
4. Christian perfection is an absolute moral quality, which must faithfully be adapted to living situations. Absolute moral integrity is fulfilled as our relative capacity grows.
5. Christian perfection can be claimed at particular points in time and as an increasing maturity.
6. Christian perfection is not absolute in the broader sense; imperfections and infirmities that come from being human do not disqualify us for Christian perfection.
7. Christian perfection must be relevant to this life. No exegesis can find textual warrant for deferring perfection to another life.
8. Christian perfection is only lived out in relationships, namely with God and neighbor. Christian perfection is necessarily relational.
9. Christian perfection is not an unhealthy legalistic perfectionism.
10. Christian perfection is not the absence of all that is less than perfect. It has the positive of love.
11. Christian perfection is more than entire sanctification. It is a lifestyle and not just an experience.[11]

THE 19TH CENTURY

Did Methodists in the 19th century hold to Wesley's doctrine of Christian perfection? This is a complex question. The early Methodists in America closely followed Wesley and were determined to keep to his doctrines. But even before his death, there was some movement away from him in light of the continuing animosity between Britain and America after the Revolutionary War. The War of 1812 only furthered the distance. Eventually Wesley was more of a founder than a father to be closely adhered to. Also, frontier conditions led to a general neglect of Wesley's special teaching on perfection. Francis Asbury in particular downplayed the education needed to make converts out of sinners by presenting the "simple gospel." Some of the deeper nuances of Christian perfection were lost on the frontier.

By 1835 there was some interest in renewing a strong emphasis on Christian perfection on the part of some leaders. Timothy Merritt published *Treatise on Christian Perfection* (which had great influence) and began a periodical devoted to Wesley's ideas (*Guide to Holiness*). The Methodist Church called for Holiness revival among its people at its General Conference in 1832. Phoebe Palmer and others worked within Methodism to not lose the doctrine. This interest reached considerable proportion by 1858.

Yet it is around this time that Methodist leaders began advising their people to be wary, even to abandon Holiness camp meetings and revivals altogether. Thus at the same time this renewed interest in Christian perfection reached a pinnacle in the 1860s, others in Methodism began to oppose Holiness teaching strongly.

After the organization of the National Holiness Association in 1867, and during the rapid increase of holiness camp meetings, periodicals, and holiness evangelists following this date, the controversy became so great that, by the close of the century, many holiness denominations had formed, while any special emphasis on perfection in the Methodist church ceased.[12]

The conclusion the Methodist Church reached at the end of the century was that sanctification should be identified with the whole process of Christian living, beginning at regeneration, and that any instantaneousness of a second work of grace should be discarded.[13] Many Holiness denominations formed to counter this position characteristic of Methodism during the last three decades of the 19th century. (This should not be taken, however, to mean that all Methodists have personally abandoned the doctrine.)[14]

Groups such as the Free Methodists, Wesleyan Methodists, and the Church of the Nazarene took what they believed to be Wesley's position on Christian perfection (as a second work of grace as well as a lifestyle) as their cardinal doctrine.[15] As these and other Holiness groups moved into the 20th century, new, non-Methodist articulations of holiness and systematic theologies were needed and written. A gross overgeneralization can be made by stating that early- to mid-20th-century expressions of Christian perfection collapsed Wesley's more inclusive view into only one meaning. Specifically, Wesley held that Christian perfection was both the instantaneous experience and the subsequent lifestyle. While most Methodists dropped instantaneousness, some Holiness writers of the early- to mid-20th century de-emphasized the Christian lifestyle as perfect love and emphasized the work of grace itself as definitive of Christian perfection.[16] When lifestyle was invoked, the focus was more on the absence of sin and less on the presence of love. Writers of this period also interpreted Rom. 7 as the life of a Christian who has yet to be entirely sanctified. This is a shift from Wesley's interpretation, as well as that of recent Holiness scholars, that Paul is referring to an unbeliever at the end of the chapter.

Wesley emphasized that Christian perfection is nothing other than "pure love reigning alone in the heart and life." It is appropriate for us to return to Wesley's emphasis on both the instantaneous work and on the life of perfect love. To do this we must go where Wesley went so often to explain the doctrine. We must approach a correct definition of Christian perfection by strongly stating what it is not.

▶ WHAT CHRISTIAN PERFECTION IS NOT

While John Wesley was adamant about proclaiming the message of Christian perfection, he was just as insistent on explaining what it is not. Most of the misunderstandings about Christian perfection can be clarified if we pay close attention to the unequivocal distinctions he made. "A failure to distinguish between sin and infirmity, puts an undue emphasis upon sin, and has a tendency to discourage earnest seekers from pressing on to a full deliverance from the carnal mind."[17] Indeed, one of the greatest discouragements that can come from the whole of Wesleyan-Holiness theology is to wrongly believe that God calls us to an absolute, angelic, or even Adamic perfection. We never become *more than* human. We become *more human* through sanctification. We never grow beyond temptation. Even Christ was tempted. We never rise above a lack of wisdom, errors or mistakes, or any number of infirmities that we suffer in mind or body. God does not expect this from us. Leo Cox aids our understanding here: "Human imperfections must never be confused with an evil moral nature. . . . This area of imperfection between perfect love and perfect performance was not passed over lightly by Wesley."[18] We shall not pass over it here. For clarity, we will divide these distinctions from perfect love into three categories: **involuntary transgressions, imperfections,** and **infirmities** (although Wesley sometimes uses them interchangeably).

INVOLUNTARY TRANSGRESSIONS

Wesley often distinguished between what he called voluntary transgressions and involuntary transgressions.[19] Similarly, he talked about "sin properly so-called"[20] and "sin improperly so-called." What he wanted to suggest by these designations is that Christian perfection deals with the moral actions and the moral center of a person. Involuntary transgressions, or sin improperly so-called, on the other hand, are actions that are not moral failures. Here Wesley's definition of sin as a willful act against a known law is very much in play. Such willful sins are those sins for which we are culpable.[21] Involuntary transgressions, however, do not change our relationship with God, while unrepented willful sins need to be addressed in this regard. We may transgress or go against the ideal in situations, but often we miss the mark of the ideal because of our human limitations, not because of our purposeful rebellious choices. Randy Maddox explains: "To understand the difference one needs to recall Wesley's identification of will and affections. Potential imperfections of obedience flowing from wrong affections would be 'voluntary' because they are effected by the will and subject to our liberty; hence, they would be sinful. By contrast, infirmities are non-moral because they are involuntary; i.e., they are not subject to our concurrence (liberty)," or free-will.[22]

Wesley himself wrote,

> I believe there is no such perfection in this life as excludes . . . involuntary transgressions which I apprehend to be naturally consequent on the ignorance and mistakes inseparable from mortality. . . . Therefore *sinless perfection* is a phrase I never use, lest I should seem to contradict myself. . . . I believe a person filled with the love of God is still liable to involuntary transgressions.[23]

We must, however, think through the issue of responsibility for involuntary transgressions, particularly in our relationships with others. If we unintentionally hurt another person, we could use Wesley's ideas to the extreme and say that we are innocent of the offense because we did not intend it. Clearly a relationship would never work in real life if based on some of the finer points we want to make theologically. Are we personally responsible for an unintentional act? We could say no in an effort to be theologically precise. But in real life, we take responsibility and apologize (repent) when we have committed even unintentional harm. A relationship would suffer if we always declared ourselves innocent based on intentionality. If we want to be theologically precise, then Wesleyans should be out in front of courtrooms picketing in an attempt to protest the punishments that are still given for unintentional acts such as manslaughter! But of course we wouldn't actually do this.

Being in a relationship implies a generosity of spirit that takes responsibility for hurting others, intentionally or not. This also applies to our relationship with God. Even unintentional acts should be confessed.

IMPERFECTIONS

Imperfections can be distinguished from involuntary transgressions because the word "imperfection" is more general in meaning than what is implied in the word "transgression." More precisely, imperfections can lead to involuntary transgressions. Wesley observes,

> In what sense [are persons] not [perfect?] They are not perfect in knowledge. They are not free from ignorance, no, nor from mistake. We are no more to expect any living man to be infallible, than to be omniscient. They are not free from infirmities, such as weakness or slowness of understanding, irregular quickness or heaviness of imagination. Such in another kind are impropriety of language, ungracefulness of pronunciation; to which one might add a thousand nameless defects, either in conversation or behaviour. From such [imperfections] as these none are perfectly freed till their spirits return to God; neither can we expect till then to be wholly freed from temptation; for "the servant is not above his master." But neither in this sense is there any absolute perfection on earth.[24]

From this we see that Wesley needed to clarify that Christian perfection does not raise us above our human limitations. We are not perfect in knowledge; we may even have intellectual difficulties. Christian perfection does not make us great orators or speakers. In countless ways we fall short of absolute perfection.

This distinction became crucial in what is known as the **perfectionist controversy** of the early 1760s. The leaders of the Methodist society in London (a very influential society) began to preach a perfection that *was* absolute, or angelic. This went against several of Wesley's own themes. First, this fanatical group believed that entire sanctification replaced any need for growth *prior* to it. Wesley always advised that entire sanctification is best pursued through attending to the means of grace. That is, the person best prepared to receive the gift of entire sanctification is the one who has grown toward it through the various ways we nurture our relationship with God—daily prayer, Bible reading, and so on. Also, the leaders of the society (Thomas Maxfield and George Bell) rejected any need for growth *after* entire sanctification. But the correct interpretation of Wesley's theology is that both gradual growth in grace and instantaneous entire sanctification must be equally emphasized. One without the other on either side perverts the doctrine of Christian perfection.

Second, they suggested that only those who have been entirely sanctified are fit for heaven, thus wholly minimizing the power of new birth. Wesley quickly removed the leaders from the society and began to preach more often against angelic perfection. This included an emphasis on human imperfections as defects *not* addressed by saving or sanctifying grace. A different type of grace is called for when we consider imperfections or more specifically what he called infirmities.

INFIRMITIES

Whereas imperfections and involuntary transgressions are a part of normal human experience, the word "infirmities" has a slightly different connotation. An infirmity implies that something has gone wrong in a more pervasive way than imperfections. Often infirmities involve the body or the emotions. Infirmities are either bodily ailments or mental illness of some sort. Wesley was before his time in recognizing that these do not have their source in the sinful actions of the person. Wesley was clear that these infirmities do not affect one's salvation or relationship with God.

> We . . . believe, that there is no such perfection in this life, as implies an entire deliverance, either from ignorance, or mistake, in things not essential to salvation, or from manifold temptations, or from numberless infirmities, wherewith the corruptible body more or less presses down the soul. We cannot find any ground in Scripture to suppose, that any inhabitant of a house of clay is wholly exempt . . . from bodily infirmities.[25]

Wesley does not explain infirmities at length in any treatise. We do find, however, in his more personal correspondence many references to bodily and mental/emotional disorders. Since most of Wesley's letters to men are about administrative or doctrinal matters, Wesley's letters and specific counsel to women illuminate the most holistic aspects of his anthropology in dealing with infirmities. As expected, Wesley offered some type of spiritual direction in most of the letters to women, but he almost as often offered advice on physical ailments and on "nervous disorders" and emotional suffering.

Wesley's spiritual counsel took many forms, from helping women with the perplexities of "working out their own salvation" to exhorting them to always continue in their works of charity; from providing consolation and comfort in some particular grief to answering intricate doctrinal questions that needed further clarification, such as about the doctrine of Christian perfection.[26] Wesley often ended his letters by asking specific spiritual questions. "Have you an uninterrupted sense of the presence of God as a loving and gracious Father? Do you find your heart is continually ascending to Him? And are you still enabled in everything to give thanks?" he asked Hannah Ball.[27]

Wesley's counsel to women also evidenced a high degree of interest in the physical condition. It can even be argued that in addition to preaching and administration, an integral part of his travels included ministering to the physical needs of his people. The preface to his *Primitive Physic*[28] makes clear he was primarily concerned about the high cost of new medicines that put medical treatment in the hands of the rich but not the poor. Wesley's "science" is close to **homeopathic** treatment. He developed it from observing the effectiveness of home remedies, remedies perhaps often devised by women. His *Primitive Physic* is a collection of remedies that would have been readily available to most Methodists and those they cared for. In many of his letters, Wesley addressed physical concerns:

> My Dear Sister—You only tell me in general that your health is declining; but you do not say in what manner or from what cause. When did you begin to feel any decay of health? In what manner was (sic) affected? What did you imagine it was owing to? How have you been since from time to time? What means of recovery have you used, and with what effect? Write to me as particularly as you can on these heads, directing to me in Dublin. It is our duty to take care of our bodily health. . . . I am, dear Patty, Yours affectionately.[29]

As in spiritual matters, the specificity of Wesley's questions is notable; the imperative here is again "particularity" and attention to intimate detail. When Mrs. Chapman answered his detailed inquiry, he penned back with confidence: "The apothecary seems to have understood your case; but you have done right in leaving off the taking of medicines. But withal you should use all the exercise you can, particularly in the open air."[30]

Wesley's long-term friend Ann Bolton suffered from various maladies throughout their more than twenty-year correspondence and friendship, and thus her health often preoccupied his letters. In 1768, Wesley wrote,

> As there is nothing new in your disorder only an increase of the same symptoms, I believe, if you will observe the directions I formerly gave, this will help you more than a hundred medicines. Oily medicines would kill you quickly; so would anything that loads your stomach. You must take care to have air enough at night: it would not hurt you to have the window a little open. When you have that tickling cough, chew a small bit of bark (as big as half a peppercorn), swallow your spittle four or five times, and then spit out the wood. So much bark as this I can allow you, but no more, at the peril of your life. Try if red currants agree with you; if they do, eat as many as you can.[31]

Not only did Wesley habitually ask direct and specific questions, but he also offered very specific, finely tuned advice. He saw himself as capable of influencing the health and wholeness of the body. Much of Wesley's advice was simple. He was adamant about not sleeping too long, getting plenty of exercise, and eating properly. At one point, Wesley went beyond the more familiar world of home remedy and proposed that people submit themselves to the latest medical technology.

In 1756 Wesley procured an "electric machine" (a device that literally shocked its user), and believed it had great medicinal value. Years later he was still an advocate. To Mary Bosanquet Fletcher, Wesley wrote, "Tis pity but you had an electric machine. It would prevent much pain . . . and supersede almost all other physic."[32] To another he wrote, "If you have opportunity to be electrified, that would remove the pain in your eye, should it return."[33] And to Ann Bolton, "At all hazards get an electric machine. It is your bounden duty. You are no more at liberty to throw away your health than to throw away your life."[34] Physical health was a spiritual discipline for Wesley and thus his advice was nearly as forceful as any spiritual exhortation. Under this rubric, an electric machine became a bounden duty.

Wesley's scheme reveals an interdependence of "spirit," "body," and "mind" (or emotions). Although Wesley testified to a high level of emotional stability, he was not unsympathetic to others who suffered from what he most frequently called "nervous disorders." Here, too, his advice was plentiful. To Mrs. Knapp he wrote:

> I have been seriously considering your case, and I will tell you my thoughts freely. Your body frequently presses down your spirit by reason of your ner-

vous disorder. What then can be done, in order to lessen at least, if not to remove it? Perhaps it may be entirely removed if you can take advice. And I think you can by God's assistance. I advise you: 1) Sleep early, never sit up later than ten o'clock for any business whatsoever—no, not for reading or prayer; do not offer murder for sacrifice. 2) Rise early: never lie more than seven hours, unless when you lie-in. 3) Beware of Satan transformed into an angel of light: he can hurt you no other way, as your heart is upright toward God and you desire to please Him in all things.[35]

As Wesley's advice reveals, he was open to possible physical causes for nervous disorders, rather than immediately naming them as spiritual in origin. He was also quick to assert that although such disorders can make the journey more trying, emotional difficulties need not doom the spiritual life. In a typical example of his spiritual triage, Wesley discerned:

If that sickness you mention came (as in the case of some) only at the time of private prayer, I should incline to think it was preternatural, a messenger from Satan permitted to buffet you. But as you find it likewise at other times, when you feel any vehement emotion of mind, it seems to be (partly at least) a natural effect of what is called weakness or nerves.[36]

Wesley maintained the possibility of spiritual victory despite physical distress or emotional disturbances. To Mrs. Downes, he wrote: "You are enabled to give a very clear and standing proof that weakness of nerves cannot prevent joy in the Lord. Your nerves have been remarkably weak, and that for many years, but still your soul can magnify the Lord and your spirit rejoices in God your Savior."[37] Wesley's optimism remained his primary hermeneutic for interpreting all aspects of human experience.

Christian perfection is a spiritual and moral condition. One can involuntarily transgress, display all sorts of imperfections common to being mortal, and suffer bodily or emotionally and still display perfect love. Wesley's point here better fits today's biological and psychological knowledge than a theologi-

FROM MERTON'S *LIFE AND HOLINESS*

To be perfect then is not so much a matter of seeking God with ardor and generosity as of being found, loved, and possessed by God, in such a way that his action in us makes us completely generous and helps us to transcend our limitations and react against our own weakness. We become saints not by violently overcoming our own weakness, but by letting the Lord give us the strength and purity of his Spirit in exchange for our weakness and misery.[38]

cal system that blames all suffering on the personal sin of the individual. It is not appropriate to tell a Christian hospitalized for a nervous breakdown that everything will be fine if he or she just confesses his or her hidden sins. It is not appropriate to believe that persons suffer physically because they do not have enough faith. Living in a fallen world means that we do not experience perfect human lives. But we can have a perfect heart that expresses itself in love for God and others. Our infirmities may even keep us from expressing that love as fully as we would desire. But God looks at the intentions of the heart and sees the purity and perfection that has been effected through the gift of grace. Purity has to do with personal morality. Perfect love has the positive content that expresses itself in the context of social ethics.

▶ THE ETHICS OF LOVE

A strong theme of this entire book is that holiness cannot be defined only as the absence of sin. While there is a place for emphasizing this absence (which is better labeled "purity"), *only* emphasizing this side of holiness will necessarily skew, distort, and kill the true doctrine. Purity can only be spoken of appropriately in a close and necessary connection to perfect love. In the last chapter, on purity, we gave attention to morality, to personal behaviors to be *avoided*. We must now turn our attention toward the *positive* content of love, which we have identified as social ethics.

Every aspect of Wesley's relentless focus on an individual's holiness was for making that individual an agent of perfect love to those around him or her. Inward transformation, if real and sustained, necessarily led to what Wesley would call "acts of mercy" performed out of genuine godly love. As he is so often quoted as saying, "There is no holiness but social holiness."[39] The call to particular acts of service in the world permeated the ethos of Methodism, not only in the time of Wesley but also in the 19th century and into the 20th. Scholars are now recognizing that well before what is known as the **social gospel movement** of the early 20th century (a movement associated with liberal Protestantism), Methodism and the late-19th-century Holiness Movement evangelized the downcast, assisted the needy, ministered to the sick, fed the poor, advocated for the oppressed, and sought liberation for slaves and women all in the name of perfect love for God and neighbor.[40] For our purposes here, we will delineate those acts into evangelism, compassionate ministry, and social justice. Wesleyan theology always drives toward touching real lives with real love.

EVANGELISM

One expression of the ethics of love is seeking the deep spiritual healing, or salvation, of others. The Wesleyan-Holiness tradition has always made evangelism one of its top priorities. It is fair to wonder: If Wesley had not been barred from Anglican pulpits, would he have ever moved to preaching in the fields, with the "world as his parish"? This brought him to real people with real needs, as it brought all his preachers face-to-face with common folk both in Britain and America.

After 1738 and Aldersgate, Wesley saw the necessity of preaching "salvation" by faith and its subsequent "assurance" wherever he went. He lined up in many ways with the great revivalists of his age, including Jonathan Edwards and George Whitefield. He called all persons to faith in Jesus Christ. His was, without a doubt, an "evangelical" call to new birth and new creation. He told his lay preachers:

> You have nothing to do but to save souls. Therefore spend and be spent in this work. And go always, not only to those that want you, but to those that want you most. Observe: It is not your business to preach so many times, and to take care of this or that society; but to save as many souls as you can; to bring as many sinners as you possibly can to repentance.[41]

But unlike his Calvinist contemporaries, Wesley's understanding of salvation, as explained earlier, in chapter 7, represents a broader, more holistic view:

> By salvation I mean, not barely, according to the vulgar notion, deliverance from hell, or going to heaven; but a present deliverance from sin, a restoration of the soul to its primitive health, its original purity; a recovery of the divine nature; the renewal of our souls after the image of God, in righteousness and true holiness, in justice, mercy, and truth.[42]

Evangelism, for Wesley, if its results were to be lasting, led to the placement of a new believer into a method of spiritual formation. The genius of Methodism, and that to which its significant and lasting growth can be attributed, is small groups (bands and classes) that connected newly confessing Christians to the means of spiritual growth.

We must be careful today not to forget the purpose and motivation of Wesley's holistic evangelistic efforts. We must be wary of consumerism, which can so easily infiltrate our work in God's kingdom and tempt us to evangelize for the "bottom line," for the sake of growing numbers instead of in the name of love. We must also be on our guard against the temptation to evangelize in the name of duty alone. If we forget that the purpose and motivation for sharing the gospel is love for the other, our evangelism can too easily become formalistic, hollow, ultimately ineffective, and dehumanizing. Love requires the type of discipleship on our part that builds an authentic and deepening relationship with such persons and integrates them totally into "body" life. This type of love costs us something. As Wesley's bands and classes show, the community of faith is absolutely indispensable in a new believer's life and Christian growth, specifically, growth in holiness and perfect love.

COMPASSIONATE MINISTRY

There is no doubt that Wesley's evangelistic concerns were directed toward the poor. However, it would have been unconscionable for Wesley to have *preached* the good news of the gospel without also attending to the basic physical needs of his listeners. But even more than that, Wesley believed that not only was the good Methodist's *service* to the poor necessary, but also life *with the poor* was requisite for the genuine Christian disciple. According to Theodore Jennings, "Wesley could no more imagine a week without visiting the hovels of the poor than he could a week without participation in the Eucharist."[43] His commitment was relentless. Wesley could say: "The honourable, the great, we are thoroughly willing to leave you. Only let us alone with the poor, the vulgar, the base, the outcasts of men."[44]

Eighteenth-century Methodists gave to the poor, lived with the poor, and preferred the poor. This was a matter of principle for Wesley, and to him it was biblically based and theologically sound. But it was driven by contact with real persons whom Wesley called his people to love in the name of Christ. The Holiness Movement evidenced a similar driving agenda. Most Holiness groups made the downcast and needy the main focus of their ministries. The work of The Salvation Army is perhaps the best expression of this. But other denominations were just as active in meeting the needs of common people.

There have been calls in recent years for Holiness denominations to go back to such roots. Our roots contain important models for us. But there must be a renewed, heartfelt concern in the here and now that stirs within us. We must not only want to do what our forefathers and foremothers did because what they did was good, but also be struck ourselves with the imperatives of the perfect love that is supposed to fill our hearts to overflowing and that compels us toward others (2 Cor. 5:14). For Wesley, as it should be for us, the evidence of a heart made pure through the sanctifying grace of God is love for God and neighbor.

And as we know, Jesus defined our "neighbor" very differently than what we might naturally be comfortable with. Jesus picked a Samaritan as the hero of the story, and the religious as those who failed. The Samaritans were a despised people for the Jews during Jesus' day. His story in Luke 10 would have cut the Pharisees down to size. But this parable, as well as countless other teachings of Christ and his interactions with people, shows that we are called to love persons regardless of their status in life. Those who love more are those who have received more mercy and grace, he implies (Luke 7:47). We are now called to re-present this love of God to any and all and to be the compassionate hands and feet of Jesus.

SOCIAL JUSTICE

Wesley was interested not only in feeding, clothing, and caring for the poor but also in rectifying and reforming the social structures that kept them poor. This was true of the Holiness Movement as well. It was, and is, not good enough to call such oppressive structures an unfortunate result of the evil in the world that came as a result of the Fall. This goes against the very essence of Wesleyan optimism. Acting, specific intentional acting, for what has come to be known as social justice must also be at the heart of Wesleyan-Holiness theology. In recent years, more than 100 million children have died of poverty. (As a reference point, 12 million people died in the Nazi Holocaust.) A holocaust of neglect plagues this world. National, political, institutional structures contribute to this horrific reality. Christians have a responsibility to work to alleviate not only the symptoms of suffering but also the *reasons* for the suffering. This applies personally, locally, and globally. At times it means acting politically.

Undoubtedly any ethical system, even the ethics of love, takes great discernment in knowing *how* principles are to be put into action. Before and during the Civil War in America, Methodists lined up on both sides of the issue of slavery, which caused a temporary ecclesiastical split. Most, if not all, Holiness people worked against slavery and became abolitionists. But there were different ways of demonstrating and expressing this belief. It is only really in retrospect that we can clearly see abolitionism as the right stand to take. At the time such ethical decisions are demanded of us, we can only act in faith believing that we are following the law of love.

An example a bit closer to our context comes from Lutheran pastor and theologian Dietrich Bonhoeffer. Although he had opportunity to leave Germany safely during World War II, he decided to stay and work against Adolf Hitler, finally deciding that the Christian thing to do would be to attempt to assassinate him. Bonhoeffer was captured and tragically executed only days before the fall of the Third Reich. His plan of action is of course highly debatable. There are those who believe that killing is never the Christian action to take. Others, like Bonhoeffer, weigh taking one life against saving countless others.

Since the 1960s, various theologies have arisen that have now come to be known as **liberation theologies**. They are characterized by the "doing" of theology from a particular context, a context from *within* a marginalized group. We sometimes speak about these issues by invoking the word "orthopraxis" as right practice in a similar way that we talk about orthodoxy as right belief (or right worship). Although some of these groups have developed complex theological reflections, for each, the practical liberation of the oppressed remains the ultimate goal. Historic examples are Black theology, feminist theology, South American liberation theology (known as S.A.L.T.), Asian theology, and Latino theology. Scholars have made connections between the ethos of these movements and the ethos of John Wesley's optimism about social transformation.

Wesley advocated for Black slaves in England and America; he is recognized as a rather progressive feminist in light of his views on men and women's spiritual and ecclesiastical equality and his sanction of women's right to preach. As has been stated, he sided with the oppressed, the poor, and the outcast of society. There is definitely a theme of *liberation* in Wesley's individual and social vision. Flowing out of his optimism about true liberation from the power of sin in this life, he envisioned social liberation for certain classes and marginalized groups and demanded that his Methodist people work for such human freedoms.

A vision of social transformation in the 19th century became even more pronounced in the United States, which evidenced a generalized utopian pull. The idea that anything was possible became the American dream. The Christian expression of this utopianism came in the form of a dedicated postmillennialism. This is the belief that the Christian church is to usher in the kingdom of God on earth by enacting kingdom principles in the here and now. That is, the church is to bring about social transformation. If the church is really the church, Christians believed, God will come. This is a very different idea from the more pessimistic premillennialism that came to dominate evangelical theology after World War I. But a shift in eschatology away from postmillennial optimism need not keep us from continuing to act for social change today. Many Wesleyan-Holiness theologians (e.g., Kristina LaCelle-Peterson,[45] Donald Dayton,[46] Douglas Strong[47]) believe that working against social structures that oppress is a crucial expression of the doctrine of perfect love.

Again, great discernment is needed to decide what path love would have us take in any given situation. It is easier to have a static list of rules that requires little thought. But love is the *dynamic* of holiness. Love sometimes does not fit into predictable patterns. But ultimately love "never fails" (1 Cor. 13:8). What we can say is that avoiding attempts to correct the *reasons* for suffering in favor of only addressing the suffering falls short of the Wesleyan-Holiness model. Holiness as perfect love, as taught and lived by John Wesley and his followers, is not only the past but also the future of the Holiness Movement—and not just the movement's distinctive but also its directive.

▶ "Shall We Drop It or Make a Point of It?"

This chapter has presented the historic doctrine of Christian perfection as understood by Wesley and the Holiness Movement. The question still remains, however, about whether the concept is still viable today.

It is still viable if we can somehow communicate to people an Aristotelian understanding of perfection so that they can adopt it. This, however, seems unlikely in the light of how strongly absolute (Platonic) perfection is ingrained in people's minds, particularly in the Western world. If Wesley had to continually explain what he meant by perfection, specifically by asserting what Christian perfection is *not*, we will have to continue to do the same.

"Perfect love" comes closer to an appropriate phraseology, because it removes the notions that sinlessness is perfection and that perfect love can be equated with entire sanctification. Again, both purity and love, in an *ongoing,* maturing relationship with God and others, must be included if we are to follow Wesley's true intent. The 19th-century Holiness Movement truncated at times this fuller meaning. But even "perfect love" can be misunderstood.

A short biblical review of the Greek words that are translated as "perfection" reveals nuances that are often not seen in English. Most Greek words that are sometimes translated as "perfect" or "perfection" mean maturity, completeness, fullness, or wholeness. At times the words imply that we are fulfilling the purpose or end that God intends for us, namely love. They are used in a few places to contrast mature Christians with "babes in Christ." In other places they imply that we are found qualified. They rarely mean good conduct; rather, they often mean the quality of our character.

Perhaps some combination of these words will better communicate the theological reality behind the phrase "Christian perfection" in the 21st century. The question, Shall we drop it or make a point of it? can possibly be answered this way: We should continue to define and refine the words and make a strong point of the truth they have attempted to convey in its rich tradition—purity and love for the sake of others and through the sanctifying, empowering grace of God. It is to this empowerment that we now turn in the next chapter.

SUMMARY STATEMENTS

1. "Christian perfection" is a term Wesley used to speak about purity of heart and outward actions of love.

2. Wesley used the term "Christian perfection" to indicate both entire sanctification and the lifestyle that follows it.

3. Wesley meant by the term "Christian perfection" the following: purity of intentions, Christlikeness, and love for God and neighbor.

4. "Christian perfection" is a moral term and excludes involuntary transgressions, imperfections, and infirmities.

5. The 19th-century Holiness Movement tended to collapse Wesley's broader meaning of Christian perfection into entire sanctification only.

6. Ethics of love have implications for evangelism, compassionate ministries, and social justice.

QUESTIONS FOR REFLECTION

1. Why did Wesley have to explain what he meant by Christian perfection so often?

2. What happened to Christian perfection in 19th-century America?

3. What aspects of Christian perfection should we maintain today?

4. Can you think of other wording to substitute in place of "Christian perfection" and still maintain its truth for the 21st century?

FURTHER READING

Cox, Leo. *John Wesley's Concept of Perfection*. Kansas City: Beacon Hill Press, 1964.

Mahan, Asa. *Scripture Doctrine of Christian Perfection*. Boston: Waite, Peirce, and Co., 1844.

Wesley, John. *A Plain Account of Christian Perfection*. Kansas City: Beacon Hill Press of Kansas City, 1966.

———. Sermon: "Christian Perfection." In *The Bicentennial Edition of the Works of John Wesley*. Vol. 2. Nashville: Abingdon Press, 1983—.

———. Sermon: "On Perfection." In *The Bicentennial Edition of the Works of John Wesley*. Vol. 3. Nashville: Abingdon Press, 1983—.

TEN

HOLINESS AS POWER

LEARNER OBJECTIVES

Your study of this chapter will help you to:

1. See power as a key aspect of holiness

2. Understand that the power of God breaks the power of sin

3. Recognize a "power for selfhood" as a gift of God to those who struggle with disempowerment, including a lack of self-esteem

4. Affirm that power is to be defined in a Christian, not worldly, way

5. Understand that God's power is made perfect in weakness and that God sometimes uses our wounds to help others

KEY WORDS

Abolitionism

Postmillennialism

Dynamism

Jesus stood before his disciples for the last time on the day of his ascension and told them, "You will receive power when the Holy Spirit comes on you" (Acts 1:8). Even before his death, he had promised them the coming of the Holy Spirit, who would comfort them, guide them into truth, and convict the world of sin. Jesus foretold the Holy Spirit's coming to *all* persons. It was the promise of the Father (v. 4) that was important to him. Strangely, Jesus did not seem to consider himself the ultimate gift to humanity, though salvation was through him alone. But he pointed to the spiritual immanence and dynamic of the promised Spirit who would bring the Christ-event to completion.

The Holy Spirit was the ultimate extension of God because by the Spirit God would be available to all persons. The Holy Spirit would fully represent Christ, who represents God, here on earth. But at Jesus' ascension, his message intensified. When the Holy Spirit comes, he told his disciples, they would receive power—specifically to be witnesses of the gospel throughout the world. Likewise, we affirm that *we* will receive power—a central theme of Holiness theology.

In the first several decades of the Holiness Movement, the theme of power was predominant in the Holiness message. Entire sanctification was connected to what happened on the Day of Pentecost. Holiness leaders and preachers in the latter decades of the 19th century focused on personal and social change, with great optimism. Pentecost was seen as an opening up of unlimited possibilities for persons from every sector of society. Often Holiness theology was joined to causes such as **abolitionism**, feeding the poor, and helping the oppressed. There was a genuine hope about ushering in the kingdom of God through societal change (known as **postmillennialism**). None of this would be possible without God's power given by the Holy Spirit in the experience of entire sanctification, and then throughout the Christian's life. The metaphor of Spirit baptism was closely connected to receiving this power to do more than what was humanly possible. Spirit baptism was essential to holiness identity.

Recently, in the late 20th century, the viability of exegetically associating the experience of entire sanctification with Pentecost and Spirit baptism has been strongly challenged.[1] Moreover, concern could arise that letting go of the centrality of the Spirit-baptism metaphor may lessen the Holiness Movement's correct emphasis on power in the sanctified life. However, relinquishing the interpretation of Pentecost as synonymous with entire sanctification does not mean abandoning the New Testament message of power—power for victory over sin, power of selfhood, and power when life goes wrong. Paul, and other New Testament writers, returns again and again to the theme of power—the *dunameōs* or **dynamism** of Christian living.

POWER FOR LIFE AND GODLINESS

His divine power has given us everything we need for life and godliness through our knowledge of him who called us by his own glory and goodness. Through these he has given us his very great and precious promises, so that through them you may participate in the divine nature and escape the corruption in the world caused by evil desires. (2 Pet. 1:3-4)

▶ POWER FOR VICTORY OVER SIN: LIFE IN THE SPIRIT

Wesleyan-Holiness theology, as we have observed throughout this book, is thoroughly optimistic about what the grace of God can do in the Christian life. Although Wesleyan-Holiness people take the power of sin very seriously, ultimately they believe that the power of grace is stronger than the power of sin in this life. In a sense, this is what distinguishes their tradition from others. Rather than wait for a better life only in heaven, people can anticipate more in life here and now—real transformation, significant growth in Christlikeness, and power over sin.

This idea is perhaps best portrayed in Paul's letter to the Romans, in chapters 5—8. The latter part of chapter 7 gives insight into the human struggle against sin. Paul describes a person whose master is sin. Whatever that person intends to do in striving for the good, he or she is unable to do. Likewise, whatever evil he or she wishes to avoid, that is what he or she ends up doing. Paul vividly depicts the internal struggle of such an individual, who Paul says is under the law and not under grace.

Interpretations of this passage differ. But most Wesleyans understand that Paul is not describing his present situation, even though he uses the historical present as his verb tense. To reach this conclusion, one only needs to read what follows in chapter 8. What Paul talks about in Rom. 7 is *not* to be descriptive of a saved, redeemed, or sanctified Christian's experience.

We may find some difficulty today relating to Paul's metaphor of mastery. We may be able to understand it intellectually, but it fails to communicate as effectively as it once did. Perhaps a more relevant metaphor would be one of addiction. Someone who is addicted to a behavior or a substance is consumed by the drive to satisfy his or her desire or craving. It is almost as if the person cannot do otherwise. Trying to ignore the addiction seems impossible. The person begins to be shaped by the addiction as it becomes central to his or her life and in turn affects and drives everything else he or she does. An overwhelming feeling of being completely out of control of his or her choices becomes dominant in the person's life.

This is the type of situation Paul describes. In his portrayal, sinful desire (the flesh) is almost personified by Paul as the entity that wars against the good and the good purposes to which all persons are called and for which we were created. Finally Paul throws up his hands and cries: "Who will rescue me from this body of death?" (Rom. 7:24). Who will rescue us from the sin that draws us strongly toward spiritual death? But clearly, Paul's question is not the end of the story. And yet, some traditions do use this passage in Rom. 7 to describe a Christian's life until he or she is rescued from life on earth and taken to heaven. Again, Wesleyan-Holiness theology strongly affirms that the rescue for which Paul cries is possible while the Christian is here on earth, through the grace of God and, more specifically, through the indwelling presence of the Holy Spirit. For this, Paul also cries, "Thanks be to God" (v. 25). He continues, "The law of the Spirit of life set me free from the law of sin and death. For what the law was powerless to do in that it was weakened by the sinful nature, God did by sending his own Son . . . in order that the righteous requirements of the law might be fully met in us, who do not live according to the sinful nature but according to the Spirit" (8:2-4).

This text encompasses three important aspects of Holiness theology. First of all, we are powerless to free ourselves from the addictive life of sin. Two words in this passage underscore for us the crucial truth of the gospel: "God did." God took the initiative to free us from a life of bondage. We cannot save ourselves, we cannot sanctify ourselves, and we cannot break the power of sin through our own strength no matter how pure our intentions.

Second, because of God's power, the "righteous requirements of the law" can be met fully in us. What is impossible through our own strength is fully possible because of what God has accomplished in Christ. Is this a call back to a type of perfectionism or legalism? If it were, Paul here would contradict the entire theme of Romans. Our righteousness comes from faith. It comes through Christ's righteousness. But it is a righteousness that goes further than the imputation of Christ's righteousness. The righteousness or holiness to which Paul calls us here is also imparted to us through grace. That is, we are truly transformed in our inner being, and in response to this transformation, holiness becomes not only possible but also real. And as Paul will state in Rom. 13, it is the law of love that enables us to fully live the holiness we proclaim.

And third, Paul clearly reminds us that grace is not a static "thing" given at particular moments in our Christian life. Rather it operates in a dynamic, living, growing, daily participation in the life of God. To express this, Paul calls us to live "according to the Spirit" (8:4). We are called to life in the

Spirit. "Those who are led by the Spirit of God are the children of God" (v. 14 TNIV).

So the Christian life, sustained by grace and the indwelling of the Holy Spirit, is a life of power, even a life of power over sin. Wesley himself was tired of the question of whether or not this implied an absolute sinlessness. He believed that the question missed the point.[2] The point is that the sanctified life is a life that is no longer in bondage to the power of sin, that is, the "sinful nature." Wesley faced a controversy in one of his societies when the leaders said directly that sanctification leaves a person *incapable* of sin. He countered this strongly and took measures to remove the leadership and set the society straight theologically. (See the perfectionist controversy in chap. 9.) Nothing will ever take away our *ability* to sin. But the sanctified, Spirit-filled life does effectively deal with our propensity to sin. The power of God is indeed greater than the power of sin, in the here and now.

▶ THE POWER OF SELFHOOD: A HOLINESS VIEW OF SELF-DENIAL

Jesus said that in order to "find" (Matt. 10:39) or "preserve" (Luke 17:33) our lives, we must lose them for him. He could have as easily said that in order to be empowered selves, we must give ourselves away. Indeed in the same text, Jesus calls us to self-denial. The Holiness Movement has, historically and theologically, had keen insight into this spiritual reality. Our focus on surrender, consecration, entire devotion, and sacrificial living are key activities, aided by the Spirit. But even more specifically, we have traditionally associated these synonyms for surrender with the experience of entire sanctification. This type of obedient surrender is hard. And yet, we must recognize that this is not a harsh message; it is not an austere life of drudgery to which we are called. No, the life of holiness is anything but severe, stark, or bleak. The Holiness message is a message of life, vitality, fullness, depth, joy unspeakable, and power. Jesus' words do not just call us to lose our lives; he promises that we will truly find them in him. Moreover, our very obedience is enabled through the Holy Spirit as we participate in the means of grace.

Grace gives us a self so that we might give that self away. And yet, although countered by the early Holiness Movement's emphasis on empowering the powerless, today we often call people to self-denial before they have experienced a self to deny. Whether it be political oppression, social structures, cultural norms, family dysfunction, even abuse, or innumerable other reasons, there are countless human beings who have been severely disempowered, even split off from any sense of personhood or even selfhood. Self-loathing, self-criticism, and unhealthy self-concepts are rampant today. And yet, there are those who say that self-esteem is unbiblical and take a pejorative view of loving oneself. But is this what the Scriptures teach? No, it is not.

Too many people have been oppressed in the name of Christianity. By way of analogy, telling a slave—who has no freedom—to choose to live as a slave is nonsense. Before the American Civil War the South even used this supposedly biblical injunction in its rhetoric to condone slavery. Or similarly, telling the poor to give up their vast wealth also makes no sense. So, in the same way, telling persons who have no sense of selfhood to deny themselves is as existentially mystifying as it is implicitly cruel. But do Christians have an alternative?

Absolutely. The biblical messages of resurrection, restoration in the image of God, empowerment for life and service, new birth, new creation, and especially holiness and sanctification all point to the power of God released into the life of the Christian, through the drenching and indwelling power of the Holy Spirit. In all its applications this drenching of the Holy Spirit never washes away our personhood! In fact, the opposite occurs. Life in God enlivens us; it brings us to real life through the liberating grace of God. We find our*selves* in God! Only as we find this godly sense of self can we then in turn give ourselves away in love. But this is not really about a loss of self, because when we lose ourselves, we again find ourselves in God. Unfortunately some historic expressions have emphasized self-denial so much that such denial seems the goal of Christianity.

As much as we have to learn from ancient ascetic spirituality and medieval mysticism, for example, Wesley demanded that such expressions of self-denial be accompanied by practical and relational service to others. Wesley deeply appreciated the mystical tradition modeled in the lives of such persons as Teresa of Avila, John of the Cross, and François Fénelon. Their experiences of God impressed him greatly. However, he concluded that they went too far.

His disagreement focused on two major points. First, he rejected the goal of the Christian experience as being unification with God. The mystics believed that a Christian can progress through certain stages of self-purgation to the ultimate experience of divine unification. Some mystics believed that the goal of unification was the complete loss of self into the essence of God. Wesley rejected both the objective and possibility of this kind of self-obliteration. Wesley was concerned that divine and human essences remain separate, theologically. We become like God, in Wesley's scheme; we do not become a part of God. Mysticism bordered on the notion that we become a part of God's self, a view untenable for Wesley.[3]

Second, and more importantly for our purposes here, Wesley wanted to refute what is known as the quietism of some ascetics and mystics, and the group of Moravians he was so indebted to for his doctrine of sola fide. Wesley never wanted to affirm a Christianity that neglected the real-life interactions with others and practical work God calls us to as those saved by grace. Some forms of quietism actually stated that such work was an affront to God's grace. Thus, quietistic expressions of Christianity can lead to such an emphasis on one's own spiritual pursuit that practical expressions of love for neighbor are neglected. Self-denial for self-denial's sake is never the goal of scriptural Christianity.

We find ourselves alive in God in order that our self-denial will lead us to a greater purpose. Thus we are called to the same self-emptying love that Jesus Christ has shown toward us. Self-emptying (kenosis) for the sake of the other is the ultimate expression and appropriate extension of selfhood and denying ourselves. Claiming *power* to empty ourselves seems paradoxical. But Christ himself shows us how this paradox works.

Christ's kenotic love never required a loss of his selfhood. It was out of his divine identity and relationship to the Father through the Spirit that Christ could empty himself on the cross, only to be filled again with the full measure of God. Indeed, Christ even now continues to empty himself for us. And there is always more of God's self in Christ to empty, as even now he intercedes on our behalf. Kenotic love is what Christ expressed and continues to express toward us and toward the world.

It is this type of love that God fully expressed in the sending of the Son to be the Savior. We use the word "kenosis" to attempt to describe this indescribable love. But we need to look further and ask the question of how such a self-giving love relates to power. Are they as antithetical as they seem to be at first glance? Or can we look deeper into this kenotic love in God and see that it requires, it demands, a different definition, a paradoxical definition of power?

Throughout his life, Jesus displayed divine power. He healed the sick and diseased, gave sight to the blind, liberated the oppressed, and even brought people back to life. He turned water into wine, fed thousands with a loaf of bread, walked across water, and calmed the sea. We can recognize the power of God—indeed we are told the power of the Holy Spirit—in Christ throughout his ministry. And we affirm the power of the resurrection; God raised the crucified Son from the dead. Paul implies in Eph. 1:18-20 that we participate in this power: The same power that raised Jesus from the dead is at work within us. Again following Paul in 1 Cor. 15, certainly orthodox Christianity has proclaimed that the Christian faith stands and falls with the truth of the resurrection of the crucified Jesus.

But Jesus himself, throughout his years of ministry, spoke a message different from one he could have proclaimed based on his ability to perform miracles or even based on the resurrection power he might have anticipated. His message, even before his death, went deeper than the superficiality, if you will, of changing the laws of nature. He spoke a message that did not negate the spiritual significance of the body or the "kingdoms of this world." Instead, his words reached beyond to the kingdom of God, which breaks open the often one-dimensional monotony of earthly life and calls us to see all of life sacramentally.

In the kingdom of God, the last will be first; the poor, the mournful, the meek, and the hungry will be blessed and filled. The powerful in the world will be the least in the kingdom of God. Indeed, the kingdom of God turns everything upside down. Authority is redefined. Mastery minimized. Power is seen in paradox.

In Mark 2, Jesus tells a paralyzed young man that his sins are forgiven, and the Pharisees grumble and cry blasphemy. Jesus turns to them and asks, "'Which is easier: to say to the paralytic, "Your sins are forgiven," or to say, "Get up, take your mat and walk"? But that you may know that the Son of Man has authority on earth to forgive sins. . . .' He said to the paralytic, 'I tell you, get up, take your mat and go home'" (vv. 9-12). Jesus seems to be saying here that in his attention to our physical needs there is something sacred, something of eternal significance, that breaks open, something that he has the power and authority to address. But how does he address it? The means by which Christ has the power to forgive sin was his choice to become powerless, obedient, even to death on the cross. Again, it is the cross that is the greatest expression of God's self-giving, self-sacrificing, indeed self-emptying love. It is this self-emptying that is to define both our personhood and our self-denial.

Holiness thus demands from us a self-emptying love that is, like Christ himself, constantly replenished by God's love for us. This is beyond observing some legalistic code and checking off a list of dos and don'ts, or arguing against what is wrong. This is about truly loving our neighbor with kenotic love and living kenotically for what is right. This all becomes possible only through God's empowerment. But it *is* possible.

We are empowered to be holy, but not for the sake of our own holiness. Holiness, most vividly expressed as kenotic love, is always costly and always for the other. We are empowered to be holy so the world might know we are Christians by our love (John 13:35)—a love that calls us, bids us, in the footsteps of Christ, to come and die so others might live. With this in mind, we now move in a different direction to talk about power in the midst of suffering.

▶ POWER WHEN LIFE GOES WRONG: "POWER PERFECTED IN WEAKNESS"

All of us are familiar with Paul's physical struggle, which most New Testament scholars believe to have been a painful eye condition. Paul tells us in 2 Cor. 12 that it was a tormenting "thorn" in his flesh. Although he asked God to heal him three times, God did not. Paul attempts to make some sense of this difficult condition. He searches for answers, as many of us do when we do not understand the suffering we must endure. Paul gives us a momentary glimpse into the whole realm of theodicy.

The book of Job gives us insight into how not to do theodicy. When Job's friends continue to challenge him again and again to connect his suffering with his sin, he refuses to take this logical path. In the end, his friends are exposed as wrong. And yet, many centuries after the writing of this wisdom book, we are still tempted to take this logical path and blame suffering on the sufferer. But there *is* innocent suffering in the world, beyond our ability to comprehend. The blind man was simply born blind—the fault of no one. Why, we ask. Why does suffering exist? Where is God? These are the questions that repeat like echoes through the centuries, the millennia of human life. *Why?* This simple three-letter word represents a question that, under the limitations of human existence, is simply beyond our ability to answer, unless we are willing to do theological somersaults that leave God practically impotent.

Paul himself tells us that he faced suffering on many fronts. Earlier in 2 Corinthians, Paul lists all the ways he has suffered for Christ. That suffering seems to have meaning for him, as he proclaims that he suffers for the gospel. But 2 Cor. 12 feels different. Why a physical difficulty that cannot be connected to his life as an apostle? This is different. And in the end, he did not arrive at some definitive answer that applies to us all. Yet he did make his way through his own suffering and took the absurd meaninglessness out of his own physical anguish. He plumbs the very depths of human experiences and gives hope to all who feel forsaken in the pool of pain. But Paul does not answer the question why. Rather, he answers the question how. How do we endure? Paul suggests a piece of wisdom that can touch even us. He says, "Power is made perfect in weakness" (v. 9). One of the many Christian mysteries we call paradox.

Here is the text in which we find these profound words:

There was given me a thorn in my flesh, a messenger of Satan, to torment me. Three times I pleaded with the Lord to take it away from me. But he said to me, "My grace is sufficient for you, for my power is made perfect in weakness." Therefore I will boast all the more gladly about my weaknesses, so that Christ's power may rest on me. That is why, for Christ's sake, I delight in weaknesses, in insults, in hardships, in persecutions, in difficulties. For when I am weak, then I am strong. (Vv. 7-10)

Our greatest temptation here is to romanticize these words—to make them heroic by sanctifying, indeed sterilizing them. The phrases "God's grace is sufficient," "power is made perfect in weakness," and "when I am weak, then I am strong" should never be thrust upon someone suffering and should never imply what some inadequate theodicies do—that God gives us suffering for our own good. Rather, a deeper theological contextualization of Paul's words is crucial if we are to avoid the meaningless dead end of redeeming God by attempting to redeem, as onlookers, the suffering and pain of others. There is much we should not say about suffering. But if we are to follow Paul, we can say grace—not sanctimoniously, but sacramentally. We can "say grace" by affirming the sufficiency of the grace of God.

IN THE FACE OF SUFFERING . . .

For those who are suffering it seems unhelpful to try to give answers on why this is happening. . . . Trying to defend God exacerbates the pain and anguish of the one who suffers. Instead of speculating about what God can and cannot do, it seems in the face of suffering we are invited to praise God through lament. Suffering is real, destructive, and gut-wrenching. In attempts to "get God off" implicitly we just keep heaping burning coals onto the head of the sufferer.[4]

John Wesley seemed always to understand what we sometimes don't. He had a category that was neither moral nor immoral. He did not, like Job's friends, see all suffering as connected to sin. He resisted the dualism that implies that poor bodily life correlates with bad spiritual health. Wesley talked compassionately about our human infirmities, without agonizing over the whys of their origins. Infirmities, he called them—those wounded and broken and hurting places in our bodies, but also in our minds, in our emotions, which do not fall under the rubric of sin. Wesley acknowledged these—in some sense long before such thinking was introduced through the medical and social sciences. Infirmities denote suffering not easily explainable but suffering that needs no less attention.

There has been a growing amount of theological literature around the issues of physical disability ever since the 1990 passing of the Americans with Disabilities Act. Nancy Eiesland has written, according to her subtitle, "a liberatory theology of disability." She acknowledges that "in American society, the temptation to hide our difficulties from others is endemic."[5] Persons with obvious physical disabilities should shake us out of our various forms of denial, but often they push us further into it. Eiesland thus continues, "Ignoring disability means ignoring life." For us all, "it is the precursor of isolation and powerlessness. . . . [The subsequent] telescoping of our lives into categorizations of good and bad, pain and pleasure, denies that the lives of people with disabilities, like all ordinary lives, are shot through with unexpected grace."[6] We could suggest that the sustaining grace of God can best be seen when pain is allowed to be pain, weakness is allowed to be weakness, and our thorns are not explained away. For far too long we have listened to friends like Job's and accepted a nonbiblical notion that Christians should not suffer.

FROM *BROKENNESS AND BLESSING*, BY FRANCES YOUNG

I could speak very personally about a radical shift in my own life. For long I struggled with the problem of evil and suffering, embodied for me in my disabled son; for how could I go on believing in a good Creator God when a newly created being was so flawed? It was not for me a question of "Why me?" but "Why at all?"—the personal and the global, the individual and the universal reflecting one another. The shift was a move beyond all that to discovering that through my son I have been brought to a very different place— for he has been the catalyst for a deeper appreciation of the core elements of the Christian tradition. I stand alongside him as a vulnerable creature, disabled and mortal, knowing my creaturely limitations and my lack of knowledge, especially of God. I know my need of God and my resistance to God's grace, the inner demons that so easily take over my interior life. Yet again and again I find myself lamed and blessed. I discern signs of God's presence; I meet God in human form; I discover glimpses of Christ in the faces of some of the most damaged and disabled human persons . . . [who, along with me] "will at last come to an entire exemption from afflictions."[7]

What makes us Christian in the midst of suffering is the affirmation that God's grace is sufficient for us. In the midst of pain and suffering we may doubt the sufficiency of God's grace. But it is real. We know about saving grace and sanctifying grace. We understand that we are saved through grace by faith alone. And even though we have had some theological problems at times with fully understanding that we are made holy by grace, for the most part we understand that we cannot sanctify ourselves—that it is God's work in us, a free gift as we make ourselves available through continual consecration and surrender. And yet, we have not articulated well the sustaining grace of God.

Perhaps we are uncomfortable with enduring suffering. We claim God's healing in every situation, and when it does not happen, we shove those suffering under the figurative rug. We cannot handle the fact that the suffering in our midst and across the world reminds us of our own mortality. We flee, particularly in United States culture and unlike most of the rest of the world, in fear from the thought of death. So sometimes we abandon the sick, the chronically ill, the aged, and the dying. We forget that while Holiness denominations affirm divine healing, they never had a "name it and claim it" theology. We find it difficult to stand humbly before our God and accept that real human suffering continues regardless of how much faith we may muster.

Only as we bring such suffering into the light, out from under the rug, can we fully understand the significance of Christ's assurance: "My grace is sufficient for you" (2 Cor. 12:9). Theologically, we must affirm that the heart of God is present to the broken and the weak. God is with those who go without, who suffer physically, who suffer at the hands of another, who suffer from mental disease—the list goes on and on. Jesus chose to spend his time with those who needed him most. And he spoke of God's concern for the poor, the needy, the captive, the blind, and the oppressed. "It is not the healthy who need a doctor, but the sick" (Matt. 9:12-13). The heart of God is present to the weak, in mysterious ways we do not often understand. And God is not only present but also powerfully active. But it is here that we must redefine power. For those with infirmities who, for whatever inexplicable reason, cannot pick up their mats and walk, an affirmation of God's power in the traditional sense seems like a cruel joke that they don't get. But if power is best characterized as God's self-emptying love for us, and if empowerment calls us to a self-emptying love for each other, there breaks forth light in the midst of suffering.

In light of God's kenosis, power can be defined as enabling a courage to endure. Paul Tillich speaks simply of the courage to be—to be at all, as the deeply Christian response to existential pain and suffering. Those who speak of the temptation of suicide often do not want to die. But they see death as the only way to end their intolerable, excruciating emotional pain—their only way to escape it. And nonbeing, if you will, seems the only way out. The choice to *be* is a courageous choice for those who suffer. But further, we must also make the courageous choice to *be* ourselves. To reflect who God has created us to *be*.

One of the greatest temptations of those who suffer from chronic and debilitating illness is to define themselves as the illness itself—to lose themselves in it. But Paul points us to the wisdom that when we are weak, then we are strong—through the power of Christ, which we must believe empowers us beyond being defined only by our circumstances. We, even in our infirmities, can find ourselves in Christ. Power means something much deeper than God's ability to remove our circumstances. Power, in the Christian sense, must also include a courage to be in the midst of it all. Here God is closer than we can articulate. God's comfort, God's presence as Paraclete, God's kenotic love enables our endurance.

This is not to imply that we compliantly accept any and all circumstances. There is an appropriate place to defy those who are causing the suffering of others. As liberation theology has shown us, a Christian's acceptance of suffering does not also mandate social passivity. It is beyond our scope here to debate the issue of passivism at length. May it suffice to say that standing against injustice, particularly on behalf of others, is thoroughly Christian. But perhaps even more relevant to the discussion here, what liberation theology (and many other perspectives as well) can teach us is a needed refusal to be a victim, even though we are being victimized. That is, God can give us a power to transcend circumstances for the sake of a higher purpose.

Another example of power redefined comes from the history of martyrdom in the early church. The martyrs' example will help make an important point. A whole genre of early Christian literature arose out of the reality of persecution and death that persons suffered under the brutality of Roman leaders. Early on, Christianity was seen as a Jewish sect, and Christians were thus afforded the same religious protections given to the Jews at this time. But as Christianity became more and more distinct from the Jewish faith because of the influx of Gentile converts and the development of its own set of sacred writings, these protections no longer applied in the minds of the authorities. As a result, when Christians did not worship the emperor or the pagan gods, they were brutally persecuted and martyred. Stories of the martyrs were recorded, often with graphic and gory details. One early church leader, Tertullian, declared that "the blood of the Martyrs is the seed of the Church."[8]

The martyrs became the symbol for the holiest of holy people. But something interesting happens in these martyrs' stories. A person's martyrdom was considered noble. But the weaker the person was, the more commendable the martyrdom. In the stratified setting of Roman society, the very highest and most admired martyrs of Christ were the very lowest in the eyes of the world. The highest and most admired martyrs were women—more than that, slave women. Thus the weaker the person, the more of God's power they displayed. A man might be able to endure the brutality of martyrdom because of his own strength. But a slave woman could only have endured because of Christ's power at work within her. It was Christ's courage, his endurance, his strength to endure the pain to the end that enabled this weakest symbol of society to die such a horrific death and keep her witness as a Christian. She was absolutely dependent on God for her "victory" in death.

Friedrich Schleiermacher, a 19th-century theologian, sometimes called the father of modern liberalism, is most known for his simple phrase: "Religion is the feeling of absolute dependence."[9] Schleiermacher believed that within every person there is the sense of dependence on something transcendent to him or her. This led him to the belief that everyone is naturally religious and that all religions, even the most primitive, are different expressions of the same search for and worship of God. This feeling of absolute dependence explains all the commonalities of religious expression. While we might want to debate the value of his reflections as a whole, we can borrow his specific expression about dependence and apply it to our context.

If holiness is anything, it is absolute dependence on God. We have done well through the decades to explore the meaning of holiness under the following rubrics: holiness as instantaneous experience; holiness as progressive character development; holiness as purity; holiness as perfection; holiness as relational; holiness as love; holiness as empowerment. These are all appropriate ways to get at the content of what holiness looks like. But holiness might be further expressed if placed under the rubric of weakness. This will accomplish a couple of things for us.

First, we need to be reminded as Holiness people that the rubric of weakness elicits and can reconnect us to a vital understanding of holiness intensely present in the early history of the Holiness Movement—this reality of being absolutely dependent on God. Absolute dependence by itself seems weak in the world's eyes. But to a Christian, that weakness is strength because it demands absolute dependence on God. The Wesleyan-Holiness tradition is able to speak in this language. Crucial in the experience of sanctification is a willingness to lay all on the altar. We speak of this through the words "consecration," "surrender," "being sold out," "making Christ Lord," or any other number of metaphors. A strong metaphor in Holiness history has been "entire devotion." This implies that God has become the very center of a person's being, the one to whom he or she pledges the deepest loyalty, and the one on whom he or she absolutely depends. This absolute dependence certainly implies a dependence on God in our spiritual life. And yet, it is certainly connected to our material and physical life as well.

But in a Western culture, it is too easy to find power, not in a dependent relationship with God, but often through position, possessions, people-connections, wealth, status, indeed, self-sufficiency. We are a far cry from the poor to whom early Holiness leaders preached. We have moved from a movement of the disenfranchised to denominations with their own form of power-structures and politics. It is an interesting question to ask: Why are Holiness churches exploding in non-Anglo contexts? Perhaps these other cultures have learned what it means to need God.

Holiness then, under the rubric of weakness, reminds us of the kind of desperate devotion to God to which and to whom we are called. Entire devotion to God necessarily draws us back to the importance of the apparently "weak" kenotic love of Christ lived out through us. If we could regrasp this sense of absolute dependence out of our own sense of neediness before God, perhaps we could once again understand the need for the means of grace, for a sacramental view of life, and for an appropriate understanding of holiness's relationship to power. It could also call us again to community, indeed communal holiness.

We are, as a community, holy people. We are the holy, though the broken, body of Christ. And when one part suffers, all suffer. When one part rejoices, all rejoice. And when one part loves, all love. We empty ourselves out for each other so that all are seen as real persons, as part of the community of faith, as parts of the body that are just as valuable as we are. Indeed, part of our own humanity is only actualized when we humanize others, when we treat others fully as subjects with dignity and not as objects over against which we define ourselves. And as we are truly the church, the image of God shines forth precisely in the weakness of us all. Christ's body was broken. The church as the body is broken. And we live not only interdependently on each other's strengths but also sacramentally through each other's weaknesses. This is the meaning of solidarity so central to the Holiness tradition; this is true community to which God calls the church. It is a meaning of holiness we have too often ignored, because we are tempted to define ourselves in worldly terms—in terms of the economy of power as judged by the world. But in the kingdom of God, we are to redefine power paradoxically in order to reflect the image of God in the church.

Holiness then, down to its very foundations, is about God's kenotic love for us even in our weakness. Under the conditions of human existence, our pain and our suffering show us all as needy. We are not whole, to varying degrees for an infinite number of reasons. But does this exclude us from holiness? Not if we redefine power paradoxically as weakness. Not if we redefine holiness as dependence; and not if we see ourselves and others through the eyes of God. We are not whole in the sense of absolute godlike perfection. But we are perfectly loved. God looks with eyes of kenotic love, we look at each other with eyes of kenotic love, and we pour ourselves out, if we can, and we are made holy together—not out of a position of power, but precisely because of our position as weak. And we treat our unpresentable parts with special honor.

Holiness, under the rubric of weakness, allows us to see that holiness and infirmity are not antithetical. Power and weakness do not stand against each other. Weakness elicits our dependence on God and our dependence on each other. Again, from Paul, Christ said to him in his suffering, "My grace is sufficient for you, for my power is made perfect in weakness." To which Paul affirms, "For when I am weak, then I am strong" (2 Cor. 12:9-10).

One final connection to our examination of power as paradoxical: Not only does the Bible say that God comforts those who need God's presence, who live in this sense of dependence, but it also affirms that God often uses the brokenness in our lives, and can redeem it. This is not to say that God causes our suffering for our own good. Rather, God being God has the power to take very difficult circumstances and "recycle" them in the kingdom. That is, the wisdom of God—which is sometimes foolishness to us—can use our brokenness, perhaps even more than our strengths. In God's economy, a different kind of healing takes place when God uses our suffering in the aid of another.

Take the woman who was sexually abused by a person in her church when she was a teen. For years and years the brokenness and deep woundedness of this experience dominated her emotional, indeed, her spiritual life. She sought healing through prayer, through trips to the altar, and appropriately through counseling. But although she made progress, any bit of wholeness seemed elusive until God started to use her brokenness to help others.

Women began to find her out—not even knowing her story. And God used her at times to make a significant difference in their lives. At the very least, she was able to offer comfort out of her ability to understand and empathize with their experiences—an ability she would never have if she had not gone through it herself.

Henri Nouwen would call her a "Wounded Healer."[10] He writes profoundly on this point—that God's grace and love work through us most strongly, not out of our wholeness, but out of our brokenness; not out of our soundness, but out of our wounds; not out of our strength, but out of our weakness. And in those moments when God touches another through us, our experiences of suffering—no less painful or absurd, at times—are *redeemed*; our mini-deaths are raised to new life in the heart of another. Paul said, "When I am weak, then I am strong" (2 Cor. 12:10). Paul said, "I will boast all the more gladly about my weaknesses, so that Christ's power may rest on me" (v. 9). Out of our own courage at times to be our unique selves despite the pain, God is able to lead us to be an instrument of powerful healing in others' lives. God is indeed a redeeming God.

SUMMARY STATEMENTS

1. An important part of our Holiness identity is the affirmation that we are empowered by the same Holy Spirit of Pentecost.

2. God's power within us "breaks the power of cancelled sin."

3. God's power can help the powerless to find a healthy sense of self.

4. We are made holy for the purpose of living out of Christ's kenotic love, as we deny ourselves daily and follow him.

5. Those with any number of infirmities are still extremely valuable in the body of Christ.

6. Holiness under the rubric of weakness keeps the church in check and away from a worldly definition of power.

7. We are most powerful when we learn to be absolutely dependent on God.

QUESTIONS FOR REFLECTION

1. What is the connection between Pentecost and holiness?

2. How might those in Western culture increase the sense of absolute dependence on God?

3. What do the "infirm" (disabled) have to teach us?

4. What wounds in your life might God perhaps use to help others?

FURTHER READING

Greathouse, William M., and George Lyons. *Romans 9-16: A Commentary in the Wesleyan Tradition.* Kansas City: Beacon Hill Press of Kansas City, 2008.

Lodahl, Michael, and Samuel Powell. *Embodied Holiness: Toward a Corporate Theology of Spiritual Growth.* Downers Grove, IL: InterVarsity Press, 1999.

McGrane, Janice. *Saints to Lean On: Spiritual Companions for Illness and Disability.* Cincinnati: St. Anthony Messenger Press, 2006.

Swinton, John. *Critical Reflections on Stanley Hauerwas' Theology of Disability.* Binghamton, NY: Haworth Pastoral Press, 2004.

Young, Frances M. *Brokenness and Blessing: Towards a Biblical Spirituality.* Grand Rapids: Baker Academic, 2007.

ELEVEN

HOLINESS AS CHARACTER

LEARNER OBJECTIVES

Your study of this chapter will help you to:

1. Understand Aristotle's concept of virtue

2. Identify the means of grace

3. Connect Wesley's moral psychology to postmodern Christianity

KEY WORDS

Virtue ethics	Continent character
Stoicism	Virtuous character
Arête	Intellectualist model
Phronesis	Will
Eudaimonia	Liberty
Material cause	Conscience
Efficient cause	Inclinations
Formal cause	Means of grace
Final cause	General means of grace
Telos	Prudential means of grace
Vicious character	Instituted means of grace
Incontinent character	Postmodernism

We begin this chapter on holy character after having already discussed the topics of morality and ethics. We have proceeded this way for several reasons. First, the earlier discussion of personal morality was appropriate in the chapter on purity, since purity is defined as the absence of sin or wrongdoing. Discussing purity would have remained abstract without some treatment of it in real, human life. Second, a consideration of social ethics was essential in the chapter on Christian perfection (defined as the presence of love) for the same reason. Finally, these two treatments of morality and ethics described the *content* of what ethical behavior might look like in a Wesleyan-Holiness theology. This chapter on character, however, has a different aim. The emphasis here is on the *how*, rather than the *what*. Rather than focusing on content, this chapter will examine the *means* by which a person is enabled to *be* moral or ethical and subsequently to perform in a moral or ethical way.

This chapter on "how" makes the whole discussion of this book on holiness complete. Without it, holiness could be seen as an ideal to strive for, with little guidance about how to reach it. Some have observed that this is precisely where the Holiness tradition has lost its way.[1] Though the Holiness tradition emphasized God's demand for a holy life, it has often failed to make clear how this is accomplished. Thus holiness has become a duty instead of the very essence and quality of our life in God. In the history of the Holiness tradition, holiness was sometimes understood moralistically or legalistically, where an external set of criteria was *the* measure of an individual's holiness. This led to the danger, often realized, of equating prescribed moral codes with personal holiness, which in reality neglected the very core of the Wesleyan message of holiness of heart and life.

During our present age of moral ambiguity, reclamation of a holistic Wesleyan ethic is imperative to the future of Holiness denominations. At the heart of this reclamation is a need to examine not only the standards or behaviors of holy living but the internal motivation for such living as well. We must move beyond an internal motivation that is driven by duty and return to Wesley's own emphasis on holy character and how it is developed. We begin with a discussion of a type of ethical theory that has endured for thousands of years: **virtue ethics**.

▶ VIRTUE ETHICS

Virtue ethics, or virtue theory, is a moral philosophy that emphasizes character development as the key element of ethical thinking and living, over against theories where rules or consequences are considered all important. This type of ethical reflection goes back to ancient Greek philosophy, most systematically in the work of Aristotle. It was the dominant theory in the ancient world and during the medieval period, interrupted only by the heavy influence of Neoplatonism and **Stoicism** in late antiquity. During the medieval period, Aristotle's reflections were Christianized through Thomas Aquinas and his commentary on Aristotle's primary ethical work, *Nicomachean Ethics*. Wesley was directly influenced by the Thomist tradition. Of note, in ancient Asian culture virtue theory can be found as well, most notably in the writings of Confucius.[2]

Important concepts are normative of the Greek model of virtue theory, including *arête* (virtue), *phronesis* (practical or moral wisdom), and *eudaimonia* (happiness, or flourishing). Virtue leads to moral wisdom, which ultimately leads to "flourishing." *Eudaimonia* is characterized by a well-lived life, or the proper human life, which can only be lived when a person attends to the virtues. It is also characterized as fulfilling our purpose, although various theorists disagree on what the purpose of humanity is. Considering that Wesley believed the goal of human life is to love God and others, *eudaimonia* is reached when we are doing this. The dual definition of this word helps clarify some of Wesley's writings. He sometimes equated holiness with happiness—happiness in the sense of living a virtuous and loving life. Wesley was deeply indebted to Aristotle's discussion of character development and virtue.[3] A brief summary of the Aristotelian tradition's ethical thought will be helpful here.

Aristotle believed that there are four causes in all objects, including the human being. There is the **material cause**, which asks the question of why something does what it does; Aristotle believed that the answer to this question was found in the tendencies of the object itself. For example, marble is the material cause for a statue. The **efficient cause** is the source of motion or change. The sculptor is the efficient cause of the marble becoming a statue. But there are still deeper causes that are definitive not only of tendencies or actions but also of nature and purpose. The **formal cause** is the nature of an object, and the **final cause** of an object determines its end, or its **telos**. The final cause asks the question, What is the purpose to which the object (person) is drawn? The formal cause is first pure potentiality that seeks to be actualized. The final cause is actualized through habituation.

Again, Aristotle believed that the telos of the human being is *eudaimonia* or happiness. But happiness or fulfillment only comes when we *act* what we know. We may know what the virtues are, and know that we are to fulfill them, and even know that our happiness depends on enacting them. But unlike Plato (who believed that "to know the good is to do the good"), Aristotle realized that to understand the virtuous life does not necessarily result in virtuous living. There is some aspect of *willing* (and willing for the right reasons) to be virtuous that is necessary, as well as the need to habituate through virtuous action the actualization of a virtuous character.

Aristotle elaborates on four types of character that potentially emerge from this tension between knowing and doing. First, there is the **vicious character**. In this instance, the person knows what he or she ought to do but chooses to do otherwise, with no remorse. The **incontinent character** describes the person who knows what ought to be done, chooses in fact to do it, but then fails to follow through, and does not act in the way decided upon. The **continent character** is closer to the ideal but misses it because of motivation. This character knows the good and does the good but only out of duty—out of the demands of the "ought to." Each of the three characters described above evidences some lack of internal harmony. The harmonious life only comes to those with **virtuous character**. The truly virtuous character knows the good and does the good for the sake of virtue itself, not out of the internal pressure of guilt, the external pressure of a fear of punishment, or even a promise of reward. The virtuous person acts in complete harmony with the knowledge he or she possesses, out of an internal desire for good, for good's sake.

Aristotle believed that there are numerous virtues for the person to seek in order to be counted as a virtuous person—virtues such as courage, temperance, generosity, and truthfulness. One solitary act of courage, however, does not make a person courageous. To become truly courageous, a person must habituate courageous acts until they become natural or actualized in his or her being. It is also important, according to Aristotle, to learn courage through watching another courageous person; thus community is crucial in Aristotle's system. So understanding or knowledge is balanced with sustained and consistent action (ethical virtue). This is the truly happy (holy) person.

Wesley's work shows deep indebtedness to this Aristotelian ethical paradigm. Again, for Wesley holiness results in happiness. And there is a deep, interpenetrating connection between holiness character and holiness acts. But how does Wesley articulate this connection? He uses the language of "tempers" and "affections." But these are truly understood only by examining Wesley's moral psychology as a whole.

▶ WESLEY'S MORAL PSYCHOLOGY[4]

Prior to Wesley's century, Anglicanism was greatly influenced by what is known as the **intellectualist model** of ethical theory. This theory suggested that reason should be the superior human attribute in all decisions about morality, with the passions (or emotions) as something to be fought. But as empiricism gained in popularity, so did the idea that emotions (or affections) are also extremely important to any internal motivation to act ethically. "This emphasis on the indispensable contribution of the affections to human action was not limited to philosophers in 18th century England. It found strong advocates as well among theologians seeking to counteract the emerging deistic reductions of religion."[5] This change away from the intellectualist model found great approval by Wesley.

Wesley developed a moral psychology that included the vital place of affections. His list of elements in the human being as related to ethical behavior included the understanding, the **will**, **liberty**, and **conscience**. A crucial distinction from an intellectualist model is what Wesley meant by the will. Wesley believed that the will was influenced not only by reason but also by the affections, perhaps *only* by the affections. That is, willing was more a function of affections than an act of "rational self-determination."[6] What did Wesley mean by the word "affections"?

Affections are made up of motivating **inclinations**, rather than just emotions. We act out of our affections. Also, theologically speaking, they are influenced by outside causes, most particularly by grace. Wesley did not stop there, however. He believed that the affections are habituated into enduring dispositions that he called "tempers." The best example of a temper was love for God and neighbor. When love is enacted, this holy temper becomes holy action—at times expressing itself in the negation of something for the sake of the other, but most often as positive loving action.

David Hume (1711-76) introduced an idea that challenged Wesley to clarify himself further. Hume, in a direct counter to the intellectualist model, believed that the passions (emotions, affections) are what motivate and direct us in our actions. But Hume placed the will so much in the passions that what he was suggesting seemed to negate free will. We act almost in a determined way with no ability to act counter to what our passions tell us. It is here that we must assert that Wesley, although he used the language of affections as where will resides, distinguished between will and liberty. Although affections can be habituated into good tempers so that we might say that we will out of those tempers, we can always act against the tempers that we have developed. Liberty is the function of deciding how to act in any situation. Habituated affections and tempers can aid our will in deciding to act for the good, but we can always act otherwise because we also possess liberty. This distinction between the will and liberty kept Wesley from the intellectualist model on one side, and Hume's determinism on the other. Most important for our purposes here is that Wesley believed that our actions flow out of our internal life. Strongly stated, holy inward tempers are the only way to truly live a holy life.

Our moral inclinations and dispositions will affect the way we live. This keeps us from believing that we come to every individual moral decision morally neutral. We are influenced by our inclinations, which have been habituated either toward holiness or toward sin. Our dispositions are influenced by our receptivity of God's grace, which we must nurture. In this way, Wesley introduces an external force, namely grace, that Aristotle excludes. But this external grace is quickly integrated into the person to such a degree that we can maintain Aristotle's condition that an internal motivation is necessary if we are to possess a truly virtuous character. "Wesley held [that] it is only in response to our experiences of God's gracious love for us, shed abroad in our hearts by the Holy Spirit, that the human affection of love for God and others is awakened and grows."[7]

> Perhaps the best way to capture Wesley's affectional view of entire sanctification, then, is to say that he was convinced that the Christian life did not have to remain a life of perpetual struggle. He believed that both Scripture and Christian tradition attested that God's loving grace can transform sinful human lives to the point where our own love for God and others becomes a free response. Christians can aspire to take on the disposition of Christ, and live out that disposition within the constraints of our human infirmities. To deny this possibility would be to deny the sufficiency of God's empowering grace—to make the power of sin greater than that of grace.[8]

▶ CHARACTER DEVELOPMENT AND CHRISTIAN PERFECTION

From Wesley's perspective, holiness begins when we come to Christ initially and are initially sanctified (see chap. 7). It could be said that our orientation is reordered toward God's original design—our proper telos, or potentiality for true holiness and agape love. This is an awakening to which we respond. As we grow in grace, our potentiality begins to progress on a long process toward actualization. Our potentiality is more and more actualized every day as we participate in the life of God. Grace enables change in our affections. Synergistic grace implies that through our intentional cooperation with God our affections become tempers over time (and are deeply impacted through attending to the **means of grace**). It is out of the tempers that our actions flow. We then continue to live out of these inclinations in the form of holy love. "God's grace does not infuse holy tempers instantaneously *complete*. God awakens the 'seed' of every virtue. These seeds then strengthen and take shape as we responsively grow in grace."[9] The seeds bear fruit in our actions, in holy living. This is why theologians often pair these two phrases when describing Wesley's scheme: holiness in *heart and life*. We change within, or more appropriately, we *are changed* within (by grace) so that we act outwardly in life from a love-inclined heart and a holy character. Sanctification, in all its aspects, is the God-enabled actualization of the potentiality of holy love.

A CHANGED CHARACTER

Grace changes our character, if we receive it and cooperate with it. The result will be actions that parallel that character. In "The Character of a Methodist" Wesley clearly shows us that our actions spring out of what God has done within us, instantaneously, and over time as we mature. The character of a Methodist:

Loves God with all his [or her] heart, soul, mind, and strength
In everything gives thanks
[Has a] heart lifted to God at all times
Loves every person as his [or her] own soul
[Is] pure in heart
[Evidences that] God reigns alone
Keeps *all* the commandments
Does all to the glory of God
Adorns the doctrine of God in all things[10]

But what does entire sanctification do in our development of holy affections, dispositions, tempers, and character? We have discussed entire sanctification as an aspect of Christian perfection, and Christian perfection as purity of intentions. Intentions, like dispositions and inclinations, require both a desire to do "the good" (and for Wesley, the good is love for God and neighbor) and willful action toward that desire. We have suggested, like Wesley, that our intentions are made pure through our synergistic cooperation with God's sanctifying work in the heart. If we apply this to an affectional model, we can also say that our inclinations and dispositions are bent toward the good (love) by the sanctifying work of God in which we actively participate. Wesley speaks of love as *ruling* our tempers. Entire sanctification breaks "the power of cancelled sin," and sin no longer *reigns*. In this sense, love replaces sin as the motivating factor in the good we actualize.

Does this mean that our inclinations were not being molded toward the good prior to entire sanctification? No. From the moment of our new birth we, in cooperation with grace, attempt to habituate love. But "sin remained." Entire sanctification is, in effect, our opening ourselves more deeply (entirely) to God's grace, and in response to our consecration, God breaks any *reigning sin* and replaces it with *ruling love*. Does this mean that our inclinations are fully perfected (in an absolute sense) and that growth is no longer necessary? No. As stated throughout this book, the sanctified life is more than a sinless life. Love is consistently present and active. Love can be more and more habituated through loving action (again, in cooperation with grace). It never reaches a completed state because opportunities for love never cease. And as with all the virtues, the more they are acted upon, the *freer* a person becomes to act out the virtue as if it is "second nature."[11] And to point out once again, where Christian virtue ethics far excel Aristotle is that grace is emphasized. Habituation is never a Pelagian act of self-will.

Like practicing a musical instrument makes playing easier and easier, and in a sense gives the musician the freedom to play at will, so also repeated acts of honesty, courage, or love make a person honest, courageous, or loving, and free to act from the heart, from the character he or she has developed. God makes us holy. We are then to consistently live like holy people because internally we have become holy people. This entails an instantaneous event that is then perpetuated. Entire sanctification makes it possible for our holy inclinations to grow more freely, without previous encumbrances. But always in the end we retain liberty at any point to choose to go against our new nature and choose to sin. If we continue to choose to sin, we begin to feed sinful inclinations once again. We always have freedom to choose.

Wesley also spoke of this crisis and process of becoming holy as taking on the disposition of Christ. This has a different connotation than being Christlike. It is possible to envision Christlikeness as the stringing together of personal choices to act as Christ would act. In a way, this would fit an intellectualist model that focuses on our decisions. Having the disposition of Christ, on the other hand, implies that not only our actions but also our inclinations have been affected to such a degree that we act out of a Christlike character. The question becomes then, not "What would Jesus do?" but "What was Jesus like?" Implied here is that while on earth Jesus acted out of who he was.[12]

Virtue ethics, rather than helping us determine what we ought to *do*, asks how and who we are to *be*. Apart from any religious appropriation, those who purport virtue ethics also demand that virtue can be developed by any common person; one should never imply that only the elite (whether in knowledge or cleverness) can be virtuous. Likewise, the virtue envisioned in Holiness theology must find connection to the lives of real people. Holiness theology must be joined to human life. One way of making this connection is through the means of grace in the life of a Christian and the church. To these Wesleyan means we now turn.

▶ Connecting the Means to the End

In Wesley's mature thought, he strongly admonished Methodists, particularly Methodist ministers and teachers, to emphasize both entire sanctification and progressive sanctification and to neglect neither. In recent years, there has been a revived interest in Wesley's understanding of the day-by-day walk in the Christian journey. This has come both from a renewed emphasis on the means of grace in the Wesleyan tradition, as well as a great interest in the topic of spiritual formation. We must note here that grace should not be seen as an abstract concept. As stated in previous chapters, grace can be equated with the activity of the Holy Spirit; as such we should see the means of grace as the means to experience and be nurtured by the very presence of God. This presence is what spiritually forms us; it spiritually *transforms* us into the holy likeness of Christ.

At the very heart of Wesley's understanding of Christian growth is his concept of the means of grace. He wrote: "By 'means of grace' I understand outward signs, words, or actions, ordained by God, to be ordinary channels whereby he might convey to persons prevenient, justifying, or sanctifying grace. . . . [Further,] all who desire the grace of God are to wait for it in the means that he has given."[13] The "means" are the ways in which we open ourselves to experience God's love and grace in our lives. It is crucial to understand that we do not earn God's grace in any way by attending to the means of grace. Wesley is clear that nothing but the blood of Christ atones for sin. But participating in the means is the way that was ordained if we are to grow in our relationship with God.

In light of our recent discussion on character development and virtue, we must strongly state at the outset that *why* we participate in the means of grace is just as important as what we specifically do. As God purifies our intentions, and as our inclinations and dispositions grow toward the virtue of love, the "why" of our obedience is transformed. We move from duty to desire. For Wesley, the more we participate in the means of grace, the more we want to participate in the means of grace, through which we draw closer to God. Too often persons remain only in the duty phase and view the means as regimented discipline simply to prove their loyalty to God. But Wesley's understanding takes us beyond sheer obedience for obedience's sake, beyond any type of works righteousness; Wesley's understanding emphasizes that participating in the means is the precise way we grow and are transformed. The means of grace are exactly what changes our affections, tempers, dispositions, and inclinations, in that God's transforming grace reaches us through the means "God has ordained." Or put differently, we become who we are created to be in Christ by attending to the means of grace.

In a way it is unfortunate that the words "spiritual disciplines" are sometimes substituted for "means of grace." It is not as if participating in the means of grace requires no discipline. But it is more than discipline. Spiritual disciplines have been explained using athletics as an analogy. Just as we must train our bodies well through discipline in order for us to be successful in sports, we must train ourselves spiritually through discipline in order to be successful as Christians. Paul himself uses the athlete as an example of perseverance. But if we are not careful, we might begin to think that we keep ourselves spiritually fit the way we keep ourselves physically fit. God then becomes just a coach to give us pointers here and there. The analogy breaks down when we need to talk about the coach being *inside* the athlete, giving the athlete all of his or her strength. "Means of grace" avoids this analogical breakdown.

Participating in the means of grace serves to remind us that all we do, all we are, and all we become is only possible through the grace of God within us through the presence of the Holy Spirit. Yes, sometimes such participation looks like discipline. But it is never our discipline alone that creates and maintains our Christlike character. Duty and discipline can focus our attention on our own efforts and away from the gracious activity of God in all facets of our lives.

THE MEANS OF GRACE

General Means of Grace
1. Universal obedience
2. Keeping all the commandments
3. Watching
4. Denying ourselves
5. Taking up our cross daily
6. Exercising the presence of God

Prudential Means of Grace
1. Particular rules or acts of holy living
2. Class and band meetings
3. Prayer meetings, covenant services, watch night services, love feasts
4. Doing all the good one can, doing no harm
5. Visiting the sick
6. Reading devotional classics and edifying literature

Instituted (Particular) Means of Grace
1. Prayer
2. Searching the Scriptures
3. Fasting, or abstinence
4. Christian conference
5. The Lord's Supper

There are three categories into which Wesley has placed certain activities. There are the general, the prudential, and the instituted (or particular) means of grace. This is how Wesley categorized Christian activities that have deep spiritual benefit. The **general means of grace** include universal obedience and keeping the commandments, watching, denying ourselves, taking up our cross, and exercising the presence of God.

Universal obedience and keeping the commandments are vital in maintaining and fostering a relationship with God. But it is a means of grace that needs to be understood. We must remind ourselves again that we are not earning grace through works or any type of works righteousness. Consider it this way. The means of grace are like a funnel or a channel that allows God's grace to flow into our lives. If we live in disobedience or continue to break the commandments of God, it is not as if God then withholds grace. Rather, we have blocked the channel through our own action. In this case, repentance is the means by which we open the channel again—open ourselves again to receive the grace we need. So if we offend God by direct disobedience, we need the forgiving grace of God, and repentance is the way we synergistically cooperate with God. Obedience and keeping the commandments, then, keep the channel open between us and the God of mercy and compassion.

Watching is the intentional act of seeking God. It implies that we are looking for God's activity in the world. We are to have our eyes fixed on what is "unseen" to a greater degree than on what is "seen" (2 Cor. 4:18). But it is too easy to forget this activity of watching, and go through our day without purposefully looking for the hand of God in our lives, in the lives of those around us, indeed, in the world. In light of our strong belief in God's prevenient grace, we should expectantly hope to see such work. Too often, sadly, we have been trained to be acutely aware of the activity of the devil around us, rather than the activity of the Holy Spirit. But watching is a means of grace that should be nurtured and deepened. This intentional attitude keeps us attuned and the channel of God's grace open.

By denying ourselves, Wesley believed that we can draw closer to God when distractions are willingly set aside. Self-denial was covered at length in the previous chapter as it relates to our ability to love others as Christ loves them. In this context, self-denial is a means of grace because it also keeps the channel open. This type of self-denial has a rich history particularly in the writings of those in the early church. They endeavored to detach themselves from worldly concerns, even legitimate concerns, in order to be better able to pursue God. This detachment is needed just as much today, if not more. In a culture often saturated with entertainment and consumerism, the ideas of simplicity, silence, and purposeful detachment are certainly countercultural. It has been said that persons who live in such a culture are attempting to numb themselves from their own generalized anxiety.[14] If nothing else, self-denial can reveal to us how dependent we are on activities that keep us numbly occupied. The simple exercise of silence can show us exactly how much we have come to need noise. Self-denial in countless forms can serve to refocus our attention and to renew our entire devotion and dependence on God.

By "taking up our cross," Wesley believed we could also draw closer to God and God's purposes, first by enduring hardships and suffering and second by doing things that go against our natural inclinations. This second meaning is the opposite form of self-denial. By feeding the poor, visiting those in prison, or taking care of widows and orphans (Matt. 25:34-36 and James 1:27), our attention is drawn to what really matters. This is a means of grace because not only do we help them, but also we ourselves benefit from a proper perspective of what it means to be a disciple of Christ.

Exercising the presence of God is the practice of being conscious of God throughout the day. This is related to watching, but different. When watching, we are looking for the activity of the Holy Spirit around us. When practicing the presence of God, we are directly communing with God in all we do. This idea was made popular by a monk named Brother Lawrence. He attempted to be aware of God's presence in every minute of every day. This did not mean that he only sat and prayed all day. But he took God with him, so to speak, into all his daily activities. From working in the garden to washing dishes, he was aware that God was with him always. Again, in light of all the distractions we face, this is a very difficult aim to achieve. But it is important to attempt it. We may not practice God's presence perfectly, but any effort is better than no effort. If we affirm that it is the very presence of God in our lives that defines spirituality and aids Christian growth, practicing that God is with us is just as important as trusting that God is with us. Many who have attempted such practice testify that it changed their hearts and lives.

For Wesley the **prudential means of grace** were those that developed over time and have been recognized as prudent or wise actions in the life of growth in grace. Most involve other persons, rather than being strictly private acts of devotion.

These include band and class meetings (small groups) where accountability is stressed. Fellowship with other believers in a variety of contexts was crucial for Wesley and should be today. Only when we engage in genuine and meaningful relationships can we grow toward our full potential. Love is never an abstract concept. And Wesley was very aware that not only do we need to love, but we also need the love of other Christians to encourage and support us. Wesley also believed that prayer meetings are a means of grace that bring the body of Christ into purposeful prayer; such communal prayer differs from our own solitary prayers. Prayer meetings are an expression of agreeing together for God's will to be done, which the New Testament says is especially efficacious.

We find this communal feature also in Wesley's covenant and watch night services, which call us to reaffirm within the church our commitment to be entirely devoted to God. Wesley's covenant service became extremely important for the Methodist people. It was a liturgy they recited, but never in a cold form. It is a deeply moving service that very much shows the warmheartedness of the Methodist tradition. Traditionally watch night services occur on New Year's Eve when people gather to pledge another year of devotement and service to God.

Love feasts were also a time of communal renewal in Wesley's Methodism. These became controversial. Wesley intended these feasts to be a type of testimony service to build up the leaders and the mature Christians. A person had to be in good standing and worthy to receive a ticket in order to attend. There was some protest as to why anyone should be excluded from these meetings. But Wesley maintained that mature Christians and leaders sometimes needed an opportunity to build each other up. Wesley was insightful at this point. Often leaders in the church spend the majority of their time taking care of the needs of the rest of the congregation (or societies, in Wesley's day). So opportunities are needed for leaders to be fed and nourished. This was Wesley's intent, and still good advice today.

Another means of grace for Wesley was "doing all the good one can, and doing no harm." Wesley is attributed for saying the following: "Do all the good you can, by all the means you can, in all the ways you can, in all the places you can, at all the times you can, to all the people you can, as long as ever you can."[15] Wesley is often quoted for the wisdom of these words. But Wesley did not propose this way of life as wise only; acting for the good is also personally transforming.

Wesley mentioned visiting the sick specifically. Why single out this good act? Clearly the sick need to be visited. This is central to any legitimate theology of pastoral care. But how is it a means of grace? In a sense, visiting the sick reminds us of our own frailty, and at times our own mortality, and in doing this we inevitably turn our minds and hearts toward the eternal. Sometimes the sick evidence God's grace in deep ways that can only affect our own sense of God's presence and sustaining power. For those who are sick and are hopeless, we can be agents of God's love and mercy. Any time we are a conduit of God's love to others, we ourselves can experience that divine love in our own hearts.

Reading devotional classics and edifying literature is also a prudential means of grace. Wesley took great care to provide his people with significant Christian writing from throughout the centuries of Christianity because he believed that God would grace those who pondered the wisdom that had come before. The grand, multivolume *Christian Library* was one of Wesley's greatest contributions to Methodist clergy education and to the spiritual nurture of laity. Although the whole collection is no longer published, individual works are still available. Books written by contemporary writers can certainly be inspiring, but like Wesley, we should be careful to also read books that have stood the test of time—sometimes centuries.

By the **instituted** or "particular" **means of grace**, Wesley refers to those means that Christ models for his disciples or directly asks them to do. Prayer and searching the Scriptures are foundational to all spiritual (trans)formation. It has been said that prayer is to the spiritual life as breathing is to the physical body. Without it, we do not survive. Wesley believed that private prayer is only one form of prayer as a means of grace. He also stressed the importance of public and family prayer.

Another fundamental means of grace is searching the Scriptures. The word "searching" implies a meditative reading in which the Holy Spirit inspires our hearts. This is different from the study of Scripture for the purpose of doctrinal truth, although such study is important. If prayer is our breath, Scripture is our food. Too often people read their Bibles out of a sense of duty. But using the analogy here, eating food is not a duty we perform. We need food in order to survive and thrive. From it we gain necessary nutrients and the energy we need to do anything. Our bodies let us know when we need to eat. If we do not eat, we become weak and start feeling the sensation of deep hunger that can lead to starvation. However, there comes a point in the starvation process when we no longer feel hungry. In a similar way, we can neglect the spiritual food we need till we no longer feel spiritually hungry. Perhaps like the physical body, it is then that we are on the verge of spiritual death. If we read our Bibles because we are supposed to or as an act of sheer obedience, we misunderstand searching the Scriptures and miss its purpose as a key means of grace.

Wesley names fasting as an instituted means of grace and not just under the prudential category of general self-denial. Wesley practiced fasting food often, at least weekly. (Besides the spiritual benefit of drawing closer to God, some have seen this as perhaps contributing to his unusually long life.) The practice of fasting seems to be waning in emphasis in the church today. The concept of prayer and fasting seems to be understood only by older generations. Fasting a meal and giving the money for that meal to the needy is more common now than fasting for the sake of seeking earnestly the heart and will of God, or as an expression of penitence or spiritual desire. But either way—to help the needy or as a sign of particular devotion—fasting is a means of grace to us.

The next instituted means of grace we refer to here is Christian conference. Wesley meant by this *Christian* conversation, or conversation about our spirituality, not just two or more Christians talking about the weather. As Christians speak about God together, grace is poured out upon them. It is fascinating, however, that we can attend church week after week and never say a word about our own personal spiritual journey. We can easily walk into Sunday School, catch up on each other's weeks, even open the Bible together and study it—all without saying a spiritually authentic thing about ourselves, or without inquiring about the spiritual lives of those attending church with us. But Christian conversation, like all the means of grace, is an intentional, purposeful, and diligent act. It is an act of love as we share our faith and live life together in the very presence of the Holy Spirit.[16] The community of believers is intended to be a means of mutual support, encouragement, and strength. To experience this, we must foster spiritual vulnerability.

The final means of grace we will discuss is the Lord's Supper (Holy Communion, Eucharist[17]). Rob Staples, in his book *Outward Sign and Inward Grace,* strongly reminds the Wesleyan-Holiness Movement of its tradition and the appropriate understanding of the Christian sacraments. In this important work, he states that the Lord's Supper should be seen as (which implies it *is*) a sacrament of sanctification. An extended quotation from Staples's book will serve us well at this point:

> Sanctification, which for Wesley has instantaneous aspects, is also a "progressive work, carried on in the soul by slow degrees, from the time of our first turning to God" [*Works* 6:74]. One important means of furthering that sanctifying work is participation in the Lord's Supper. [William] Willimon is correct in saying:
>
> > The Lord's Supper is a "sanctifying ordinance," a sign of the continuity, necessity, and availability of God's enabling, communal, confirming, nurturing grace. Our characters are formed, sanctified, by such instruments of continual divine activity in our lives.[18]
>
> Persons brought up in Wesleyan Holiness churches have generally not been well instructed as to the potential of the Eucharist as a means for the promotion of holiness. For them, the very normality, regularity, and ritualistic nature of the sacrament militates against such an understanding. The invitation to the Lord's Supper is not particularly heard as a call to holiness. . . .
>
> > [And yet] Sanctification asserts that the Christian life ought not to be formed in a haphazard way. It takes constant, life-long attention, habits, and care to employ this character. The normality, the constancy of the Eucharist is part of its power. This meal need

not be special, nor exhilaratingly meaningful (though sometimes it is both). This is the normal food of Christians, the sustaining, nourishing stuff of our life"[19] . . .

. . . Whereas baptism is the sacrament of *initiation* and consequently is not repeated, the sacrament of *sanctification* is to be celebrated again and again from baptism until death.[20]

In Wesley's sermon "The Duty of Constant Communion," he strongly states that the Eucharist should be celebrated "constantly." He argued tenaciously against those who feared that its frequency would diminish its efficacy: "If we do it too often it will lose its meaning."[21] Wesley could argue against this way of thinking because he saw Holy Communion as an extremely significant *means of grace.* Should we pray less frequently because we fear it will lose its meaning? Should we read our Bibles less, go to church less, minister to others less? Of course not. Then why fear that celebrating Communion often will make it less meaningful?[22]

The Eucharist in Wesley's eyes is a means by which the soul is "peculiarly nourished." This does not mean that Wesley believed in a transubstantiation or real change of the elements.[23] The act, which involves memory as well as the direct activity of the Holy Spirit, is an immediate way (as in immediacy) of participating in the ongoing transforming grace of God. As such, it should not be neglected. And yet, as Staples suggests, it seems as though those of us in the Holiness tradition have not made this connection. However, it is now being recognized historically that at the close of revivals and camp meetings across the country in the 19th century, Communion was often served. Perhaps these Holiness prescribers were not as disconnected to Wesley's understanding of the sacrament of sanctification as assumed. Either way, a renewed focus on the Eucharist is needed as we preach holiness in the 21st century, for it is a vital means of progressive sanctification and growth in grace.

▶ CHARACTER IN A POSTMODERN WORLD

Long gone are the days when religion was reduced to what we might reason about God. This Enlightenment-based modern paradigm is hardly ever permitted by those who have recognized and embraced the philosophical shift known as **postmodernism.** Modernism was firmly planted in the tendency to exult human reason over against human experience and human emotion. Even empiricists were systematically rational about their discoveries in the modern period! But "reason" over "affect" is no longer the dominant mode of thought. Although some still struggle, and struggle hard, to keep modernism alive and well, it really is dying if not dead.

The postmodern understanding expressed here calls into question the legitimacy of the intellectualist model of moral psychology. The intellectualist model leans strongly into a modernist vision. In contrast, Wesley's affectional moral psychology is in many ways akin to postmodern thought. In the book *John Wesley on Religious Affections*, Gregory Clapper makes the observation that while Christianity for Wesley involved right doctrine (orthodoxy) and right action (orthopraxy), there is something deeper in his vision of faith. Clapper writes, "What is missing [in these two descriptions] is what I term ortho*kardia*—the right heart. . . . Without such a 'right heart' there is no Christianity on Wesley's terms."[24] Similarly, Theodore Runyon first suggested the term "orthopathy" when trying to describe Wesley's experiential model of Christianity.[25] Wesley himself directly stated that true religion is never a matter of intellectual assent only. By itself the rational mind could only produce "faith of a devil . . . , a train of ideas in the head."[26] It is the heart that believes. The heart is moved to action. Simply, the heart is the home of the affections.

Whatever term is employed—"orthokardia" or "orthopathy"—the warmheartedness of Wesleyanism sets it apart from other traditions. It mediates between faith as a set of doctrines (however true) and faith as a set of actions (however noble). All belief and all activity must come from the heart. That is, faith is a deep trust in Christ that transforms who we are so that we act out of the character Christ has formed within us.

This emphasis on the heart, as well as on experience and the equal place of the emotions in Wesley's affectional psychology, match the desires of postmodern Christians. They want to emphasize an experiential faith that leads to meaningful action in a broken world. They seek genuine and authentic relationships, with God and others. They focus much more on *being* and *becoming* as the essence of human life, instead of just *thinking* or *doing*—or instead of either intellectual belief or blind moral action as constituting Christianity. Perhaps above all, they seek out as their models those who are true in character rather than those who hold true concepts. They hunger and thirst after a righteousness defined by Christlike love. Yet this *is* the very message of holiness.

If holiness has ever been relevant, it is relevant now. Perhaps what we need to communicate well is not a renewed emphasis on crisis moments or a renewed interest in progressive sanctification. Perhaps what we need to communicate this doctrine of Holiness well in the here and now is to live genuinely what we already know—live it fully and live it deeply, from the heart. Living it is the only way to save its credibility.

It is possible to talk holiness into a grave. To know its content requires a corresponding obligation to do its truth. When this fails the doctrine becomes a head-stone to the grave of those who have betrayed it.[27]

SUMMARY STATEMENTS

1. Wesley was deeply concerned about character development and looked to Aristotle and the moral theology of the Thomist tradition that followed Aquinas in his own views.

2. Wesley finds a middle way between an intellectualist model of ethics and a type of ethical determinism.

3. Wesleyan-Holiness theology believes holy, loving action can only really come from a holy, loving character. We are to live from the inside out.

4. The means of grace include the general, prudential, and instituted means of grace.

5. Holy Communion should be seen as a sanctifying sacrament.

6. Wesley's understanding of affectional character development and the means of grace are compatible with postmodern Christianity.

QUESTIONS FOR REFLECTION

1. Does a person's motivation make a difference in the quality of his or her action?

2. What might it mean to live from the "inside out" or "from the heart"?

3. What means of grace have been the most helpful in your spiritual growth?

4. How is Communion a sacrament of sanctification?

FURTHER READING

Clapper, Gregory. *John Wesley on Religious Affections*. Metuchen, NJ: Scarecrow Press, 1989.

Knight, Henry. *The Presence of God in the Christian Life*. Metuchen, NJ: Scarecrow Press, 1992.

Staples, Rob. *Outward Sign and Inward Grace: The Place of Sacraments in Wesleyan Spirituality*. Kansas City: Beacon Hill Press of Kansas City, 1991.

Steele, Richard. *"Gracious Affection" and "True Virtue" According to Jonathan Edwards and John Wesley*. Metuchen, NJ: Scarecrow Press, 1994.

TWELVE

HOLINESS AS LOVE

LEARNER OBJECTIVES

Your study of this chapter will help you to:

1. Connect holiness and love

2. Identify the essential characteristics of God's love for us

3. Understand how we best love God

4. Identify the essential qualities of our love for others

KEY WORDS

Praxis

Shema

Entire devotion

As suggested throughout this book, any definition of holiness must include love. We could go so far as to say that *holiness is (holy) love,*[1] both in reference to God and to the holiness that God works in us. We have put forward that God's most essential characteristic is love. "God *is* love," John says simply and yet most profoundly. We may modify God's love with the word "holy." But this adds little to an understanding of God because by nature God's love is holy. The modifier "holy" does remind us, however, that God is beyond us as other than us. God *is* holy and always different from us in nature.

And yet the scriptural message of salvation is that this holy God comes near to us, most powerfully in the incarnation of the Son and most perpetually through the presence of the Holy Spirit. The Wholly Other becomes "just as we are" because of love (Heb. 4:15), while never sacrificing the quality of otherness, even in the incarnation. And yet there is more to the message.

The God of holy love desires to make us holy as well. Here it is absolutely essential (when speaking of human holiness) that we do add the word "love." Holiness without love is no holiness at all.[2] We have discussed at length why this is so in previous chapters. If we simply define human holiness as sinlessness, we have defined it only by an absence (namely, the absence of sin). But holiness is never a passive state; nor is it vacuous. There must be the presence of love in the holy life to which God calls us. Holiness and love cannot be separated. In this sense, this is a book as much about love as it is a book about holiness.

However, the close reader will realize that nowhere in the book has love been defined completely. Certainly "we love because [God] first loved us" (1 John 4:19) and love is most clearly seen in the love of God in Christ. But in reality, on a human level, a full comprehension and explanation of love seems an impossible task. While we could certainly list the qualities of love as set forth in scriptures such as 1 Cor. 13, and as important as such definitions are, we tend to "know" love intuitively. And the intuitive is hard to gather up into concrete propositions. But we aim here toward a definition nonetheless. With that intention, we will first explore what it might mean to place love at the center of Wesleyan-Holiness theology. This exploration will serve a summational as well as a directive purpose.

▶ LOVE AT THE CENTER

It is critical to our discussion of love and holiness to understand that placing love at the center will have profound effects on a theology of Holiness. If love is firmly placed at the center of its theology, such theology will evidence certain qualities. Five are elaborated here.[3]

1. A strong theology of Holiness will be "affectual" as well as cognitive and behavioral

There is something within us that knows that love is more than what we think or even what we do. The cognitive and behavioral aspects of love are important: we know what love is through rational analysis, and we affirm that love is best expressed through volitional actions—love acts. But understanding love only from these two perspectives takes the heart out of love and, in essence, the heart out of Wesleyan-Holiness theology. That is, our affections, which can be defined as habituated emotions (see chap. 11), influence our ability to love. Wesleyan-Holiness theology is never stoic; it does not seek to suppress the emotional element of life. It affirms that God uses our emotional experiences just as much as our rationality and our liberty. If love is at the center of Holiness theology, then we must recognize that love includes affect.

Love, then, includes emotions such as affection, delight, and even desire. Love feels true affection for the other. This makes love genuine and avoids any hint of love as mechanistic or diffused. God's grace makes heartfelt affection possible. Further, according to theologian Gary Charter, "Love as delight finds it a good thing—indeed, a wonderful thing—that the other exists; simply knowing of the other's reality can be a source of pleasure, even joy."[4] As God changes our inclinations from within, love becomes less laborious and more delightful. This is not to say that love does not still require much of us, even to the point of loving dutifully. But it does mean that God can instill joy, and thus fulfillment, in our love for others. In a similar way, love can also include desire.

"Love as desire seeks closeness, intimacy with the other, freely given, and acknowledges the value . . . of the gift of presence."[5] This desire is most often experienced in reciprocal relationships such as friendship (*philios*), the fellowship found in Christian community, or in the *eros* in marriage. These relationships especially can be a means of grace to us as we seek to love from a pure heart. Certainly, love always genuinely desires the best for any other and does not desire the other as object but always as subject. Overall, love (*eros, philios,* and even *agape*) involves the affections.

2. A strong theology of Holiness will be existentially relevant

Love is always existential. Love is not only felt affectually and affectionately but also experienced at the deepest levels of our being in the realm of meaning and purpose. We were created to love. This is our telos. But it is also our present calling. Love is the very definition of the *imago Dei* that God renews within us. The very purpose of our humanity is to love, and we are only truly human when we love by humanizing others and love our Creator above all else. Existential love takes us deeper than the superficiality of the law, or rules. Love fulfills the law. Further, to use Aristotle's model, we cannot truly love even if we have a *continent* character (i.e., the person who does the right thing but for the wrong reason). Only the virtuous person, who has been made virtuous through participation in God's grace, can love in the fullest sense.

Wesleyan-Holiness theology not only needs to be existentially directed but also needs to be existentially relevant. That is, Holiness theology must be correlated to the context in which it finds itself. True love for the other motivates this desire for correlation. Any theology can be logically coherent, perfectly organized, and precisely argued. But if it is not relevant to its context, it is of little worth. Even theology without love is nothing, only a "clanging cymbal" (1 Cor. 13:1). Holiness theology must be adapted. This does not threaten the integrity of the doctrine but allows it to come to life in the hearts and lives of the wide variety of people who encounter it. Keeping love at the center of Holiness theology is key to maintaining its relevancy.

Love toward other persons, then, includes the qualities of respect, identification, and equality. Love as respect recognizes the dignity and worth of every individual. Out of this respect, love goes all the way to the other. Just as God came all the way to us, love as respect is willing to reach toward the other without condition. There is no sense of waiting until the other meets us halfway. Each human being deserves this type of outflowing respect for no other reason than he or she, too, is created in the image of God and is loved equally by God. Love also seeks to identify with the other, to see life from his or her perspective, and to embrace him or her with empathy. There is a shared humanity in which we all participate, and thus love is never xenophobic. Ultimately, love recognizes the equality of all humans as created by God.

3. A strong theology of Holiness will be relational and communal

It is unfortunate that only certain persons have been labeled "relational theologians."[6] But if we consider the issue closely, who would want to identify himself or herself as an *un*relational theologian? Holiness abstracted from human relationships is nonsensical. Holiness has everything to do with how we relate to God and others and implies that the nature of these relationships is founded on love. Disembodied holiness is always a danger; indeed disembodiment negates true holiness. Love always cherishes the particular relationship.

It is also dangerous to separate holiness from community. The Christian community is essential to each person's pursuit of holiness and love. It is to this community that our love is uniquely owed.[7] There is no such thing as a solitary Christian life. God intends for the church to truly act as one and for every part to serve the rest. This is why the majority of Paul's references to love are in the context of the church—being the church together requires genuine love. It is also appropriate to identify the church as a whole as holy.

The love, then, that is central to a strong Holiness theology is always interdependent in the body of Christ. Here especially is where the reality of equality is mutually expressed (Gal. 3:28). According to 1 Cor. 12, each part, no matter how great or small, needs every other part. Love also is intense in affection and loyalty. Paul writes, "Be devoted to one another in brotherly love. Honor one another above yourselves. . . . Share with God's people who are in need" (Rom. 12:10, 13). The Greek word for "devoted" refers to the mutual affection found in a family (see ESV and NRSV) and implies a deep and reciprocal loyalty and trust. Love trusts. Love always perseveres. We might wonder what Paul would think about the "body amputations" that occur so frequently in a consumeristic culture where people change churches so frequently. Love, particularly within the body of Christ, "always trusts, always hopes, always perseveres" (1 Cor. 13:7). Love is loyal and devoted and ultimately eternal.

4. A strong theology of Holiness will be praxis-oriented

Holiness always involves what we do and how we act. Perhaps this is so obvious that it goes without saying. But it is possible theoretically to develop a theological framework that has little to do with human life. Early Scholastic theologians were accused of theological speculation to an extreme degree. It is feasible to imagine a nonpractical theology. But the heart of Wesleyan-Holiness theology is always and *necessarily* practical. From Wesley himself to Wesleyan theology today, every theological formation leads to the question: How does this apply to life?

The word **praxis** in theology does have certain connotations. The emphasis is usually on social transformation such as compassionate ministries or social justice issues, but it need not be limited to only these areas. "Praxis" can be an all-inclusive term that covers what theology *does*. A theology that is praxis-oriented cannot leave things as they were before. Theology, if it is relevant and true, is demonstrated, indeed embodied. We might say that a theology is validated by its praxis. Praxis is validated when human lives are impacted and changed for the good. Wesleyan-Holiness theology is a theology that works, a theology that is practical and transformative. Theology "puts on overalls" as one theologian has said.[8] It moves out from its center into the nooks and crannies of life. A theology of love brings those who need spiritual freedom and redemption to God, and God to them.

In the Wesleyan-Holiness tradition, during both the 18th and 19th centuries, praxis was predominantly directed toward the needy, principally toward the poor. Many within the tradition have called it back to its roots and to a renewal of the early praxis that seemed to naturally flow from its theology of Holiness. Steven Land uses a powerful illustration that should challenge us today. When he was a pastor, a person came to him and said he was very concerned about the poor. Land replied, "Really, you love the poor? Then give me three of their names and addresses. Tell me what you know about their kids, hopes, fears, and when and how you've prayed for them."[9] We cannot love the poor without loving poor people. Love is never an abstraction. Love as praxis is always personal. Love as praxis always extends to the neediest.

The love, then, that remains at the center of Wesleyan-Holiness theology includes the components of compassion, care, and service to the other. In the story of the Good Samaritan (Luke 10) Jesus describes the Samaritan by contrasting him to the more officially religious characters of the priest and the Levite. Unlike them, the Samaritan feels compassion for the wounded one left by the side of the road. Here the Greek word for compassion is *esplagxnisthē*. This word speaks of deep feeling that arises from the very "bowels" of our being. It is more than feelings of pity or sympathy. It is a word that implies deep motivation toward action, almost as if we are compelled to offer care to the one in need. The same word is used to describe Christ's compassion for us.

The word "compassion" itself is a compound word that means "to suffer with." Compassion entails entering into the suffering of the other. Love never waits by the sidelines. Love is moved (both affectually and behaviorally) toward action. Love cares for the needs of the other, even, as Christ's parable shows, the needs of the stranger. Love serves the other and takes on the attitude of servanthood. Love expresses itself through praxis.

5. A strong theology of Holiness will be integrated with spirituality

Wesleyan-Holiness theology is confessional theology. It never stands outside the confessional circle seeking to be solely, rationally objective.[10] Faith is necessarily subjective in nature. This is another way to say that any theology of Holiness must be integrated with spirituality, or personal piety—the theologian's included! Just as Holiness theology necessarily acts out in praxis, Holiness theology necessarily moves inward toward matters of devotion and trust. As we have suggested throughout this book, we live our Christianity from the inside out.

Spirituality involves intentionality. Spiritual life is only fully lived when reflected upon and intentionally nurtured. Spirituality is aided by an introspection that can lead to deliberate and purposeful change. Also, as presented in chapter 6, the theological anthropology of Wesleyan-Holiness theology emphasizes a holistic understanding of the human being. That is, a person's spirituality is not some compartmentalized aspect of himself or herself. The self is spiritual in its entirety, through and through. Personal piety must be an integral part of Wesleyan-Holiness theology.

And the love, then, that remains at the center is intentional and holistic. Love never succeeds by accident. Love comes out of an intentional willingness on behalf of the other. Also, one loves with one's whole being with a love that is directed toward the whole being of the other. This is why it is impossible to evangelize the soul but neglect a person's physical needs (James 2:14-17). Love surfaces from a deep, personal spirituality.

This section presented love in the context of a strong Holiness theology and focused generally on holy love for others. We now turn more precisely to God's love for us and to a more Trinitarian discussion of holy love. We will examine God's love in greater detail—God's love *for* us, *with* us, *in* us, and *through* us.

▶ GOD FIRST LOVED US

GOD'S LOVE FOR US: STEADFAST LOVE

The God of love is for us. This is one of the most foundational messages of the Bible and key to Holiness theology. But before we immediately jump to a discussion of *what* God has done for us, we must pause to consider the impact of this simple statement on its own. God is for us. God is not our enemy; even when we were estranged and lost, God was for us, and all of us. It is an essential aspect of Wesleyanism's Arminian roots to affirm that God is for the whole world, not just for certain elected people. God so loved the *whole* world.

Despite the way we are trained to think, sometimes from an early age, if we are in Christ, we are not vulnerable before God, for God is *for* us. Vulnerability has to do with the possibility of harm. Vulnerability has to do with fear. But God's love is completely trustworthy. God's love is entirely dependable. God's love is absolutely reliable. We may feel vulnerable before God, but John steps in and reassures us, "If anyone acknowledges that Jesus is the Son of God, God lives in him and he in God. And so we know and *rely* on the love God has for us. . . . There is no fear in love. But perfect love drives out fear, because fear has to do with punishment" (1 John 4:15-16, 18, emphasis added). And Paul reassures us:

> If God is for us, who can be against us. . . . Who shall separate us from the love of Christ? Shall trouble or hardship or persecution or famine or nakedness or danger or sword? . . . I am convinced that neither death nor life, neither angels nor demons, neither the present nor the future, nor any powers, neither height nor depth, nor anything else in all creation, will be able to separate us from the love of God that is in Christ Jesus our Lord. (Rom. 8:31, 35-39)

Because of love, God's power willingly concedes to God's compassion; God's wrath willingly surrenders to God's mercy; God's majesty willingly submits to God's grace, as God gives Jesus Christ up for mere human beings like us.

And so what has God done for us? The most profound activity of God for us, poured out from God's heart, is found on the cross. God's love in Christ justifies us, reconciles us, redeems us, and adopts us as children. God has given us everything we need for salvation, life, and godliness (2 Pet. 1:2-4), through the Son. God's gifts for us are given through him: prevenient, saving, and sanctifying grace and even creation itself, for "through him all things were made" (John 1:3). God is for us, always for us.

GOD'S LOVE WITH US: IMMANENT LOVE

Not only is God's love for us; God as love is also with us. From the symbols of God's presence in the Old Testament to the outpouring of the Holy Spirit at Pentecost, God has been a God with us. Christ as Emmanuel in the person of Jesus on earth was the immanent presence to whom all of salvation history pointed. God became human in order to truly be with us, in order to fully communicate with us, and to fully understand us from a position of actual empathy. From a Wesleyan-Holiness perspective, the incarnation is as important as the atonement. The Word dwelt among us. It is only through this immanent and embodied presence of God on earth that Jesus Christ can serve as our high priest—representing us to God through a true identification with us as human and representing God to us through true identity in nature with God. It is this scandal of God's particularity in Jesus that changed and continues to change everything.

God was potently with us in Jesus Christ. And God is perpetually with us through the Holy Spirit. And the Holy Spirit represents and transmits God's love for us. Pentecost is rightly seen as the birth of the faith of the church, because the Holy Spirit was manifested is particular ways. But the Holy Spirit continues to offer faith, give birth to faith, and nurture faith in the heart of every Christian. The Holy Spirit remains with us. The Holy Spirit is truly the one "called alongside" us as comforter. The Holy Spirit abides with us. God is with us. It is also the Holy Spirit that breathes life *into* us and transforms our perception from God as with us, to God as truly in us.

GOD'S LOVE IN US: TRANSFORMATIVE LOVE

God's love through Christ and the Holy Spirit is a love that is for us, with us, and also *in* us. One of the important emphases of Wesleyan-Holiness theology is the indwelling of the Holy Spirit. It is fair to say that there are other traditions that focus more on God as for us than on God within us. But one of the strengths of Wesley's early Methodism and the Wesleyan-Holiness Movement from its beginnings is a robust pneumatology that underscores what God does *in* us. And what does God do in us? God works our sanctification. God transforms us from within and breaks the power of cancelled sin. God purifies, perfects, and empowers us. God alters our inclinations, indeed, our very nature. God builds our holy character from within as we practice the virtues and participate in grace. God's grace not only forgives us but also changes us and genuinely sanctifies us.

But all these acts of God in us are *not* to be seen as ends in themselves! God sanctifies us so that we can be filled with love, to overflowing. We are to re-present Christ to those who cannot see him. We are to be the presence of Jesus Christ for those who cannot touch him; we are to be his body—his hands, his feet, his heart—to those who most need him. God's love transforms us so that God can love others through us.

GOD'S LOVE THROUGH US: OUTPOURING LOVE FOR NEIGHBOR

Hopefully this book has been able to communicate effectively that holiness is nothing if it is not lived out *through love* in the context of a broken world. Holiness is Christlikeness at its core.

> We know that we have come to know him if we keep his commands. Those who say, "I know him," but do not do what he commands are liars, and the truth is not in them. But if anyone obeys his word, love for God is truly made complete in them. This is how we know we are in him: Whoever claims to live in him must live as Jesus did. (1 John 2:3-6 TNIV)

God sanctifies us to make us authentic messengers of the gospel. God sanctifies us to purify and make effectual the love we offer to others. God sanctifies us to work through us. We have misread the Bible if we believe that God sanctifies us only for our own betterment or eternal salvation. There is no such thing as sanctified selfishness, even when it comes to heaven. Paul, in Rom. 9, says something almost unbelievable on this point: "I could wish that I myself were cursed and cut off from Christ for the sake of my brothers, . . . the people of Israel" (v. 3). Paul, who has lost everything to gain Christ, is even willing to lose Christ for the sake of those he loved so deeply. It would be tempting to doubt him, except that he makes a special point to preface this statement with these words, "I speak the truth in Christ—I am not lying, my conscience confirms it in the Holy Spirit" (vv. 1-2). He means this.

It is one thing to give up one's life. It is another to give up one's eternal destiny. Paul's words are an incredible expression of love. It is only the love of God through him that would make this sentiment possible. It is God's own self-emptying love that works not only in us but also through us. God's love for us, with us, and in us flows through us and enables us truly to love our neighbors. The fact that God first loved us also moves us to love God in return.

▶ LOVE AS ENTIRE DEVOTION TO GOD

How do we love God who first loved us? There have been good arguments that have suggested that the only way to love God *is* to love our neighbors. This is basically an interpretation that collapses the first and second commandments into one. This is one option. The way we express love to God is through service to others. But is this all there is to loving God? When Jesus identifies the two greatest commandments, he takes each from two distinct passages in the Old Testament.

For millennia before Jesus, the Israelites had been saying the **Shema**, found in Deut. 6: "Hear, O Israel: The LORD our God, the LORD is one. Love the LORD your God with all your heart and with all your soul and with all your strength" (vv. 4-5). It is from a passage in Leviticus that Jesus derives what he calls the second greatest commandment. That the Shema stands firmly on its own should at least make us pause and ask *how*—how do we love God with our whole being? It is here that some aspects of the love we direct toward fellow human beings fall away. Do we need to care for God's physical needs? Does God need compassion or empathy? Indeed, does God *need* anything from us? In some ways we do need to explain our love for God different from our love for others. But rather than pursue many possible paths of speculation on this point, we will address an aspect of love for God that is firmly planted, with roots in the Wesleyan-Holiness tradition.

One way that described the life of holiness in the 19th century as the Holiness Movement congealed was **entire devotion** to God. It became a centralized theme in the language of sanctification from the mid-1800s onward. At its heart, the phrase expressed a love for God so deep that it was unmatchable by any other experience. The phrase had several different connotations.

First of all, entire devotion was seen as the only proper and fitting response to God's love for us. If we truly understand God's love in a deeply personal way, and have known ourselves accepted and forgiven, a deep heartfelt love as entire devotion will be our response. As we grow in that understanding of what God has done for us and in us, our love for God will grow as well. According to Wesley's interpretation of Rom. 8, when Paul felt assured of God's love, the Spirit testified to his spirit that he was a child of God. And what was Paul's response to this deep sense of acceptance? He cried out to God with passion and a sense of intimacy, "Abba." In this sense, a deep affectual love for God will come from our experience of God's love for us. This is as true for today as it was for Paul, for Wesley, and for the Holiness Movement.

Second, entire devotion was directly connected to the complete consecration and surrender requisite of the experience of entire sanctification. Multiple metaphors were used to describe this type of absolute surrender. From Phoebe Palmer's placing all "on the altar of Christ" to being "sold out for Jesus," the Holiness Movement placed emphasis on a decision point where a total commitment was made. This moment was sometimes described as entire devotion to God. And it was this moment that allowed God to do the deeper work of entire sanctification. This moment played itself out in day-to-day life. Entire devotion meant a deep, consistent love for God. The phrase is just as meaningful today.

Third, this kind of complete surrender necessarily implied then, and implies now, that there are no rivals and no idols vying for God's appropriate place in the heart. This was a key emphasis early in the Holiness Movement. Love for God as entire devotion displays a singleness of heart toward God. This book has defined sin primarily as idolatry—idolatry of self or idolatry of others. Entire devotion is its cure.

Again, to use Phoebe Palmer as an example, Palmer was keenly aware that children and husbands vie for the "uppermost place in a woman's heart." She can make them into idols, and by doing so, she can prohibit the flow of sanctifying grace. But rather than taking the radical measure of leaving children and husband behind (as was the case in some instances of women ascetics in the early centuries of Christianity), or choosing not to marry at all (as John Wesley advised so many Methodist women), Palmer called for a radical internal shift. A woman's complete loyalty and entire devotion to God allows her to overstep traditional dependency on male religious authorities. God was her direct authority. Not coincidentally then, women in the Holiness Movement were allowed full ordination from the inception of most Holiness denominations. This came not only out of an entire devotion that defeated idols but also out of an entire devotion and desire to completely obey God (and God's calling on their lives). This of course applies to both men and women.

Entire devotion also demanded (and demands today) a full willingness to obey God with the attitude of "not my will, but thine be done." Love for God necessarily involves our obedience. To be clear, God's love for us is not dependent on our obedience, but our love for God is expressed in our desire to do God's will. "If you love me, you will obey what I command" (John 14:15). But as said above, our love for God does not come out of fear. Indeed, entire devotion is never inspired by fear. The entire devotion that leads to deeper levels of sanctification and Christian perfection changes the inclinations of our hearts. We keep God's commandments because we truly desire to do so. Obedience is a response of gratitude for the grace we have been given. And a deep reception of grace inspires not only obedience but also obedience over the long haul. That is, our gratitude for grace prompts a deep and lasting loyalty. Entire devotion is not a flash in the pan experience. Entire devotion denotes a lifetime commitment.

Entire devotion as an expression of love for God is put forward as unwavering loyalty. This is why Holiness theology, particularly in its 19th-century expression, was so optimistic about Christian perfection being maintained. Through our love and entire devotion to God, and through God's progressively sanctifying grace, our character changes and we are moved toward true virtuous living. As discussed at length in the previous chapter, this makes us freer to continue in the path of obedience and loyalty and makes it significantly harder to fall away (although our liberty can always make that choice). God's love and grace for us transforms a person into one capable of entire devotion, obedience, and loyalty over time. We might say that this is the place where Holiness theology can place its hope in a type of eternal security. It is not in God's sovereign election for some to be saved that makes us secure. It is the immensity of love that God lavishes on us, that changes us from within and makes us capable of a deep and loyal love in return. Love for God expresses itself as entire devotion.

▶ CONCLUSION

What then have we said about love? At the beginning of this chapter we suggested that love is affectual; love experiences emotions such as affection, delight, and desire. In the context of humanity in general (yet still speaking of the particular), we referred to love as respect for and identification with the other and as the acknowledgment of the equality of every person. In the context of Christian community, we pointed to a love that is interdependent, trusting, and loyal as each part is devoted to every other part of the body of Christ. Love meets the needs of the other, even the stranger, through compassion, care, and service. We have also suggested that Christian love, if it is to be truly Christian, arises out of a spirituality that loves intentionally and holistically. When we consider God's love for us, with us, in us, and through us, these characteristics expand even more significantly. So what do we want to conclude about love and, consequently, about holiness? Certainly,

Love is affectual.
Love is respectful.
Love is empathetic.
Love is equalizing.
Love is trusting.
Love is loyal.
Love is compassionate.
Love is caring.
Love is active.
Love is intentional.
Love is holistic.
Also,

God's love is steadfast.

God's love is immanent and ever-present.

God's love is transformative.

And,

Our love for others flows out of our love-filled hearts.

Our love for God is expressed as entire devotion.

Each of these descriptions adds to the whole as we seek to define a love that seems ineffable; so do the following familiar characteristics: "Love is patient, love is kind. It does not envy, it does not boast, it is not proud. It does not dishonor others, it is not self-seeking, it is not easily angered, it keeps no record of wrongs" (1 Cor. 13:4-5 TNIV). "Love must be sincere" (Rom. 12:9). All of these descriptions are helpful. But none represent an all-encompassing definition. Is love ultimately still elusive in the end? Is holy love so indefinable after all? John, again so simply but most profoundly, says in 1 John 3:16: "This is how we know what love is: Jesus Christ laid down his life for us. And we ought to lay down our lives for one another." Love lays down one's life; love is willing to die; love "empties" the self "of all but love."[11] This is the heart and soul and strength of love.

It is in this sense that we understand what it means to say that holy love, *in essence*, is kenotic. God as Father, Son, and Holy Spirit loves the world with kenotic love. Love is at the center of God's very being. For no other reason than this, love should be at the center of Wesleyan-Holiness theology. We venture to say here that a Wesleyan-Holiness theology that is not centered on the love of God is not really Wesleyan-Holiness theology at all. Love at the center keeps the holy in Holiness. But much, much more importantly, love should be at the center of the *holy person*. Only with love at the center of our being are we ever enabled to reflect the holy God and be holy as God is holy. Rob Staples, speaking on love, in a recent presentation titled "Things Shakable and Things Unshakable in Holiness Theology," concludes,

> I submit that the meaning of love can be better captured in descriptions and examples than in formal definitions. I would want to say that the love that is the "core distinctive" of holiness is the love of the Crucified God! It is the kenotic divine love of the suffering Servant who, says Isaiah, "poured out his soul unto death" (Isaiah 53:12). It is the self-denying, cross-bearing love of Matthew 16:24. It is the love depicted by Dietrich Bonhoeffer who said: "When Jesus calls a man to follow him, he bids him come and die." It is the love of the lowly Galilean, washing the feet of his followers, emptying himself, making himself of no reputation, taking the form of a servant, and becoming obedient even to death on a cross. The love that is the core distinctive of holiness is a cruciform

love. It is the love described so graphically in the 15th chapter of Luke: a love that goes out into the darkness of night, searching amid the hills and valleys, among the briars and the brambles, looking for that one lost sheep; a love that looks in every corner, sweeping in every nook and cranny, searching for that one lost coin; a love that stands forever out by the gatepost gazing yearningly, longingly, down the long road that leads in from the far country. That is love . . . That is holiness! That is what Wesleyan [Holiness] Theology calls "perfect love." That cannot be shaken.[12]

This then is the essence of holiness, the holiness to which we have been called. To be called unto holiness is to be called to kenotic love. Love at the center of it all. Love at the center of us all. Self-emptying love outpoured into the world: This has been our past; this can be our future.

Therefore, as God's chosen people, holy and dearly loved, clothe yourselves with compassion, kindness, humility, gentleness and patience. Bear with each other and forgive one another if any of you has a grievance against someone. Forgive as the Lord forgave you. And over all these virtues put on love, which binds them all together in perfect unity. (Col. 3:12-14 TNIV)

SUMMARY STATEMENTS

1. Love at the center of Holiness theology affects such theology in distinct ways.
2. God's love for us is steadfast, immanent, and transformative.
3. We love our neighbors only as God fills us with love.
4. Our love toward God can perhaps best be expressed as entire devotion.
5. Our call to be holy is God's call for us to love kenotically.
6. When we love, we are who God created us to be.

QUESTIONS FOR REFLECTION

1. What are the five qualities of a Holiness theology centered on love?
2. In what ways does love work?
3. What characteristics of love does this chapter list? Are there others you would include?
4. Why is it so important to say love is essentially kenotic?

FURTHER READING

Charter, Gary. *The Analogy of Love: Divine and Human Love at the Center of Christianity.* Exeter, Devon, U.K.; Charlottesville, VA: Imprint Academic, 2007.

Collins, Kenneth. *The Theology of John Wesley: Holy Love and the Shape of Grace.* Nashville: Abingdon Press, 2007.

Wynkoop, Mildred. *A Theology of Love.* Kansas City: Beacon Hill Press of Kansas City, 1972.

NOTES

Foreword

1. John Leland Peters, *Christian Perfection and American Methodism* (New York: Abingdon Press, 1956), 47-48.

2. That is, the issue of crisis vs. process, or instantaneous vs. gradual sanctification.

3. Diane Leclerc, *Singleness of Heart: Gender, Sin, and Holiness in Historical Perspective* (Landover, MD: Scarecrow Press, 2002).

Introduction

1. See Kevin W. Mannoia and Don Thorsen, eds., *The Holiness Manifesto* (Grand Rapids: Eerdmans Press, 2008).

2. Ibid., 18.

3. Ibid., 19.

4. For an insightful commentary of just such an occurrence, see the Introduction to Donald Dayton, *Discovering Our Evangelical Heritage* (Peabody, MA: Hendrickson Publishers, 1976).

5. Jay Akkerman, conversation with Diane Leclerc.

6. Henry H. Knight III, "John Wesley and the Emerging Church," in *Preacher's Magazine* (Advent/Christmas 2007): 34.

7. Ibid.

8. Ibid.

9. Modernism can be loosely defined as a cultural and philosophical paradigm that penetrated into most academic fields, including art, literature, and even theology. It immediately predates postmodernism. Scholars differ on a precise date when modernism began. Some would suggest that it is the period that follows the medieval period. Others would date it only to the 19th century. It is characterized by an emphasis on the systemization of thoughts and beliefs, and the quest to make generalizations about knowledge. Science and empiricism are the primary sources of knowledge. However, this is not to imply that modernism did not influence Christian thought. Some aspects of modernism that affected Christianity are the tendencies to use deductive thought, to organize theology through presuppositions and "truth statements," to focus on right belief, and to see Scripture as an answer book. In a way, it can be associated with what is known as Protestant Scholasticism.

10. Letter to Dr. Burton, October 1735 (http://wesley.nnu.edu/john-wesley/the-letters-of-john-wesley/wesleyrsquos-letters-1735).

11. Albert Outler, ed., Introduction in *John Wesley* (New York: Oxford University Press, 1964), 11.

12. John Wesley, *Journal* (March 4, 1738) in *The Works of John Wesley*, ed. Thomas Jackson, 14 vols., CD-ROM edition (Franklin, TN: Providence House, 1994), 1:86, hereafter cited as *Works* (Jackson).

13. From John Wesley, *Journal* (May 24, 1738).

14. This is Wesley's preferred term. See "The Scripture Way of Salvation," *Works* (Jackson) 6:43-54.

15. These phases include prevenient grace, awakening, repentance, salvation (or new birth), progressive sanctification, entire sanctification, and final sanctification. Each of these will be considered in precise detail in future chapters.

16. Significant to the optimism expressed here is the Wesleyan idea of the "new creation." This term in Wesley more deeply reflects the source of optimism. The optimism of grace comes not only from sins forgiven or a new relationship with God but also from the reality that an individual is truly transformed from within; the old has gone and the new has come because of a regeneration powerful enough to effect a real, not relative, change in the person.

17. Theodore Runyon, *The New Creation: John Wesley's Theology Today* (Nashville: Abingdon Press, 1998), 71.

18. Wesley, "Catholic Spirit," *Works* (Jackson), 5:492-504.

19. Ibid., 497.

20. Ibid., 497-99.

Part I
Chapter 1

1. It is important to hear George Lyons on Wesleyan interpretation when he writes, "The reference to 'the Wesleyan interpreter' suggests a non-existent uniformity among those who choose so to identify themselves, whether this uniformity is conceived in terms of presuppositions, methodology, or conclusions. There is no generally agreed upon or distinctively Wesleyan hermeneutic or attitude toward an application of the so-called 'higher criticism.'" George Lyons, "Hermeneutical Bases for Theology: Higher Criticism and the Wesleyan Interpreter," in *Wesleyan Theological Journal* 18, no. 1 (1983): 63.

2. Randy Maddox, *Responsible Grace: John Wesley's Practical Theology* (Nashville: Kingswood Books, 1994), 37.

3. Scott J. Jones, "The Rule of Scripture," in *Wesley and the Quadrilateral: Renewing the Conversation*, W. Stephen Gunter, et al. (Nashville: Abingdon Press, 1997), 56-57.

4. Joel Green, "Is There a Contemporary Wesleyan Hermeneutic?" in *Reading the Bible in Wesleyan Ways*, eds. Barry L. Callen and Richard P. Thompson (Kansas City: Beacon Hill Press of Kansas City, 2004), 125. Rob Wall adds, "When I speak of a Wesleyan reading of Scripture, then, I do not mean that Wesleyans simply adopt as normative Wesley's particular reading of Scripture or return to a crude, uncritical version of proof-texting." Robert W. Wall, "Facilitating Scripture's Future Role Among Wesleyans," in *Reading the Bible in Wesleyan Ways*, eds. Barry L. Callen and Richard P. Thompson (Kansas City: Beacon Hill Press of Kansas City, 2004), 119.

5. Scott J. Jones, *John Wesley's Conception and Use of Scripture* (Nashville: Kingswood Books, 1995), 18.

6. George Lyons writes, "In opposition to Lutheran [Protestant] orthodoxy the pietists called for a truly biblical theology which was to be found inductively in the Bible and not to be influenced deductively by dogmatic and philosophical presuppositions." Lyons, "Hermeneutical Bases," 66.

7. Robert W. Wall, "Toward a Wesleyan Hermeneutic of Scripture," in *Reading the Bible in Wesleyan Ways*, 50-51.

8. Donald Thorsen, "Interpretation in Interactive Balance: The Authority of Scripture for John Wesley," in *Reading the Bible in Wesleyan Ways*, 81.

9. For further reflection on how Wesley interpreted Scripture in light of Methodist women's call to preach, see Diane Leclerc, "Introduction: The Wesleyans and Holiness Roots of Women Preachers," in *I Am Not Ashamed: Sermons by Wesleyan Holiness Women*, ed. Diane Leclerc (Point Loma, CA: Point Loma Press, 2005), 15-25.

10. 2 Timothy 3:16, *Explanatory Notes upon the New Testament* (London: Epworth Press, 1950), 794.

11. See George Lyons, "Presidential Address: Biblical Theology and Wesleyan Theology," in *Wesleyan Theological Journal* 30, no. 2 (1995): 24.

12. This is not to imply that biblical criticism is dangerous in and of itself. George Lyons reminds us that "higher criticism—a designation seldom used by contemporary practitioners, unfortunately often carries a largely negative connotation of a destructive attack upon the authority of the Bible." Lyons, "Hermeneutical Bases," 1. Lyons rightly implies here that this is not necessarily true.

13. Wall, "Toward a Wesleyan Hermeneutic," 44.

14. Charles Wesley, Hymn No. 461, in *The Bicentennial Edition of the Works of John Wesley* (Nashville: Abingdon Press, 1983—), 7:643-44, hereafter cited as *Bicentennial Works*.

15. Larry Shelton proposes this term "sacramental" in relation to Wesley's conception of Scripture. See "John Wesley's Approach to Scripture in Historical Perspective," in *Wesleyan Theological Journal* 16, no. 1 (1981): 23-50.

16. Wall, "Toward a Wesleyan Hermeneutic," 47.

17. Ibid., 47-48.

18. John Wesley, *Explanatory Notes upon the Old Testament* (repr., Salem, OH: Schmul Publishers, 1975), ix.

19. Wesley, *Works* (Jackson), 14:253.

20. Wall, "Toward a Wesleyan Hermeneutic," 53.

21. Ibid.

22. For a full discussion of the relationship of biblical interpretation and the church, see Richard Thompson, "Community in Conversation: Multiple Readings of Scripture and a Wesleyan Understanding of the Church," in *Reading the Bible in Wesleyan Ways*, 173-86.

23. This section should not be taken to imply that these principles were unique to Wesley.

24. Wesley, *Preface to Notes upon the New Testament*, par. 10.

25. This is in essence the approach of contemporary so-called biblical theology or the theological interpretation of Scripture. See Kevin J. Vanhoozer, ed., *Dictionary for Theological Interpretation of the Bible* (London: SPCK, 2005), esp. 19-25. See also James K. Mead, *Biblical Theology: Issues, Methods, and Themes* (Louisville, KY: Westminster/John Knox, 2007), 242.

26. Wall, "Toward a Wesleyan Hermeneutic," 42.

27. Jones, *John Wesley's Conception*, 53-54.

28. This is not to be confused with the doctrine known as dispensationalism. Wesley simply means by the word a particular era of time.

29. Wesley, *Works* (Jackson), 11:110.

30. John Wesley, "Letter to Dean D—," 1785, *The Letters of John Wesley*, ed. John Telford (London: Epworth Press, 1931), 7:252.

31. Wesley, *Notes upon the New Testament*: 1 John 2:8.

32. The "Hermeneutic of Love" is a phrase borrowed from Mildred Bangs Wynkoop. See *A Theology of Love: The Dynamic of Wesleyanism* (Kansas City: Beacon Hill Press of Kansas City, 1972).

33. These four are used most often. Wesley at times lists only three: original sin, justification by faith, and holiness. He has also used repentance, justification, and sanctification. It is important to note that each of these imply the *ordo salutis* (the order of salvation).

34. Scott Jones states in full, "If holiness of heart and life is the dominant emphasis of Wesley's hermeneutics in his early ministry, it occupies a different place after 1738. The theological transaction Wesley made during that year altered his understanding of faith and its relationship to holiness. From that time on, he insisted that faith alone was necessary for

salvation, though he continued to emphasize that good works were both the fruit of faith and a necessary condition for its continuance" (*John Wesley's Conception*, 53).

Chapter 2

1. I have received invaluable help in this chapter from conversations with my colleague George Lyons. For an extremely helpful summary of the important hermeneutical issues around the topic of holiness, see George Lyons, *More Holiness in Everyday Life* (Kansas City: Beacon Hill Press of Kansas City, 1997), esp. chap. 1.

2. This phraseology is sometimes broadened to "scriptural Christianity," which still implied a strong theology of Holiness.

3. Walter Brueggemann, *Theology of the Old Testament* (Minneapolis: Fortress Press, 1997), 267.

4. Ibid.

5. Ibid., 108.

6. Ibid.

7. Ibid., 312.

8. William M. Greathouse, *Wholeness in Christ: Toward a Biblical Theology of Holiness* (Kansas City: Beacon Hill Press of Kansas City, 1998), 13. Originally from Augustine, "Questionum in Heptateuchum," in *Patrologiae cursus completus, Series Latina* 34.2.73; see www.sant-agostino.it/latino/questioni_ettateuco/index.htm.

9. Lyons, *More Holiness*, 28.

10. Brueggemann, *Theology of the Old Testament*, 288.

11. One of the best examples of apophatic theology is found in the work of Gregory of Nyssa.

12. Brueggemann, *Theology of the Old Testament*, 277-80.

13. George A. Butterick and Keith R. Crim, ed. *The Interpreter's Dictionary of the Bible: Vol. 2:E-J* (New York: Abingdon Press, 1980), 618. Also see Katharine Doob Sakenfeld, ed., *The New Interpreter's Dictionary of the Bible: Vol. 3:I-Ma* (New York: Abingdon Press, 2008), 202-3.

14. George Allen Turner, *The More Excellent Way* (Winona Lake, IN: Light and Life Press, 1952), 31.

15. See Ronald M. Hals, *Grace and Faith in the Old Testament* (Minneapolis, MN: Augsburg Publishing House, 1980).

16. David Thompson, "Old Testament Bases of the Wesleyan Message," in *Wesleyan Theological Journal* 10 (1975): 39. All quotations used by permission of the publisher.

17. Greathouse, *Wholeness in Christ*, 21.

18. Thompson, "Old Testament Bases," 43.

19. Ibid., 42.

20. Greathouse, *Wholeness in Christ*, 21.

21. Thompson, "Old Testament Bases," 43.

22. See Leclerc, *Singleness of Heart*, chaps. 3 and 4.

23. Thompson, "Old Testament Bases," 44.

24. Kenneth L. Waters, "Holiness in New Testament Perspective," in *Holiness Manifesto*, 40.

25. Ibid., 41.

26. A brief discussion of entire sanctification, as it has been interpreted historically by Holiness exegetes, may be helpful here. Holiness thinker Daniel Steele was the first in a long line of scholars who connected the aorist tense to entire sanctification. Persons such as W. T. Purkiser, H. Orton Wiley, Richard Howard, and Olive Winchester followed Steele's assertions. However, the basis of Steele's initial use of the aorist tense, it has been argued by

Randy Maddox, was based on his misunderstanding of a Greek grammar published before the turn of the 20th century. Here is Steele's argument: the aorist tense in New Testament Greek always implies that an action has been completed. Thus when the word for sanctification is put in the aorist in certain New Testament passages, it means that the work of sanctification has been instantaneously accomplished. Maddox explains the significance of this: "The difference [is] between expecting the aorist to be referring to a crisic event unless it can be proven otherwise [and] the reverse of only assuming crisic content in the aorist when the context demands it. The first position has been that of the majority of holiness proponents. The second is the position of the leading Greek grammarians [today] and, I believe, the one true to the Greek language." Maddox does not suggest that the context will never support the use of this meaning of the aorist. He simply argues that it should not always be used in this manner. According to him, "A proper understanding of the aorist tense can be very instrumental in helping to find a balance in the present debate between the crisis and the process of sanctification in holiness thought. . . . It shows that the distinctions between crisis and process are not arrived at or defended on the basis of grammar but rather on the basis of thorough theological exegesis." Entire sanctification is on shaky ground if it is only based on a verb tense. There are, however, stronger reasons to interpret the whole of the New Testament as supportive of this primary Wesleyan-Holiness doctrine. This doctrinal position will have greater integrity when it is based on the best exegesis possible. Maddox quotes are from "The Use of the Aorist Tense in Holiness Exegesis," in *Wesleyan Theological Journal* 16, no. 2 (1981): 106-18.

27. David Kendall, "Jesus and the Gospel of Holiness," in *Holiness Manifesto*, 58.

28. For more on this see Kent Brower, "The Holy One of God and His Disciples: Holiness and Ecclesiology in Mark," in *Holiness and Ecclesiology in the New Testament*, ed. Kent Brower and Andy Johnson (Grand Rapids: Eerdmans Publishers, 2007), 57-75.

29. Lyons, *More Holiness*, 100.

30. Kendall, "Jesus and the Gospel of Holiness," 64. See Matt. 23:27-30.

31. See Kent Brower, *Holiness in the Gospels* (Kansas City: Beacon Hill Press of Kansas City, 2005), 99-101.

32. Richard Thompson examines the Lukan depiction of Jesus in the meal scenes as discussions of holiness. See Richard Thompson, "Gathered at the Table: Holiness and Ecclesiology in the Gospel of Luke," in *Holiness and Ecclesiology in the New Testament*, 76-94.

33. Brower, *Holiness in the Gospels*, 59.

34. Robert Wall, "Purity and Power According to the Acts of the Apostles," in *Wesleyan Theological Journal* 34, no. 1 (1999): 66-67.

35. Ibid., 67.

36. Werner Georg Kummel, *The Theology of the New Testament* (Nashville: Abingdon Press, 1973), 262.

37. Brower, *Holiness in the Gospels*, 68.

38. Clark Pinnock, *Flame of Love: A Theology of the Holy Spirit* (Downers Grove, IL: InterVarsity Press, 1996), 31.

39. D. Moody Smith, *The Theology of the Gospel of John* (Cambridge: Cambridge University Press, 1995), 129.

40. For a discussion of John's mysticism (or lack thereof), see C. K. Barrett, *The Gospel According to John* (London: SPCK, 1962), 71-74.

41. Greathouse, *Wholeness in Christ*, 91.

42. Lyons, *More Holiness*, 100.

43. For further elaboration of this point, see George Lyons, "Modeling the Holiness Ethos: A Study Based on First Thessalonians," in *Wesleyan Theological Journal* 30, no. 1 (1995): 187-211.

44. Lyons, *More Holiness*, 100.

45. F. F. Bruce, *The Epistle to the Hebrews,* in *The New International Commentary on the New Testament,* ed. F. F. Bruce (Grand Rapids: Eerdmans Publishing Co., 1973).

46. David Peterson, *Possessed by God: A New Testament Theology of Sanctification and Holiness* (Grand Rapids: Eerdmans Publishing Co., 1995), 34. As quoted by William Greathouse, *Wholeness in Christ,* 156.

Part II
Chapter 3

1. See Peter Brown, *Society and the Holy in Late Antiquity* (Berkeley, CA: University of California Press, 1982).

2. Tertullian, *Apologeticus,* chap. 50 in *The Ante-Nicene Fathers,* ed. Alexander Roberts and James Donaldson (Peabody, MA: Hendrickson Publishing, 1994), 3:55. This is the common phrase that is often quoted. Tertullian actually says, "The blood of Christians is seed."

3. Not in any reductionist way. "New martyrdom" is a common way to refer to asceticism by patristic scholars. For one example among many, see Aideen M. Hartney, *Gruesome Deaths and Celibate Lives: Christian Martyrs and Ascetics* (Devon, Exeter: Bristol Phoenix Press, 2005), 57.

4. There were also desert mothers. See Benedicta Ward, *The Sayings of the Desert Fathers: The Alphabetic Collection* (Collegeville, MN: Cistercian Publications, 1987).

5. For more on Irenaeus and succession, see Robert Grant, *Irenaeus of Lyon* (New York: Routledge, 1997), 7.

6. I am indebted to the work of Christopher Bounds in this section, especially his most recent article, "The Doctrine of Christian Perfection in the Apostolic Fathers," in *Wesleyan Theological Journal* 42, no. 2 (2007): 7-27.

7. Ibid., 22.

8. Ibid.

9. Ibid., 23.

10. Ibid.

11. Justin, "First Apology," in *Ante-Nicene Fathers,* 1:165.

12. Ibid., 168.

13. Ibid., 177.

14. "The Martyrdom of Perpetua and Felicitas," 6.8, in *Ante-Nicene Fathers,* 3:697-706.

15. Henri Rondet, *Original Sin: The Patristic and Theological Background,* trans. Cajetan Finegan (Staten Island, NY: Alba House, 1972), 40-41.

16. Irenaeus, *Against Heresies,* as quoted in Rondet. This quote is actually Finegan's English translation of Rondet's French translation of the Latin in W. Wigan Harvey, *Sancti Irenaei Libri Quinque Adversus Haereses* (Cambridge: Cambridge University Press, 1857).

17. See Michael Christensen, "Theosis and Sanctification: John Wesley's Reformulation of a Patristic Doctrine," in *Wesleyan Theological Journal* 31, no. 2 (1996); Michael Christensen, *Partakers of the Divine Nature: The History and Development of Deification in the Christian Traditions* (Grand Rapids: Baker Publishing Group, 2008); and K. Steve McCormick, "Theosis and Chrysostom and Wesley: An Eastern Paradigm of Love," in *Wesleyan Theological Journal* 26 (1991).

18. Irenaeus, "Against Heresy," in *Ante-Nicene Fathers,* 1:526.

19. William M. Greathouse and Paul M. Bassett, *Exploring Christian Holiness, Vol. 2: The Historical Development* (Kansas City: Beacon Hill Press of Kansas City, 1985), 44-45.

20. Clement of Alexandria, *The Instructor,* in *Ante-Nicene Fathers,* 2:215.

21. Ibid.

22. Ibid., 217.

23. Clement of Alexandria, "The Stromata," in *Ante-Nicene Fathers,* 2:426.

24. See Rowen Williams, "Does It Make Sense to Speak of Pre-Nicene Orthodoxy?" in *The Making of Orthodoxy*, ed. Rowen Williams (Cambridge: Cambridge University Press, 1989), 1-23.

25. Peter Brown, *The Body and Society: Men, Women, and Sexual Renunciation in Early Christianity* (New York: Columbia University Press, 1988), 163.

26. See Rebecca Lyman, *Christology and Cosmology: Models of Divine Activity in Origen, Eusebius, and Athanasius* (Oxford and New York: Clarendon Press, 1993).

27. Ibid., 165.

28. See Elizabeth Clark, *The Origenist Controversy* (Princeton, NJ: Princeton University Press, 1992).

29. Lyman, *Christology and Cosmology*, 66-67.

30. On Wesley and his Eastern influences, see Arthur MacDonald Allchin, "Our Life in Christ, in John Wesley and the Eastern Fathers," in *We Belong to One Another: Methodist, Anglican, and Orthodox*, ed. Arthur MacDonald Allchin (London: Epworth, 1965), 62-78; Bassett Greathouse, *Exploring Christian Holiness*, Vol. 2; Ted A. Campbell, *John Wesley and Christian Antiquity: Religious Vision and Cultural Changes* (Nashville: Kingswood Books, 1991); Ted A. Campbell, "John Wesley and the Asian Roots of Christianity," *Asian Journal of Theology* 8 (1994): 281-94; Seung-An Im, "John Wesley's Theological Anthropology: A Dialectic Tension Between the Latin Western Patristic Tradition (Augustine) and the Greek Eastern Patristic Tradition (Gregory of Nyssa)" (PhD dissertation, Drew University, 1994); David C. Ford, "Saint Makarios of Egypt and John Wesley: Variations on the Theme of Sanctification," *Greek Orthodox Theological Review* 33 (1988): 285-312; Luke L. Keefer, "John Wesley: Disciple of Early Christianity," in *Wesleyan Theological Journal* 19, no. 1 (1984): 23-32; Randy Maddox, "John Wesley and Eastern Orthodoxy: Influences, Convergences, and Differences," in *Asbury Theological Journal* 45 (1990): 29-53; K. Steve McCormick, "John Wesley's Use of John Chrysostom on the Christian Life: Faith Filled with the Energy of Love" (PhD dissertation, Drew University, 1983); John G. Merritt, "'Dialogue' Within a Tradition: John Wesley and Gregory of Nyssa Discuss Christian Perfection," in *Wesleyan Theological Journal* 22, no. 2 (1987): 92-116; Albert C. Outler, "John Wesley's Interests in the Early Fathers of the Church," in *The Wesleyan Theological Heritage: Essays of Albert C. Outler*, ed. Thomas C. Oden and Leicester R. Longden (Grand Rapids: Zondervan, 1991), 55-74; Mark Anthony Smith, "John Wesley: A Pattern of Monastic Reform" (PhD dissertation, University of Kentucky, 1992); and Howard Snyder, "John Wesley and Macarius the Egyptian," in *Asbury Theological Journal* 45 (1990): 55-59.

31. See note 17 above.

32. See Merritt, "'Dialogue' Within a Tradition."

33. Saint Gregory of Nyssa, *Ascetical Works*, trans. Virginia Woods Callahan, in *The Fathers of the Church: A New Translation*, Vol. 58 (Washington, DC: Catholic University of America Press, 1967), 121.

34. Ibid.

35. That is, Gregory was Neoplatonic.

36. See Nyssa, "On Perfection," in *Ascetical Works*, in *The Fathers of the Church*.

37. Messalians are considered a heretical Christian sect that originated in Mesopotamia ca. 360 CE. They were condemned for their beliefs on the Trinity, believing that God used only one hypostasis to relate to "the perfect." A Christian is perfected through prayer and not the church, according to the Messalians; this was probably the primary reason for their condemnation. If it is true that Pseudo-Macarius was a Messalian, we may have difficulty defending him. However, much of his theology of Holiness seems very orthodox. Thus Wesley (who of course would have thought the author to be Macarius) praised him.

38. *Pseudo-Macarius: The Fifty Spiritual Homilies and the Great Letter*, "Preface" by Kallistos Ware (New York: Paulist Press, 1992), xii.

39. Ibid., xiii.

40. John Wesley's diary for July 30, 1736.

41. *Pseudo-Macarius*, sermon 4, sec. 6.

42. Ibid., sermon 4, sec. 8.

43. Ibid., sermon 44, sec. 9.

44. Ibid., sermon 47, sec. 1.

45. Ibid., sermon 11, sec. 9.

46. Ibid., sermon 15, sec. 8.

47. Ibid., sermon 18, secs. 2-3.

48. This is of course open to interpretation.

49. See Peter Brown, *Body and Society*, 309.

50. Vigen Guroian, "Family and Christian Virtue in a Post-Christendom World: Reflections on the Ecclesiastical Vision of John Chrysostom," in *St. Vladimir's Theological Quarterly* 35 (1991): 328, 341.

51. Brown, *Body and Society*, 306.

52. Elizabeth Clark, "Introduction," in *On Virginity; Against Remarriage*, by Saint John Chrysostom in *Studies in Women and Religion* (Lewiston, NY: Edwin Mellen Press, 1983), xiv.

53. See F. X. Murphy, "*The Moral Doctrine of St. John Chrysostom*," *Studia Patristica* 11 (1972): 52-57.

54. See Leclerc, *Singleness of Heart*, 36-41.

55. Columba Stewart, *Cassian the Monk* (New York: Oxford University Press, 1998), 43.

56. Ibid., 44.

57. Ibid.

58. For a detailed account of Jerome's theology of virginity, see Demetrius Dumm, *The Theological Basis of Virginity According to St. Jerome* (Latrobe, PA: St. Vincent Archabbey, 1961).

59. Jerome, *Adversus Jovinianum*, 1.3, in *Nicene and Post-Nicene Fathers* (NPNF), eds. Philip Schaff and Henry Wace (Peabody, MA: Hendrickson Publishing, 1994), 6:348 (PL23:222-24).

60. Jerome, "Against Jovinianus" in *NPNF*, 6:348.

61. Elizabeth Clark, "Theory and Practice in Late Ancient Asceticism: Jerome, Chrysostom, and Augustine," in *Journal of Feminist Studies in Religion* 5 (1989): 30.

62. Elaine Pagels, *Adam, Eve, and the Serpent* (New York: Vantage Books, 1988), 95.

63. See Clark, *Origenist Controversy*, 121-50.

64. Clark expounds, "Surprising to the modern reader is Jerome's seeming lack of comprehension of Origen's theology" (*Origenist Controversy*, 139).

65. Caroline White, *Christian Friendship in the Fourth Century* (Cambridge: Cambridge University Press, 1992), 131.

66. Clark, *Origenist Controversy*, 122.

67. Ibid., 121.

68. Brown, *Body and Society*, 383.

69. For those who might doubt the applicability of the term "optimism" when applied to Jerome, consider Peter Brown's analysis: "For all his shrill sense of sexual danger, Jerome had been a monk of the old school. The intense physicality of his descriptions of the ascetic life contained an unadmitted optimism" (*Body and Society*, 419).

70. Ibid., 386.

71. Ibid.

72. See Campbell, *John Wesley and Christian Antiquity*, 46-53; Campbell, "John Wesley and the Asian Roots of Christianity," 281-94.

73. Greathouse and Bassett, *Exploring Christian Holiness*, 121-22.

74. Ibid.

75. See Mary O'Driscoll, "Catherine the Theologian," in *Spirituality Today* 42, No. 1 (Spring 1988): 4-17.

76. Ibid.

Chapter 4

1. See Maddox, *Responsible Grace*, 176-91.

2. John Fletcher, *The Works of the Reverend John Fletcher* (repr., Salem, OH: Schmul Publishers, 1974), 2:633.

3. Adam Clarke, *Christian Theology* (Cincinnati: L. Swormstedt and A. Poe, 1856), p. 184.

4. See Peters, *Christian Perfection*, 107.

5. See Greathouse and Bassett, *Exploring Christian Holiness*, 2:248-49.

6. Richard Watson, *Theological Institutes*, Part II, chap. 29, point 5, http://wesley.nnu.edu/wesleyan_theology/watson/watson_p2_ch29.htm.

7. Peters, *Christian Perfection*, 159.

8. See Thomas Langford, *Practical Divinity: Theology in the Wesleyan Tradition* (Nashville: Abingdon Press, 1983), 66-70.

9. Phoebe Palmer's critics, for example, accuse her of Pelagianism.

10. See Greathouse's review of Pope, in *Exploring Christian Holiness*, esp. 256-57.

11. See C. C. Goen, "The 'Methodist Age' in American Church History," *Religion in Life* 34 (1965): 562-72; Winthrop Hudson, "The Methodist Age in America," *Methodist History* 12 (1974): 3-15. A. Gregory Schneider summarizes, "This new organization [the Methodist Episcopal Church] became a vessel that both contained and spread a major portion of the remarkable spiritual effervescence that flowed from what is called the Second Great Awakening in America. This Awakening marked the transition from the 'Puritan Age' to the 'Methodist Age' in American church history. There is a simple statistical reason for such a statement. In 1784 . . . the Methodists were a small and insignificant sect. By 1850 . . . there were more Methodists in America than any other kind of Protestant. There is also a more sophisticated reason for the statement. When historians speak of the nineteenth century as the Methodist Age in American religious history they refer to a popular religious style that characterizes Methodists but was not limited to them. Indeed, this style of religion penetrated virtually all of Protestant church life and virtually every region in America" (*The Way of the Cross Leads Home: The Domestication of American Methodism* [Bloomington, IN: Indiana University Press, 1993], xx).

12. Dennis C. Dickerson, "Richard Allen and the Making of Early American Methodism," in *From Aldersgate to Azusa Street: Wesleyan, Holiness, and Pentecostal Visions of the New Creation*, ed. Henry Knight III, 1. This is a compilation of papers from the Wesleyan, Holiness, Pentecostal Consultation, 2003-9. Book forthcoming from Wipf & Stock Publishers.

13. Ibid., 3.

14. Ibid., 2.

15. Thomas N. Ralston, *Elements of Divinity* (Nashville: Abingdon-Cokesbury Press, 1924), 470.

16. Ibid., 467.

17. See Introduction by Thomas Oden, ed., in *Phoebe Palmer: Selected Writings* (New York: Paulist Press, 1988).

18. See Randolph Foster, *The Nature and Blessedness of Christian Purity* (New York: Land and Scott, 1851), chap. 6.

19. Greathouse and Bassett, *Exploring Christian Holiness*, 278.

20. Langford, *Practical Divinity*, 111-12.

21. Ibid., 112.

22. Ibid.

23. Greathouse and Bassett, *Exploring Christian Holiness*, 313.

24. See John Allen Wood, *Perfect Love* (n.p., n.d.), 87-88.

25. Ibid., 88-89.

26. See Harold Raser, *Phoebe Palmer: Her Life and Thought* (Lewiston, NY: Edwin Mellen Press, 1987).

27. Invaluable to the writing of this and the next section was William C. Kostlevy, ed., *Historical Dictionary of the Holiness Movement* (Lanham, MD: Scarecrow Press, 2001). This book has been an incredible contribution to Wesleyan-Holiness studies.

28. Douglas Cullum, "Gospel Simplicity: Benjamin Titus Roberts and the Formation of the Free Methodist Church" in Knight, *From Aldersgate to Azusa Street*, 4.

29. Palmer never took an abolitionist platform. In fact, she was preaching in England through the entire Civil War. Interestingly, her *Four Years in the Old World* says next to nothing about the war or what is going on in America in her absence.

30. Amanda Berry Smith, *An Autobiography: The Story of the Lord's Dealings with Mrs. Amanda Berry Smith, the Colored Evangelist* (Chicago: Meyer and Brother Publishers, 1893), 116-17.

31. Barry Callen, "Daniel Sydney Warner: Joining Holiness and All Truth," in *Wesleyan Theological Journal* 30, no. 1 (1995): 92-93.

32. Floyd T. Cunningham, ed., *Our Watchword and Song: The Centennial History of the Church of the Nazarene* (Kansas City: Beacon Hill Press of Kansas City, 2009), 179.

33. Ibid.

34. Ibid., 179-80.

35. Langford, *Practical Divinity*, 137.

36. Neoorthodoxy refers to a theological movement after World War I. It is also sometimes known as dialectic theology or theology of crisis. It is a reaction to the liberal theology of the late 19th century. Neoorthodoxy has a strong doctrine of sin and reinvigorates the theology of the Protestant Reformation. Neoorthodox theologians include Karl Barth and Emil Brunner.

37. Following Wynkoop, this is one of the hermeneutics guiding this present book.

38. See Mark Quanstrom's discussion in "The Credibility Gap," chap. 7 in Mark Quanstrom, *A Century of Holiness Theology: The Doctrine of Entire Sanctification in the Church of the Nazarene, 1905 to 2004* (Kansas City: Beacon Hill Press of Kansas City, 2004), 137-69.

39. Kostlevy, *Historical Dictionary of the Holiness Movement*, 250.

40. Rob L. Staples, "The Current Wesleyan Debate on the Baptism with the Holy Spirit," TS, 38 pp., The Rob L. Staples Collection, Nazarene Archives, Lenexa, KS.

41. I am indebted to Barry Callen for this information. Callen spoke to Massey on his 80th birthday, January 4, 2010.

42. Kostlevy, *Historical Dictionary of the Holiness Movement*, 241.

Part III
Chapter 5

1. To be clear, I am not calling for a return to any traditional view of God simply because it is traditional. There are aspects of the traditional God that emanated from a type of hypersyncretism to past cultures and that need to be released. The critiques that come from the various forms of liberation theology need to be seriously considered. But such consideration does not necessitate a release of an understanding of God's transcendence.

2. Another way of expressing this is to talk about how God's fullness or *pleuroma* spills out; this makes creation inevitable.

3. I am not attempting to be insensitive to cultures where having children is a necessity to family work and thus survival. I am speaking more in psychological/emotional terms.

4. I am indebted to my colleague Brent Peterson and our discussions around this point.

5. Other chapters will further elaborate on an aspect of self-sacrifice that needs to be heard. My comments here come out of the influence of liberation theologies in my own work. I would assert that sacrifice without first experiencing the liberating work in God, which gives us a truly renewed self, can reinforce structures of oppression. And yet, a renewed self can then pour out itself in sacrificial living. See my book for elaboration, *Singleness of Heart: Gender, Sin, and Holiness in Historical Perspective.*

6. E.g., Rom. 8:35-39; Heb. 13:5; Matt. 18:19-20; Phil. 1:6.

7. See Augustine, *On the Trinity*, ed. Garreth B. Matthew, (Cambridge: Cambridge University Press, 2002).

8. See especially John B. Carman, *Majesty and Meekness: A Comparative Study of Contrast and Harmony in the Concept of God* (Grand Rapids: Eerdmans Publishing Co., 1994), 213. In Luther, see the theme in his commentaries on Genesis, Romans, and Galatians.

9. George Lyons, e-mail to Diane Leclerc, November 26, 2007.

10. A title of a famous sermon by Jonathan Edwards.

11. I am using this in the sense that Wesley did. Wesley allowed for a category he called "sin, improperly so-called," which included infirmities. For Wesley these are amoral.

12. It is key for Wesley and Wesleyans that this second aspect of repentance is only possible *after* faith, and only through the assistance of God. Otherwise, we would inappropriately connect salvation to our own efforts at righteousness. It is only grace, through faith, that enables us to repent in this second sense.

13. See Paul Tillich, "We Are Accepted," in *The Shaking of the Foundations* (New York: Charles Scribner's and Sons, 1948), 153-63.

14. This a concept from John Wesley. He believed that when the heart overflows with the love of God, there is no more room for sin.

15. Charles Wesley, "And Can It Be?"

16. The Church of the Nazarene changed its language regarding sanctifying grace. The word "eradication" was deleted, and the word "cleansed" was added in its place. I hold that "cleansing" is a vital part of our theology and is that which distinguishes us from our Keswickian cousins.

17. "Article X," *Manual of the Church of the Nazarene.*

18. With the exception of Jesus himself, of course. As Luke tells us, Jesus was filled with the Holy Spirit from birth.

19. Perhaps most notably, Asa Mahan. John Fletcher, of course, proposed this a century earlier.

20. See Rob Staples, *Outward Sign and Inward Grace: The Place of Sacraments in Wesleyan Spirituality* (Kansas City: Beacon Hill Press of Kansas City, 1991), for a very pertinent discussion of the sacrament of Holy Communion not just as a means of grace, but as a means of *sanctifying* grace.

Chapter 6

1. Portions of this chapter are reprinted and adapted from Diane Leclerc, "Holiness: Sin's Anticipated Cure," in *The Holiness Manifesto,* ed. Kevin W. Mannoia and Don Thorsen © 2008 Wm. B. Eerdmans Publishing Company, Grand Rapids, Michigan. Reprinted by permission of the publishers, all rights reserved.

2. See Warren Brown, Nancey Murphy, and H. Newton Maloney, eds., *Whatever Happened to the Soul? Scientific and Theological Portraits of Human Nature* (Minneapolis: Fortress Press, 1998).

3. Mildred Bangs Wynkoop, *A Theology of Love* (Kansas City: Beacon Hill Press of Kansas City, 1972), 122-23.

4. The Origenist controversy, interpreted in a radically Platonic sense, can be seen as exalting the incorporeal while disparaging the flesh. In reaction to this denial of God Incarnate, other monks adopted an equally heretical notion called anthropomorphism, ascribing a human form to God as God, and thus interpreting the *imago Dei* as a physical body. See Elizabeth Clark's discussion in "Images and Images: Evagrius Ponticus and the Anthropomorphite Controversy," in *Origenist Controversy*, 43-84.

5. Wynkoop, *Theology of Love*, 116-24.

6. H. Ray Dunning, *Grace, Faith, and Holiness* (Kansas City: Beacon Hill Press of Kansas City, 1988). Although Dunning does mention these four relationships, he cautions against love for self, and "the world" is portrayed as dangerous. Many following Dunning, this author included, have modified these last two relationships by stating that God desires an appropriate love for ourselves, and our love for "the earth" as its stewards.

7. For an extensive discussion on this issue of sin as "privation," see Leon O. Hynson, "Original Sin as Privation," in *Wesleyan Theological Journal* 22, no. 2 (fall 1987), 65-83. Hynson analyzes Arminius, Wesley, and scholars from Richard Watson to H. Orton Wiley, and states that for Wesleyan theology, being deprived of our primary relationship with God results in a modified depravity. (Interestingly, Hynson criticizes Wesley for not being consistent on this point.) This relational understanding has been supported by scholars later than Wiley, including Clarence Bence, Craig Blaising, Barry Bryant, H. I. Smith, and Rob Staples. See Maddox, *Responsible Grace*, 296, n. 118.

8. See Dunning, *Grace, Faith, and Holiness*, 157-59.

9. This is not to imply that Wesley rejected the Reformed position. Maddox writes, "How bad is this corruption of our faculties? In Reformed theology it became common to describe it as 'total depravity.' This phrase could easily be misunderstood to suggest that every human person is as evil as one could possibly be. Such was not its intent. Reformed theologians meant only to affirm that the corruption of sin decisively affects every faculty of the human person, leaving us incapable of living in God's likeness—or even truly desiring to—through our debilitated powers alone. Even construed in these more limited terms, the affirmation of total depravity was broadly rejected outside Protestant circles. Not by Wesley (at least after 1738)! While not always using the specific term, he repeatedly affirmed the point that Inbeing Sin's corruption pervades every human faculty and power, leaving us utterly unable to save ourselves. Fortunately, however, God the Great Physician can heal our diseased nature" (*Responsible Grace*, 82).

10. See Sermon IX, "The Spirit of Bondage and Adoption," in *Works* (Jackson), 5:98-110.

11. See John Wesley, "Farther Thoughts upon Christian Perfection," in *Works* (Jackson): 11:418.

12. Mildred Bangs Wynkoop, *An Existential Interpretation of the Doctrine of Holiness* (unpublished, 1958), 2-3.

13. Ted Campbell writes, "Wesley's attitude toward Pelagianism was considerably more ambiguous. He could recognize 'Pelagianism' as being as dangerous an extreme as Calvinism, but he was not sure that the historical Pelagius (so to speak) could be handily condemned as a heretic, if for no other reason than that none of Pelagius's own writings had survived. Moreover, Wesley argued, Augustine was angry at Pelagius, and for that reason Augustine's account of Pelagius could not be trusted. . . . Elsewhere Wesley stated his guess that Pelagius

was 'both a wise and holy man' [*Letters* (Jackson), 12:240] whereas of Augustine he wrote: 'A wonderful saint! As full of pride, passion, bitterness, censoriousness, and as foul-mouthed to all that contradicted him' [*Sermons* (Jackson), 6:328-29]. Pelagius, Wesley wrote to John Fletcher, 'very probably held no heresy than you and I do now' [*Letters* (Telford), 6:125] . . . Wesley may have felt that Pelagius was a kindred spirit, accused (as Wesley was accused) of denying the priority of grace in his stress on the necessity of following God's law" (*Wesley and Christian Antiquity*, 6).

14. Leclerc, *Singleness of Heart.*

15. See Sermon 44, "Original Sin," in *Works* (Jackson), 6:57-62.

16. Ibid., 6:60.

17. Ibid.

18. Sermon 78, "Spiritual Idolatry," in *Works* (Jackson), 6:441.

19. George Price, *The Narrow Pass: A Study of Kierkegaard's Concept of Man* (New York: McGraw-Hill Book Company, Inc., 1963), 35.

20. Ibid., 40. Italics mine.

21. Wynkoop, *Existential Interpretation of the Doctrine of Holiness* (unpublished), 254-56; edited.

Chapter 7

1. Portions of this chapter are included and adapted from the author's contribution to Clergy Development, Church of the Nazarene, *Becoming a Holy People* (Kansas City: Nazarene Publishing House, 2004). Used by Permission.

2. Some scholars (e.g., Edwin Crawford, professor of philosophy, emeritus, Northwest Nazarene University) are calling for the Holiness denominations to distinguish themselves from evangelicalism today, because evangelicalism often now means Reformed theology and fundamentalism.

3. From the Charles Wesley hymn "O for a Thousand Tongues to Sing."

4. John Wesley, "A Plain Account of Christian Perfection," in *Works* (Jackson), 11:426.

5. John Wesley, "The Great Privilege of Those That Are Born of God," Sermon Nineteen, in *The Sermons of John Wesley*, ed. Thomas Jackson, Wesley Center Online, http://wesley.nnu.edu/john_wesley/sermons/019.htm.

6. See George Croft Cell, *The Rediscovery of John Wesley* (New York: H. Holt and Company, 1935), 347. Cell is often quoted when he writes that Wesley represents "an original and unique synthesis of the Protestant ethic of grace and Catholic ethic of holiness." Albert Outler writes of Wesley's synthesis by calling it "evangelical Catholicism." Wesley, according to Outler, "glimpsed the underlying unity of Christian truth in both the Catholic and Protestant traditions. . . . In the name of Christianity both Biblical and patristic, he managed to transcend the stark doctrinal disjunctions, which had spilled so much ink and blood since Augsburg and Trent. In their stead, he proceeded to develop a theological fusion of faith and good works, Scripture and tradition, revelation and reason, God's sovereignty and human freedom, universal redemption and conditional election, Christian liberty and an ordered polity, the assurance of pardon and the risks of 'falling from grace,' original sin and Christian perfection" (*John Wesley* [New York: Oxford University Press, 1964], viii).

7. See Raser, *Phoebe Palmer*, 35. Raser later adds, "This is not to say that Palmer did not teach that genuine conversion and holiness involve a 'mystical,' felt relationship to Christ. Her understanding of Christianity was too much suffused with pietism for that to occur. And in her writings one can find many examples of the language of religious emotion. . . . Yet, these are somehow less 'convincing,' and appear more like deliberate recitations of a familiar formula than spontaneous expressions of religious rapture" (266). I am unconvinced that her language is "less convincing" and "deliberate" (read, insincere) on the issue of religious emotion.

Part IV
Chapter 8

1. In his *Preface to James*, Luther writes, "But this James does nothing more than drive to the Law and to its works. Besides, he throws things together so chaotically that it seems to me he must have been some good, pious man, who took a few sayings from the disciples of the Apostles and thus tossed them off on paper. . . . In a word he wanted to guard against those who relied on faith without works, but was unequal to the task." In a translation of Martin Luther's writings, *The Prefaces to Luther's German Translation of the New Testament* (1522) we read the following on James: "Firstly, because, in direct opposition to St. Paul and all the rest of the Bible, it ascribes justification to works, and declares that Abraham was justified by his works when he offered up his son. St. Paul, on the contrary, in Romans 4[:3], teaches that Abraham was justified without works, by his faith alone, the proof being in Genesis 15[:6] which was before he sacrificed his son. Although it would be possible to save the epistle by a gloss giving a correct explanation of justification here ascribed to works, it is impossible to deny that it does refer Moses's word in Genesis 15 (which speaks not of Abraham's works but of his faith, just as Paul makes plain in Romans 4) to Abraham's works. This defect proves that the epistle is not of apostolic provenance" (John Dillenberger, *Martin Luther: Selections from His Writings* [New York: Anchor Books, 1962], 35).

2. Thomas Cook, *New Testament Holiness* (London: Epworth Press, 1950), 43.

3. For more on sin as substance see Wynkoop's discussion in *Theology of Love*, 149-64. It should also be noted that some scholars have accused Wesley of seeing sin as a foreign substance. See Maddox, *Responsible Grace*, 296, n. 117. Maddox lists R. Newton Flew, J. Ernest Rattenbury, and William Sangster as Wesley's critics on this point.

4. John Wesley, *A Plain Account of Christian Perfection* (Kansas City: Beacon Hill Press of Kansas City, 1966), 117-18.

5. Ibid., 19.

6. See Søren Kierkegaard, *Purity of Heart Is to Will One Thing* (Radford, VA: Wilder Publications, 2008).

7. Wesley, *Plain Account* (Beacon Hill Press of Kansas City), 19.

8. See Article Nine, www.anglicancommunion.org/resources/acis/docs/thirty_nine_articles.cfm.

9. Wesley, "On Sin in Believers," in *Bicentennial Works,* 1:320-210.

10. Ibid., 321.

11. Wesley, "Repentance in Believers," in *Works* (Jackson), 5:156-71.

12. Ibid.

13. See Maddox, *Responsible Grace,* 185-86.

14. Wesley, "Rules of the Band-Societies," in *Bicentennial Works,* 9:77-78.

15. See http://www.darkness2light.org/KnowAbout/statistics_2.asp. And http://www.prevent-abuse-now.com/stats.htm#Links for databases of further statistics. Also see Dr. Nancy Nason-Clark, "When Terror Strikes the Christian Home"; Keynote Address at "The Awakening Conference," Fort Lauderdale, FL (October 7, 2006).

Chapter 9

1. L. Tyerman, *The Life and Times of the Rev. John Wesley, Vol. 2* (New York: Harper & Brothers Publishers, 1872), 306.

2. "Westminster Shorter Catechism," Center for Reformed Theology, http://www.reformed.org/documents/WSC.html. The Westminster Confession of Faith, which is the basis for the Shorter Catechism, is a confession of faith in the Calvinist tradition. It was written in 1646 by the Westminster Assembly of the Church of England; but it became and remains the standard of doctrine in the Church of Scotland and within Presbyterian churches worldwide.

In 1643, the English Parliament called an assembly at Westminster Abbey. These meetings, over a period of five years, produced this confession of faith. It is clear at this time that the Anglican Church was influenced by the Calvinism of some of its leaders and thinkers. For more than three centuries, various churches around the world have adopted the confession as their standard of doctrine. The Westminster Confession of Faith was modified and adopted by Congregationalists and Baptists in England. English Presbyterians, Congregationalists, and Baptists would come to be known as Nonconformists, because they did not conform to the Act of Uniformity in 1662, which established the Church of England as the only legally-approved church, even though they were in many ways united by their common confessions, built on the Westminster Confession. This does not imply that Arminianism was absent before and after the Westminster Confession was written.

3. Thomas Merton, *Life and Holiness* (New York: Image Books, 1963), 4.

4. Reuben Welch, *We Really Do Need Each Other* (Nashville: Impact Books, 1973).

5. John Wesley, "Christian Perfection" and "On Perfection," in *The Bicentennial Edition of the Works of John Wesley* (Nashville: Abingdon Press, 1984—), 2:99-124 and 3:71-87.

6. Wesley, *Plain Account* (Beacon Hill Press of Kansas City), 61.

7. This is the greatest difference in Wesley before and after Aldersgate in 1738. Prior to that experience, Christian perfection was only a goal to be sought after and never to be realized in this life. After 1738, Wesley envisioned Christian perfection as not only possible, but needed in the Christian's life.

8. This date is given by Harald Lindstrom. Timothy Smith dates the sermon at 1761; Albert Outler at 1784 (see http://wesley.nnu.edu/john_wesley/sermons/chron.htm).

9. According to Harald Lindstrom. See Harald Lindstrom, *Wesley and Sanctification* (Wilmore, KY: Francis Asbury Publishing Co., 1950).

10. Ibid., 131-32. Also see "On Perfection," in *Works* (Jackson), 4:411-23. Most of these characteristics can also be found in Wesley's *Plain Account*.

11. See Wynkoop, *Theology of Love*, 294-301. I have summarized her points and made them clearer where helpful.

12. Leo George Cox, *John Wesley's Concept of Christian Perfection* (Kansas City: Beacon Hill Press, 1964).

13. Elmer Clark, *What Happened at Aldersgate?* (Nashville: Methodist Publishing House, 1938), 58: "Vital holiness was passing out of Methodist faith and practice. Finally all traces of the doctrine were carefully eliminated from the songs of the church in the hymnal published in 1935. For example, in Charles Wesley's great hymn 'Love Divine, All Loves Excelling,' which appeared in the hymn books since 1747, a line in the second stanza reading 'Let us find that second rest,' was altered by the hymnal commission to 'let us find the promised rest.' Nothing was allowed to remain that might remind Methodists that their church had ever endorsed a second work of grace."

14. I am indebted to Leo Cox's analysis of the work of Leland Scott, Elmer Gaddis, John Peters, Timothy Smith, Delbert Rose, and Robert Cushman in his review of Christian perfection in America in the 19th century. See Cox, *John Wesley's Concept of Christian Perfection*, 182-90.

15. It is historically interesting that in the latter part of the 20th century there were those within these Holiness denominations who wanted to move to a more progressively oriented form of sanctification. Elmer Clark said of the Methodists at the end of the 19th century, "Nothing was allowed to remain that might remind Methodists that their church had ever endorsed a second work of grace." (See endnote 12.) One might wonder if this will be said of Holiness churches in the coming century?

16. Mark Quanstrom places this emphasis on the instantaneous act as definitive of sanctification as early as H. Orton Wiley. See Mark Quanstrom, *A Century of Holiness Theol-*

ogy, 80-85. Quanstrom does show that Wiley still affirmed the importance of perfect love even when defining sanctification narrowly as entire sanctification. Quanstrom points out that there was a need in the 1940s and 1950s to modify the "exaggerated" claims of early 20th-century theologians (regarding the effects of entire sanctification on sin) by authors more in touch with "Christian Realism" relevant for a new historical period (see pp. 97-108). I would argue, however, that this occupation by authors on being corrective had the effect of de-emphasizing the positive aspects of Christian holiness as a loving lifestyle.

17. H. Orton Wiley, *Christian Theology, Vol. 2* (Kansas City: Nazarene Publishing House, 1941), 508 (see first footnote on page).

18. Cox, *John Wesley's Concept of Christian Perfection*, 182.

19. Since Wesley developed the meaning of these distinctions over time, what is presented here should be seen as his most mature thought on the subject.

20. Wesley offered an explanation of this term in a letter of May 31, 1771, to Miss March. Wesley, responding to her letter, replied, "There cannot be a more proper phrase than that you used, and I will understand your meaning; yet it is sure you are a transgressor still—namely, of the perfect, Adamic law. But though it be true all sin is a transgression of this law, yet it is by no means true on the other hand (though we have so often taken it for granted) that all transgressions of this law are sin: no, not at all—only all voluntary transgressions of it; none else are sins against the gospel law" (Letter to Miss March [31 May 1771], *Letters* [Telford]), http://wesley.nnu.edu/john-wesley/the-letters-of-john-wesley/wesleys-letters-1771.

21. Technically speaking, Wesley did say that involuntary transgressions need the atoning blood of Christ, in a general sense. But these actions do not change our relational status before God whereas a willful act would.

22. Maddox, *Responsible Grace*, 184.

23. Wesley, *Plain Account* (Beacon Hill Press of Kansas City), 54.

24. Ibid., 23.

25. Ibid., 36.

26. For only a few examples of Wesley's advice regarding Christian perfection and entire sanctification, see Letter to Ann Foard (12 October 1764), *Letters* (Telford), 4:268-70; Letter to Mrs. Bennis (29 March 1766), *Letters* (Telford), 5:6; Letter to Miss March (14 March 1768), *Letters* (Telford), 5:81-2; Letter to Mrs. Barton (8 October 1774), *Letters* (Telford), 6:116.

27. Letter to Hannah Ball (5 November 1769), *Letters* (Telford), 5:153.

28. John Wesley, *Primitive Physic* (Philadelphia: John Dickins, 1791; repr., Nashville: United Methodist Church Publishing House, 1992).

29. Letter to Martha Chapman (15 March 1775), *Letters* (Telford), 6:145.

30. Letter to Martha Chapman (5 April 1775), *Letters* (Telford), 6:147.

31. Letter to Ann Bolton (7 June 1768), *Letters* (Telford), 5:92.

32. Letter to Mary Bosanquet (15 January 1770), *Letters* (Telford), 5:176.

33. Letter to Penelope Newman (23 October 1772), *Letters* (Telford), 5:342.

34. Letter to Ann Bolton (13 July 1774), *Letters* (Telford), 6:97.

35. Letter to Mrs. Knapp (25 March 1781), *Letters* (Telford), 7:52.

36. Letter to Ann Loxdale (14 July 1781) *Letters* (Telford), 7:73.

37. Letter to Mrs. Downes (21 November 1783), *Letters*, (Telford), 7:197.

38. Merton, *Life and Holiness*, 31.

39. See John Wesley, "Preface to 1739 Hymns and Sacred Poems," in *Works* (Jackson), 14:321.

40. See Timothy L. Smith, *Revivalism and Social Reform* (Nashville: Abingdon Press, 1957).

41. Wesley, "Minutes of Several Conversations," in *Works* (Jackson), 8:310.

42. Wesley, "A Further Appeal to Men of Reason and Religion," in *Works* (Jackson), 8:47.

43. Theodore Jennings Jr., "Wesley and the Poor: An Agenda for Wesleyans," in *The Portion of the Poor: Good News to the Poor in the Wesleyan Tradition,* ed. M. Douglas Meeks (Nashville: Kingswood Books, 1995), 21.

44. "A Farther Appeal," in *Works* (Jackson), 8:239.

45. See Kristina LaCelle-Peterson, *Liberating Tradition: Women's Identity and Vocation in Christian Perspective* (Grand Rapids: Baker Academics, 2008).

46. See Donald Dayton, *Discovering Our Evangelical Heritage.*

47. See Douglas M. Strong, *Perfectionist Politics: Abolitionism and the Religious Tensions of American Democracy* (Syracuse, NY: Syracuse University Press, 1999).

Chapter 10

1. Rob Staples, "Things Shakeable and Things Unshakeable in Holiness Theology," The Edwin Crawford Lecture, Northwest Nazarene University's Wesley Conference: *Revisioning Holiness*, February 9, 2007. See nnu.edu/Wesley.

2. See John Wesley, "Farther Thoughts upon Christian Perfection," in *Works* (Jackson): 11:418.

3. See discussion of Wesley and the unification of God in Robert G. Tuttle Jr., *Mysticism in the Wesleyan Tradition* (Grand Rapids: Francis Asbury Press, 1989), 70, 124-25, and especially 132. S. Diamond adds, "Wesley's character stopped short of mystical ecstasy and neither the mystic death nor union can be said to describe any experience in Wesley's life" (S. Diamond, *The Psychology of the Methodist Revival* [London: Oxford University Press, 1926], 77).

4. Brent Peterson, e-mail to Diane Leclerc (September 15, 2008).

5. Nancy L. Eiesland, *The Disabled God: Toward a Liberatory Theology of Disability* (Nashville: Abingdon Press, 1994), 13.

6. Ibid.

7. Frances M. Young, *Brokenness and Blessing: Towards a Biblical Spirituality* (Grand Rapids: Baker Academic, 2007), 59. Quote by Macarius, *Fifty Homilies,* "6:4, as translated in Wesley, *Christian Library*" (see n. 44 for chap. 2 in Young, *Brokenness and Blessing,* 132).

8. Tertullian, "The Apology," in *Ante-Nicene Fathers,* 3:54-55.

9. Friedrich Schleiermacher, *On Religion: Speeches to its Cultured Despisers,* trans. John Oman (London: Kegan Paul, Trench, Trubner & Co., 1893), xliv.

10. See Henri Nouwen, *The Wounded Healer* (New York: Doubleday, 1972).

Chapter 11

1. See Randy Maddox, "Reconnecting the Means to the End: A Wesleyan Prescription for the Holiness Movement," in *Wesleyan Theological Journal* 33, no. 2 (1998): 29-66.

2. This is important because Asian Wesleyans need not adopt a Western philosophical model as the only means of discussing the importance of virtue.

3. For example, see Randy Maddox, "A Change in Affections: The Development, Dynamics, and Dethronement of John Wesley's 'Heart Religion,'" in *"Heart Religion" in the Methodist Tradition and Related Movements,* ed. Richard Steele (Metuchen, NJ: Scarecrow Press, 2001), 3–31 (and the whole of Steele's book). For a more philosophical review, see Philip Cary, "A Brief History of the Concept of Free Will," in *Behavioral Sciences* 25 (2007): 165-81.

4. I am deeply indebted to Randy Maddox for this entire section, as well as the next. See his remarkable article, "Holiness of Heart and Life: Lessons from North American Methodism," in *Asbury Theological Journal* 51 (1996): 151-72.

5. Ibid., 152-53.

6. Ibid., 153.

7. Ibid.

8. Ibid., 154.

9. Ibid., 154, emphasis mine.

10. The list here comes from *Plain Account* (Beacon Hill Press of Kansas City), 17.

11. For a keen study of the difference between inclinations and instincts see Joseph Bankard, "Human Biology and Moral Instincts: Do We Have an Innate Moral Grammar?" forthcoming in his doctrinal dissertation from Claremont.

12. Wesley's own thought is problematic here. Wesley has been charged with a "practical monophysitism" because he emphasized Jesus Christ's divinity sometimes more than his humanity. There are odd points in Wesley's writings where he clearly de-emphasized Jesus' human responses and emotions. But to be consistent with language of "taking on his disposition," Jesus' humanity is vital. We cannot become divine. Thus to imitate Christ in our character, we must imitate the perfection of his humanity—as a full human being.

13. Wesley, "The Means of Grace," in *Works* (Jackson), 5:185-201.

14. See Henri Nouwen with Michael J. Christensen and Rebecca Laird, *Spiritual Direction: Wisdom for the Long Walk of Faith* (New York: HarperCollins, 2009), 17; and Henri Nouwen, *Here and Now* (New York: Crossroads Publishing Company, 1994), 76-77.

15. Though this is so often credited to Wesley, there is no direct quote in existence. Also see William J. Federer, *America's God and Country: Encyclopedia of Quotes* (St. Louis: William J. Federer Publication), 683.

16. See Dietrich Bonhoeffer, *Life Together* (New York: Harper and Row Publishers, 1954).

17. "Eucharist" literally means thanksgiving.

18. William Willimon, *The Service of God: Christian Work and Worship* (Nashville: Abingdon Press, 1983), 125.

19. Ibid., 127.

20. Staples, *Outward Sign and Inward Grace*, 204-5.

21. See Wesley, "The Duty of Constant Communion," in *Bicentennial Works*, 3:428-39.

22. Ibid.

23. For a full treatment of how Wesley interpreted the Eucharist, see Staples, *Outward Sign and Inward Grace*, and Ole E. Borgen, *John Wesley on the Sacraments* (Grand Rapids: Francis Asbury Press of Zondervan Publishing House, 1985). I interpret Wesley as between the theory of "spiritual presence" and the "memorialist" view. Key to interpreting Wesley's understanding of Communion is his pneumatology. I am not sure these connections have been explored to the fullest.

24. Gregory Clapper, *John Wesley on Religious Affections* (Metuchen, NJ: Scarecrow Press, 1989), 154.

25. See Theodore Runyon, "A New Look at Experience" (*Drew Gateway* 1987), 44-55. Credit should also be given to Steven Land, who wrote a paper with Runyon during his doctoral program.

26. Wesley, "Salvation by Faith," in *Bicentennial Works*, 1:120.

27. Mildred Bangs Wynkoop, *Existential Interpretation*, 301.

Chapter 12

1. This is not to refute Wynkoop's assertion that the terms "holiness" and "love" are to remain distinct. She writes, "Holiness and love are two different words for two different things. In the realm of formal definition each is distinct. They cannot be interchangeably used in any one context. But this is in the realm of words as words. In the realm of existential meaning something of their relatedness begins to come through" (Wynkoop, *Theology of Love*, 24).

2. And certainly conversely, "Love without holiness is no Love at all" (Steve McCormick, correspondence with editor, April 23, 2009).

3. This list is a combination of concepts offered by Mildred Bangs Wynkoop and Gary Charter, as well as my own thoughts. See Wynkoop, *Theology of Love*, and Gary Charter, *The Analogy of Love: Divine and Human Love at the Center of Christianity* (Charlottesville, VA: Imprint Academic, 2007), 14-15.

4. Charter, *Analogy of Love*, 2.

5. Ibid. Desire has unfortunately been too closely associated with lust by some; lust should be understood as a sinful distortion of desire. Again, this confusion can lead to an unhealthy stoicism and distort healthy sexuality in particular. See "Excursus" in chapter 8 on purity.

6. For example, Mildred Bangs Wynkoop and Rob Staples—labeled as such by others; or Tom Oord, who takes the name for himself (see Thomas Jay Oord and Michael Lodahl, *Relational Holiness* [Kansas City: Beacon Hill Press of Kansas City, 2005]).

7. See John Wesley's sermon "The Catholic Spirit."

8. A statement made by Rob Staples.

9. Spoken by Steven Land, president of Church of God Theological Seminary at a consultation of Wesleyan-Holiness-Pentecostal historians in Kansas City, October 2006.

10. Paul Tillich invokes the image of the "theological circle" to imply that true theology always stands in the service of the church. He writes: "The theologian . . . claims the universal validity of the Christian message in spite of its concrete and special character. . . . He [or she] enters the theological circle with a concrete commitment. He [or she] enters it as a member of the Christian church to perform one of the essential functions of the church—its theological self-interpretation" (*Systematic Theology, Vol. 1* [Chicago: Chicago University Press, 1951], 9-10).

11. This sentiment is expressed in Charles Wesley's hymn "And Can It Be?" The second verse reads: "He [Christ] left His Father's throne above, / so free, so infinite His grace! / *Emptied Himself of all but love*, / and bled for Adam's helpless race." Also see chapter 10 for a full examination of the concept of self-emptying.

12. Staples, "Things Shakeable and Things Unshakeable in Holiness Theology."

GLOSSARY

Abolitionism—A reform movement that arose in America connected with the anti-slavery movement. The antislavery movement sought to keep slaves from being traded from Africa to America and Western Europe and sought emancipation for those already slaves.

Adoption—Wesley strongly affirmed the significance of being a child of God and co-heir with Christ. This aspect of salvation also implies that persons are born into a family, i.e., a community of brothers and sisters in Christ. This prevents people from imagining salvation as a purely private event in life.

Affections—In Wesleyan terms, the affections are the inclinations that motivate human action, and as such they are indispensible. (See Inclinations, as well as Tempers.)

Analogy of faith—The connecting themes of Scripture. For Wesley this was reduced to four particular truths: the corruption of sin, justification by faith, the new birth, and present inward and outward holiness. These elements unify Scripture and act as an interpretive guide to problematic passages.

Antinomianism—The idea that a Christian is saved by grace alone (sola fide), and not by works; but further, it means that a Christian is then free from all moral law or obligations, and free to sin. Literally, it means anti-law.

Apokatastasis—Origen's belief that everyone will be saved in the end, including Satan. He was deemed heretical for this and other beliefs after his death. Still, Origen is considered a church father, and not a heretic today.

Apology—A style of writing in the early church (and since) in which the author seeks to defend aspects of Christian doctrine or Christianity as a whole. Apologetics sought to find common ground with critics in order to appeal to their reason. Philosophy, history, and science were used to convince the opposing party that Christians should not be condemned as unreasonable and, therefore, not be condemned to death. Such efforts were usually futile.

Apophatic theology—This theology was employed by Christians as far back as the early church. It states that any positive statement about God is impossible; we can only state what God is not. It is sometimes called negative theology.

Apostolic fathers—The second generation of Christians; that is, those persons (usually men) who wrote significant works just after the writers of the New Testament. Some of their works were even considered for inclusion in the canon. Most would claim that they were taught by the apostles or someone who had been close to Jesus.

Arête—Greek term meaning "virtue" or "excellence." Used mainly when speaking of the virtues of human character.

Asceticism—The practice of extreme forms of self-denial.

Aseity—A doctrine that holds that God is entirely self-sufficient. God is not dependent on any other being or thing, either for God's existence or for God's nature.

Assurance—See Witness of the Spirit.

Awakening—In an individual's life, it is the conviction that brings personal repentance. It can also reference a time when society at large has been impacted by an extraordinary season of religious interest (e.g., the First and Second Great Awakenings). Charles Finney emphasized an awakening as a return of the church from its backsliding, and the conversion of sinners to the reality of the presence of the Holy Spirit in ordinary everyday life.

Baptism with the Holy Spirit—Long associated with entire sanctification, this term is based on biblical passages stating that the baptism Jesus Christ would perform surpasses water baptism; he would "baptize with fire" (e.g., Matt. 3:11). It is also based on the disciples' experiences at Pentecost. The phrase is not to be confused with "baptism in" or "baptism of" the Holy Spirit, which is used by Pentecostals to signify tongue speaking.

Biblical criticism—A form of inquiry that seeks to make discerning and discriminating judgments about the biblical text, based on the various contexts of the text.

Biblical interpretation—The process of discovering what the original author of a text sought to convey to his original readers. The goal of interpretation is to make the biblical text and thus the author's original point applicable to the present world.

Biblical theology—This field of study stands between exegesis and hermeneutics, on one side, and systematic theology, on the other. Biblical theology presents the grand themes of Scripture in an organized way. It is often broken down into smaller chunks, such as Old Testament or New Testament theology, or even the Theology of the Prophets, Johannine theology, or Pauline theology.

Cenobitic monasticism—The type of monasticism that was practiced in a community of other monks or nuns, as contrasted with eremitic monasticism—the solitary life of a hermit.

Christian perfection—Wesley himself strongly affirmed Christian perfection as a real possibility for every Christian who had been justified by faith. Wesley defined Christian perfection as "pure love" that reigns alone in the heart and in the life of an individual.

Christian Platonist—This person ascribes to a type of theology that takes the best of Plato's philosophy and "Christianizes" it. Examples of Christian Platonists include Justin Martyr and Augustine.

Condescension—A voluntary becoming equal with a person or persons who are otherwise regarded as inferior or other than (e.g., God becoming flesh). This was particularly emphasized by Martin Luther.

Conscience—An internal compass that helps persons discern what is right or wrong. The conscience is the awareness of right or wrong. It is argued that it either is formed by experience or inherently present within every person. Christian theology usually affirms that it is God-given.

Consecration—In the theology of the Wesleyan-Holiness tradition, this term refers to the absolute surrender or entire devotion of one's life to God.

Continent character—From Aristotle. A person who lacks internal harmony or who suffers from internal dissonance. The continent person is said to have reached a decision within a particular occasion of events, and having reached this decision, is able to carry it out despite pressure from the appetites or passions. The continent agent is able to resist these pressures and is thus able to stick with a reasoned decision, but they act for the wrong reasons. This contrasts the virtuous person who acts for the right reasons.

Covenant—An agreement between persons, and/or, between God and persons, wherein the covenanter binds himself or herself to the promise he or she makes with the covenantee. In relations between God and humans, God makes a self-imposed obligation to covenant with people. This covenant made between God and people becomes a mutually binding agreement between both parties wherein the people are called to live lives of faithfulness, trust, and loyalty.

Deism—The theistic belief that God created the universe and everything that exists therein, but that God does not now interfere with creation. God is like a clockmaker who created the clock and then allows it to run without further intervention. God and world are separate entities. Deism is belief in God based on the application of reason to the laws of nature; it is thus belief in God on purely rational grounds.

Depravity—A word to describe the condition of humanity after the Fall. It is usually connected to the phrase "total depravity," which connotes humanity's hopelessness apart from the grace of God.

Deprivity—A Wesleyan perspective holding that human beings are sinful and that they are without God. Human beings are incapable of being or becoming righteous on their own. However, human beings are not unchangeably sinful because they can be transformed by God's grace. God's prevenient grace (a grace that goes before any human knowledge of it) restores humanity's freedom to will. It differs from total depravity, in that humanity's main problem is estrangement from God, not its internal corruptness.

Dispensations—Understood within theology to be a divine order of things taking place at a particular time within history. Dispensationalism originated among the Plymouth Brethren namely, John N. Darby. This theory is popular in evangelical churches and is essentially pessimistic about the condition of the world. It is characterized by three main points: (1) the division of history into eras [usually in sevens]; (2) mention of a dual Second Coming including a secret rapture before a public revelation; and (3) the division of the church into Gentile and Jewish churches.

Dispositions—The tendency of someone or something to act or to react in a certain manner or in characteristic ways, under certain given situations. Can be understood also as *prevailing* tendencies or inclinations.

Divinization—See Theosis.

Double inspiration—The belief that the Holy Spirit inspired the original writers of Scripture and that the Holy Spirit continues to inspire the present-day reader so that the passages read come to life.

Dynamism (from Greek *dunamis*)—A biblical term that usually refers to the power of the Holy Spirit in the life of a Christian as the Christian cooperates with such power.

Eisegesis—When a person interprets and/or reads something into a text (including Scripture) that the author of the original text did not intend to convey. It is equivalent to taking a verse out of context.

Empiricism—Reliance on observable data gained through the five senses to establish truth.

Entire devotion—Another word for consecration or surrender in the commitment made at the point of entire sanctification. It also is descriptive of the life lived thereafter.

Epistemology—The philosophical discipline concerned with the nature, manner, and validity of human knowledge. It asks the question, How do we know what we know?

Eremitic monastics—The type of monasticism characterized by extreme solitude; the life of a hermit.

Eudaimonia—A central concept in virtue ethics that often translates as "happiness" or "to flourish," i.e., the flourishing of a human being, not to be mistaken with the flourishing of plants and animals.

Exclusivism—The view that there is only one way to salvation, and thus to God, and that this way is through faith in Jesus as the Christ. In effect, it denies prevenient grace.

Exegesis—The study of Scripture to discover its original, intended meaning.

Experience—One part of the Wesleyan quadrilateral. Experience refers to the experience of God's grace. This experience is regarded as such when it is or has been affirmed within the Christian community—both past and present.

Forensic salvation—The notion that persons are saved by grace in the sense that God's goodwill and kindness has freed a person (saved by grace) from the consequences of his or her action(s). Grace is spoken of as the free gift of God. Salvation as justification is emphasized.

Gnosticism—An early church heresy that produced writings and theology that stressed very odd ideas about creation and about Christ that the church declared heretical.

God's incomparability—This is a theological tenet that God is unique. In God's whole being, God is unlike any other creature.

Hagiography—A biography written about a holy person. Hagiographies are not objective accounts of a person's life but are written for the purpose of showing how the person is extraordinary in various ways.

Hamartiology—The doctrine of sin. It comes from the Greek word *hamartanein*, which refers to an archer missing the target or the mark at which he or she was aiming. It is the study of how sin originated, how it affects humanity, and the consequences of sin here and now, as well as after death.

Heresy—That which is counter to whatever is deemed orthodox.

Hermeneutic of love—This is the belief held by many Wesleyans that the most important theme in Scripture is love: God's love for us, and our love for God and others.

Hermeneutics—The science and art of interpreting a text and applying it to the present-day context. Based on exegesis.

Homeopathic—An approach to physical sickness that focuses on the use of herbs, "home remedies," and advice for holistic living. Wesley's book *The Primitive Physic* is a collection of such advice that covers a wide variety of ailments.

Idolatry—When our relationship to other things or persons takes the primary place instead of our relationship with God.

Imago Dei—Literally, "image of God." Mildred Bangs Wynkoop, interpreting Wesley, defines the image of God in humanity as the capacity to love, in the context of a relationship with God, others, self, and the earth.

Immanence—This term denotes the very nearness and/or presence of God in the creation. God as immanent is personal or personable (the opposite of transcendence [see Transcendence]).

Imparted righteousness—A gracious gift of God given at the very moment of the new birth of an individual person. God begins the process of making us holy. This is different from imputed righteousness.

Impassibility—A term used within classical theism as well as Christian Orthodoxy wherein God is viewed as not being capable of being acted upon or affected by others.

Imperfections—A category in Wesley's thought that was not equivalent to sin, similar to involuntary transgressions and infirmities. Imperfections refer to human limitations that do not have a moral quality. For example, an imperfection could be a lack of omniscience, a physical ailment, or mental defect.

Imputed righteousness—The righteousness of Jesus credited to the Christian, which then enables the Christian to be justified. God sees the person through Christ's righteousness, but it does not speak to the inner transformation and cleansing of the individual by God.

Inclinations—Broadly understood as a person's tendency to act or to feel a certain way (see Affections).

Inclusivism—The position that only one religion is true, but that salvation is possible outside of this one true religion. An example of this position is a Christian inclusivist who maintains that Jesus is the only way and that Christianity is the true religion, but that persons of other faiths can be saved because of prevenient grace, even if they do not explicitly believe in Jesus. Paul seems to imply this in Rom 2.

Incontinent character—A person/agent who lacks internal harmony or who suffers from internal disorder. The incontinent person is said to have reached a decision within a particular occasion of events, and upon having reached this decision, said person experiences pressure from the appetites (also known as emotions), which are not fully controlled by reason. The incontinent person is less able, or rather, less successful than the continent person in resisting the pressures of the appetites, and therefore, will be persuaded by the appetites and not follow through with the decision.

Inductive (interpretation)—The process of exegeting the biblical text and then drawing theological conclusions. A different approach than deductive interpretation.

Infirmities—Physical or mental weakness. Wesley distinguished between willful sin and infirmities that may keep us from doing all the good we can. Infirmities have an amoral quality.

Intellectualist model of moral psychology—This refers to a shift away from Wesley's "affectional model" of character development toward a model that emphasizes the rational mind and the exercise of the will in being virtuous.

Involuntary transgressions—Acts committed that are still considered transgressions but are not properly understood as sins because they are committed out of the ignorance and mistakes inherent and inseparable from humanity.

I-Thou—Philosopher Martin Buber coined this phrase in a book titled *I-Thou*, wherein Buber's dominant theme concerned how a person is to relate to other persons and to God. In the above-mentioned work, Buber discusses two possible relations that exist in the world—"I-it" and "I-thou" relations. Buber argues that one relates oneself to another properly in recognizing the other as a "thou." "I-it" relations are relations wherein others are or become objects or means to one's end. Buber also affirms that a person comes in contact with an eternal "Thou." This eternal "Thou" is God who cannot be turned into an object or a means to one's own gain without the relationship being threatened.

Justification—A concomitant of salvation that implies that our sins are forgiven. The guilt of our sin is taken away. God no longer condemns us for our transgressions. Wesley affirmed justification. However, he believed that fuller salvation goes beyond justification to address the underlying problem or disease.

Late antiquity—The period in history that corresponds to the development of the early church. It refers to the time when Rome ruled the empire.

Legalism—Understood within theology as the overemphasis on moral law, codes of conduct, etc., as preeminent principle of redemption over and above God's mercy.

Liberation theologies—A term first used by the Roman Catholic priest Gustavo Gutierrez, who argued that the Gospel message calls for a preferential option for the poor and the oppressed in this life. Following this understanding, liberation theology demands that Christians follow Christ through seeking ways to liberate the poor and oppressed.

Liberty—A person's freedom to refuse to perform an inclination (see also Affections).

Love, agape—A love not conditioned by the object of one's love, it is therefore unconditional. Early Christians defined agape as the self-sacrificing love of God for humanity, to which they were called to imitate in their own lives toward others. This self-sacrificing love is not conditioned, i.e., it is given both to friends and to enemies.

Love, eros—Greek term for "passionate love" beyond the love of friendship. Physical attraction is not always necessary for this kind of love. Eros is understood under Platonic thought as helping the soul to *recognize* beauty as well as to *recall* beauty.

Love, philia—Greek word for "friendship." Also understood as fondness or loyalty to and for friends and family.

Marcionism—A heresy originating within a sect from the second and third centuries CE from the teachings of Marcion of Sinope. Marcionism condemned and rejected the Creator God of the Old Testament who was deemed righteous, inconsistent, jealous, and wrathful. Marcionism accepted the God of the New Testament who is a God of goodness. Christ was understood as the Son of the good God, and not as the Son of the God of the Jews.

Material, efficient, formal, and final causes—Aristotle believed that there are four "causes" in all objects, including the human being. There is the "material cause," which asks the question of why something does what it does; Aristotle believed that the answer to this question was found in the tendencies of the object itself. For example, marble is the material cause for a statue. The "efficient cause" is the source of motion or change. The sculptor is the efficient cause of the marble becoming a statue. But there are still deeper causes that are definitive of not only tendencies or actions but also of nature and purpose. The "formal cause" is the nature of an object, and the "final cause" of an object determines its end, or its *telos*. The final cause asks the question, what is the purpose to which the object (person) is drawn? The formal cause is first pure potentiality that seeks to be actualized. The final cause is actualized through habituation.

Means of grace—Understood in Wesleyan thought as outward signs, words, and/or actions that serve as ways/channels/means by which a person opens himself or herself up to God and thus to receiving or preventing justifying (or sanctifying) grace.

Means of grace, general—Certain activities suggested by Wesley for living the Christian life, such as the exercise of the presence of God, taking up one's own cross, denying oneself, and watching.

Means of grace, instituted—Those means of grace believed by Wesley to be evident in the life of Jesus, namely, the Lord's Supper, prayer, fasting, Scripture, and Christian conversation.

Means of grace, prudential—These means of grace are considered to be wise, although not directly commanded. They include class meetings, covenant services, prayer meetings, and visiting the sick. Prudential means of grace vary between different times, among different cultures, and also from person to person.

Midrash—An ancient commentary containing a compilation of homiletic teachings on parts of the Tanakh (Hebrew Bible).

Modalism—An interpretation of the doctrine of the Trinity wherein its proponents insisted on an undivided Sovereign/God. The proponents of modalism did not want to divide God into three distinct persons; therefore, they argued that the three terms were names applied to the different *modes*. Modalism was deemed a heresy.

Moral attributes of God—Those attributes of God where God has a choice to act. For example, God could choose to be merciful or not be merciful.

Natural and moral image in humans—The idea that humanity is the counterpart of God's person, and thus takes part in the economic life of God. Persons reflect the *imago Dei* in the world, and thus, one is able to discuss the nature (natural image), and the character (moral image) of humankind.

Natural attributes of God—Those attributes of God that describe what makes God God. If these attributes cease to exist in God (hypothetically) God would cease to be God. For example, God cannot cease to be good without ceasing to be God.

Natural, legal, and evangelical states—In Wesleyan thought the *natural state* is understood as the way God created humanity before the Fall; the *legal state* is the person under the law; *evangelical state* is the state of the regenerated. The natural state then, is more of a hypothetical state except in the case of Jesus Christ who was born without original sin.

Natural theology—Talk about God, or a doctrine of God, that is constructed without appeal to faith or to special revelation. Natural theology is based on reason and experience alone.

New birth—The point in a person's life when he or she is born again or regenerated.

Omnipresent—Literally means "all present." God is present and active everywhere, in all things, across time and space.

Ontological—A branch of metaphysics that studies the nature of being, existence, and/or reality.

Ordo salutis—Literally means "order of salvation." Since this is often considered a series of steps in the Christian life, some scholars prefer *via salutis*, or way of salvation to emphasize the fluidity of one stage to another.

Origenism—Followers of Origen who took his speculative theology to its extreme, to the point that it became heretical.

Original sin—The doctrine that considers the inherited sinful condition passed down from Adam.

Panentheism—God *is in* all things. The universe is contained in God's "body," but God's awareness and/or personality is greater than the sum of all the parts of the universe. God is therefore in all things, yet God is also more than those things that God is in.

Pantheism—A doctrine that holds that all things—all beings—constitute God. God and nature are identical, i.e., there is no distinction between the two. God *is* all things.

Paraclete—Name of the Holy Spirit found within the Gospel of John. Signifies the Spirit of God that will strengthen the faithful and guide them into all truth. It comes from two Greek words that mean "called alongside."

Patripassionism—A form of modalism wherein the Son is viewed as the human part of Jesus as the Christ, and the Father is seen as the Christ; the Father thus took on the form of Jesus by becoming born of a virgin and then suffered and died on the cross.

Patristic—The period of history that refers to the era of the church fathers. It usually refers to the time from the post–New Testament period to the fall of Rome in 430 (longer in the East).

Pelagianism—This term refers to the teachings of British monk Pelagius pertaining to the relationship between divine grace and human will. Pelagius seems to have denied the doctrine of original sin, thereby viewing humanity as basically good, and unaffected morally by the Fall; thus Adam's disobedience had significance only for himself.

Pentecost—The day the Holy Spirit fell upon the disciples in a new way, which led them to witness to those gathered in Jerusalem for the Jewish celebration of Pentecost (a harvest celebration). To all Christians, it has been called the birthday of the church. For those in the Wesleyan-Holiness and Pentecostal traditions, it has been associated with the baptism with, or of, the Holy Spirit.

Perfectionist controversy—Wesley's emphasis on Christian perfection, that is, to love God with one's whole heart, soul, and mind, and to love one's neighbor as oneself, came under attack. Many of the disagreements grew out of a misunderstanding of terminology, with "perfection" understood as a finished and even angelic state after entire sanctification. This misunderstanding was promoted by the London Society in the 1760s. Wesley strongly disciplined them, and dismissed their leaders.

Phronesis—Greek term meaning "practical wisdom." In Aristotle's Nichomachean ethics *phronesis* was considered an intellectual virtue. Phronesis is the capability to determine which mode of action to take at a particular time, thereby enabling a person to discover the Golden Mean. In terms of action and the virtuous life then, *phronesis* means doing the right thing, at the right time, in the right way, to the right person, to the right degree, and for the right reason.

Platonic realism—The theory that abstractions of objects (forms or ideas) exist as real entities, yet they exist in another dimension beyond the concrete world.

Pluralism—The view that all world religions are equally valid and lead to God and thus to salvation.

Positional holiness—This is a phrase associated with a Calvinist form of Holiness theology such as Keswickianism. It is distinct from Wesleyan-Holiness theology because it claims that holiness is "imputed" to Christians through their relationship with Christ. It does not imply that Christians are actually made holy inwardly through grace—imparted righteousness.

Postmillennialism—Human cooperation in history is crucial to bringing about God's kingdom on earth.

Postmodernism—A term used to designate the era beyond modernity. This era is said to be one of relativity, of holism or wholism, and of interdependence. This is an era that calls into question the ideals of modernity and that is concerned with *process* and with *becoming* rather than with the *conclusions* and *closure* that modernity concerned itself with.

Poststructuralism—Whereas structuralism sought and argued for a way of knowing, of speaking, and of acting—that is to say, a structure—that extended over a number of domains of human activity (e.g., linguistics, anthropology, psychology, philosophy, etc.), poststructuralism understood language, society, etc., to be influenced by systems but disagreed and deconstructed any notion of an underlying structure that could explain the entirety of the human condition or the unity of the different domains mentioned above. Continental philosophers, critical theorists, and deconstructionists are said to fall within the era of poststructuralism. Examples of such persons are philosophers Michael Foucalt and Jacques Derrida.

Praxis—A theological word that is used to focus on the practical aspects of faith, sometimes referring to the political implications of theological constructs.

Premillennialsim—This is a theory of eschatology that was popular in the 20th century following World War I. It holds that the world is getting worse and worse as we anticipate Christ's coming, which is opposite to the position of postmillennialism.

Prevenient grace—In Wesley's mature thought, this sort of grace was that which gives a certain amount of light to every human being and that which awakens the spiritual senses. It allows Wesley to emphasize God's saving activity and stay out of Pelagian territory. Prevenient grace means that God takes the initiative in the matter of conversion, inclining us to turn, wooing us, giving us opportunity for repenting and believing, but never irresistibly.

Quietism—A belief among some Pietistic groups that the life of holiness should be one of meditation and "stillness." Works of piety and pursuit of means of grace are discouraged in favor of a private, nonworking devotion.

Rationalism—Reliance on reason for the establishment of religious truths, often recognizing innate knowledge.

Reason—One part of the Wesleyan quadrilateral. Reason is that which enables a person to interpret, organize, and communicate truth from Scripture, Tradition, and Experience.

Recapitulation—A theory of the atonement developed early in the history of the church. It focuses on Jesus Christ as the second Adam. This theory focuses on more than the cross; it envelopes all of Christ's life, lived obediently for God. What Adam did wrong through disobedience, Jesus does right through obedience. The cross is the greatest expression of that obedience. Jesus, in a sense, redeems human life by giving us a model for living the life fully committed to the will of God.

Reconciliation—This is a theme that we find in John Wesley's writing, and also in Charles's hymns. This is the sense that the alienation and estrangement from God implicit in sin is overcome when we come into a new relationship with God.

Redemption—Implies liberation from sin. Exodus acts as a metaphor for redemption. Redemption also implies receiving a new purpose, namely, to love God with all our being, and our neighbor as ourselves. Our lives are redeemed from sin and for love.

Regeneration—Wesley's favorite term for salvation is "new birth." This concept implies that we are regenerated, born again, and are new creations in Christ. Wesley never wanted his doctrine of sanctification to minimize the power and significance of new birth.

Sanctification, entire—The central doctrine of the Holiness Movement. A second crisis experience following regeneration; it is an experience that cleanses one from original sin, or cancels out the carnal nature and the bent toward sinning, thus enabling an entirely sanctified person to significantly progress in a life of holiness, or virtuous living.

Sanctification, final—Only takes place in glorification or in glory. It is in final sanctification that a person is removed from the very presence of sin.

Sanctification, initial—Wesley never actually used this term, but it signifies his belief that the moment of salvation begins the process of being made righteous.

Sanctification, progressive—This is the process *prior to* entire sanctification that brings the individual into a gradual knowledge of his or her inbeing sin, or original sin. Once the person, through the Holy Spirit, comes to a complete renunciation of inbeing sin, an instantaneous cleansing [entire sanctification] takes place, and gradual sanctification continues until one dies. Thus this is also a process of growth in the likeness of Christ and the deepening of holy character *following* the moment of entire sanctification.

Shema—The extremely important Jewish text found in Deut. 6. It is a statement about monotheism and about loving God with one's whole being. It is the center of prayer for the Old Testament Hebrews. Jesus refers to it when asked about the greatest commandments.

Social gospel movement—A religious movement that arose in the second half of the 19th century. This movement arose out of a developing social concern among American Protestants from the influence of persons abroad (e.g., Scottish theologian and philanthropist Thomas Chalmers). The central doctrine of this religious movement was the kingdom of God here and now. Although the leaders of the social gospel movement did not have a unified point of view, with the centrality of the kingdom of God at the forefront, they sought to hold meetings to inform people—mainly Protestants—about the industrial conflict that was taking place (Protestants were generally the wealthy people during this day, and so they were unaware of the lot of the laborer/worker). Upon informing these people about the state of industries, the leaders of the social gospel movement called these people to share their wealth (money, land, food), as well as to fight for the rights of labor. The call was to follow Jesus' example of enacting or bringing about the kingdom of God in the *here* and *now*.

Sola scriptura—"Scripture alone." A doctrine developed in the 15th century by Reformers Martin Luther and John Calvin in a reaction to the authority of the Catholic Church. Such a principle insists that Scripture alone is the source of authority for the Christian and the church.

Soteriology—The branch of theology that deals with the doctrine of salvation.

Spiritual senses—The God-given human capacity to know of God's existence and spiritual realities. Every human has spiritual senses, but they must be awakened by the Holy Spirit.

Stoicism—A philosophical movement of the Hellenistic period that was founded in Athens by Zeno of Citium. The Stoics defined virtue as the telos (end) of a thing. In addition they taught that virtue is the highest good and is based in knowledge or in reason. The Stoics taught that a divine reason governs all things, and that the wise person will live in harmony with this divine reason. In addition, the Stoics taught that one should accept one's situation in the world in a manner of *apathia* or of resignation, recognizing his or her situation as a reflection of the divine reason of things.

Subjective interpretation—This type of interpretation has become increasingly accepted in biblical scholarship in recent years. It is the open acknowledgement that readers come to the text with biases and perspectives resulting from their life experiences, that is, their own subjectivity. This type of interpretation is related to what is known as reader-centered interpretation.

Synergism—In theology, the idea that God and humans cooperate toward human salvation. God's grace is not overpowering, but initiates a relationship to which humans must respond.

Teleological—The philosophical study of design and purpose. Can also be understood as a discourse on the end purpose or a final cause for all that exists.

Telos—A Greek word literally translated as "end," "purpose," or "goal."

Tempers—In Wesleyan thought they are human affections that are focused on and strengthened into enduring dispositions.

Thematization—This aspect of biblical interpretation happens when the interpreter assimilates the extensive information and exegesis of a multitude of individual texts and generalizes about the themes that emerge from the whole. For example, to talk about Pauline theology requires thematization that outlines the main theological points throughout Paul's correspondence.

Theodicy—The problem of evil. Theodicy is an attempt to justify the goodness of God in the face of the presence of evil and innocent suffering in the world.

Theological anthropology—The branch of theology that deals with humanity's metaphysic and moral being.

Theosis—A belief in early Christianity (particularly in the East) that "God became human that we might be like God." Also known as divinization and deification. Interpreted by Wesley, it closely relates to the process of sanctification—to be made holy as God is holy.

Tradition—One part of the Wesleyan quadrilateral. It refers to the early councils and creeds of the church that are used to judge Christian orthodoxy.

Transcendence—"Surpasses" or "goes beyond." God as transcendent is wholly other, unknowable, and impassible. God transcends the world; its polar opposite is *immanence*.

Trinity—A doctrine from the 4th century that states that there are three eternal and essential distinctions—three persons in one substance. The Father, Son, and Holy Spirit who are co-eternal, co-equal, and share one divine reality.

Via salutis—See *ordo salutis*.

Vicious character—A person/agent who does not attempt or rather who outright refuses to do what a virtuous person/agent would do. (See also Continent, Incontinent, and Virtuous character.)

Virtue ethics—Theories of morality in which "virtues" play a central role. Virtue ethics is concerned less with rules that should be followed, and more with helping people develop good character.

Virtuous character—A person/agent who takes pleasure in exercising his or her intellectual skills in decision-making and is not distressed at the giving up of appetites. A virtuous agent is thus not internally divided and carries out the good.

Wesleyan quadrilateral—The criteria by which theological ideas can be tested for truth. This name for Wesley's practice of checks and balances was a later designation, but throughout his works there is evidenced a method by which Scripture, reason, tradition, and experience together testify to truth.

Wholly Other—This term was coined by theologian Rudolf Otto and implies that God is unlike any creature. The term is used to reinforce God's absolute transcendence.

Will—The part of the human being that makes decisions. For Wesley, the will works in combination with the affections.

Witness of the Spirit—Commonly referred to as the doctrine of assurance. Wesley described this experience as the Spirit of God's direct impression on his soul of the certainty of his being accepted and loved by God.